Strengthening
Adult and Continuing
Education

Alan B. Knox

Strengthening Adult and Continuing Education

A Global Perspective on Synergistic Leadership

Jossey-Bass Publishers · San Francisco

132914

Substantial discounts on bulk quantities of Jossey-Bass books are available to corporations, professional associations, and other organizations. For details and discount information, contact the special sales department at Jossey-Bass Inc., Publishers. (415) 433-1740; Fax (415) 433-0499.

For sales outside the United States, contact Maxwell Macmillan International Publishing Group, 866 Third Avenue, New York, New York 10022.

Manufactured in the United States of America

 The paper used in this book is acid-free and meets the State of California requirements for recycled paper (50 percent recycled waste, including 10 percent postconsumer waste), which are the strictest guidelines for recycled paper currently in use in the United States.

The ink in this book is either soy- or vegetable-based and during the printing process emits fewer than half the volatile organic compounds (VOCs) emitted by petroleum-based ink.

Library of Congress Cataloging-in-Publication Data

Knox, Alan Boyd, date.
   Strengthening adult and continuing education : a global perspective on synergistic leadership / Alan B. Knox.
      p.   cm.—(The Jossey-Bass higher and adult education series)
   Includes bibliographical references (p.   ) and index.
   ISBN 1-55542-537-2
   1. Adult education—Cross-cultural studies. 2. Continuing education—Cross-cultural studies. 3. Educational planning.
   4. Educational leadership. I. Title. II. Series.
   LC5215.K635   1993
   374—dc20   92-41687
                                                              CIP

FIRST EDITION
HB Printing   10 9 8 7 6 5 4 3 2 1   *Code 9340*

The Jossey Bass
Higher and Adult Education Series

Contents

Preface

Educational programs for adults affect every aspect of life in the United States. One or two generations ago, most adult and continuing education programs were largely invisible to the general public. (After all, adult learners typically study on a part-time or short-term basis, concurrently carrying out their responsibilities in the family, job, and community.) Today, by contrast, adult education is referred to routinely in the mass media and is part of every type of organization and institution. Adult and continuing education is increasingly recognized to be of central rather than marginal interest to society in many other countries around the world, as well. Accelerating social change and concern over inequities have contributed to the growing centrality of educational programs for adults, and the trend seems likely to persist into the coming decades. Lifelong learning is an essential feature of society as we enter the twenty-first century. (In this book, the terms *adult education, continuing education, extension, nonformal education, popular education,* and *lifelong learning* are used interchangeably to refer to all types of educational programs for adults, although the preferred terminology varies according to country and provider agency.)

Past success in educational programs for adults can be attributed above all to inspired instructors and coordinators, whose own roles often gradually changed from learning (as adults) to instructing other adults to coordinating other instructors. These adult educators developed their vision and expertise through experiential learning and on-the-job training, supplemented perhaps by their reading of articles or attending an occasional conference. That gradual training process served them well, because experience of and reflection on the adult learning process contribute greatly to responsive instruction. Moreover, successful instruction is a valuable prerequisite for program coordination and work with other instructors, especially when they teach similar material, to adults from similar backgrounds.

In addition, long association with one provider agency gives such instructors thorough understanding of its strengths and weaknesses—a familiarity that provides the key to the internal aspects of strategic planning and implementation.

Leadership and Strategic Planning in Adult Education

Effective leadership and strategic planning entail more, however, than understanding the past functioning of an organization. Leadership and strategic planning require projecting future directions for the external context or service area in which the agency operates, along with the threats and opportunities that affect the agency. Significant societal influences are difficult to recognize unless a leader has a comparative perspective, based on familiarity with other education providers and societal contexts.

The essence of leadership lies in gaining agreement on goals and encouraging their attainment. Strategic planning is the means by which leaders attain that end. Because the intended outcome of strategic planning is agreement on mission and goals, strategic planning (in contrast to long-range planning) encourages continuous participation in the planning process by both internal and external stakeholders (in this case, the people who will help implement the plans) to increase their understanding, involvement, and commitment. The valuable perspective brought by internal stakeholders—learners, instructors, and program administrators—has been noted. The involvement of outside stakeholders, such as policy makers and public members of advisory committees, can also greatly enrich the planning process.

Background of This Book

Strengthening Adult and Continuing Education is based on an extensive cross-national effort to understand the functioning of local educational programs for adults. This collaborative study was called "World Perspective on Adult Education." Cooperating colleagues from other countries analyzed pertinent case descriptions from the joint project and drew conclusions for adult education in their country (Clark and Rooth, 1988; Reischmann, 1988; Tuomisto, 1987). The book builds on the comparative findings to arrive at recommendations for strengthening planning in U.S. provider agencies.

The basic ideas for such a project were formulated in the mid 1980s in conversations with a longtime friend, Dušan Savićević, now professor emeritus of adult education, University of Belgrade (at the time a visiting Fulbright scholar at the University of Wisconsin), and with my wife, Linda Bock Knox, an experienced adult education practitioner. Conversations at international conferences and correspondence with colleagues in adult education from many countries led to a preliminary project plan, which provided a basic format for each case description and a general framework and schedule.

The crucial ingredient, however, was the people who participated in the project. One person engaged in adult education volunteered to serve as case coordinator in each country where there was interest in the project (Resource B). The case coordinators arranged for people knowledgeable about specific program areas to write case descriptions of the adult education organizations. The coordinators also worked with the authors, helping with preparation (or even publication) of some case descriptions, and shipped the materials. The time and expenses contributed by case coordinators and authors from each country subsidized this project in an essential way. External funding would probably never have materialized; the cost of the project would have amounted to far more than $1 million.

My own analysis was enriched by visits with case coordinators and some of the authors of case descriptions. The ERIC Clearinghouse published a preliminary review of the literature (Knox, 1987a).

Audience and Purpose for the Book

The main audience for this book is thoughtful leaders in adult and continuing education who want to strengthen the impact of their work through collaborative, comprehensive programs. The comparative perspectives on societal influences presented here can improve leadership of such programs. The fundamental tenet of comparative education is respect for important features of each distinctive society. Needless to say, a program transplanted to a new national setting will require major adaptation. The illustrations from various countries are intended to encourage North American practitioners to use contextual analysis to strengthen strategic planning and implementation. Examples were included neither because they were especially representative or successful nor because they provide a current profile of the country or situation. Rather, they illustrate societal influences on agency functioning at a specific location and time and reveal certain influences and implications for planning. (Even though case examples were gathered over the past decade or more and the programs and countries discussed have subsequently experienced changes, most case examples are described here in the present tense, in the interests of readability.) Major efforts have been made to include examples from all over the world, but more come from industrialized countries in North America and Europe than from other regions. The case descriptions, combined with examples and overviews from the literature review, reflect the variety of adult education practice worldwide. These extensive and detailed data were used for the basic comparative analysis.

Overview of the Contents

In most countries, the broad field of adult and continuing education is fragmented. Most practitioners work in just one of the sectors described in the book, and many have little familiarity with or interest in other sectors. Although, as previously stated, my intent is to show why it is important for adult education leaders to gain a comparative perspective of the field and of national settings to strengthen strategic planning and implementation, readers interested in specific program areas (basic education, distance education, or rural development) may choose to read only the relevant chapters, in any sequence. The sequence of chapters is designed to juxtapose contrasting program types. Some types of programs, such as self-directed learning, are not included.

The earlier chapters explore basic societal influences and implications for planning. The later chapters build on those discussions to examine more comprehensive, synergistic approaches that entail collaboration by multiple providers. The sequence of chapters allows each to build on the strategic planning concepts developed in the preceding chapters.

Chapter One states why it is important to strengthen agency planning and impact and how a comparative perspective can help agency leaders improve contextual analysis and recognize major issues and societal influences. The chapter also defines and explores basic concepts discussed in the subsequent chapters.

Chapters Two through Thirteen all follow a similar format. Each focuses on a specific program area and the pertinent planning issues. After an introduction to clientele, providers, program characteristics, and planning issues in the program area, an example from the United States helps readers relate international examples to planning in the U.S. context. Examples from other national settings follow. A general overview of adult education in the featured country serves to orient readers who are unfamiliar with the variety of practice in the field and provides the background for references in other chapters to its specific adult education practices. Each of these chapters concludes with implications for strategic planning.

Chapter Two, on part-time study at educational institutions, emphasizes relations between the mission, staff, and methods of the adult education agency. I also assess priorities of the parent institution, as well as ways to broaden stakeholder support and collaborative relations with other providers.

Chapters Three and Four focus on less-advantaged participants. Chapter Three, on adult basic education and literacy, discusses the provider's values and priorities concerning social change, financial support, staff roles, serving hard-to-reach participants, and social stratification.

Chapter Four deals with cultural minorities. Among other

topics, it covers staff leadership, social change, diversity, alternative goals, economic conditions, and public policy that influence minority subpopulations.

Chapter Five reviews educational technology, funding, staff expertise, and quality standards in distance education.

Chapter Six covers human resource staff development training programs. It concentrates on enterprise productivity and on educational activities for higher-level staff members who face issues of change and obsolescence.

Chapter Seven discusses the influence of penal institutions' organizational culture on the teaching-learning transaction. Adult educators in correctional institutions must try to relate to both inmates and prison staff. Four approaches to correctional education are considered: punishment, remedial actions, coping, and alternative culture.

Chapter Eight on cultural programs treats quite different participants and purposes: it focuses on ways of obtaining resources for and commitment to programs on family life, religious beliefs, and the arts that touch on the personal search for meaning and shared cultural values.

Chapter Nine covers continuing professional education. It addresses occupational concerns such as obsolescence and the contributions of adult education to self-directed learning and actual work performance as professionals progress from novice to expert status.

Chapter Ten deals with education for elders, focusing on mutual aid methods for the subculture of older adults, whose status in society is changing and varies from country to country.

Rural development is the subject of Chapter Eleven, which emphasizes comprehensive approaches to improving the quality of rural life through education, especially for the poor.

Chapter Twelve considers leadership in health education, including cooperative approaches to provide educational activities about life-style-induced health problems. The chapter explores both personal and cultural values.

Chapter Thirteen examines leadership and mission as they relate to community problem solving. Adult education providers must undertake participatory research and other community development procedures, especially when change is resisted by powerful elites. Political, economic, and social factors may make it a special challenge to mobilize participation.

Chapter Fourteen analyzes societal influences, presented in all the preceding chapters, that have implications for strategic planning. The examples in this concluding chapter emphasize identifying external threats and opportunities. Ten guidelines for strategic leadership of adult education agencies stress comprehensive programs that make a real impact. Adult education leaders can use the guidelines to strengthen their collaboration with major stakeholders in a planning process that results in a shared and compelling vision of agency mission and in stakeholder commitment to implementing plans.

Resource A provides information about the 175 case descriptions from thirty-two countries around the world, including procedures for obtaining copies of case descriptions. Citations in the text to the case descriptions list their location in the book (Resource A), followed by the author's name.

Resource B lists the case coordinators.

Resource C lists the main types of societal influences identified in the project as a whole and indicates which chapters discuss each type. The example in Chapter One of adult education to overcome hunger, for instance, includes all thirty-three categories of societal influence assessed during the project, emphasizing the systemic perspective on leadership of adult education agencies that is especially important for collaborative efforts.

Acknowledgments

Central coordination of the project at the University of Wisconsin was covered from various sources. The logistical support for translating, duplicating, mailing, and related coordination and dissemination of the international exchange of case materials was supplied by the W. K. Kellogg Foundation and reflected the vision of Arlon Elser. I was assisted by a sabbatical leave from the University of Wisconsin and a Fulbright scholarship in Yugoslavia.

I would like to extend thanks to the thousands of individual people who contributed to this book in various ways, especially my wife, Linda, a partner throughout, to whom this book is dedicated; World Perspective team members who helped with project planning and implementation; experts on comparative adult education who critiqued the preliminary project plan, case descriptions, and the draft manuscript; case coordinators who arranged for preparation of case descriptions; authors who prepared case descriptions and articles; people in many countries who provided support for the project; and adult education practitioners around the world whose dedication and leadership are reflected in the examples throughout the book and provide a continuing source of inspiration. To all these friends and colleagues, I freely express my appreciation.

Madison, Wisconsin   Alan B. Knox
May 1993

The Author

Alan B. Knox chairs the Department of Continuing and Vocational Education at the University of Wisconsin, Madison, where he has been a professor since 1981. He received his bachelor's degree (1952) in arts, two master's degrees (1953 and 1955), in arts and adult education, respectively, and his doctorate (1958) in adult education, all from Syracuse University. The university awarded him its Distinguished Alumnus Award in 1980. During the past forty years, he has held teaching, research, and administrative positions at Syracuse University; the University of Nebraska; Teachers College, Columbia University; and the University of Illinois, Urbana–Champaign. He has published more than one hundred articles, chapters, and books on many aspects of the broad field of adult and continuing education. Between 1979 and 1984, Knox initiated and served as editor-in-chief of the Jossey-Bass quarterly series New Directions for Continuing Education; since then, he has served as consulting editor for Jossey-Bass books on adult and continuing education.

In addition to doing research, teaching graduate courses, and conducting workshops over the years on leadership, administration, and supervision of educational programs for adults, Knox has held leadership positions in both professional associations and universities. He served as president of the American Association for Adult and Continuing Education, founded the Adult Education Research Conference and the Illinois Council on Continuing Higher Education, was president of the New York Adult Education Council, and chaired the Commission of Professors of Adult Education and the policy boards of leadership projects for the Association of American Medical Colleges and the National University Continuing Education Association. He has been a continuing education administrator at Syracuse University, associate director of the Nebraska Center for Continuing Education, director of the Center for Adult Education Research at Teachers College, and associate vice-chancellor for academic affairs and director of continuing education and public service at the University of Illinois. His publications concerning leadership and administration include *Leadership Strategies for Meeting New Challenges* (1982), *Developing, Administering, and Evaluating Adult Education* (1980), a chapter in *Adult Education: Evolution and Achievements in a Developing Field of Study* (Peters, Jarvis, and Associates, 1991), and articles in the *Journal for Higher Education Management, Adult Education*, the Jossey-Bass New Directions for Continuing Education series, the 1979 *World Yearbook of Education*, and the 1985 *International Encyclopedia of Education*. He also served as coeditor of a special issue of the *International Review of Education* (1977).

In addition to teaching graduate seminars on comparative adult education, Knox has acted as a consultant on the subject in countries around the world. He has participated in many international conferences, including a world assembly of the International Council for Adult Education, and has worked on special assignments for the United States Information Service and UNESCO. He was the recipient of a Fulbright research fellowship for Yugoslavia in 1987.

Strengthening
Adult and Continuing
Education

1

Building Strategic Leadership for Effective Adult Education

Leaders of adult education agencies in North America confront many challenges. As we enter the twenty-first century, lifelong learning has become essential to deal with change and to foster cooperation in family, work, and community. The vision, tasks, and effectiveness of leaders reflect their roles as agency directors, program coordinators, and advisory committee chairs. Strategic planning and implementation provide a major vehicle for involving other people who should have a stake in addressing those challenges by strengthening agency functioning and increasing program impact. The aspects of strategic agency planning that pertain to *internal* strengths and weaknesses tend to be learned informally as leaders make routine decisions within a familiar organizational context. By contrast, *external* aspects of planning regarding contextual opportunities and threats tend to be neglected because they depend on a broader comparative perspective that requires explicit situational analysis of societal influences such as demographic trends, economic conditions, and activities of other adult education providers. It is typically assumed that because little can be done about such societal influences, attention to them is not warranted.

A contrasting view is provided by Bogard (1989, 1991, 1992) from the context of the Council of Europe (COE) project on adult education and social change. The following highlights from recent COE project reports have provocative implications for adult and continuing education leaders in North America, with the prospects

1

of a North American common market composed of Canada, the United States, and Mexico.

The COE reports were based on analysis of selected adult education activities in various European countries since 1989, in which adult educators from participating countries contributed to the assessment and exploration of implications. Even before the diverse European nations moved toward the formation of the European Community, each nation state had experienced fundamental and ongoing social, demographic, economic, and political changes. Shifting East-West relations and the rise of regionalism had been accompanied by tensions associated with subcultural movements within and across nation states.

The reports concluded that respect for pluralistic values has been important in appreciation of national differences, decentralized decision making, and multicultural connections by individual adults. Adult and continuing education is increasingly recognized and employed to help people negotiate new social contracts. In the face of massive social change, adult education has helped to increase social cohesion and democracry, as a bridge between individuals, social groups, and institutions. Individualized and responsive adult education programs have also been used in a broader context designed to promote occupational and social integration. This lifelong learning commitment to ongoing socialization to promote solidarity in relation to family, work, and community is especially important to offset polarization into a two-class society.

The COE project members recognized that such a comprehensive mission for adult education required unprecedented professionalization of adult education leaders to enable them to understand the global context in which program planning and implementation occurred. Central to such professionalization was a systemic view of adult education, in contrast with delivering programs to individuals on demand. The synergistic approach also went beyond providing programs to target groups (such as the unemployed or elderly); it included educational programs that addressed societal influences such as causes of unemployment or social exclusion. This approach entailed holistic forms of adult education with characteristics of organization and community development.

Because of the fragmentation among the various types of

adult education providers, adult education leaders confronted a special challenge to work with multiple stakeholders and resource systems to plan and conduct comprehensive programs aimed at important social issues. Planning for comprehensive programs gave systemic attention to relationships between various categories of learners associated with an issue. For example, to help resolve an unemployment issue, educational programs would be aimed not only at unemployed adults but also at adults in families, enterprises, social service agencies, media, and public policy. Recommended planning guidelines included local initiatives, organizational and financial flexibility, emphasis on shared values, cooperation among providers, and attention to the continuum of education (Bogard, 1991, 1992).

Comparative Perspectives

This brief overview of a current approach to adult education in Europe reflects the main ideas with which the entire book deals. In the United States, most adult education practitioners enter the field with little formal preparation and then learn on the job (Peters, Jarvis, and Associates, 1991; Peterson and Associates, 1979). For many aspects of practice, this informal process can be very satisfactory. Experience as a learner, instructor, or coordinator can contribute to both empathy and expertise. However, some aspects of agency leadership depend on larger perspectives on the societal context and desirable directions. Comparative understanding of other segments of the field and national settings contribute greatly to such breadth of perspective. The examples and rationale for agency planning and implementation can help reflective practitioners recognize societal influences that affect local adult education providers in other locations. Practitioners can use a comparative perspective to engage in contextual analysis of major societal influences as a basis for strengthening their strategic planning and implementation (Bennett, Kidd, and Kulich, 1975; Fordham, 1986a, 1986b; Gelpi, 1979a, 1979b, 1985; Kidd, 1970; Levine and White, 1986; Lichtner, 1988; Lowe, 1975; Schuller and Megarry, 1979; Titmus, 1989).

International examples contribute to a comparative perspective that can stimulate new program directions. Examples from other program areas can stimulate innovation and also promote collaboration with other types of providers in comprehensive approaches.

Educational programs for adults have become as timely and pertinent as newspaper articles and television programs. Every month, U.S. mass media refers to myriad adult education programs. Although most programs are related to both social issues and personal concerns, one or the other is emphasized. The following dozen examples based on recent news reports and features are placed in sequence to parallel the topics of the following chapters.

- University—U.S. universities adapt videotapes from engineering and management courses for part-time students; the tapes are to be used by universities in Central and Eastern Europe and the former Soviet Union to help engineers and managers there adapt to market economies.
- Literacy—Two university departments assist various community agencies engaged in adult basic education by providing staff development activities for paid staff, community volunteers, and university students who tutor and assist functionally illiterate adults to improve their reading, writing, and math.
- Minorities—A community college, community agency, and several religious institutions cooperate in offering educational activities such as English as a foreign language and vocational education for refugee families from several countries and subcultures that must make similar adjustments.
- Distance—A public broadcasting station announces several new program series and study guides that provide opportunities for adults who might otherwise have been deterred by location or other commitments.
- Workplace—An enterprise expands its retraining and staff development activities to increase economic productivity and quality improvement.
- Corrections—A correctional education program at a state prison is reduced because of overcrowding, combined with cuts in state funding that formerly allowed a local community college to provide instructors for adult education courses in the prison.
- Family—A social worker works intensively for months on edu-

cational activities for an entire family to reduce dysfunctionality as an alternative to placing the children in foster homes.

- Professions—A professional association conducts a workshop for members on new knowledge, implications for professional practice, and benefits for clients.
- Elders—A private organization announces upcoming domestic and international study tours for increasing numbers of better-educated and affluent older adults who seldom attend activities at local senior citizens centers.
- Rural—The Cooperative Extension Service offers a wide variety of educational programs and services in a rural county on agricultural production, conservation, family life, nutrition, leadership of youth groups, and community problem solving.
- Health—Major features of Alcoholics Anonymous's twelve-step program, such as individual responsibility and peer support, are adapted to other self-help groups concerned with drug dependency, weight loss, smoking cessation, and various health conditions.
- Community—Community groups and government agencies collaborate on a series of nonformal educational sessions to explore causes and possible solutions following violence in a poor neighborhood.

These examples indicate the variety of current educational programs for adults and opportunities for comprehensive collaborative planning. Adult education agency leaders seek to increase program responsiveness and effectiveness to help people deal with important issues. Agency planning entails contributions by various people who each have a special stake in program success and who (as the foregoing examples indicate) may be from various organizations. In addition to program administrators, who typically take the lead in strategic planning and implementation, effective leadership of comprehensive programs includes people from various categories of stakeholders. Included are instructors who help adults learn, adult learners who participate, representatives of cosponsoring organizations, and policy makers and supporters from the parent organization and society generally.

Leaders of educational programs for adults obtain agreement

on important goals (planning) and encourage contributions to goal achievement (implementation). Such leaders tend to be oriented toward obtaining results and seek to make a difference. The outcomes of adult education that leaders seek to achieve (impact) may take the form of improved individual performance or changes in group, organizational, or community settings. Effective leaders realize that they can not achieve such changes by themselves; they must do so with and through others who have a stake in achieving the desired goals. Including these people in decision making for planning and conducting adult education can be synergistic to the extent that cooperative efforts increase the energy contributed and results achieved. The whole can be greater than the sum of the parts.

In the process of strategic planning and implementation, leaders involve stakeholders in achieving agreement on a compelling vision of a desirable mission and direction for the provider agency with which the leader is associated. The participation of stakeholders in planning encourages their help with implementation. Adult education occurs in conjunction with various types of organizations and institutions. In most instances, the agency offering adult education is a dependent part of a larger parent organization. Examples include the adult education office of a school system, the continuing education department of a community college, the extension division of a land-grant university, the college of continuing education of a private urban university, the adult services department of a library or community agency, the training and education department of an enterprise, or the adult education office of a religious institution or voluntary association. Adult education practitioners include both full-time program administrators and many other instructors, counselors, and volunteers who help adults learn, typically on a part-time or short-term basis (Merriam and Cunningham, 1989; Votruba, 1981, chap. 1).

Strategic leadership for an adult education agency entails inclusion of internal stakeholders such as participants, instructors, program coordinators, and parent organization leaders in the planning and implementation process. The breadth of perspective that is desirable for agency strategic planning contrasts with that necessary for an instructor to plan a course or workshop, for which accumulated experience with the teaching-learning transaction may be sufficient. The focus of this book is on agency planning. Agency leadership includes not only attention to internal strengths and weaknesses but also to threats and opportunities in the external environment. As adult education leaders deal with their parent organization, other providers in their service area, and major societal influences in a turbulent and changing context, strategic planning helps clarify the distinctive contribution that the provider agency can make and assists in identifying the external influences that help or hinder. The lack of a clear mission and performance indicators for most agencies makes strategic planning more difficult but more important. Inclusion of external stakeholders (such as policy makers, funders, and cosponsors) in strategic planning can contribute to understanding of social, political, and economic influences and can increase external support. External stakeholders typically care about adult education as a means to address broader societal issues and specific personal benefits.

A broad perspective on the adult education field and the societal context in which it functions is especially important for collaborative approaches required to influence organizational or community change. In these approaches, two or more providers cooperate, sometimes by serving several categories of adult learners related to an issue. For example, effective functional literacy programs raise consciousness, improve role performance, incorporate interesting materials, and lead to postliteracy activities—in contrast with just helping adults learn to read. Staff development that increases the productivity of the enterprise (private business or public department) usually includes organization development of work teams, rather than the specialist training of individuals. Agricultural extension that increases productivity and well-being of poor farmers is concerned with nonformal education regarding farming and rural development, not only with dissemination of technical information. Effective health promotion includes education for people at risk, family members, health professionals, and mass media, in contrast with patient education only. Educational programs that benefit older adults involve attention to self-help by the elderly and assistance by professionals, younger adults, and educators; they are not programs just for seniors.

Successful leadership of such comprehensive educational

programs depends on greater insight into societal influences than practitioners typically acquire from experience alone. Most people take their societal context and outlook for granted and do not consider other perspectives. One way to gain a comparative understanding of adult education leadership is to become familiar with similar educational programs for adults as they function in other program areas and national settings. Cross-national comparative analysis of similarities and differences between adult education agencies and programs can enable leaders to identify crucial societal influences in their own service area and to reflect this insight in their strategic planning. Internal strengths and weaknesses are easier to recognize than external threats and opportunities. Therefore, the emphasis in this book is on fostering leaders' understanding of *societal* influences as a basis for strengthening external aspects of strategic planning to guide reflection, planning, monitoring, and retrospection. The value of a comparative perspective is heuristic (provides suggestive examples from which we can learn); it comes not from adopting practices from another setting but from appreciating the cultural values and traditions that shape the functioning of an adult education program elsewhere and then being stimulated to ask more productive planning questions about one's own situation and local contingencies. Such contextual analysis to specify local contingencies (such as economic conditions, population characteristics, alternative providers, and availability of adult education staff) is a neglected aspect of strategic planning (Bhola, 1988; Brown, 1981; Faure and Associates, 1972; Hall and Stock, 1985; Hoggart, 1982; McLean, 1986; National Institute for Educational Research, 1986, Reed, 1987; Rogers and Shoemaker, 1971; Titmus, 1989).

Familiarity with similar adult education agencies and programs in contrasting settings can help adult education leaders engage in *contextual analysis* to identify the salient contingencies in their own program area. For example, familiarity with Israeli adult education programs for recently arrived Ethiopian Jews can help U.S. adult educators be responsive to Hmong refugees in adult education programs, even though there are differences as well as similarities in the two situations. This constructivist viewpoint recognizes the multiple realities perceived by the various stakeholders with whom leaders interact in the strategic planning and implementation process. People act on their perceptions, which are shaped by experience and values and are thus socially defined. The heuristic value of comparative perspectives lies in the impetus leaders gain to clarify the specific local contingencies that warrant special attention in agency planning and implementation. Familiarity with quality circles in Japan and learning enterprises in Sweden can help U.S. enterprises use training and education to improve quality improvement efforts, not by adoption of foreign practices but by adaptation to U.S. circumstances. Although conclusions from scholarly research may have limited general applicability, they can be very valuable in helping leaders simplify complex situations (by focusing on important relationships and emerging trends) and interpret current local experience against the broader perspective provided by comparative analysis (Charters and Associates, 1981; Liveright and Haygood, 1968; Maydl and Associates, 1983; Maydl and Savicky, 1986; Titmus, 1976; Ulich, 1965).

The importance of the themes in this book was underscored by the dramatic August 1991 political events in the Soviet Union. By contrast with the relative stability of the societal context in which most adult education agencies usually function, the agencies that have provided educational opportunities for adults in the Soviet Union experienced an abrupt shift in the political, economic, and social conditions within which they functioned. Many of the changes pertained to the transition from a centralized to a pluralistic nation state. For more than seven decades, the Union of Soviet Socialist Republics typified a large country with highly centralized political and economic systems. The 1917 revolution was also a dramatic period of transition for the sprawling, culturally diverse, but largely rural country. Yet Communist party rule had at least two features similar to the previous centuries under the czars. In both regimes, political power was highly centralized, and citizens were relatively passive. A monolithic, planned economy resulted after 1917. During the 1980s, major adult education providers in the Soviet Union utilized both central planning and selective decentralization in dealing with the great social and cultural diversity among republics. This approach is illustrated by the Russian examples of Znanie (an all-union knowledge society that provided cultural, political, and scientific education for adults) described in Chapter Eight, and of continuing medical education in Chapter Nine.

In recent years, similar trends toward decentralization and pluralism in Yugoslavia and other Central and Eastern European countries have affected adult education providers in those countries. For example, programs related to staff development (Chapter Six), minorities (Chapter Four), and continuing professional education (Chapter Nine) that drew heavily on examples from pluralistic countries with market economies may have increased relevance for nations in the process of decentralization. In recent years, adult educators from North America and Europe have been working with their counterparts in the former Soviet Union, and in Eastern European countries. This assistance has taken several forms. One form of help has been to share content to be taught to adult education participants regarding pluralistic political, social, and economic practices to accelerate progress in the transition toward democracy and a market economy. Another form of help has been suggestions about how to transform centralized adult education organizations to enable them to become more responsive to the new realities in that region of the world. Their experience with adult education during a period of rapid change may also have implications for understanding agency functioning elsewhere, including the United States. In all instances, social change disturbs long-standing habits and assumptions, and efforts to understand and cope with new realities help to make explicit broad societal influences as they relate to specific local contingencies that leaders confront in their strategic planning and implementation.

Strategic Leadership

In the former Soviet Union, the United States, and most countries, strategic leadership for adult education depends on a vision of emerging directions. As adult education leaders (and members of professional fields generally) become more expert, they combine knowledge from their educational experience with that gleaned from their practical experience to deal effectively with the specific problems, opportunities, and contingencies in their situation (Houle, 1980). This level of expertise, which we might call wisdom, gives attention to desirability of goals as well as effectiveness of procedures. In most types of adult education programs, leaders seem to link client systems with knowledge sources that help participants (learners) alternate over time between action and knowledge. This approach further broadens the range of stakeholders with whom effective leaders deal and includes people from both client systems (such as family members or work associates) and resource systems (such as policy makers and representatives of community agencies).

Expert leaders engaged in such systemic linkage understand the complex aspects of temporary coalitions and integrated systems. Leadership tends to be shared among stakeholders, and strategic planning is a procedure for encouraging such cooperation. Leadership entails influence on matters of organizational relevance, usually cycles of activity by program stakeholders such as participants, instructors, coordinators, funders, and policy makers. It can be exerted by people in one role or in several. Leadership is necessary to help members deal with societal change, incompleteness of organizational arrangements, and interpersonal relations. Strategic leadership is oriented toward the future and emphasizes collaboration to achieve implementation.

Agency administrators can make valuable contributions to leadership as they formulate policies to guide agency decision making, relate to external constituencies, acquire and allocate resources, evaluate programs in relation to contextual influences, and encourage cooperation. Staff development for adult education practitioners and volunteers can be a powerful adjunct to leadership and strategic planning, and one that is often neglected. Such staff development can occur within the agency, through professional development conferences and courses conducted by adult education associations, or through university graduate programs with specializations related to adult education. Topics can include comparative perspectives on societal influences and strategic planning, as well as adult learning and teaching, program development, and coordination (Bhola, 1988, chap. 11). Current quality-improvement rationales emphasize that staff members should recognize learning as an important part of doing their job.

One contribution of leadership vision, policy making, and staff development is to help people understand that sometimes simple solutions to complex problems do not work. In such instances, leaders may shift the focus from the teaching-learning transaction to the provider agency level to achieve broader collaboration. Strategic planning can be a vehicle for such commitment, concerted effort, and collective impact. Many staff members are realizing that their organizations are undergoing fundamental changes in mission and culture. Continuing education leaders who help create fundamental changes in their own provider organization (or who enable adult learners to do so in their own context) depend on their personal mastery and mental models to articulate a compelling future vision that will inspire commitment by stakeholders (Beckhard and Pritchard, 1992; Senge, 1990). Changing the essence entails going beyond internal modification of organizational strengths and weaknesses. Leadership of continuing education agencies for the next century also requires contextual analysis to understand major societal influences. The range of such influences is suggested in the following section on various adult education activities related to hunger.

Adult Education Related to Hunger

The example furnished here suggests some of the ways in which strategic planning can identify societal influences and work with various providers in a collaborative adult education approach to issues related to hunger. It can also illustrate ways to use comparative insights regarding societal influences for synergistic planning of comprehensive educational programs for adults. This example foreshadows (and cites) the societal influences on local adult education agencies listed in Resource C. Of course, each provider agency can address only a few aspects of the problem.

For hundreds of millions of people around the world, threat of starvation is a stark reality (Resource C, #26: *health*). The threat is increasing. In all of Africa, more than two million people died of starvation in 1984. In 1992, an estimated thirty million were at risk, as dramatized by the famine relief efforts in Somalia. Hunger has been recognized as a major social problem for millennia. The images have been graphic—from one of Revelation's four horsemen of the Apocalypse, to fund-raising ads with the photograph of a little hunger victim with bony limbs, bloated belly, hollow eyes, and empty outreached food bowl (Resource C, #11: *image*). What can educational programs for adults do to ameliorate such a complex problem? As with peace education, it is hard to know where to begin. Hunger includes chronic malnutrition, seasonal hunger, and famine. With each, it is important to think globally but act locally (Hunger Project, 1985; Lappé and Collins, 1986). The following analysis suggests places to initiate the dialogue.

If one could allocate massive resources to assist educational activities related to hunger and starvation, how would they be deployed? No one would advocate allocating all the resources to educational programs for the victims. To give them only food for thought in response to their urgent need for food and drink would be a cruel joke. Yet although such actions seem foolish, similar ones have been used. There are adult literacy campaigns that spend everything on teaching reading and writing while ignoring postliteracy opportunities, functional connections with family life and occupational performance (Resource C, #3: *enterprises;* 30: *role*), in-service education for literacy staff and volunteers, and staff development for elementary and secondary teachers. In the face of widespread structural unemployment, some occupational retraining programs try to prepare left-over workers for left-over jobs and fail to take into account the societal influences that make such a solution unlikely—such as inadequate economic growth, job creation, and opportunities for upward mobility all along the job ladder (Resource C, #20: *stratification;* #30: *role*).

Another target for help might be education aimed at the potential donors to whom the hunger relief ads are aimed (Resource C, #6: *volunteers*). The happy result would be that deepened understanding would encourage them to send more money or food (Resource C, #22: *social services*). An educational effort for donors might address the urgency of the problem, the grave need for their contributions, and the benefits for recipients. However, as beneficial as such aid is, it is not a long-term solution to the problem of starvation. In the spring of 1992, U.S., Japanese, and European donors at a general conference pledged half a billion dollars in aid to drought victims in eleven countries in southern Africa, but it was only 60 percent of the need. Some aid programs forestall development because they foster dependence and weaken local systems. As the old saying goes, "Give a man a fish, and he eats for a day; teach a man to fish, and he eats for a lifetime." This advice reflects a curative and preventive educational emphasis in contrast to treating the symptoms of the fundamental problem.

We know that the personal tragedy of starvation is part of a more global scene. As we move away from a close-up on starving victims and food donors, we can identify various societal influences on food supply, demand, and consumption. A provider's educational goal is to increase understanding of connections between personal problems and public issues.

The usual companion of malnutrition and starvation is poverty (Resource C, #20: *stratification*). In a famine, the poor are most vulnerable. Because reduced starvation entails improved living conditions, major causes and effects of poverty should be considered. This analysis should include the pattern of social stratification in each society, the number and extent of disadvantage of people in the lower strata in comparison with middle-class families, and opportunities for upward mobility. This issue has both a personal and a social face. In countries with widespread poverty and few opportunities for productive work, provision of educational opportunities tends to result in apathy because of pessimism about resultant improvements or in unrealistic expectations followed by disillusionment (Resource C, #33: *expectations*). A comprehensive effort to reduce poverty as a way of combating hunger must provide educational programs for affluent citizens and policy makers regarding the national stake in reducing inequalities through increased economic growth, income redistribution, land reform, and job creation (Resource C, #10: *economy;* #20: *stratification*). In general, less hunger contributes to more security for the affluent.

A typical proposed solution to inadequate food supply is to produce more. As all types of countries have discovered, major improvement in agricultural production is very complicated and involves more than simple commitment, quotas, and dissemination of technical information on topics such as soil types, fertilizers, pest control, and improved seeds or breeding stock. The green revolution boosted production but did not solve malnutrition. In many developing countries in which more than three-quarters of the adult population is engaged in subsistence agriculture, improvements in personal living standards and in national economic growth are tied to modernization of commercial agriculture (Resource C, #25: *modernization*). This entails access to supplies, equipment, credit, and markets. Thus, successful educational programs to help farm families increase production cover a variety of such decision areas as part of comprehensive rural development that also includes nonfarm rural enterprises and provision of social services (Resource C, #13: *urban-rural relations;* #22: *social services*).

However, famine conditions are sometimes produced not by agricultural practices but by natural hazards that cause sharp drops in food production. Examples of such hazards include too much or too little rainfall or temperatures that are too high or too low or poorly timed (Resource C, #14: *geographic characteristics*). Regional drought in Africa is a current dramatic case. Educational programs to help reduce such natural hazards to stable food production extend far beyond farmers to include policy makers, engineers, enterprise managers, and many others concerned with conservation and prevention. Projects include dam, dike, and canal systems for flood control; irrigation systems for drought control; technology to keep a late freeze from ruining a fruit crop or to filter the intense summer sun; and conservation or reclamation projects to offset environmental degradation in many forms (such as topsoil erosion, loss of trees, disruption of tropical rain forests, and water pollution). Research and new technological knowledge can guide such projects (Resource C, #24: *knowledge*). In addition to agriculture, such large joint projects can benefit power generation, recreation, and industrial development. Educational programs for adults can help the general public, policy makers, and leaders in the nonagricultural sectors of the economy understand the human causes of much environmental degradation and the multiple benefits of such development projects (Resource C, #1: *policies*). In-service education can help increase the capability of the people who implement such projects once development plans are approved and funded.

The foregoing influences on hunger have emphasized the food production side of the equation. The other side is food consumption. Hunger, starvation, and famine are a threat when production falls much below consumption requirements; that threat is greatly reduced when there is satisfactory balance and distribution. In some developing countries, high levels of population growth make it difficult if not impossible to achieve a satisfactory balance (Resource C, #27: *age distribution;* #28: *population change*). At some point, trying to solve the hunger problem by increasing production while ignoring population control reaches a point of diminishing return when modern food production procedures are being used on all arable land. In the extreme, sole reliance on increased food production to deal with very high levels of population growth can lead to widespread famine when food production reaches its capacity at the same time that population size continues to increase rapidly. Exploding population is a major problem for many reasons and has causes similar to hunger.

Family planning and birth control to restrict excessive population growth have been an even more intractable problem than agricultural production (Resource C, #31: *family*). In many developing countries, large family size is associated with tradition and high infant mortality rates, as well as the dependence on sons for family continuity, use of offspring for agricultural labor, and reliance on younger family members as the main social security for elders (Resource C, #22: *social services;* #31: *family*). In countries that value individual freedom, education is the major means to teach parents to restrict family size and to reach people in many other roles related to health and social services; it then becomes possible for parents to have only a few children and perhaps no sons to run the farm and yet still be provided for in old age (Resource C, #16: *values*). In the United States and in some other Western countries, zero population growth reflects the tendency of a large middle class to have small families and for immigrants and guest workers to provide a supplementary labor supply (Resource C, #15: *international influences*). Even the zero population growth projected for the United States a few years ago was recently revised to a 50 percent increase in population in the next six decades, due largely to immigration and continued high childbearing rates for minority subpopulations. The social change from a society oriented toward a rural, feudal, extended family to an urban one oriented toward a nuclear family is so pervasive that resistance is great and pace is slow (Resource C, #29: *social change;* #31: *family*). Even the dramatic transformation of Japanese family life took about three generations. Educational programs can be directed to older as well as younger generations because of their interdependence; they can also be aimed at those in the helping professions (who in urban settings perform functions similar to those performed by rural families) and at policy makers as a basis of their understanding and support for educational activities to address the interrelated issues associated with population control.

A societal influence on hunger, agriculture, population, and other economic and social conditions is public policy (Resource C, #9: *government*). In centralized political systems, the government and ruling party are the main source of public policy. In pluralistic political systems, nongovernmental organizations also affect public policy (Resource C, #32: *associates*). More and more political systems are becoming pluralistic, such as the former Soviet Union and Central and Eastern European countries since 1990 (Resource C, #17: *pluralism*).

Public policy regarding food has many aspects. Trends in food consumption are more stable than production, in which variations in weather and other conditions can produce large fluctuations in production (Resource C, #14: *geographic characteristics*). Some agricultural policies have been designed to increase stability in the food supply—to reduce surpluses as well as shortages (Resource C, #1: *policies*). Such policies include production quotas; fixed prices; price supports; assistance with storage, transportation, and supplies (such as fertilizer); and the extent to which rural people share the benefits of agricultural productivity (that sharing does not occur when there is a cheap-food policy and when resources are used to enhance quality of life in cities but not in rural areas). Mismanagement of national development efforts can compound the hunger problem. Quality of life can mean many things, including access to educational, cultural, recreational, and health resources, as well as to electricity, water, transportation, and housing. In some locations, huge disparities contribute to high rates of migration from rural to urban areas (Resource C, #13: *urban-rural relations*). In addition to massive urban unemployment and money spent on the resultant urban ills that is not available for national development, the depleted rural work force may help to depress agricultural production

(Resource C, #10: *economy*). In extreme conditions such as civil war, governments may restrict food supply to try to subdue rebellious regions (Resource C, #19: *minorities*). Sometimes governments refuse international assistance because they prefer not to acknowledge that famine conditions exist (Resource C, #9: *government*).

Another pervasive influence is economic conditions because they affect all aspects of the causes and effects of hunger (Resource C, #10: *economy*). A healthy, expanding economy allows allocation of resources to reduce problems associated with famine conditions, such as by accumulating surpluses beforehand as a buffer and by purchasing food from outside the country. Desirable economic conditions also allow investment in the infrastructure: flood control, irrigation, mechanization, and transportation projects that can undergird agricultural development and increased food production. A healthy economy also allows development of social services that contribute to population control (Resource C, #22: *social services*). Other economic reforms to reduce hunger have included combinations of free and regulated markets for inputs and outputs, attention to small as well as large producers, and commitment to democratic economic life and civil liberties. By contrast, a stagnant economy or runaway inflation compounds the problems of the victims of hunger and reduces the resources from either government or non-government organizations to help with short-term relief or long-term solutions.

Regarding both political and economic influences on hunger, educational activities can address multiple audiences— from policy makers and administrators to the people in many roles upon whom policy implementation depends (including members of the general public in democracies whose understanding of public policy issues can affect the options considered by policy makers and leaders). Although the providers and program formats typically vary with the audiences, because each is associated with part of an interrelated social system, it is important for planners of educational programs related to hunger to understand how the parts can fit together.

Increasingly, political, economic, and agricultural affairs are international (Resource C, #15: *international influences*). In developing countries, farmers who shift from subsistence to commercial agriculture are subject to international market forces, so that distant decisions related to supply, demand, and price can have an even more devastating impact on their lives than the weather. Without bargaining power, exports may not be profitable. Passing concerns in North America about pesticides used on fruit imported from South America can have a calamitous effect on sales for one or more seasons. Of course, governmental policies and assistance can soften the impact on growers and exporters. Because importing and exporting food is so extensive, international relations can be part of both the hunger problem and the solution. Some large agricultural agribusinesses provide their own extension services for local farmers with whom they work, in addition to national agricultural extension services (Resource C, #2: *parent organization;* #3: *enterprises*). Foreign aid has contributed to agricultural development, and international nongovernmental organizations are active in hunger relief (Resource C, #8: *financing*). Greater appreciation of ways in which international activities help or hinder national efforts to improve the world hunger situation can provide the basis for well-meaning people to help. Educational programs within a country can explore the tradeoffs of costs and benefits likely to be associated with various international agricultural arrangements.

National and international efforts to reduce hunger are interconnected. Many countries with widespread hunger have the capability to feed more people. In addition to the foregoing influences, the current famine in Africa has been worsened by civil war; transience; high prices for food, feed, and livestock; and poor education, especially of women (Resource C, #21: *educational level*). Although hunger can breed passivity, the resourcefulness of people facing survival can be impressive. International interdependence is reducing the presumed benefits to economically developed countries of the low wages that create hunger in developing countries. Increased appreciation of causes, conditions, and results of hunger has contributed to progress. Between 1960 and 1985, forty-one countries ended hunger as a social problem, though they were economically developed countries. Successful long-term efforts have been comprehensive, such as China's attention to agricultural production, family planning, flood control, literacy, health, and nonfarm rural enterprises. Even short-term crises, such as the current famine in

Africa, can benefit from comparative perspectives: stockpiling of food supplies regionally to improve responsiveness and recognition that conflicts elsewhere will divert attention. Adult education about hunger can even inform the emerging international economic order so that adequate attention is given to human and ecological considerations (Hunger Project, 1985; Lappé and Collins, 1986).

The preceding review suggests some of the complexity of an issue such as hunger and the variety of interrelated audiences for educational activities to address aspects of it. There are a number of useful implications from this example for policy and planning of comprehensive educational programs for adults in the United States. Although it may be important to provide educational programs on topics and for adults at strategic points in the social system, this does not mean that a gigantic centrally coordinated program is warranted. Especially in a diverse and pluralistic country such as the United States, such a monolithic approach is contraindicated. Instead, the main benefit of a systemic perspective on education for social change is that many independent providers of educational programs for adults contribute their special expertise as a part of their mission to a concerted effort (Resource C, #4: *educational institutions;* #5: *other organizations*).

Even though each provider can focus on only one or a few aspects of a problem, leaders in each organization should have an overview of needed educational programs and the ways that they can complement each other in symbiotic ways to effect social change. A comparative perspective on societal influences on similar programs in other settings can alert leaders to unexamined dynamics in their own situation and to opportunities for collaboration. Although it is a challenge to prepare an insightful and locally relevant analysis of an issue for which a comprehensive set of educational programs for adults is needed, once one or several are prepared, they can be of great value to leaders in each contributing provider organization. Such assessments can be disseminated through talks, journal articles, organization newsletters, and special mailings. The interested audiences may be very specialized. They may use such an overview in several ways, such as strengthening their rationale regarding the salience of the issue to people in the United States, understanding how various educational programs related to the issue are complementary, inventorying available programs in their service area that address the issue, identifying gaps in existing programs, selecting a market niche for their current and new programs that reflects their mission and resources, and preparing the justification for external financial support of a pertinent program that requires subsidy.

Some of the major influences on hunger worldwide are not prominent causes in the United States. One benefit of a comparative perspective is to enhance understanding of the specific cultural context. For example, about 3 percent of the work force produces all of the food and fiber for the U.S. population, with surpluses for storage and export. This figure compares with 70 or 80 percent of the population of some developing countries engaged in all aspects of agriculture (Resource C, #10: *economy*). In the United States, there have also been substantial investments in the agricultural infrastructure. Examples include irrigation, flood control projects, manufacture of farm equipment, transportation capacity for harvests, grain elevators, and many other agribusinesses, such as food processing and production of fertilizers and pesticides. In addition, affluence allows importing special foods from around the world (Resource C, #15: *international influences*). Clearly, inadequate food production is not a major cause of hunger in the United States.

Also, population control does not seem to be part of the problem. Average birth rates have dropped since the postwar period to zero population growth levels, and the current boomlet reflects larger numbers of young adults having children, not higher average numbers of children. Although illegal aliens pose various problems, recent immigration levels have helped alleviate tight labor markets in some regions and are projected to continue to do so into the next century. Rapid population growth is not a major current cause of hunger in the United States (Resource C, #28: *population change*).

Paradoxically, in a land of plenty, starvation exists next to affluence (Resource C, #23: *elites*). Average levels of production and consumption mask the distribution problem. Unlike regional famine caused by crop failure or civil war, malnutrition, hunger, and starvation in the United States are more localized and often occur in poverty areas that adjoin well-to-do neighborhoods (Resource C,

#20: *stratification*). It reflects breakdowns not in supply and demand but in the functioning of individuals, families, neighborhoods, and public and private sector "safety nets" designed to assist people in distress. Other situations create or compound the conditions that lead to hunger or starvation. One example is the unwillingness of unemployed coal miners in remote areas of the Appalachians to relocate to find work. Another is homeless or solitary old people without family support or welfare assistance. Deinstitutionalized adults who are mentally retarded or emotionallly disturbed can also become part of the problem of hunger in America. Unemployed urban minority youth are another major part, as was dramatized in the riots in May 1992. All of these factors are compounded by alcohol and drug addiction. The U.S. drug problem is affected by production in rural areas of developing countries because of its profitability and by distribution by international drug cartels. However, drug and alcohol abuse is so destructive and widespread at all levels of society that major causes are associated with demand rather than supply (Resource C, #26: *health*). The use of drugs and alcohol reflects a deeper hunger for enduring satisfaction and hope by individual people, which if satisfied would make drug use an unattractive option for them.

Despite the severity and complexity of hunger in America, there are a number of components of a comprehensive synergistic strategy that are already in place upon which a provider of educational programs for adults could build. The problem does not seem to have a solely individual solution, or the appropriate educational programs would be for the hunger victims only. There is growing recognition of the extent and urgency of the problem for the families that are affected, as reflected in the conferences, books, and media coverage during the past decade. It is apparent that the causes and cures of the pockets of hunger in the United States are different than for the regional famines that occur in developing countries. Also, U.S. policy makers have explored both public and private sector solutions in contrast with countries with centralized political-economic systems, some of which have revealed their hunger problems in recent years. U.S. educational efforts to combat hunger are seldom linked to direct assistance such as food stamps and school lunch subsidies to children of low-income families. Nutrition information is seldom tied to such direct assistance.

Some religious congregations have connected education and assistance, but usually for the donors rather than the recipients (Resource C, #18: *religion*). For instance, they provide adult religious education activities and materials for congregation members on topics related to hunger in America and encourage members to make monthly donations to the local free food pantry. Otherwise, the expanded food and nutrition education program of the Cooperative Extension Service (CES) is an example of education for recipients (Resource C, #4: *educational institutions*) not connected to religious groups. The program is aimed at rural and urban low-income homemakers and uses paraprofessional nutrition aides under the supervision of professional home economists. The aides periodically visit the homemakers to discuss choices of foods for recent meals and possible changes that would help stretch the food dollar while at the same time increase nutritional content and appeal to family members. The content is practical, and follow-up studies indicate that it results in enduring improvements in understanding and family nutrition. During adverse economic conditions, some of these families would be at risk regarding malnutrition.

If a provider of educational programs for adults wants to address an aspect of hunger in America, what are some promising possibilities? Suggestions include the following:

1. Several providers and experts might help the mass media offer programs to increase public awareness of the nature and extent of hunger in America along with sources of assistance to people at risk and opportunities for staff and volunteers to work in that area (Resource C, #12: *media*).
2. Providers with expertise in nutrition education might create or expand individual or small-group programs for high-risk adults, as a supplement to the CES nutrition education program for low-income homemakers.
3. Providers with community development expertise and interest in a local hunger problem might mobilize local interested organizations and individuals to study the current situation and then marshal resources to achieve improvements.

4. Members of religious institutions, voluntary associations, and community agencies (such as the YMCA and YWCA or a senior citizens center) might participate in educational activities conducted by their organizations to help the members understand the problem and ways they can contribute their time and money as volunteers and donors to local efforts.
5. Interprofessional continuing education programs might alert members of the helping professions to the high-risk populations that they are likely to encounter and what they can do, including referrals.
6. Higher education institutions and appropriate associations might cosponsor conferences and consultations for policy makers to explore the hunger aspect of various social problems and programs, to critique current efforts, and to recommend improvements in policy and delivery (Resource C, #4: *educational institutions*).
7. A university might invite opinion leaders interested in many aspects of hunger in America to a forum to explore multiple views on the issue (Resource C, #7: *priority*).

If, in a service area, continuing education leaders interested in hunger could gain a comparative perspective on the issue and current adult educational programs on this topic, there might be several benefits. Individual providers could decide the specific subjects and audiences that warranted new or expanded programs. Multiple providers could cosponsor programs, which would then be more likely to succeed. Most importantly, a comprehensive perspective can enable cooperating providers to engage in synergistic and developmental planning likely to make a difference. Hunger is only one of many problem areas that a comprehensive adult education program could address. The example illustrates major societal influences on problem areas that need collaboration by multiple providers, which in turn requires strategic leadership and comparative perspectives. The small but growing number of adult education leaders with such an understanding are both oriented toward the future and able to understand how their provider agencies function in relation to other providers and major societal influences in their service area. Such systemic thinking emphasizes contextual analysis of external opportunities and threats to a greater extent than most adult education practitioners have in the past. Strategic planning and implementation provide a useful means to do so.

Open Systems

Strategic planning should provide a broad perspective on the open system that includes the agency providing adult education, its parent organization, other providers, client systems, and resource systems. Planning should increase responsiveness to major issues and societal influences in the service area. Such influences affect agency functioning and our understanding of it. It is important, therefore, to analyze the flow of inputs (such as participants, instructors, money, and other resources) into the agency; the transformations that occur as these ingredients are combined; the outcomes that result; and the feedback and reactions that have an impact on the flow of inputs. Adult education leaders who understand their provider agency in such systemic terms are able to strengthen agency functioning. Agencies can produce similar results in different ways. Leaders can use integrative thinking for planning systemically with synergistic release of energy and cooperation (Bhola, 1983; Bhola, 1988, chap. 6; Bogard, 1992; Botkin, Elmandjra, and Malitza, 1979; Senge, 1990).

External aspects of strategic planning entail analysis of major societal opportunities and threats and their implications for the provider agency. A range of economic, political, and social influences affect adult education provider agencies. A comparative perspective helps agency leaders identify salient influences to analyze and monitor, amid the myriad forces that are less important in their context. Economic influences include the general state of the national and local economy, as well as specific features of local work force supply and demand that have implications for adult education. Political influences encompass public policies and resource allocations at local, national, and international levels. Social influences involve both broad demographic shifts (such as immigration trends or an aging society) and traditional practices related to family, religion, or health.

Many of such societal influences that can be analyzed separately reflect widespread cultural values that have an impact on the functioning of adult education agencies and can be addressed in the content of their programs. Examples include distributions of power in society and individualism versus community (Bellah and others, 1985; Bock and Papagiannis, 1983; Dahrendorf, 1979). Educational programs can encourage participants to reflect critically on their assumptions and beliefs and to question societal procedures and expectations (Apps, 1988). The fabric of society is composed of many and diverse subcultures related to such distinctions as social class, religious beliefs, gender, age, place of residence, racial and ethnic groups, and language. Clientele analysis can help identify subpopulations of participants in order to strengthen program responsiveness. Programs can also address the benefits of unity as well as encourage appreciation of diversity. Unity and cohesion are enhanced by the experience of individual participants as members of multiple and overlapping subcultures. For example, feelings of social distance regarding someone of a different race or income level can be mitigated by a sense of solidarity based on shared place of residence, gender, and religion.

The transformations that provider agencies seek to help adult learners accomplish are seldom solitary journeys. Most people are accompanied on their developmental journey by a caravan of family, friends, and associates whose support or resistance can help or hinder transformations. Educational interventions on behalf of such transitions are analogous to rites of passage, which typically include both the person making the transition and members of the community. Comprehensive educational programs aimed at major personal, organizational, or community development include both the primary audience of adult learners and people in related roles whose support is essential for constructive and enduring progress. It is helpful for adult education leaders to reflect on this developmental process of change and the importance of addressing multiple categories of participants related to a problem area (Davis, Thomson, Oxman, and Haynes, 1992).

Reflection also helps practitioners to be critical of the past as they analyze agency mission and performance in a changing context. Critical reflection can contribute to emerging opportunities and create new program visions for the future. The following example of enterprise training and education demonstrates a relationship between social change and agency functioning. It provides a contrast with the preceding example and illustrates links between community, organizational, and personal change.

Change and Impact

Sweeping technological changes are creating new realities in education and training within enterprises (including private businesses and government organizations). For generations, newly hired office workers could learn to use new equipment and procedures while old timers could do their work in traditional ways. This was the case because work changes occurred slowly enough to be accommodated gradually through personnel changes. This situation changed abruptly during the past generation.

Today, new technology such as word processing, is affecting the social system of the work organization. Workplace education is thus required to address the systemic changes and societal influences that are altering the fundamental nature of work. The accelerating pace of technological and social change is reducing the time frame for an alteration in work practices and is increasing the frequency and extent of retraining. Staff training and education are among the most rapidly expanding segments of adult education. In some occupations, it takes the equivalent of a day a week to learn new developments and avoid obsolescence (Willis, Dubin, and Associates, 1990). Such widespread changes affect more than work skills. Also affected are the specialized knowledge base for each job, interpersonal relations among the people with whom each worker interacts, and the policy framework within which the work occurs (Zuboff, 1988).

As a result, planning of educational activities for staff members should be forward looking and comprehensive, not just reactive and piecemeal. An educational objective should be to help staff members understand and deal with broader views of societal change and personal adaptation. This understanding involves an appreciation of ways in which various categories of staff members interact as team members and as parts of an interdependent social system. Categories include those newly hired, experienced workers, supervisors, policy makers, and support staff in departments such as finance, personnel, and data processing. The impact of education and training is typically greater if it goes beyond specialized staff development for individuals to reflect comprehensive planning. Educational planning is comprehensive to the extent that it includes people in the various interdependent roles who should have a stake in the organizational improvements to be achieved. Marketing concepts and procedures can encourage such participation. Planning and implementation are synergistic to the extent that key stakeholders are included in interrelated educational activities that produce cumulative improvements in team and system performance. This approach is reflected in current attention to total quality improvement. As successful directors of musical ensembles and coaches of athletic teams well understand, individual improvement is a necessary but not sufficient condition for effective performance by the group. Organization development activities can help align personal, team, and organization efforts.

There is another important relationship between comprehensive and individual educational activities that should be noted. The main strength of a comprehensive educational program is that the inclusion of major stakeholders is generally a more powerful way to achieve systemic changes than one limited to individual progress. However, such an approach can be tyrannical and discourage individual creativity and dissent. Fortunately, comprehensive and individual activities are not mutually exclusive. When a larger-scale educational program is warranted to achieve systemic change, it is important also to encourage individual educational opportunities as a safeguard. For example, some enterprises reimburse members for costs of participation in outside educational programs.

Strategic planning should provide an efficient way to understand the functioning of an adult education agency in its changing societal context. Historical studies of agencies analyze similar sets of complex trends and influences on certain issues (Charters and Hilton, 1989; Titmus, 1981). Leaders typically focus on the present and future and face the even more difficult task of identifying *emerging* trends and implications without the benefit of hindsight. Environmental scanning and futures forecasting are designed to extract from the mass of detailed complex information some insights to guide today's planning and implementation decisions for tomorrow's realities (Ascher, 1978; Callan, 1986; Morrison, 1987; Theobald, 1987). In this book, the focus is on agency functioning in its service area, although this of course occurs within the broader context of national policies, plans, and conditions, and also depends on planning decisions made by individual instructors and participants. In leadership and planning, it is important to recognize the hierarchical level on which to focus. Strategic planning combines features of long-range planning with planned change by involving people who are to implement plans. This involvement of stakeholders can enrich the planning process and increase the likelihood of implementation. Perspectives and commitment from involvement in strategic planning can help stakeholders gain understandings of agency purposes and procedures so that leadership is amplified (Mackenzie, 1991). Strategic planning is ongoing but tends to be most concentrated and visible when plans are being prepared and updated.

Adult education agencies and programs vary greatly in their relative focus on individual, group, organizational, or community change. The focus that is selected has many implications for leadership. They include the definition of potential participants, specification of intended outcomes, selection of educational methods, involvement of stakeholders, and development of evaluation procedures to assess impact. Such attention to change and the contribution of education entails more than analysis of structural features of the agency and its relation to society. Systems analysis stresses current assumptions and conditions. Strategic planning also includes attention to what ought to be (such as power relations) and should contribute to a rationale for whether evolutionary or revolutionary change is warranted. Leadership for planned change depends on understanding the internal and external forces at work (Senge, 1990).

Leadership of educational programs for adults is strategic to the extent that multiple stakeholders contribute to future planning and implementation. It is comprehensive to the extent that two or more adult education providers cooperate to serve two or more categories of adult learners related to a problem area, where a concerted effort is more likely to have an impact than separate programs. An understanding of societal influences is especially important in such comprehensive efforts. Collaboration among providers is more likely to be successful if leaders have a comparative perspective to understand how the other providers function as social systems related to their client and resource system. Contextual analysis and environmental scanning can help adult education leaders strengthen the external aspects of strategic planning and implementation.

There are many benefits to strategic planning and implementation in addition to agency survival, wise use of resources, and stakeholder support. Strategic leadership can contribute to effective collaboration when appropriate and can increase client and societal benefits. The desired result of an enhanced understanding of societal influences is synergistic adult education leadership to achieve an impact.

2

Part-Time Study
at Educational
Institutions

Ensuring that educational opportunities for part-time students have a central place is a crucial challenge to leaders of adult and continuing education provided by educational institutions. Parent organizations greatly influence such programs of schools, colleges, and universities, especially part-time study in the evening or at outreach locations in credit courses to earn diplomas and degrees. Unlike innovative noncredit programs that are mainly described in other chapters, part-time study in credit courses is constrained by requirements, procedures, and expectations that have evolved in preparatory education programs for young full-time students and that are imposed on adult education programs to assure "quality." As a result, part-time study in educational institutions includes some of the least innovative and responsive adult education programs. However, it is useful to begin with such programs when exploring planning and leadership. This chapter describes basic themes of provider agency functioning (especially relations with both parent organization and clients) that recur in various forms in subsequent chapters.

Increasing Access

A long-standing issue for practitioners who plan and coordinate the adult education offerings at formal education institutions has been how to serve adults who want to study part time in an educational institution oriented toward the preparatory education of young people who study full time. This issue involves the types of educational opportunities that adults seek, the problems of access that they confront, and the societal influences that affect efforts to improve access for adult learners. Attention to this issue is vital because current arrangements for all adult education providers in the United States are widening the gap between the "haves" and the "have nots." Relations with the parent organization are important for planning because they are part of the problem and of the solution.

A century ago, schools and colleges typically served young people who studied full time to prepare for careers or further education. This situation was so in the United States and in most other countries. During this century, a steadily expanding proportion of students served by U.S. public elementary and secondary schools and by higher education institutions have been adults of an increasingly broad age range who study on a part-time or short-term basis. Today, such adult learners who enroll in higher education degree credit courses now outnumber traditional younger students who come directly from secondary school. Who makes up this new majority of adult part-time students, why do they return to school, and what problems of access remain that warrant strategic planning? How do institutional practices affect access?

Early in this century, adult education participants in educational institutions were mainly from less advantaged subpopulations, and remedial programs predominated. Public schools started vocational education courses for farmers and blue collar workers, and in cities with large immigrant populations schools offered adult basic education and Americanization programs. Land-grant universities created the Cooperative Extension Service to help rural adults; other public universities initiated extension courses to reduce spatial barriers; and urban colleges and universities increasingly offered evening courses to overcome time constraints. By midcentury, growing community college systems accepted many students not traditionally included in higher education, half of whom attended part time.

The part-time participants in the adult education agencies of educational institutions early in the century were predominantly young, male, and undereducated. By contrast, more women than men attend today. There is a wide age range (with average ages in the thirties or early forties); an increasing number of retired people attend; and voluntary participation rates are higher for adults with high levels of formal education than for those with low levels.

What attracts so many adults to part-time study in educational institutions? Of course, there are many benefits sought by this new majority, and the reasons for attendance vary. Those who pursue a diploma, certificate, or degree anticipate that it will enhance their career, education, and general quality of life. This trend appears to be very beneficial to providers, so what is the problem? The adult education practitioner confronts at least two issues that require planning attention. One is that some adults who want to study part time at an educational institution still confront barriers that could be reduced. Another is that adult education practitioners in educational institutions often struggle with institutional constraints regarding not only adult students but also policy, staffing, and resources. Practitioners who understand both the dynamics between the adult education agency and its parent organization and the major societal influences can improve their educational leadership.

Educational institutions vary greatly in their acceptance of adult and continuing education as an important part of their mission. At one extreme is private schools and colleges whose predominant mission is to serve young people who attend full time. At the other extreme are community colleges and land-grant universities, which have a dual commitment to both preparatory and continuing education. Between these extremes, there is a continuum of institutions in which the adult education function ranges from being marginal to central. Especially in institutions in the middle of this continuum, adult education practitioners must contend with potential barriers that affect adult part-time students directly or indirectly. Educators must ensure that courses and conferences are scheduled at convenient times and locations and that evening hours are available for related services such as library materials and advisement. Another problem is finances. When the adult education function is central, the agency receives financial subsidy so that tuition and fees are minor deterrents (for example, the Cooperative Extension Service subsidizes noncredit programs, and community colleges subsidize credit courses). The financial obstacle for students can be reduced by practices of the institution, government, and employers. Institutional practices can permit students to pay tuition in installments, government student loan policies can allow financial assistance for part-time enrollment; and some students' employers have tuition reimbursement policies. Less tangible barriers include institutional images and policies discouraging faculty members from teaching courses that meet in the evening, on weekends, or off campus.

Broad societal trends influence institutional priority for adult education. A recent one has been the decline in the numbers of young people (following the post–World War II population bulge), which has resulted in smaller enrollments by traditional preparatory education students and increased priority for adult part-time students to fill classrooms, occupy teachers and meet budget requirements. Another trend is demand for education by adult learners due to shortages of qualified workers for specialized occupations.

Practitioners who are committed to serve adult learners value equity and are distressed by the extent to which annual participation rates in *all types* of educational programs for adults reflect levels of formal education that adults have already achieved. Each year in the United States, about one out of twenty adults who have not completed elementary education takes part in some adult education activity—compared with one out of four adults who finished secondary school and one of two adults who completed a year or more of university studies beyond an undergraduate bachelor's degree. With voluntary adult education, higher participation rates by those with the most formal education indicate both their personal commitment and the encouragement they receive. This situation is even more true in adult education offered by educational institutions than in programs by most other providers (business enterprises, labor unions, and religious institutions). Regardless of reasons, the unfortunate result for individuals and society is that instead of narrowing the gap between the haves and the have nots, adult education programs are helping to *widen* the gap.

To strengthen the continuing education function to better serve adult learners, effective practitioners seek to increase support from other parts of their institution and to address broader societal influences. To explore strategic planning challenges, concepts, and procedures that are related to part-time study in educational institutions, this chapter next presents an example from community colleges. This is followed by an overview of planning for adult education by U.S. schools and universities. The subsequent section analyzes similar programs in Sweden, from which practitioners in the United States can learn much about policy support. This discussion is followed by one of planning issues and efforts in other countries that have implications for strengthening U.S. practice. The chapter concludes with a synthesis of strategic planning guidelines with an emphasis on relations with the parent organization.

The examples and rationale in this chapter concentrate on four interrelated aspects of strategic planning. These are clarifying agency goals and missions, strengthening relations with the parent institution, attracting participants, and collaborating with other organizations. In addition, attention is given to vision and leadership provided by adult education practitioners as they deal with other internal aspects of agency functioning (such as attracting participants and staff) as these local contingencies are affected by external influences: economic conditions, government policy, and practices in other countries.

Community College Continuing Education

In the late 1980s, an innovative, collaborative effort to strengthen education of adults and young people in its service area was made by a midwestern community college in conjunction with three other educational institutions. They were the public schools, the public library, and the local museum. In 1988, their plan to strengthen personal, family, community, and economic development through organizing a communitywide learning and information process was submitted to the citizens, institutions, and professionals of the area.

The community college served the rural area and small city in a county with a population approaching 150,000, of whom about 36,000 lived in the city. The community college, which had an enrollment of about five thousand students, provided a variety of credit and noncredit adult education programs.

The following overview and rationale for the plan illustrates a synergistic planning model for strengthening educational programs for adults in a local area, in which a community college is a major partner. This section then gives a summary of U.S. community colleges as providers of part-time educational opportunities for adults, along with societal influences on such programs that strategic planning should address.

In collaboration with the local public schools, library, and museum, the college evolved a holistic vision of an educative community in which children and adults could learn in many settings: individually, in the family, at work, in educational institutions, through the mass media, in religious institutions, and in various community organizations and voluntary associations. The four institutions used a planning process designed to achieve broad community involvement to explore this vision for strengthening learning opportunities and to obtain commitment to a plan of action. They incorporated a nonprofit entity, which they called the Educational Maintenance Organization (EMO), as a mechanism to link individual learners, local educational providers, and a national electronic information delivery system (an education utility). On behalf of the EMO, the college helped convene planning meetings, provide staff assistance, achieve agreement on a community agenda for strengthening learning opportunities, and contract with the education utility for modern telecommunications technology such as video and computer networks and data bases. The EMO goal of helping local people to become more self-directed, goal-centered lifelong learners reflected the U.S. emphasis on individualism (Bellah and others, 1985). Another EMO goal of using modern telecommunications technology to support efforts to strengthen local educational opportunities demonstrated a local effort to integrate emerging technological capabilities, such as computers, video monitors, data bases, electronic mail, and training. The third EMO goal of synergistic linking of individuals, educational providers, and community organizations arose from a conviction by the EMO organizations about the importance of a comprehensive perspective on learning opportunities to offset the many incentives that encourage specialization and fragmentation.

The rationale for the plan was based on the ideas of Niebuhr

(1984), who identified several societal shifts promoting a general movement toward increased individual responsibility for lifelong learning. According to Niebuhr, the challenge to increase economic productivity was stimulated by the shift to high technology and intense international competition. The search for new life-styles and rules for family relation had occurred as a result of high individualism and a sense of loss of family stability. The need for increased civic literacy was increased by urban loss of communal identity and by media-based politics accompanied by declining participation. The intent of the EMO was to encourage community-wide cooperation to strengthen lifelong educational opportunities to pursue such goals. With the bewildering array of learning opportunities, community-based educational counseling was also becoming important to help people make informed choices (Heffernan, 1981).

The EMO planning process was designed to achieve a broad base of community agreement and support. In developing and implementing the plan, the college, schools, library, and museum drew on many people and organizations that had a potential stake in its success. The plan was distributed, discussed at meetings, and reported in the media to the general community. Because the plan was to benefit young people in school as well as all types of adult education, the process included a range of providers of formal and nonformal education, along with enterprises, religious institutions, community agencies, and families. Meetings convened people from various organizations to encourage cooperation, and training programs were provided to foster use of technology (Crookes and Associates, 1988).

The early planning led to preparation of a proposal for a very large foundation grant, which after several years of effort was not approved. Following this frustrating hiatus, the community college pursued a more limited low-technology project that could be initiated and sustained with local resources. One lesson that could be learned from this experience was the importance of allowing new programs to evolve gradually. More recently, in a southern state, a similar collaborative effort focused on environmental education was initiated, but it avoided dependence on external funding of a large proposal; instead, it began small, with evolving support from local resources. Collaborators included the school system, a local education foundation, the chamber of commerce's economic development department, a data systems company, a cablevision company, and a state technology grant of $200,000. During 1991–92, telecommunications were used to serve school students and their families in a community of ninety thousand people. In the 1992–93 school year, they plan to expand service to community groups and enterprises.

The midwestern community college was distinctive in some respects but shared many characteristics with most other such institutions across the country (Merriam and Cunningham, 1989, chap. 24). Although the first public community college in the United States dates to the turn of this century, most were started in the late 1950s and 1960s during the great expansion of higher education institutions. Except for those in large metropolitan areas, most community college districts include at least one urban center and the surrounding rural area. Community colleges fill a distinctive niche in formal education by providing postsecondary education opportunities for those who do not enroll in four-year bachelor's degree programs at colleges and universities. Course offerings include two-year associate degree transfer programs, which constitute the first two years of a bachelor's degree program, and many shorter-term certificate and noncredit vocational education programs. Almost from the outset, more than half of the students in credit and degree programs have been adult part-time participants, and many other adults take part in noncredit programs. Because adult students make up a large proportion of the students, adult education is a responsibility of all parts of many community colleges, in contrast with other types of educational institutions that have a separate continuing education division to coordinate outreach programs.

Collaboration has been a widespread feature of community colleges. They have provided cooperation in vocational education and location of outreach courses with the public school systems in the district, articulation for transfer students to four-year colleges and universities in the state, and cooperation with enterprises and community agencies. Collaboration has been especially prominent in the continuing education and community service function.

Community college adult education is affected by some major societal influences. State legislation has authorized most community colleges. Typically, state appropriations support about one-third of costs, with the other two-thirds coming from local taxes and from student tuition. Degree-credit courses for part-time students are equivalent in tuition, facility requirements, and most other respects to courses for full-time students. Many noncredit programs are subsidized by external funds, such as the Federal Job Training Partnership Act for job retraining for the underemployed. However, other noncredit programs, especially nonoccupational ones, may require full-cost recovery from participant fees. Some enterprises provide tuition reimbursement that reduces financial deterrents for interested employees. Employment trends affect enrollments; for example, there has been an expansion of service occupations and the need to cope with technological changes in many occupations. Community college adult education is usually quite responsive to social and economic trends and issues that affect their districts. The dramatic expansion of enrollments during the decades following World War II was a result of the increasing numbers of young people and the rising proportions of secondary school graduates who continued on to higher education (a number that reached about one-half the graduates). The gradual drop in community college enrollments since 1982 indicates declining numbers of young adults. Many community college and public school adult education programs offer programs in response to community demand, so that they are greatly shaped by enrollments. In addition, adult education administrators have made agreements with enterprises, community agencies, and other organizations for cosponsored programs. Examples include in-service education for allied health personnel in hospitals and educational programs for older adults in senior centers. Participation by older adults and by minorities reflect demographic trends in the society, trends that are likely to continue through the coming decade or two.

Educational Programs for Adults by Schools

All types of educational institutions in the United States provide adult and continuing education programs, not just community colleges. The proportion of effort devoted to adult part-time students

varies greatly. Although some public school adult education programs are extensive, they constitute a small portion of the school
system budget, in part because they depend mainly on part-time
staff on annual contracts, on student fees, external funding from
federal and state sources, and contract funds from local organizations. Private secondary schools, which seldom receive external
funding for the purpose, offer little adult education. By contrast,
proprietary schools, such as private business colleges, depend heavily on part-time enrollments. During the past decade or so, declining numbers of secondary students have helped accelerate the
increasing proportion of part-time college and university students.
In many institutions, adults are the new majority, and in some
instances there have been gradual changes toward more responsive
programs and organizational arrangements. Some colleges, faced
with serious enrollment and financial problems, have made dramatic changes to attract adult students, such as small rural institutions opening extension centers in urban areas.

In addition to basic skills programs (covered in Chapter
Three), public schools in the United States have provided a variety
of adult education programs, including community education, vocational education, and cultural programs (Merriam and Cunningham, 1989, pp. 287–302, 278–489). The extent and type of adult
education offerings by a local school system depended on relations
between the adult education department and the remainder of the
school system. Some of these relationships have been shaped by
population characteristics in the district and by school system policies regarding long-term commitments to full-time adult education
staff. Although the following generalizations identify widespread
societal influences to consider for planning purposes, there are of
course exceptions within and among states. District population
characteristics are especially influential because they affect learner
demand, school system resources, and competing providers.

For example, in affluent suburban school districts, budgets
are generally higher than average, even in states with differential
state aid to help equalize school funds across districts. In addition,
affluent families in such districts are willing and able to contribute
volunteer time and extra funds for supplemetary facilities, programs, and services. District policies are set by elected local school

boards that emphasize local commitment to lifelong learning and furnish some subsidy of adult education through free use of facilities and some basic staff salaries. By contrast, in most rural and large city school districts where people have less formal education and family income, there are lower levels of resources and commitment to adult education. In poorer districts, there are also fewer full-time and long-term staff positions for adult education teaching and administration. Instead, the main reliance has been on people with part-time adult education positions, a situation that results in less continuity and innovation than is possible in other, generally more affluent, districts. Local adult education offerings are also affected by other providers, such as a YMCA or YWCA or community colleges whose programs can supplement or extend those of the schools. Another local influence is the employment base and economic conditions. Adult education opportunities are enhanced by larger enterprises with tuition reimbursement, by high employment rates that encourage adults to study for advancement, and by cooperation between schools and enterprises (such as in vocational cooperative work-study programs).

There are also societal influences on adult education beyond the local district, in addition to national and international economic conditions that affect the local economy. One example is federal and state legislation and appropriations for adult education. In addition to external financial assistance for adult basic education and for immigrants (that are described in subsequent chapters on basic education and minorities), there are several laws related to adult vocational education, which include formula funds distributed each year based on population to be served and special grant funds in response to proposals. States vary greatly in their additional support for public school adult education.

The vitality of public school adult education programs especially reflects the leadership of the director of adult education and key staff members. Staff members with a compelling vision of the importance of adult education for both the community and the school system, combined with organizational effectiveness, can harness positive influences (such as support from the school board and the school superintendent). They can also minimize negative influences (for example, a rise in unemployment can increase adult education enrollments in the short run, but after unemployment benefits run out and people lose hope of finding jobs, unemployment can depress enrollments). Because of the potential contribution of such local leadership and program vitality, some states have provided incentives to local school districts to appoint full-time or at least half-time directors of adult education and have supported professional development opportunities for adult education staff.

The foregoing overview suggests some of the potential stakeholders whom adult education leaders can include in strategic planning, some of the ways they can do so, and some of the societal influences to consider. One category of stakeholder is school district teachers, administrators, and school board members whose support and assistance for adult education programs is likely to depend on their understanding of benefits for both district and community. Another category includes state-level adult education administrators, who in addition to dispensing formula funds can assist with special-project grants and staff development. A third is directors of other providers of adult and continuing education in the district whose collaboration can strengthen and supplement school programs. A fourth category of stakeholder consists of members of a representative adult education advisory committee, which can contribute to contextual analysis, needs assessment, and priority setting that take into account major threats and opportunities. An essential aspect of strategic leadership is inclusion of people from such stakeholder categories in the planning and implementation process.

University Continuing Education

Further insights for strengthening part-time study opportunities are gained by consideration of university continuing education. Large American comprehensive universities with graduate schools and various professional colleges usually provide extensive continuing higher education programs under somewhat decentralized organizational arrangements. In this chapter, the focus is on part-time study by adults in undergraduate and graduate degree credit and certificate programs. In practice, many more adults are served by noncredit programs that may be even more decentralized and less visible because they usually serve specialized audiences. Although evening or extension credit course offerings in public universities may receive some financial subsidy, noncredit programs (aside from the Cooperative Extension Service) are generally provided on a cost-recovery basis from student fees (Merriam and Cunningham, 1989, pp. 303–315).

A central issue in continuing higher education is shared governance; continuing education staff must try to deal with both representatives of client groups and university administrators and faculty members. This issue underlies questions of priority for continuing education participants and programs, resource allocations, and type of organizational structure and extent of control (such as centralized administration combined with decentralized program decision making by faculty members). Strategic leaders seek agreement on priorities as they try to achieve a mutually satisfactory linkage between client and resource systems. Effective program development is collaborative, with major participation by learners and their representatives on planning committees. Institutional support depends on programmatic congruence with university priorities, benefits, and procedures. In the past, continuing education administrators have performed this linkage between client needs and institutional resources most creatively and effectively when they were relating well with both clients and institution (Knox, 1982b; Votruba, 1981).

A recent study of undergraduate programs for adults, with direct implications for the University of Maryland, University College, helps identify external influences and suggestions for planning (Keeton, 1990). A major theme is the importance of understanding the distinctive characteristics of adult part-time students as a basis for assuring access to responsive programs serving diverse learners with competing responsibilities. This emphasis on adapting procedures for adult learners, while retaining goals similar to those for full-time, younger students, is one of the options identified by Houle (1973) in his book on external degrees. Keeton (1990) recognizes that the goals and procedures of continuing higher education programs should vary according to differing contingencies and stakeholders. In Keeton's survey responses, faculty development is acknowledged as the most important administrative service; other research has also confirmed its desirability but decried its neglect (Apps, 1988; Chickering and Associates, 1981; Schlossberg, Lynch, and Chickering, 1989). Faculty development depends on staffing arrangements to attract regular faculty members from the university and adjunct experts from the community to teach continuing education courses. During the post–World War II expansion of higher education, some continuing education administrators were dismayed that faculty shortages prompted resident instruction administrators to abrogate teaching commitments on behalf of continuing education; this is a caution to consider in view of the prospect of looming faculty shortages beginning in the 1990s.

Another theme in Keeton's analysis is the desirability of equitable financial aid to part-time students. He urges continuing higher education leaders to be persuasive with institutional and public policy makers about this matter. He notes that in the interest of productivity and competitiveness of the nation's advanced economy, stakeholders should recognize that adult students need less financial assistance per course, repay loans more quickly, and pursue studies more directly related to career goals than do full-time students. Keeton's report includes an exemplary if unusual review of trends and experience elsewhere, with specific implications for institutional planning.

A contrasting approach to environmental scanning for continuing education at the University of Georgia is provided by Simerly and Associates (1989). The scanning and futures forecasting procedures used to understand relevant emerging trends in the state sought to identify early signals to guide program planning and organizational relations. Planning for scanning by the continuing education division included administrative commitment to costs and benefits, clarification of organizational mission and the purpose of scanning, and provision of a coordinator whose role included reinforcement of staff commitment to the process. An early orientation workshop emphasized voluntary and open staff involvement as the participants discussed the mission of the division, the value of environmental scanning, trial use of scanning procedures, and their willingness to volunteer to help with the scanning effort. The detailed design of the scanning process (beyond broad, voluntary participation) included explanation of responsibilities and procedures for use of a taxonomy to select and code content of publications and media. The four major taxonomy categories were social, technological, economic, and political (STEP) trends and events. Each scanner reported on specific media and prepared single-page abstracts that also assessed implications for the division. At least three times a year, interested staff members reviewed abstracts to identify a manageable number of themes (about six to ten) and to discuss ramifications for planning. The analysis procedures included delphi procedures, cross-impact analysis, and scenario development. In addition, there was documentation of actions taken in the division as a result and feedback to staff to encourage use of conclusions and continued cooperation (Morrison, 1987).

Adult education leaders in other institutions also try to use study findings to be responsive to learners and expectations within their parent organization. Regional, national, and cross-national studies help illuminate relationships between student expectations and institutional programs that have implications for strategic planning. In a study of full-time students at the University of North Dakota, somewhat older returning students were found to be surpisingly similar to traditional-age students. Undergraduate students prior to career commitment wanted faculty members to confirm them as people; more advanced students with career commitments wanted faculty members to confirm course content (Slotnick, Pelton, Fuller, and Tabor, 1992). A national study of adult (mostly part-time) students in regular higher education courses during the 1970s, indicated trends toward increased inclusion of adult students, women, older students, and minorities and discovered greater similarity in reasons for participation given by men and women.

One conclusion is that higher education programs for traditional age and adult students should be responsive to their diverse life goals and educational needs. Students are selecting artistic and creative goals less frequently than those related to status, social, family, business, and personal reasons (Solmon and Gordon, 1981). The arts and creative activity are one aspect of general or liberal adult education in the United States and United Kingdom, but other ones emphasize higher adult education for liberation and social transformation—a goal seen as possible within higher education institutions in Britain but less so in the United States. In both countries, liberal arts education has been declining in recent de-

cades, as requirements for cost recovery from student fees has shifted
the program balance toward continuing professional education
(Taylor, Rockhill, and Fieldhouse, 1985).

A study of graduate-level credit and noncredit continuing
professional education has concluded that program vitality and effectiveness are associated with educational leadership that includes
attention to both institution and clientele. Continuing education
administrators can function on the creative margin of the university
to promote mutually beneficial exchanges between institution and
community. Many of the changes in higher education institutions
have been in response to external pressures (Millard, 1991). Such
external pressures can provide leverage for continuing education
leaders (Knox, 1982a).

A comparative perspective on the foregoing overview of part-
time study in the United States is provided by the following sections
on similar programs in Sweden and in other countries.

Adult Education in Sweden

Swedish adult education has many features, such as high participation rates and solid government policy and financial support, that
make it attractive to practitioners in other countries. Although some
distinctive national characteristics prevent transplantation without
adaptation to other countries, even in Europe and North America,
Swedish success has great heuristic value. This section provides a
brief review of the national context for adult education in Sweden,
followed by more detailed examples of adult education in secondary
and higher education. It concludes with a short discussion of other
major providers of Swedish adult education, some of which will be
considered in greater detail subsequently.

Sweden's geography has influenced its adult education. Its
large size, northern climate, and sparse and homogeneous population (with Stockholm as its only large city) influence the country's
economic base and sense of national identity. Sweden is a prosperous nation that enjoys one of the highest standards of living in the
world. It has a mixed economy: about 90 percent of the industry is
privately owned; however, as a welfare state Sweden has one-third
of its work force in the public sector (which accounts for about 60

percent of the gross national product). A transformation, which began more than a century ago, has changed the economy from one concentrating on agriculture, mining, and forest products to one emphasizing high-tech industry. Sweden did experience some economic stagnation during the 1980s and retrenchment in the early 1990s. Recent increases in the inflation rate and concerns about the impact of the European community are unsettling political coalitions and raising questions about Sweden's economic and social welfare system.

From the early 1930s, almost continuously until the mid 1970s, the Social Democratic political party was in power. The labor government concentrated on equity, industrial peace, and a policy of public investment and social services, including adult education. Although the role of adult education in popular movements and educational associations goes back well into the nineteenth century and legislation important to adult education was enacted in 1914 and 1923, a 1947 law provided a major impetus for the field. The perceived high value of and priority for adult education reflected a public policy commitment to social justice and equity across generations and rural-urban areas, given rising levels of formal education in the general population. Swedish inventiveness contributed to early progress in advanced technology, which helped transform Sweden from an industrial to an information society in which continuing education created access to knowledge, the capital of modern times and a basis for occupational flexibility and productivity. During most of the past thirty years, government furnished leadership on behalf of growth and change of adult education (Peterson and Associates, 1982; Swedish National Board of Education, 1990; Titmus, 1981).

Legislation has helped establish what the Swedes term municipal adult education to provide educational opportunities for older adults who have not completed the basic nine years of formal education. The major legislation was in 1967, but municipal adult educational programs have benefited from other legislation and policies, such as a 1975 act that granted employees the right to an educational leave and the initiation in 1971 of a training course for municipal adult education staff by Stockholm College of Education. Municipal adult education expanded rapidly at the outset and more gradually during the past decade or so.

In addition to part-time study to complete upper-secondary courses for entry to university study, programs include basic education and vocational education, which complement other long-standing programs. The rationale for municipal adult education emphasizes learner- and problem-centered programs, though in practice they tend to be teacher- and subject-centered. This outcome results from the practice of using preparatory education teachers who teach adults part time, because such a staffing practice has seemed cost effective. Adult participation in these programs reflects both the quality of instruction and modernization trends. Technological change has influenced modernization, which has stimulated educational participation, especially by adults with relatively high levels of formal education who recognize the resulting professional or family benefits. More women than men use municipal adult education to complete an upper-secondary diploma, and they have the same ratio of continuation as men to higher education. Over the years, government-supported research has helped to provide documented feedback about the extent to which adult education has been advantageous to participants and society, and the research reports contribute to ongoing policy making (Hoghielm, 1986).

Municipal adult education and other Swedish educational programs for adults have been helped by the high priority given adult education, which in turn reflects two clusters of influences—a high value accorded to equity and generally favorable economic conditions. Among the many contributors to the important place of equity and democratic values in public policy have been a Protestant religious tradition and the importance of the two major trade union–employee associations in government and social policy (such as welfare state social services and efforts to reduce social class differences, including barriers to adult education participation). Commitment to equity has interacted with the other major influence on adult education (economic conditions) by undergirding the rationale for adult education's priority in competition for scarce resources. Fortunately, democratic values and a healthy economy have provided strong justification for high levels of support. Over the years, a generally healthy and expanding economy has allowed high levels of public policy and financial appropriations support by the government for municipal and other forms of adult education. The favorable economy has also enabled enterprises, organizations, and individuals to help finance programs. Shared values regarding equity encouraged collaboration among adult education providers and with formal education institutions. Relatively independent municipal adult education programs have in recent years explored relations with local upper-secondary schools. Relative priorities for clients and programs have shifted as the number of adults without basic education have shrunk, as the numbers of undereducated immigrants have increased, and as the threshold regarding desirable levels of higher and further education has risen. Because of political support for adult education related to values such as equity and democracy, there has been balanced support for both occupational and general education.

Recent Swedish National Board of Education (1990) plans regarding opportunities for upper-secondary education have emphasized that it is a responsibility of municipalities and a right of individual adults (as reflected in recent decentralization of even greater responsibility to the local level). Collaboration is also stressed, including attention to complementarity of cooperation among adult education providers and improvement of articulation between upper-secondary and higher education.

During the early 1990s, major shifts in education policy have further affected adult education. The current national government, which closed the National Board of Education in July of 1991, has decided to strengthen preparatory education (elementary through graduate school) and work-related adult education. By contrast, there have been substantial cuts in subsidies for municipal adult education, nonoccupational adult education, trade union education, and paid study leaves.

Yet over the years Sweden has done more to encourage adult study in standard higher education courses than other Western European countries. Following gradual increases during the 1950s and 1960s, between 1970 and 1980 the proportion of adults increased from one-quarter to one-half of higher education enrollments. Major reasons included free tuition, technological change, maintenance grants, study leaves, higher education reform, and declining numbers of young adults. During the 1980s, there was concern about competition between adults and young people for spaces in higher education because of economic stagnation (which restricted tax funds) and increased youth unemployment (even though the total unemployment rate was only 1 or 2 percent). In the early 1990s, unemployment increased to about 5 percent in less than two years. In recent decades, Swedish higher education policy has reflected the country's familiarity with innovations in Europe and North America, especially the U.K. Open University (Abrahamsson, 1986; Henriksson, 1991; Swedish National Board of Education, 1990; Titmus, 1981).

A distinctive and well-known form of adult education in Sweden is study circles, which are neighborhood lay-led study discussion programs, mainly on cultural topics. In 1947, government funds for the major associations that conduct study circles were increased, an indication of the distinctive combination of public funds and local control. Geography and climate have contributed to the emphasis on friendship and a sense of community. A related effort to strengthen study circles is the provision of leadership training by Linkoping Training College. In recent years, government subsidy of study circles has been about 80 to 90 percent.

Another provider of adult education that is distinctive and widespread in Sweden and throughout Scandinavia is the folk school. Dating from the mid-nineteenth century, folk schools originally provided general education for rural young adults during the winter months. Over the years, their programs have become more urban, diversified, and short term for a broader age range of participants. Participation has been so extensive that a decade or so ago, a majority of the members of the Swedish legislature had been participants or staff members in a folk school, a fact that contributed to government understanding and support.

In recent decades, the most rapidly expanding segment of adult education has been the education and training that enterprises provide for the people who work there. Participation in such programs has become comparable, per capita, to those in the United States and has also become more extensive than all other types of adult education in Sweden combined. Recent discussion of this segment of the field has emphasized the concept of the learning organization because educative activity has become central to the successful functioning of most types of enterprises.

Other aspects of adult education include basic education and literacy, trade union education, distance education, and mass media. When all types of educational participation by adults on a part-time or short-term basis are considered, more than half the total adult population participates each year, one of the highest rates in the world. This uncommon achievement merits attention by adult education planners in other countries; they should seek to understand societal influences on the high levels of public policy and financial support that have contributed to this success, along with similarities and differences in the national context that should be taken into account in adapting programs for other national settings. Consideration should be given to the combination of policy makers and adult educators who have sustained a supportive policy consensus for so many years and to recent economic and political forces that have played a part in recent reversals.

Other Countries

Adult education practitioners who seek to strengthen part-time study opportunities at formal education institutions can also learn much from relevant experience in countries other than Sweden. The following brief examples each identify aspects of program functioning that have implications for strategic planning elsewhere.

United Kingdom

The United Kingdom shares with the United States varied and decentralized forms of higher education. In Britain, continuing higher education opportunities have been provided by universities, polytechnics, colleges of education, colleges of further education, residential colleges, and community colleges. During the past two decades, the Open University has become one of the main providers of university education for part-time students (it will be analyzed in more detail in Chapter Five, which deals with distance education). Each institution in Britain furnishes continuing education for its own region. The 1944 and 1945 Education Acts stimulated expan-

sion of university continuing education and loosened its historic
connection with the Workers Education Association (which had
arisen because of the earlier focus on liberal education) by adding
largely noncredit occupational education. During the past decade,
university continuing education programs have been helped by declining cohorts of traditional-university-age students but have been
hindered by government budget cuts, which they absorbed disproportionately. (This parallels recent cuts of nonoccupational adult
education in Sweden.) The greater acceptance of part-time study by
the more egalitarian Scottish universities, in contrast with most
other U.K. universities, illustrates the importance of relations with
the parent institution for strategic planning (Bryant, 1984).

In each of the other types of U.K. higher education institutions, continuing education programs have been affected by institutional and societal influences. The polytechnics have emphasized
full-time younger students, but—especially in Birmingham and
London where there are more part-time students—links with industry have encouraged continuing education. In colleges of further
education and technology, cooperation with labor unions and the
Open University has contributed to increasing part-time study.
Nonoccupational studies tend to be administered separately. In the
1972 James Report, provision of continuing professional education
for teachers was basic to the proposed reform of colleges of education; the report recommended that they integrate their programs
more with the remainder of higher education by connecting continuing education to the early years of practice. Community colleges
or schools, which began in the United Kingdom between the two
World Wars, are similar to community colleges and schools in
America (as programs and facilities attached to secondary schools).
The intent is to provide external educational opportunities for
adults and out-of-school youth. In practice, the community college
principals and teachers mainly work for and are oriented toward the
secondary school program, and the community college arrangement
generally benefits the school more than adult education and the
community.

International influences have been especially prominent in
residential colleges for adults. The first to be established, in 1899,
was Ruskin College for workers, founded in Oxford by two Amer-

icans. It has continued to stress labor studies and is governed by a council composed mainly of labor union representatives. (Such residential adult education occurs worldwide, and the experience in Scandinavia has been especially influential on programs in other countries.) In Britain, residential colleges have been especially vulnerable to closing on the grounds that their expenses are high and the benefits of the residential experience are intangible. Other parts of the U.K. mosaic of continuing higher education include short-term colleges and summer schools. As a way of helping adults deal with the very decentralized U.K. higher education, the Council for National Academic Awards has granted degrees to students who satisfactorily complete all degree requirements, but at various higher education institutions other than universities. Continuing higher education is also served by university graduate programs that conduct research and prepare leaders for the field (Armstrong, 1985; Brett, 1987, Flude and Parrott, 1979; Hutchinson and Hutchinson, 1986; Kulich and Kruger, 1980; McIlroy, 1987; Newman, 1979; Legge, 1982; Titmus, 1981).

People's Republic of China and United States

In various countries, examinations provide one means for adults to receive credit for proficiencies acquired from various sources, including self-study. (A U.S. example is the College-Level Examination Program of the Educational Testing Service, which is one way to validate the results of experiential learning and apply it to meeting degree requirements.) With its long history of civil service and university examinations, China has used an examination system to reduce barriers to adult higher education related to distance, work, and other responsibilities. During the 1980s, the People's Republic of China Higher Education Commission set up an external degree program for working adults in which adults used various study opportunities, including self-study, to prepare to take standard examinations. The commission largely establishes policy and plans in collaboration with higher education institutions, enterprises, and other organizations that assist adults in their studies in preparation for the exam (Resource A, Lin).

Australia

A widespread issue in Australia, as in many developed countries, is how best to help returning adults make the adjustment to higher education after some time away from formal education. A program begun in 1983 by the continuing education staff of Darling Downs Institute of Advanced Education in Queensland, Australia, is the Preparatory Studies Program. This uses distance education procedures to help returning adults strengthen skills in academic study and examination taking, mathematics, and communications. Government priority for increasing adult access to higher education has helped continuing education staff obtain support for the Preparatory Studies Program by institute faculty and administrators. The program is planned and conducted by institute faculty and division staff, who devote part time to it. Participants pay fees that cover full costs because they want to succeed in higher education but doubt that their preparation to do so is sufficient; they also appreciate the ease of distance study. In the early years, almost 90 percent of those who completed the program passed all of their higher education courses (Resource A, Crock and Cottman).

For many years, adults have been able to study part time at various Australian universities, although there are restrictions in some professional fields (Neumann and Lindsay, 1986). For example, in 1992, at the University of Technology, Sydney (UTS), part-time students made up 47 percent of undergraduate enrollments, and the average age of UTS students was twenty-eight. Many mature students enter the university through the Technical and Further Education (TAFE) system, sometimes with credits for prior study.

Germany

Secondary education programs for adults in Germany have also been used to help them gain entry to higher education, but such programs may be seen as competition to traditional secondary education (as has happened with General Education Development (GED) high school equivalency programs for adults in the United States). For example, in Germany, passing the higher secondary school final exam (Abitur) was the traditional route to university admissions. In 1967, an independent evening high school was founded in Reutlingen to enable adults (who had taken noncollege preparatory secondary education) to pass the Abitur exam, which was necessary for admission to both higher and professional education. About half of the adults who began the evening high school program worked hard, completed it successfully, passed the exam, and valued the experience. Over the years, there has been resistance to the program on the grounds that higher education was not expected to be able to accommodate all young graduates of the traditional higher secondary schools, so additional applicants should be discouraged. The program has continued, but it has been forced to emulate the traditional higher secondary program too much and to be responsive to the adult learners too little. Staffing has also been a problem because long-term commitments to faculty have not been possible and high teacher unemployment has caused the regular schools to restrict additional part-time teaching at the Evening High School (Resource A, Taigel).

Norway

Gender differences also affect adult education participation and benefits, as seen in the following Norwegian example. Women constituted most of the people who successfully completed at least two courses a year between 1973 and 1982 in an Oslo program designed to help adults without college preparatory education to enter higher education. This situation came about as increasing numbers of women sought higher secondary education completion for entry to higher education and career advancement. Program completion was beneficial, since most of those finishing their secondary education went on to higher education. However, the women were less likely than men to find employment commensurate with their postsecondary education (Gooderham, 1988).

Yugoslavia

Relations between the preparatory education of young people and continuing education of adults can influence adult education program functioning in various ways. In what was Yugoslavia, following World War II, there was much innovation to make educational programs responsive to adults as learners, including elementary and secondary education programs for adults. As part of the education reforms in the mid 1970s, a period of worsening economic conditions, responsibility for these programs was given to the traditional school systems for young people. As a result, the adult education programs were made to conform to preparatory procedures regarding class size and instruction, and they became less responsive to adult learners.

Canada

Planning for part-time study by adults at formal educational institutions entails more than analysis of current circumstances (Wolf and Waldron, 1986). It should also include projections of emerging societal trends and implications for strengthening continuing education (Apps, 1988). Some Canadian projections were based mainly on American literature and are equally relevant to the United States. Baskett, Hamilton, and Bruce (1985) state that knowledge is becoming a more central focus of society than products, that job dislocation will continue, and that work and learning are becoming inseparable. The postwar baby boomers are moving into middle age, and the aftermath is reducing the flow of young people studying full time in higher education and increasing the numbers of adults studying part time. Also, competition is growing among providers of adult education as they become larger and more numerous. The authors conclude that these facts call for greater mission clarity by continuing higher education providers and more collaboration with other providers. They also suggest that continuing education practitioners reframe their relations with their universities because higher education is changing. This reframing presents challenges to continuing higher education divisions related to the overall institutional mission.

Adult education practitioners seek to help participants pass examinations and succeed in their studies, but they must also seek to relate effectively with parent organizations that are sometimes in transition. There is sometimes resistance from the parent organization, which indicates the importance of leadership and mission clarity to strengthen internal support for adult education. The U.K. examples indicate the diversity of higher education institutions and the differing contingencies associated with them. Because adult education agencies work closely with influential people in many aspects of their service area (industry, agriculture, government, labor unions, professions, community agencies), these contacts constitute potential stakeholders for adult education who are also important to leaders in the parent organization. Collaboration with various stakeholders helps increase support. In the past, practitioners have benefited from familiarity with practice in other settings, in their county and abroad. In the future, there is likely to be increasing international interchange. A comparative perspective can help practitioners adapt ideas and programs from one national context to another (Jourdan, 1981; Knoll, 1981; Kunzel, 1985; Rivera and Dohmen, 1985; Rubenson, 1977; Williams, 1977).

Strategic Planning

The foregoing selective cross-national review of reciprocal relations between preparatory and continuing education by educational institutions has implications for strategic planning and strengthening part-time educational opportunities for adults. The following discussion of relevant planning concepts is organized in relation to agency goals, relations with parent organization, attracting participants, local contingencies (economy, priority, values, support, staffing, facilities), and collaboration.

Goals

The adult education agency of an institution is composed of adult learners, along with the full- and part-time administrators, instructors, and other people who help plan and conduct educational activities for adults. A fundamental issue for planning is the centrality versus marginality of an agency in relation to the remainder of its school system, college, or university. The problem of marginality was most severe in the examples from Germany and the former

Yugoslavia. Planning should consider congruence of both goals and procedures for achieving goals.

Although it is desirable that agency goals be fundamental to the mission of the parent organization, there should be some differentiation between them. Otherwise, a separate agency or division to serve adult part-time students would not be warranted. An effective way to demonstrate congruence of goals is through evidence of benefits from agency efforts in achieving the mission of the parent institution; potential agency goals that are likely to be most highly valued by the institution should be emphasized. This was a major recommendation in the Canadian report on continuing higher education (Baskett, Hamilton, and Bruce, 1985).

The primary outcome of an adult education agency is enhanced proficiencies for participants that help them, their associates, and society. Another result of continuing higher education programs is service to community organizations. These are educational outcomes that should be valued by educational institutions. However, a problem for educational planning generally is the lack of clear and specific performance indicators for use in impact evaluation. Where obtainable, findings from summative evaluation can be combined with anecdotal information to improve programs as well as increase the understanding and support of stakeholders in the parent organization and service area. There are also secondary outcomes that assist the parent institution if the adult education program is of high quality. Included are positive public relations, increased enrollments, income, use of facilities, and benefits to other adult education providers and community organizations. Agency planning should review such outcomes to assure future priority for agency programs that are sufficiently compatible with institutional mission to make their continued support likely. This approach is illustrated by the examples from the University of Maryland and from Sweden.

Parent Organization

Adult education agencies function within partly implicit institutional demands and constraints, which affect both goals and procedures. When both goals and procedures are the same (as in evening high schools, community college degree-credit courses, and university evening colleges), the agency retains institutional course and degree objectives as well as content and methods; what is altered is mainly time and place so that the program is accessible to the part-time student. When goals are the same but procedures differ (as in granting of degree credit for experiential learning or distance education credit courses), the agency retains the objectives but alters the procedures for achieving them (examples from Australia, Germany, and Norway). When the same procedures are used to achieve different goals (as when standard credit courses are grouped in a special certificate program), the agency and students retain course content and methods but use courses as building blocks to achieve goals related to adult roles (such as art and philosophy courses for retirees or sociology, counseling, and management courses for personnel administrators). When both goals and procedures differ (as when a new program is designed for people active in community projects to prepare them for positions of major public responsibility), the agency provides a credit or noncredit educational program especially for adults. Strategic planning by an agency should consider the extent and type of congruence between agency and institutional goals and procedures that is desirable to both maintain institutional support and allow responsiveness to the participants.

It is not only that the agency is influenced by the parent organization; the opposite is also true. For example, the existence of career-long occupational education opportunities makes it unnecessary to include all content in preparatory education; faculty development occurs as instructors use insights gained from teaching adults when they instruct younger people in preparatory courses; community support for the institution increases as adults gain personal experience with institutional staff and program; and the freedom to experiment that can exist in adult education agencies can result in innovative programs that may become part of the institution. Agency planning should emphasize its potential for the kind of organizational change likely to be valued by the institution.

Participation

Typically, adult education agencies have more permeable boundaries than the rest of the parent organization. Organizations vary in the extent to which they maintain boundaries; these may take the form of rules and expectations for organization members and restrictions on the ease with which outsiders can influence and participate in the organization. Educational institutions tend to have high boundary maintenance, as exemplified by fortress urban schools or ivory-tower rural colleges. By definition, adult education agencies allow different access and procedures than in traditional preparatory education for young full-time students. In contrast with the separate facilities and full-time students and staff in preparatory education, most adult education agencies share facilities, and most instructors and staff members are on a part-time basis, along with the students. As a result, the agency can have a weak subculture and an indistinct public image. Boundary maintenance varies among agencies. On the one hand, there are private evening colleges with high community demand, entrance standards, and autonomy from the parent institution; on the other, there are programs sponsored by public schools, held at scattered sites, and offering courses in response to community requests that are open to any adult in the district. Agency planning should consider the extent of permeability that is desirable from the point of view of both community participation and institutional support.

Agency priorities should reflect institutional mission and resources as well as client needs and demand. Strategic planning can help achieve a satisfactory balance. School and college adult education agencies in the United States have long been characterized as responding more to an enrollment economy and to participant demand than their parent organizations (Knox, 1982a). Agency planning thus includes attention to characteristics and needs of potential participants, along with influences on their decision to enroll. (This was an objective of the University of Maryland project.) Some influences are personal, such as ability, expectations, and awareness of educational opportunities. Other influences also reflect situational factors such as role changes, perceived cost benefits in relation to alternative activities, social-class level, and richness of social space. Understanding characteristics that differentiate successful participants from nonparticipants and those who fail to complete programs can enable practitioners to better attract and retain their clientele. Information about events that trigger partic-

ipation and about sources of influence on students' decision to enroll is especially useful to attract similar participants. Information
about deterrents to participation provides additional assistance to
attract and retain nonparticipants (Aslanian and Brickell, 1980;
Farmer, Knox, and Farmer, 1977; Frischkopf and Braun, 1981; Merriam and Cunningham, 1989; Knox, 1987b). For strategic planning,
specification of segments of the adult population that fit agency
mission (such as educational level, gender, age, reasons for participation, and place of residence) is important for effective marketing.
Such specifications also have implications for relations with the
parent organization. For example, many adult education programs
that prepare people to pass the GED high school equivalency exam
have minimum age limits and other restrictions by the schools to
discourage their use by young people who drop out of secondary
school in the belief that the GED route is more desirable (Beder,
1991).

Contingencies

Contingency leadership recognizes the importance of dealing with
distinctive circumstances associated with a specific time and place.
Such time-related, local contingencies arise from characteristics, traditions, and trends in the parent organization and the service area.
Strategic planning entails selection of a few major contingencies to
consider from among many (Knox, 1982a). In addition to assessment of agency strengths and weaknesses, strategic planning includes attention to major threats and opportunities in the societal
context that tend to be more difficult to identify and influence. The
international examples in this chapter, and especially the diverse
higher education institutions in Britain, indicate the wide-ranging
contingencies that adult education practitioners confront.

Economic conditions tend to be a major influence because
they affect so many agency stakeholders. They may have an impact
on participants' interest in further education and ability to pay;
enterprises' educational assistance and advancement opportunities;
potential instructors' interest in part-time teaching; and availability
of subsidy funds from government, parent institution, and benefactors. During the 1990–1992 recessionary period in the United States,

part-time higher education enrollments increased initially, as they typically do under similar circumstances. This is a useful generalization for planning purposes. The connection between continuing education and increased economic productivity can also be a useful part of the rationale for planning decisions, especiallly during adverse economic conditions when competing demands for resources and scrutiny of budget requests increase. (Economic influences were apparent in the examples from Sweden, Germany, and the former Yugoslavia.)

Government priorities are another major influence, as reflected in enabling legislation and appropriations, especially for public educational institutions that receive tax funds. Strategic planning should consider the substance of proposals that emphasize public benefits, as well as the timing and base of support reflected in the proposals. An advantage of environmental scanning to identify emerging trends is that the conclusions allow practitioners to propose programs and needed support at an early stage when the trends can capture the imagination of policy makers, instead of doing so belatedly when their attention is turning to other matters. As illustrated by the initial community college example, the request for external subsidy may be too large, and it may be better to begin on a smaller scale.

Societal influences produce threats as well as opportunities. For example, some of the critical issues that face community educators are trends that adversely affect their programs as well as the problems they address (Merriam and Cunningham, 1989). Societal issues include declining school enrollments, changes in family structure, general economic conditions, fiscal constraints in school budgets, and public unrest and dissatisfaction with the schools. Unfortunate recent trends are decreases in community education centers, staff in state education departments, and external foundation support. Strategic planning can enable advocates to support the importance of adult education activities with rationales that harness opportunities and deflect threats.

Planning and marketing activities to win and maintain stakeholder support should also apply to relations with the parent organization, but they are affected by the institution's mission in relation to the adult education function. Now that adult learners, who generally study part-time, have become the new majority in higher education, an increasing number of higher education institutions are developing a dual commitment to both preparatory and continuing education. Strategic planning and leadership by continuing education practitioners can accelerate the process and evolve arrangements that also serve adult participants well. However, as the German example indicates, traditional institutions can also resist part-time study.

The main theme of this chapter has been planning by adult education staff members to strengthen their agency for the benefit of part-time students, especially in relation to the remainder of the educational institution. Strategic planning is one means of doing so and involves stakeholders in gaining commitment to shared goals and encouraging contributions to achievement of goals. Such leadership is an interactive and transformative process that extends beyond the people who have management responsibility and includes all stakeholders. As several of the international examples demonstrate, adult education practitioners can experience resistance from their parent organization, so a special challenge for the adult education agency is to strengthen that linkage between client needs and institutional purposes (Baden, 1987; Keller, 1983; Simerly and Associates, 1987). Examples from other national or international settings can help clarify institutional and societal influences. Projections of emerging trends are also useful to make current decisions to guide agency directions (Baskett, Hamilton, and Bruce, 1985). Of course, actual leadership decisions are specific in relation to agency functions such as staffing, student services, resource allocations, and collaboration (Knox, 1982a).

Staffing decisions can be especially important because program quality depends upon them; they can also be difficult because many staff members work part time with the agency but full time with the parent institution, so there is dual reporting. A useful concept for planning regarding selection of part-time instructional staff is congruence between agency and candidate expectations. Although team teaching and staff development can be used when no one is available who is prepared for an entire instructional role, such arrangements are time consuming for program coordinators. Thus, they emphasize staff selection. Because, as previously stated, adult education instructors are often part of the faculty of the parent institution or are outside experts hired from the community on an adjunct basis, the agency can usually decide whom to hire, and a potential instructor can decide whether or not to accept. However, both decisions are influenced by the parent institution. The agency coordinator considers guidelines from the parent institution and specifications based on program requirements, along with the number and qualifications of alternative candidates. Each candidate assesses the position in relation to other possibilities. A match occurs if the candidate and the coordinator have the same expectations of various aspects of the position. These might include purposes, content competence, teaching style, pay, time schedule, agency image, and previous obligations. This matching process is more problematic when an instructor's administrator in the parent institution (with which policy dictates that the agency coordinator must work) seeks to force upon the agency an instructor whom the coordinator believes to be unsatisfactory for adult learners.

In addition to the results of staff selection, program quality reflects staff development and rewards, which are also influenced by the parent institution. Because commitments to instructional staff are typically part time and short term, the main process achieving staff quality is to not reappoint instructors who are unsatisfactory and to work informally and gradually with those who are satisfactory, to enhance their proficiency (Knox, 1979). In addition, special staff development activities can be provided (Schlossberg, Lynch, and Chickering, 1989). Institutional commitment to the adult education function influences each of the foregoing aspects of staffing but has an even greater impact on the basic reward system for those faculty members who teach in continuing education programs. There are various incentives and rewards for people who help adults learn. One is extra income, which institutional policies tend to restrict, and another is the personal satisfaction and recognition that many adult education instructors receive from working with adult learners on topics and projects that the teachers value. However, for full-time higher education faculty members who teach adults part time, a major reward is positive decisions about promotion, tenure, and base salary increases; institutional criteria have in the past either ignored continuing education or in some instances discriminated against it. In recent years, there has been progress in improving institutional reward systems by developing appropriate criteria for judging the quality of continuing education and public service performance so that faculty members who do well are fairly treated (Eastman, 1989; Lynton and Elman, 1987; Votruba, 1981). The basic conclusion is that some improvements in agency functioning require policy changes in the parent institution.

There are similar implications for strengthening student services, resource allocation, and collaboration. As illustrated by the College-Level Examination Program (CLEP) and GED exams in the United States, the use of exam-based study programs in the People's Republic of China, and the preparatory studies programs in Australia, Germany, and Norway, the success of the adult education activity depends on some acceptance by preparatory education institutions. Without this, learner aspirations are frustrated. The challenge to adult education leadership is to earn this acceptance while serving the adult learners well.

Institutional support is also important in regard to resource acquisition and allocation, such as financial aid for part-time students, agency use of institutional classrooms and other facilities, and approval of grant proposals. Continuing higher education administrators have been frustrated by federal and state policies that restrict student aid to full-time students—policies that higher education institutions have generally supported because they did not want such external assistance shifted to part-time students. Continuing education leaders were encouraged in 1990, when New York State eased restrictions on financial aid to part-time students in higher education. This decision reflected a shift by higher education institutions, in part because about half of the students attend part time.

Decisions about allowing agency use of institutional facilities and equipment (versus requiring separate facilities) and about providing these free to the agency as a form of subsidy (or whether they must be rented) also depend on a matching process between agency and parent institution. For the agency, considerations include the desirability and feasibility of shared or separate facilities based on program and clientele location, timing, and program requirements, along with the availability of alternative facilities. For the institution, considerations are the availability of facilities that would be satisfactory for the agency (after the requirements of the resident instruction program are met) and the institutional priority of the agency as something to be subsidized rather than as a source of income to the institution. Again, institutional priorities and policies constitute major influences that can be addressed by strategic planning. Institutional support also affects the funding of agency proposals for special funds from the institution or from external sources such as foundations and government agencies (Buskey, 1981). The Swedish example indicates the positive influence that high government priority can have but also the results of a policy shift. One reason for including key people from the parent institutions as stakeholders in strategic planning is to increase such support.

Collaboration

Most continuing higher education activities are individual courses or workshops that are planned and conducted by one or a few people. Yet some of the most challenging programs for continuing education leaders are collaborative efforts that can entail multiple providers and audiences. Some consist of cooperation among similar providers, such as an interuniversity network to produce instructional materials (videotapes for use by each institution). However, difficulties sometimes arise because each institution wants to make similar contributions and to receive similar benefits. By contrast, some of the most successful collaborations combine educational institutions such as a school or university (using faculty members and educational facilities) with noneducational organizations (such as a labor union or a professional association with members who want help learning). The result can be complementary partnerships in which each partner seeks what the other wants to provide. Planning for such collaboration should include identification of mutual goals, complementary contributions, and shared benefits (Knox, 1982a). As stated previously in relation to the midwestern community college EMO, it is desirable to begin on a manageable scale and allow the project to evolve. However, the EMO example also illustrates the importance of a compelling vision that generates cooperation—an essential feature of leadership. Strategic planning should help to develop such a vision and commitment to it.

Essential features of strategic planning discussed in this chapter include leadership that conveys a distinctive agency mission. The process of strategic planning can include internal stakeholders from the parent institution and external stakeholders from the service area in the formulation of an agency mission that is compelling to both. The resulting commitment to future directions can strengthen agency functioning in relation to both parent organization purposes and procedures and to expectations and benefits as viewed by agency clients and other external stakeholders. As a result, adult education agencies can use planning to strengthen their linkages with both client and resource systems. Strategic planning also includes analysis of societal influences likely to affect future directions, including both local contingencies (employment conditions, competing adult education providers) and more remote influences (domestic and international political and economic conditions), because they affect the opportunities and threats an agency confronts (Morrison, Renfro, and Boucher, 1984).

This chapter has explored concepts and examples regarding strategic planning related to part-time educational programs for adults associated with educational institutions. A major theme has been strengthening support from the parent institution. For this purpose, the focus has been on part-time study in credit and degree programs, in which institutional cooperation is especially important. However, adult education agencies associated with educational institutions provide many other types of largely noncredit educational programs for adults. For example, schools and community colleges offer adult basic education and programs for minorities. Land-grant universities include the Cooperative Extension Service, which is a major provider of educational programs for rural development. Universities have extensive programs of continuing professional education and staff development programs cosponsored with enterprises and occupational associations. Many types of agencies associated with educational institutions provide programs for elders, on cultural topics, and for community problem solving although such activities constitute a small proportion of their total adult education effort. Examples of such *noncredit* programs by educational institutions are included in these chapters.

3

Basic Education
and Literacy

A U.S. newspaper article appearing in May 1991 probably surprised some readers. The article referred to a UNESCO report that during the 1990 International Literacy Year the estimated number of illiterate adults in the world was almost one billion, though the number was a few million less than the 1985 estimate. The current number is more than one-quarter of the total adult population. Compared with a 1970 estimate of almost 40 percent illiterates, UNESCO concluded that there had been progress toward its goal of eradicating illiteracy, but it had been painfully slow. The surprising sentence at the end of the article was that International Literacy Year raised awareness that functional illiteracy in industrialized nations was estimated at between 10 and 20 percent of the adult population.

Extent of Illiteracy

Most readers of the article probably assumed that adult illiteracy in the United States was close to the 1 or 2 percent routinely reported in international statistics. So what accounts for the wide range of estimates of the size of the U.S. illiteracy problem? The lack of precision is partly definitional and partly contextual. At the turn of this century, the criterion was the ability to write one's name. Using a minimal standard, such as the ability to read English at a level equivalent to the average third grader in school, fewer than 10 percent of American adults are illiterate. (This may be a satisfactory level for rural adults in some developing countries.) In the United States, as in other countries, illiterate and very low-literate adults include older adults with little schooling, recent immigrants, and school dropouts.

However, standards for literacy, numeracy, and other basic skills are contextual and depend on the abilities that are necessary for adults to derive meaning from symbols and function in their societal context (Beder, 1991; Harman, 1987; Merriam and Cunningham, 1989, chap. 35; Wagner and Puchner, 1992). During this century in the United States, the threshold of literacy and basic skills has been rising so that by World War II it was equivalent to six or eight years of schooling and by 1990 it was equivalent to secondary school education. With inadequate basic education, adults are unable to function satisfactorily as workers, parents, consumers, and citizens in today's high-tech information society. With the rapid rate of social change, older adults who were functionally literate a generation ago, but who did not continue to learn, may not be so today. Thus, if adults with marginal levels of basic education do not advance, they may be below a rising functional threshold in a decade or so. Of course, some low-literate adults function well in family, work, and community (Harman, 1987; Valentine, 1986).

Adult basic education has both personal and societal aspects. Basic skills consist of communications and numeracy abilities such as reading, writing, listening, speaking, and use of basic mathematics. Also included in these skills are concepts and vocabulary to deal with basic expectations in work, family, and community. Such fundamentals enable adults not only to perform at least minimally in response to role expectations but also to learn and progress to respond to emerging opportunities. These competencies can be acquired through personal abilities and life chance, but they also reflect societal influences. Undereducated adults vary greatly in abilities and outlook. Compare a bright, young person with a learning disability who has supportive family and friends and optimism about advancement with a similarly disadvantaged person whose family and friends discourage further education and whose poverty and hopelessness about advancement deter educational participation. Many reasons for nonparticipation pertain to negative attitudes. Learning generally is an active search for meaning. One function of leadership for adult basic education is to help undereducated adults gain a compelling yet realistic vision of the benefits that further learning can help them achieve in themselves and their situation. Such benefits include greater independence, identity, and communication ability (Harman, 1987).

However, there are also societal influences on adult basic education programs provided by schools, community colleges, voluntary associations, libraries, enterprises, and religious institutions. The variety of these providers produces different emphases. Some societal influences respond to cultural values, such as enabling adults to become more productive workers, more informed citizens, more effective parents, and more caring people. Other societal influences may be negative. For example, there is the stigma of illiteracy. Other social services compete with adult education for time and resources. Some feel concern that overeducated workers will become too assertive or mobile, and there are always many barriers to participation by the least literate. International comparative analysis helps us understand major societal influences that affect planning of such basic education programs, which are also referred to as functional literacy programs, and also contributes to a broad rationale for social transformation efforts to assist undereducated adults.

A special challenge to strategic planning and implementation is to attract and retain hard-to-reach participants who are especially influenced by peers and who can be persuaded that further education will make an important difference. Because many potential participants are poor as well as undereducated, program subsidy is essential. This entails both economic support and postliteracy opportunities for those completing programs. Availability of governmental resources depends on public policy priorities. Educational leaders can increase policy support by pointing to the rising threshold of functional basic skills and projections of labor shortages in a decade or so.

The examples and rationale in this chapter focus mainly on some interrelated aspects of strategic planning crucial to strengthening adult basic education. They reflect political and economic conditions that affect local contingencies and broader social change that can influence the goals of both provider agencies and functionally illiterate adults. Various stakeholders that can help attract participants, staff, and resources are identified. The concluding section highlights information about personal and community goals, attraction and retention of participants, recruitment and development of staff, inclusion of major stakeholders, and attention to local contingencies that can be included in strategic planning.

Public School Adult Basic Education

An overview of typical relations between an adult basic education program, the public school system of which it was a part, and the community that it served is provided by the following case example (Resource A, Knox (c)). The school system served a small city and the nearby suburban and rural area with a population of a quarter-million. The district had a mixed economic base, unemployment fluctuated between 6 and 10 percent, and about 20 percent of the adult population was functionally illiterate; another 20 percent (mostly older adults) did not have a high school diploma.

The adult basic education program followed federal, state, and school system guidelines, but its administrators and instructors had been given wide latitude on program decisions. The general goal was to help undereducated adults increase their educational level so they could function satisfactorily in work, family, and community. The main content areas were communications, mathematics, consumer issues, health, and prevocational education. In addition to the director and three part-time supervisors, the staff included fourteen full-time instructors, twenty part-time instructors, four paraprofessional aides, and three secretarial and support staff members. (The proportion of full-time staff was higher than in most programs. Nationwide, about 40 percent of leaders are volunteers, about 50 percent are part time, and fewer than 10 percent are full time.) Most of the staff members had backgrounds in education, many with school-teaching experience and certification. Some aides and support staff members were former participants in the program. Uncertain funding from year to year, combined with mixed attitudes by the school system, created problems for program staff. These included lack of benefits for part-time staff and year-to-year appointments for full-time staff. (Uneven funding is a major problem for most adult basic education programs.) Although staff members were quite committed to the program, each year some left for more attractive and secure positions. As the school system's own enrollment and related financial problems worsened over the years, the subsidy for the program was reduced below the minimum required for matching state and federal funds. As a result, the director increased collaboration with other providers and tried to diversify funding.

Prior to the start of federal funding for adult basic education in the mid 1960s, the only similar program was a small English and Americanization program for naturalization. Since that time, federal funds allocated to the district each year by the state continued to be the main source of financial support for the program. State funds and special federal grant funds for retraining unemployed adults were supplementary sources. A positive image and high priority for basic education were reflected in a relatively stable level of appropriations. In constant dollars, there were some declines during the 1980s, when support for many other social programs was being reduced even further. Priority reflected general cultural values in support of literacy and education and about the economy and society generally. Participants paid none of the program costs because it was assumed that functionally illiterate adults had high unemployment rates and low levels of family income.

Those working on the program encouraged participation by undereducated adults in part because they realized that if enrollments declined, some staff members would lose their jobs. However, they also realized that given budget and upper-enrollment limits, it was undesirable to attract many more participants than they could accept because this practice would result in discouragingly long waiting lists. In recent years, about 1,400 people participated, of whom more than one-third were new to the program; about 40 percent dropped out. Attendance was somewhat irregular, so that average weekly attendance was about 800. (Nationally, about 8 percent of eligible adults participate; see Beder, 1991).

About half of the participants were native-born whites, and the remainder were various categories of immigrants and ethnic minorities such as blacks, Hispanics, and Asians. Participants were more affluent and had higher reading levels than nonparticipants.

There were a number of positive influences on participation in and general support for adult basic education. One was increasing public understanding of the extent of the illiteracy problem. Contributions to increased awareness were made by publications, prominent advocates, state governors, adult education associations, mass media, and Project Literacy U.S. Another influence was social change, as reflected in a rising threshold of functional literacy. A third positive influence was optimism about the potential benefits of literacy.

A negative factor was that without other societal and personal changes, people who completed this program were still not able to make progress in their occupation and level of living. Though most of the adults who completed this program reported satisfaction with its benefits and their goal achievement, some experienced disappointment regarding the actual opportunities for advancement in the face of unemployment, job discrimination, health, and other problems associated with poverty. The goals that brought some adults to the program turned out to be unrealistic. Even passing a GED high school equivalency exam did not necessarily lead to progress. Because illiterate adults have been marginal to society, they lack power, and their voices are seldom heard.

The program director considered the contributions of other local providers of basic education and related services: a community college with a developmental education program, the library with materials and services for adult new readers to encourage postliteracy activity, volunteer literacy groups, and community agencies. Some activities were cosponsored with these other providers, and some programs were sequential. In addition, some organizations, such as employment services or health clinics, referred undereducated adults to the program, and successful participants were helped to find jobs in local enterprises or to continue their further education.

The foregoing example suggests some of the societal influences on a program that should be considered in strategic planning. The extent of planning assistance from the state education department varies greatly from state to state. The preceding case is not from California. However, in 1989, California completed an exemplary strategic plan to meet the state's long-term adult education needs; this plan gave substantial attention to adult basic education (Best, 1989). (Other states, including Massachusetts, Michigan, New Jersey, and New York have also done strategic planning; see Beder, 1991). Both the planning process and the resulting California report had heuristic value for practitioners elsewhere who wanted to strengthen state-level planning to assist local programs. The report summarized the state's participatory and ongoing planning process and indicated the importance of combining an agreed-upon mission with attention to long-term needs to combat the skill gap, to serve more people, to increase access and delivery options, and to balance and diversify programs. While acknowledging the diversity of independent providers to be considered, the report concentrated on public adult education that received state funds. The planning process focused on four goals to guide planning at state and local levels during the coming decade. These were improving access to learners, accountability, program quality and responsiveness, and planning and coordination. Each of these broad goals incorporated four or five themes that had been identified in earlier planning. For each of these goals, two to five action steps were recommended. Examples of recommendations included funding for innovations, provision of educational information services, an education access card for adults (enabling them to obtain easily individual educational records and program eligibility status from an integrated data system), quality standards for program review and improvement, staff development, and collaborative planning. The report concluded with phased implementation steps and a rationale for building partnerships among stakeholders.

Not all parts of even a well-developed plan and process can be implemented without difficulty. The result of planning should be broad agreement among local and state stakeholders on a desirable vision for the future and specific steps to help accomplish it. Although such agreement can be difficult to accomplish, the synergistic results can be substantial. For local directors of adult basic education, such a state plan provides a framework for cooperation at local and state levels with people associated with related aspects of publicly funded adult education in addition to adult basic education.

Local efforts to strengthen adult basic education receive assistance from federal as well as state levels. Paralleling the preparation of the California strategic plan for all public adult education, a report entitled *Jump Start: The Federal Role in Adult Literacy* was also being prepared (Chisman, 1989). This report was based on a series of technical reports by experts and the suggestions of a distinguished advisory group. It proposed that the federal role should be to stimulate more attention to adult basic skills. Considering that an estimated twenty to thirty million adults currently in the U.S. work force have serious problems with basic skills, the report concluded that there would be dire economic consequences unless there were a forceful national effort to help.

Although adult literacy has received generally low federal priority and has been fragmented at national, state, and local levels, the report urged a new outlook and higher levels of support for adult basic education. It concluded that there was enormous latent political support for a vigorous pluralistic national initiative. Recommendations included leadership by the executive branch especially on behalf of workplace literacy, a legislative initiative including innovative training and technology, reinforced federal-state cooperation, and strengthening of the intellectual base by establishing a national center for adult literacy. The report also recommended greater emphasis on adult basic education in more than a half dozen federal programs. (Between 1988 and 1992, there was increased federal funding through various programs, largely oriented toward economic development.)

The *Jump Start* report had a substantial impact in helping to galvanize understanding of the problem of adult illiteracy and commitment to solutions. Other reports helped prepare the way, such as a report by the National Assessment of Educational Progress called *Literacy: Profiles of America's Young Adults;* this work specified the extent of the illiteracy problem, especially among minority young adults (Kirsch and Jungeblut, 1986). The *Jump Start* report led to a book entitled *Leadership for Literacy: The Agenda for the 1990s* that developed a more detailed and balanced approach for strengthening adult basic education at all levels, but with a national emphasis (Chisman and Associates, 1990). Chisman and his colleagues concluded that the essence of the problem was that many low-literate adults lacked the basic skills required to function effectively in society, and many of them suffered from economic and social distress associated with the lack of these skills. The authors cited humanitarian and civic reasons but emphasized the economic stake as warranting support by all Americans for a national effort to solve the problem. The authors' suggested strategy was to build on the opportunity presented by the current widespread recognition of the situation, using pluralistic leadership by people associated with the issue.

A major theme throughout the book was that a comprehensive approach was essential if the effort was to be successful, and this endorsement of pluralism was reflected in their recommendations. Instruction by providers with various approaches and goals related to family, work, and community problem solving should be combined with attention to poverty, health, housing, and vocational development. Policy makers at local, state, and national levels should also be part of the effort. Professional development for adult basic education practitioners should be conducted by providers, government, and literacy organizations; and it should include attention to standards. Participatory research was urged that would include learners, practitioners, and policy makers, as well as scholars, to produce findings that improve practice in all its aspects. Use of educational technology required a broad base of collaboration to achieve economy of scale. Cooperation by enterprises in workplace literacy should be part of a lifelong learning perspective on basic skills to provide continuity with postliteracy opportunities and ongoing occupational development.

Chisman concluded with a proposed agenda based on a larger vision that literacy leaders should help to generate. He urged solving the illiteracy problem before the demographic deadline imposed by the retirement of the baby-boom generation starting in 2010, which will place great demands on the productivity of the smaller work force that remains. The agenda included providing functional literacy for the several million adults who are completely illiterate and removing limited language proficiency as a barrier to opportunity by expanding English-as-a-second language programs. The larger goal was functional literacy for the 10 or 20 percent of adult Americans unable to meet everyday social demands or hold jobs that provide decent wages and reasonable opportunities. The long-term solution regarding basic skills was integration with life-long learning programs. The challenge to leadership was to shift the paradigm so that current attention to illiteracy was used to shift basic skills education from the margin through a comprehensive strategy of informed pluralism. (Further commentary on this rationale is provided in the section on strategic planning at the end of this chapter.)

This section has suggested some of the ways in which planning by local public school adult basic education programs is related to contingencies in their service area and to state and federal planning as well. However, informed pluralism involves relations with other adult education providers, and this issue is the focus of the next section.

Other U.S. Providers of Adult Basic Education

Comprehensive planning for adult basic education includes consideration of the various providers; their complementarity regarding distinctive goals, methods, and clientele; the points at which close collaboration is merited; and connections with the remainder of adult education and with family, work, and community. Family literacy occurs within the context of libraries and schools. Workplace literacy is achieved within enterprises and labor unions. Community literacy programs are provided by voluntary associations and community agencies. Cooperation by these providers and by religious institutions, ethnic groups, and other organizations has been encouraged by local literacy councils and adult education round tables that bring representatives of providers together to promote collaborative planning, professional development, educational counseling, fundraising, and encouragement of participation. The following examples identify distinctive features of agency functioning that have implications for planning.

As providers of adult basic education opportunities, public libraries offer a useful contrast to public schools, which typically hire teachers for courses. Instead, libraries generally provide materials and encourage individualized tutoring by volunteers (Mathews, 1987). Unfortunately, services and materials for adult new readers have had low priority in most local public libraries due to the competition with services for active readers and severe financial constraints. A notable exception occurred during the 1980s in the Wierton, West Virginia, public library. This institution was founded in 1958 in a steel mill city and serves a rural two-county population of 72,000 people. The library had long been active in providing services to special populations. With about 11,000 functionally illiterate adults in the service area, the staff began to plan adult literacy activities in 1975, and two years later, staff members and volunteer tutors began using Laubach literacy materials (which are discussed later in this chapter). The unusually high commitment to adult literacy had been created through support by the library board, director, a literacy coordinator, staff members, volunteers, and cooperation with other providers (such as the schools, community college, and a literacy coalition).

Priority for helping undereducated adults increased in 1982 when the eight thousand employees of the Wierton Steel Corporation (the largest manufacturer in West Virginia) acquired the company through a stock-ownership plan. This acquisition prompted high levels of cooperation and learning to meet the new demands of self-management. External support, including federal, state, and local funds, supported the literacy effort, so that more than 10 percent of the library budget was devoted to adult literacy education, along with more than a thousand volunteer hours. External support included educational technology such as videotapes and computer materials. The library literacy program coordinator was instrumental in planning, staff development, acquisition of outside funding, and facilitation of local collaboration. (Recently, some community apathy about the importance of literacy education, combined with uncertainty about outside funding, has raised questions about continuation of the literacy education coordinator position.) In addition to benefiting from the coordinator's leadership, undereducated adults were encouraged to participate in literacy activities by a number of factors: a positive image of the library, use of educational technology, personal values and anticipated benefits, and (especially) heightened expectations related to self-management (Resource A, Johnson (b)).

This example of library-based literacy education touched on two other aspects of adult basic education: educational technology and family literacy. Library and information science has been one of the fields that has started to use technology for educational purposes. In addition to circulation, record keeping, and data base searches, computer technology is utilized for adult basic education, as noted in the Wierton public library program. Other providers of literacy education (such as schools, community-based volunteer literacy agencies, community colleges, and enterprises) are beginning to use educational technology for basic education—an advance from several decades ago, when print materials for elementary school children were widely employed. A broad base of collaboration among providers has been desirable for computer technology because economies of scale are essential to reduce unit costs to feasible levels, given the large investment for equipment and programs. For much investment to occur, stakeholders must understand costs and benefits as they pertain to decisions by learners, providers, and funders (Chisman and Associates, 1990). Libraries, along with school-based intergenerational programs, are well suited for family literacy programs. Reading to children can be a source of motivation and reinforcement for both parents and children in the spirit of lifelong learning. Family literacy programs can contribute to the success of such intergenerational efforts.

Adult basic education has been provided by many types of organizations in addition to schools and libraries, which in some states may not even be major providers. Other ones have included community colleges, enterprises, religious institutions, voluntary associations, and community agencies. In each instance, provider characteristics have influenced program goals, methods, and clientele. Strategic planning can identify other major providers in a service area. This is part of the rationale for informed pluralism and a comprehensive approach that local literacy or adult education councils can help promote. Strategic leadership adds to the complementarity of contributions as the special strengths and missions of various providers become apparent.

Community Colleges

In some states, public community college districts have received higher levels of state financial assistance for adult education and have served larger geographic areas than do public school systems. Circumstance encourages providing adult basic education through the community colleges instead of the schools. Community colleges, in justifying their provision of adult basic education, point to a more positive adult-oriented institutional image (in contrast with the schools in which some undereducated adults failed earlier) and closer connections with postliteracy educational opportunities (such as a prevocational theme in basic education that leads into postsecondary educational opportunities for adults).

Workplace

Workplace literacy can allow even closer connections between basic and vocational education by emphasizing vocabulary and reading skills that workers need to know, which are then reinforced in occupational tasks (Chisman and Associates, 1990; Merriam and Cunningham, 1989, chap. 35). Occupational literacy programs in business, government, and military settings are quite diverse and reflect local contingencies, which contribute to their relevance and success as functional literacy programs.

Religious Organizations

Religious institutions have long supported literacy and other educational programs, partly in a belief that literate people have greater access to religious writings and concepts, which can contribute to faith development (Merriam and Cunningham, 1989, chap. 30; Niebuhr, 1984). Adult literacy programs have been even more prominent in foreign missions than in local benevolences. Early in the century, Frank Laubach, a Methodist missionary in the Phillipines, developed each-one-teach-one procedures for literacy education, which spread to many developing countries. In recent decades, Laubach Literacy has developed and published materials through New Readers Press, supplied leadership training, and worked with local adult literacy providers, including religious institutions, libraries, community agencies, and voluntary associations. Literacy Volunteers of America (a secular association) is a similar organization that originally separated from Laubach Literacy to offer a wider range of instructional procedures but that also relies on volunteer tutors.

Community-Based Organizations

The Madison Literacy Council (MLC), the local affiliate of Laubach Literacy, serves the metropolitan area of the Wisconsin state capital, which has a population a third of a million people. MLC is similar to many nongovernmental organizations (NGOs) that depend on fundraising by United Way and other philanthropy. In the course of a year, five hundred MLC volunteers tutor as many undereducated adults on a one-to-one basis. A small staff and a policy board coordinate the program, recruit learners and tutors, provide tutor training, and raise funds to support the program. MLC is one of a dozen adult literacy providers that belong to a county Literacy Consortium that promotes cooperation, public awareness, financial support, and training for staff and volunteers. Other organizations that have taken part in monthly consortium meetings include the county library system, community college, community agencies, and community ethnic groups such as the Urban League and Centro Hispano. This variety of community-based organizations has reached more people than any one provider would have.

Participatory Programs

Participatory literacy programs have emphasized active involvement by adult learners in decisions to plan and conduct programs (Fingeret and Jurmo, 1989). Although this orientation could occur in relation to any type of provider, it has special applications when literacy education is part of community problem-solving activities and empowerment of economically less advantaged adults is a related goal. A concern of some literacy education leaders has been that there has been too much focus on remedial efforts for learners and too little attention given to structural features contributing to unemployment and poverty (compounding the illiteracy problem and confounding efforts to solve it).

This brief review of some U.S. adult basic education programs illustrates the differing contexts in which they occur and suggests why informed pluralism is a desirable strategy. In a society such as America, this strategy has been responsive to diverse population characteristics and learner needs and accommodates a variety of providers. However, fragmented provision has a weakened impact on policy making and resource allocation. The next two sections describe some literacy education in other countries. These examples explore ways in which a holistic understanding of societal influences on local programs can be used to plan successful, comprehensive efforts. These should include the multiple stakeholders whose contributions can have a synergistic effect to strengthen the many local providers of adult basic education and raise basic skills to a functional level.

Adult Education in India

Adult basic education and literacy are an important part of an extensive and diverse educational program for adults in the large and pluralistic country of India. Other program areas range from continuing higher education, distance education, and continuing professional education to agricultural extension, rural and tribal development, and nonformal education by nongovernmental organizations concerned with issues such as health and social welfare. Although most of these programs are associated with separate ministries, funding, and providers, a community development orientation can be seen in instances of collaboration between literacy education and program areas (for example, agricultural extension, family services, and rural development). India is a country of contrasts, which are reflected in various views of adult education program success.

The people of India are understandably proud of their ancient and colorful cultural heritage. Although that heritage and the experience of British rule have created an overlay of national unity, traditions and practice also contribute powerfully to fragmentation of subpopulations that can be seen in adult education programs. Sources of stratification include regional differences, urbanization, language, education, occupation, age, religion, politics, affluence, and the religio-cultural caste system. There are fifteen officially recognized languages, and many people understand neither Hindi (the national language) nor English. These differences are generally divisive; however, because a person may have differing statuses within various categories, some of the distinctions may contribute to coherence within the total fabric of society. For example, especially in urban areas, adults from lower-caste families who attain higher levels of education and occupational prestige may feel increased solidarity with people with similar attainments but different caste categories (despite their reinforcement by cultural traditions, language usage, and family practices). Although stratification tends to be more rigid in rural areas, being a family elder and local political leader can also strengthen solidarity among people from different stratification categories.

Population is another major factor. Although India has less than 3 percent of the earth's land mass, it contains more than 15 percent of the world's population. In 1989, the population estimate was more than 835 million, second only to China, which has slowed its rate of population increase. India's estimated doubling time is now thirty-three years, and the population is projected to be one billion, 225 million in twenty years. The country continues to have one of the world's most serious population growth problems, despite more than thirty years of family-planning programs. Especially in rural areas (where more than 70 percent of the population resides), lack of social security provisions for elders and with ancient cultural and family traditions relying on sons to provide economic security and family continuity have been major deterrents to reduction of family size and population growth. There has been mounting agreement that the future success of family-planning policies depends on their being part of a general development strategy that includes attention to education and social welfare, especially in rural areas.

In recent decades, food production has increased greatly, but great disparities exist between levels of living and consumption in the substantial and increasing middle class, compared with members of a much larger proportion of people who live in poverty. Poverty is a major problem in India. Educational level and poverty are associated, and about 60 percent of the adult population is illiterate. Poverty and rural residence are also linked. Adult education can contribute to improvement, as demonstrated by studies in which literacy level has been positively associated with agricultural production and health conditions.

For decades, there has been rhetoric on behalf of literacy education but token funding and effort. Even though the percentage of literate adults has begun to increase slightly in recent years, the actual numbers of illiterate adults have also increased because of rapid population growth. In October 1978, the national government recognized literacy education as a high priority for the first time since independence. The following paragraphs summarize the main features of this effort and briefly describe the program in the state of Tamil Nadu, whose part of the national effort was the object of several contrasting critiques. The example concludes with highlights from the critiques that are interesting for educational planners because they illuminate the importance of assumptions when evaluating success.

Most of the five-year plans since independence contained verbiage about the seriousness of illiteracy, unrealistic recommendations about voluntary efforts and the extent to which illiteracy was to be reduced during the plan period, and so little money allocated for the purpose that few people took the words seriously. The share of all national educational expenditures for adult basic education fell from 4.3 percent in the first plan, to 1.5 in the second, to 0.1 in the fourth plan, by which time the amount allotted to adult education had dropped to 45 million rupees. Yet in 1978, the allocation for adult education jumped to 2,000 million rupees—more than four hundred times the amount set aside just a few years earlier. The sixth five-year plan (1980–1985) greatly increased the funding for adult literacy education and elementary education in the context of an increased emphasis on a minimum needs program; this emphasized comprehensive rural development, including social services and facilities such as health, nutrition, housing, water supply, electrification, and roads. The response to the increased priority for literacy education was generally positive. The recommendations from the organization's conference in October 1981 indicated the willingness of the Indian Adult Education Association to cooperate at the local level with the government in literacy education programs that were part of an integrated development effort. In June 1983, the Central

Advisory Board of Education recommended increased adult education, combined with massive community participation, so that all illiterates would be reached by 1990. Implementation plans focused on the fifteen to thirty-five age group. Nevertheless, even though the funds allocated for literacy education constituted a large increase from the past, they were estimated to be about 5 percent of the amount actually required to achieve minimal goals for the decade.

National Adult Education Program

The National Adult Education Program (NAEP) was started in 1978 during the two-year period when Indira Gandhi was replaced as prime minister by Morarji Desai of the opposition Congress party and then the Janata coalition. A son of a village teacher in Gujarat Province, Desai initiated NAEP. When Mrs. Gandhi returned as prime minister and found that the program had considerable popular support she was reluctant to eliminate it but changed its name and restricted its funding. In the mid 1980s, there was great dissatisfaction with the results of educational programs in India generally, including literacy education. However, adult literacy remained a priority in the seventh plan. During the 1980s, underfunding of NAEP was widely acknowledged. There was also general agreement on several other features and influences related to the effort. National economic conditions and lack of political commitment contributed to meager national funding and support for local efforts that were token in relation to needs and goals. Although funds were provided through several ministries for efforts related to literacy education, a major part of the NAEP relied on funds from the University Grants Commission in New Delhi to Indian universitites in support of literacy education. The universities collaborated with various organizations to provide resource centers that contributed to planning, materials, and staff development. The staffing was aimed especially at young people with secondary education who were attached to local communities. They received nonformal instruction and stipends that were attractive in relation to local rural wage levels but were quite low in relation to other people who worked in the program. Poverty and illiteracy were recognized as interconnected. Because they were interested in functional literacy, recognized modernization trends, and received encouragement from associates, some participated, but they constituted a very small portion of illiterate adults. For most, pessimism about connections between stratification, poverty, illiteracy, and lack of occupational opportunities led to conclusions that there were few likely benefits worth the effort (Bhola, 1986; Dave, Ouane, and Perera, 1986; Duke, 1985; "Adult Education," 1982; Gugnami, 1985).

Before comparing several critiques of the NAEP in Tamil Nadu, several characteristics of this coastal state in southeast India should be noted. Tamil Nadu is in the middle range of state population with about 50 million, compared with more than 110 million in Uttar Pradesh and fewer than one million people in four other states. Tamil Nadu is a bit more urban (33 percent) than the national average (27 percent), partly because its state capital and major city, Madras, has five million people in its metropolitan area. The state is more industrialized than many, with almost one-third of its domestic product coming from the secondary sector and another third from the tertiary sector. However, much of the state is rural. Tamil Nadu is one of the states in the India Union that implemented a literacy program more extensively than most. In the early 1980s, the adult education program in the state was composed of the Rural Functional Literacy Project (funded by the central government) and the state Adult Education Program (funded by the state budget). By the end of 1982, more than 33,000 local adult education centers had been in operation for ten months; these reported serving one million learners. Another 120,000 learners were reportedly served by an additional 4,400 local centers operated by voluntary agencies, universities, and Nehru Youth Centers.

One of the related programs was based at the University of Madras and provided literacy education assistance to rural villages in the adjacent Chigkeput District, which has a population of more than four million people (Resource A, Jayagopal (a)). A distinctive feature of this university-based program, a small part of the total literacy education effort in Tamil Nadu, was the use of graduate students majoring in adult education as local field staff members. During a six-month internship period with the program, each student worked with one or several local field staff members called animators, who conducted literacy activities in one or more villages, and the program supervisor for that area. The animators were typically secondary school graduates who received ongoing inservice education from a literacy resource center in the district, including a major orientation at the outset and another after five months. Animators prepared and implemented lesson plans with a conversational emphasis related to reading, writing, numeracy, health, and artisan skills for cottage industry. The supervisor, resource center, and other agencies helped them with methods, materials, plans, and evaluation. The graduate students began their internship by observing the animator and attending the resource center, then began assisting the animator, and finally worked as an animator in a local village. As part of their internship experience for the university, students prepared written reports that evaluated educational needs and program functioning, which contributed to program improvement.

The annual program budget from the University Grants Commission was the equivalent of $6,000 dollars, almost half of which was for local instructional costs related to the animators, who received small stipends, in line with national policies. The remainder was for program coordination, including staff development and help with preparation of a twice-weekly television series entitled *Education for Life,* which participants were encouraged to watch. Each year, the literacy education program served about five hundred participants, about half of whom completed it. Most of those who started were illiterate and had not attended school. About half of those who completed the program achieved basic goals in reading, writing, and numeracy. Attrition was due to participants' leaving the village to seek work during the off season and to dissatisfaction with instructional or organizational aspects of the program. Some animators departed from program guidelines for nonformal functional literacy activities and used more formal classroom procedures. Most participants believed that achieving basic literacy alone would contribute little toward a better life, but it was difficult for the organizers to achieve a really functional program to affect basic conditions of poverty.

Many practitioners throughout India apparently believed that small appropriations in relation to stated goals and implicit government expectations were inconsistent with the rhetoric of empowerment and dramatic improvement in poverty conditions; they felt that the actual program objectives were to make gradual increases in literacy. After 1980, the rhetoric of massive social change may have been viewed as a means to obtain appropriations and not as realistic objectives.

External Evaluation

A contrasting appraisal by Ramakrishnan, based on an evaluation of the NAEP in all of Tamil Nadu, appeared at about the same time (Duke, 1985). The report began with a review of the rationale for the nationwide literacy effort and then focused on all programs in the state of Tamil Nadu, of which the preceding university-based program was a small part. Unlike some practitioners who dismissed the rhetoric of empowerment and structural change as an unlikely result of a literacy program and as more likely to result from comprehensive rural development efforts by various ministries, Ramakrishnan accepted the statements of policy makers as actual program goals against which to assess impact. Some policy makers seemed to believe that increased literacy alone could result in massive socio-economic improvements for numbers of people living in absolute poverty. One result of this differing basic assumption was that he perceived the glass as half empty instead of half full. The national NAEP objectives were to impart literacy skills to illiterates aged fifteen to thirty-five, to facilitate upgrading of functional skills, and to help poor and illiterate people become aware of their rights to help achieve social and cultural change. Although Ramakrishnan acknowledged that NAEP was not explicitly expected to reduce poverty, he reviewed policy statements expressing hopes that NAEP might contribute to consciousness raising and empowerment and might work with various ministries to encourage poor people to play an active role in social change. He concluded that these statements implied objectives beyond increased literacy such as an improved standard of living and quality of life.

Ramakrishnan acknowledged that to accomplish such ambitious goals funding was meager; too much was used for administrative costs and too little for local instructional activities by animators, whose stipends were modest but well above average local income levels. Partly as a result of the modest stipends, it was difficult to attract and retain local animators in some areas to organize and teach groups of illiterate adults. Some animators, who had typically completed secondary education and were economically better off than participants, reported being hesitant to engage in counsciousness raising with participants for fear that this would cause conflict with local elites who might terminate the program. Interestingly, after orientation, animators became less convinced that social change was more important than increased literacy. The program goals raised expectations that it would have direct economic benefits; however, in practice it dealt mostly with improving literacy skills, and there was little attention to increased ability of participants to increase their incomes.

Staff members reported difficulty trying to attract illiterates. Only approximately 10 percent of all illiterates in the area attended at least once. In some areas, efforts to organize a group were abandoned for lack of interest. Some of those who attended mainly wanted to be able to read books of movie lyrics. It appeared that the poverty that the program was supposed to ameliorate served as the major barrier to participation. For both nonparticipants and dropouts, preoccupation with work discouraged involvement. Half of those who started were school dropouts, and half were total illiterates. A large minority were in their teens. In the early years, in trying to reach a maximum number, the program would be moved to serve a new area after ten months, a practice that reduced continuity and postliteracy activities. Only about one-fifth of the initial participants achieved their objectives.

The reasons for the only limited success reflected goals, plan implementation, and funding. Ramakrishnan concluded that because poverty resulted from structural features of society, improvements required structural changes in the economic system. He concluded that reduction of absolute poverty required a comprehensive approach to individual and collective life in which adult education was not a brief campaign but an ongoing activity; also necessary were preparatory education, health, and other direct efforts to reduce poverty.

Rural Poor

A third approach to poverty and the literacy education in Tamil
Nadu during the same general time period was provided more recently by program leader Sugirtharaj (Duke and others, 1990,
pp. 169–195). He drew his rationale from many sources, including
Christian and neo-Marxist, along with Gandhi, Freire, and Alinsky.
Sugirtharaj combined Freire-like Christian commitment to equality
and working with poor people for their liberation with Alinsky-
type organization of landless agricultural laborers through an association for the rural poor (a nongovernmental organization in the
form of an agricultural laborers movement). Association staff received assistance from various sources, including the Tamil Nadu
Society for Rural Education and Development. Staff trained many
people as rural development workers, about half of whom were
from church-related groups. They also trained village-level animators. Staff members and rural education workers lived in poor villages for extended periods, working day and night to organize
landless agricultural laborers to encourage and help them to improve their own conditions. The staff also trained many local village leaders who subsequently took charge of the agricultural
laborers movement. This was an especially important feature because efforts to empower the poor were resisted by landlords and
successful farmers who benefited from the low wages that the laborers received. Cooperation between separate categories of agricultural laborers was difficult because caste organizations wanted to
maintain their separate identities.

Literacy education was a subsidiary part of this NGO effort
to help the rural poor. Sugirtharaj questioned the usefulness of
large-scale literacy campaigns because the high costs and frustration
did not result in much improvement of socio-economic conditions.
Instead, he urged use of literacy education as one of several ways to
raise consciousness of poor people about their oppression, as part
of a political education and empowerment effort.

Bhola's Assessment

In a paper for the African Studies Association, Bhola (1986) expressed his hope and fear regarding literacy education in India. His

hope reflected his conviction that functional literacy and basic skills had finally been recognized as one essential part of a necessary national effort to reduce poverty. Popular support was so great that policy makers were reluctant to talk against it. Although the NAEP had failed to achieve its unrealistic goals, and a 1985 ministry of education report on the challenge of education was very critical of educational programs generally, there were some program successes and wide agreement on the importance of decentralized efforts and active participation by the masses. His fear concerned growing violence associated with factional conflict and insufficient commitment to functional literacy education that could produce substantial improvement. Government leaders and program administrators had provided too little funding for the attempted program and relied too much on volunteerism by middle-class young people. Recent reports of modifications to the national literacy program continue to complain about uneven political and financial support, but refer to improved pace, quality, management, collaboration, and student involvement; there has also been some success associated with a committed staff and with postliteracy activities.

Contrasting Assessments

These four perspectives on literacy education by Jayagopal, Ramakrishnan, Sugirtharaj, and Bhola serve to illuminate the influence of positions, assumptions, beliefs, and expectations on assessments of the desirability of program goals and methods, along with success achieved. The authors differ in their views of the importance of trying to promote structural change in society, a fact that underscores how important it is for planners to clarify assumptions and beliefs early. A theme prominent in these writers' work is the desirability of comprehensive efforts that include literacy as part of collaborative programs, such as integrated rural development that responds to multiple needs and categories of people who must learn and grow if social change efforts are to succeed. Such collaborative efforts require recognition of the many other adult education providers and programs in India (International Council on Adult Education, 1982; Rangaswami, 1984; Wagner and Puchner, 1992).

With the second largest population in the world and great

regional differences, India is a pluralistic country with many separate educational programs for adults. These programs are connected with many government ministries. Regarding literacy education and basic skills, as already noted, there are various providers and programs exclusively or partly engaged in literacy. Along with the National Adult Education Program, these include state functional literacy projects, women's education programs, Nehru Youth Centers, and nongovernmental organizations. Rural development educational programs for adults include agricultural and rural extension: for example, training and visit procedures; farm training centers; rural health, nutrition, and family life programs; and tribal development projects. Voluntary agencies and nongovernment organizations provide adult education on various health and welfare topics. Adult vocational education is offered as part of state adult education programs. Although Indian colleges and universities have been oriented toward the elite and have produced an oversupply of graduates, they have conducted some adult education programs and leadership training for the field. Distance education using standard mass media and special satellite transmission has served adult learners. Additional adult education activities have been furnished by many other types of organizations: libraries, enterprises, labor unions, and religious institutions (Bannerji, 1981; Dave, Ouane, and Perera, 1986; Wagner and Puchner, 1992).

Some of these other adult education programs have worked with people and topics involved in the social change that a comprehensive effort entails. For example, in-service education for elementary school teachers can both improve their current classroom performance and increase their lifelong learning orientation, including assistance with adult literacy activities. Since 1975, government-operated Nehru Youth Centers for out-of-school youth have provided small stipends and in-service training for educated youth who serve as leaders of programs that encompass recreation and community service, along with various educational programs including literacy and postliteracy activities.

In spite of a societal predisposition to cast rural women into narrow stereotypes, rather than to liberate them, a women's literacy movement has had a rationale that has extended beyond reducing illiteracy, poverty, hunger, and exploitation. It is intended to achieve consciousness raising, empowerment, liberation, and higher standards of living (Bhasin, 1984). In such instances, broader synergistic approaches include literacy in more comprehensive programs with attractive goals.

Adult education leaders in the United States and other countries can reflect on the contrasting perspectives on literacy education in India and consider the differing assumptions that are made in their own context.

Other Countries

The foregoing overviews of adult basic education in the United States and in India reveal both similarities and differences related to national context that have implications for strengthening literacy education in each country. American experience with state and federal policy support, with participatory literacy, and with collaboration among providers could be used to enrich literacy planning in India. Likewise, Indian experience with connections between illiteracy and poverty and with contrasting assessments of the role of literacy education in producing structural changes in the socioeconomic system could be used to clarify assumptions and issues that are seldom examined in the United States. Inclusion of policy makers in strategic planning can help them discover ways in which adult education is likely to help achieve goals they value.

Reports from other countries that analyze the functioning of local adult basic education programs in their national context also contain insights useful for planning literacy education programs elsewhere. Comparative adult education writings include examples that illustrate coping by immigrants in Germany and the Netherlands, influence of economic conditions in Nigeria and Hong Kong, contributions of television in the United Kingdom, and ideological prerequisites of literacy campaigns in Cuba and Nicaragua. The following discussion of literacy education in Sweden, Saudi Arabia, Ireland, Australia, China, and Canada identifies both some distinctive national features and some shared characteristics that suggest provocative questions for planning in the United States. Juxtaposition of contrasting countries provides insights beyond those gained from focusing only on literacy education in industrialized countries or in economically developing countries (Adult Literacy and Basic Skills Unit, 1987; Barron and Mohan, 1979; Ellis, 1984; Neves, 1982; Rojo, 1984; Wells, 1985). Strategic planning can include comparative analysis to help leaders provide responsive programs for contrasting populations of functionally illiterate adults in the United States. For some participants, group solidarity is an overriding value (as it is in many developing countries), an idea conflicting with some individualized instructional methods (Bhola, 1981, 1988; Huang, 1985; Kahler, 1978; Limage, 1986; Lind and Johnston, 1986; Ryan, 1985).

Sweden

In view of its commitment to equity and democracy, Sweden might seem to be an unlikely country in which to find an illiteracy problem. As noted in Chapter Two, for more than a century, Sweden has had a strong tradition of generally widespread educational opportunities, which for more than half a century has included one of the highest levels of policy and financial support for adult education. The right to education for all people is widely understood, and the threshold of basic education has been broadly defined to include not only reading, writing, and numeracy but also proficiencies related to occupation, citizenship, and cultural heritage comparable to nine years of preparatory education. This is a level of basic education deemed necessary for satisfactory functioning as an adult in contemporary Swedish society. Varied and responsive educational opportunities for adults are available from many public and private providers (including enterprises), and each year more than half the adult population participates. By 1990, only an estimated 18 percent of Swedish adults had completed less than the equivalent of nine years of schooling, a big improvement from 65 percent in 1960 (Abrahamsson, 1990a, 1990b).

Half of the participants in Swedish adult basic education programs are native born; the other half are immigrants, many of whom are from developing countries and have limited education. Priority and appropriations for adult basic education result from a policy promoting absorption of immigrants as part of a broader commitment to use education to enhance equity and reduce social stratification. Adult basic education priority, planning, and appropriations also reflect cultural values central to national identity and to appropriate use of technology in planned change. Favorable economic conditions have allowed strong appropriations of tax funds, which have been the main source of financial support for much of adult education, aside from staff development by enterprises. An economy that has been sluggish in recent years and concerns about an increasingly interdependent European community beyond 1992 may be contributing to current reorientation and devolution of Swedish adult education. Legislation in providing study leaves for immigrant workers in 1973 and establishing occupational proficiency standards and adult basic education programs in 1987 correspond to increased support for adult education in other European countries during the 1970s (Resource A, Thang (a)).

Saudi Arabia

Societal influences on adult basic education in Saudi Arabia might not be expected to be very similar to those in Sweden (Al Sunbul, 1985; Sobeih, 1984; Resource A, Al Rasheed and Al Sunbul). However, there are some major similarities. In recent years, as the monarchy increased priority for education as important for achievement of national goals, the result has been a fairly unified direction similar to that provided by the Swedish National Board of Education under a social democratic government. A strong Islamic religious tradition contributes to cultural unity, which is reflected in educational content and procedures. Favorable economic conditions in Saudi Arabia have also allowed substantial increases in appropriations for adult basic education. A variety of nonformal education activities for adults is viewed as part of a desirable combination of broad development and modernization efforts, although in practice adult basic education programs have tended to be fairly separate from other types of educational programs for adults. Illiteracy is viewed as an impediment to technological modernization for increased rural and urban productivity. Literacy education has progressed substantially since 1970, as a result of 1972 legislation and subsequent increases in policy support, funding, and coordination.

Of course, there are also major differences in these two countries' societal influences on literacy education, as well as in their climates. Many of the differences pertain to a more restricted view of education than in Sweden. Illiteracy rates have been high in Saudi Arabia, especially for women, whose roles have been traditionally differentiated from men's. Nevertheless, some urban women's organizations have conducted educational programs for women. Literacy is not highly prized in the general population, a fact that discourages participation in adult basic education. Preparatory education for young people has not been oriented toward lifelong learning. The literacy education curriculum has been characterized as traditional, lacking relevance for adults, and slow to change. This situation is partly due to the predominant use of elementary school teachers, who are little oriented toward active methods of adult education (but instead emphasize passive learning) and for whom too little inservice education is provided. In addition to relatively low policy and financial support for literacy education in comparison with preparatory education of young people, adult basic education is quite separate from other types of adult education. This situation is reflected in the few postliteracy opportunities for participants and little university support for adult education staff. Some of the strongest criticism of adult basic education has been aimed at inadequate staff development that should be helping teachers to become more responsive to adult learners. Although the administrative responsibility for the national adult basic education effort lies with the ministry of education and the main local provider is the schools, there is policy support for cooperation from most pertinent ministries and help from other local providers. The foregoing comparison between Sweden and Saudi Arabia illustrates the importance of strategic planning to help stakeholders recognize connections between adult education and pressing societal problems. This is one purpose of the California state plan for adult education.

Republic of Ireland

A recent literacy project in a rural county in the midlands of Ireland demonstrates a way to include many people associated with a local program and strategic planning (Hautecoeur, 1990). Volunteers helped to bring the adult illiteracy issue to public attention in the 1970s. In 1973, Ireland officially recognized that illiteracy was a problem for an estimated 100,000 adults. In 1977, a variety of people concerned with the problem (including adult education practitioners, volunteers, and retired teachers) organized the National Adult Literacy Agency (NALA) as a support agency for local literacy work. Its four hundred members included literacy students, tutors, organizers, and people from schools, libraries, and labor unions. In 1986, the Department of Education increased its estimate of the number of adult illiterates to 400,000 (18 percent of the population). According to a 1987 NALA survey, surprisingly, 63 percent of the NALA program participants were between sixteen and twenty-five years old.

During 1987–88, NALA worked with the County Offaly literacy program in central Ireland on an action research project that involved many people associated with the local program in evaluation for planning. Both the findings and the commitment that resulted from the evaluation contributed to many program improvements. For example, many participants and potential participants felt the stigma of illiteracy and the need for confidentiality in the individual tutoring arrangements the program provided. The study findings pointed to ways to assure confidentiality and lack of competitive pressure while also providing small-group activity for support, encouragement, and recognition for progress. The study also discovered the great amount of time entailed in assisting volunteer tutors, most of whom did not continue. As a result, several organizers were added, and an increasing number of paid tutors began meeting with volunteer tutors for purposes of encouragement, staff development, planning, and materials development. This action research project illustrated a procedure for various stakeholders in a local program to analyze its current functioning and to implement plans to improve the match between participants, program, and staff.

Local literacy programs, such as the one in County Offaly, reflect a growing recognition of the importance of adult basic education and its integration into a national program for economic and social progress. Government commitment as a major stakeholder in adult education is obvious in a 1992 discussion draft by the minister of education in preparation for a policy paper and proposed legislation. Literacy education is discussed as an important aspect of the continuum of lifelong education, served by a network of providers including vocational education committees, adult education boards, community training workshops, prison education service, NALA, the National Association for Adult Education, universities, voluntary associations, and community agencies. Reports by the Organization for Economic Cooperation and Development (OECD) have helped clarify the extent of the functional literacy problem in Ireland; also, the Irish Adult Literacy and Community Education Scheme, operated through the Vocational Education Committees, received a boost in 1990 with a doubling of its budget, with additional funding for tutor training provided in 1991 and continued support for the grassroots scheme and its evaluation through 1992. Continued tutor training has involved multiple stakeholders, including a government department, university, and NALA. Such local projects reflect increased national commitment in recent decades (Kenny, 1983; Murchu, 1984; National Association for Adult Education, 1986).

Australia

Three years after the New South Wales, Australia, Education Department recognized the extent of the illiteracy problem, a thousand adults were participating in the literacy program in 103 locations, including colleges of technical and further education (TAFE) and community centers. After official recognition, funds were appropriated, basic education specialists were appointed, and commonwealth education funds were used to employ literacy teachers and coordinators whose responsibilities included planning, communication, staff development, and encouragement of collaboration. As the level of priority for literacy rose, so did cooperation from community groups in the form of additional assistance from volunteers. Workshops and newsletters were utilized to orient volunteers and to help teachers modify their methods for illiterate adults. Educational technology was used in distance education procedures to serve isolated adults. Increased priority, subsidy, and collaboration resulted in subsidized programs. By 1987, two hundred people were working full time in the program in New South Wales alone (Resource A, Wickert).

Another predominantly urban adult literacy program in Victoria has focused on workplace literacy (Resource A, Newcombe and others). Leadership by the adult education council led to government funding of a collaborative workplace-based education program that includes writing as well as reading with an emphasis on work-related vocabulary and use. The Australian economy was healthy enough in the late 1980s for the Department of Labor to allocate funding for the project and for enterprises to invest in human resources, such as release time for participation. Program planning has been collaborative and has drawn on the adult education council; Australia's strong labor unions, which emphasize further education as part of workplace democracy; and enterprises, many of which had employees with low literacy and educational levels. Staff development and educational technology have helped staff performance, and functionally illiterate adults have been encouraged to participate by changes in work requirements, program content and methods, encouragement by peers, and anticipated benefits. In each of these Australian examples, the focus has been on individual learners. Educational technology has sometimes been used to serve undereducated adults (Wilson and Hooper, 1986).

People's Republic of China

The current stage of China's long struggle against illiteracy, especially in rural areas, provides some perspectives on social mobilization planning that contrasts with the earlier examples from the United States, India, Sweden, Saudi Arabia, Ireland, and Australia (Department of Adult Education, 1990; Hopkins, 1986; Hunter and Keehn, 1985; Wang, Lin, Sun, and Fang, 1988; Yong-Fan, 1982; Resource A, Dong and Zhu (b)). In spite of the major destruction of education generally during the so-called cultural revolution, the adult illiteracy and semiliteracy rate has declined from about 80 percent forty years ago to about 16 percent in 1990. Of the current illiterates, about 90 percent live in rural areas, and about 70 percent are women—figures that partly reflect early marriage for rural girls. Simplification of characters in the written language has made basic mastery of reading and writing less difficult, and the objectives of adult basic education have been broadened to include the range of proficiencies prerequisite to modernization.

Because of China's huge population and great regional diversity, functional literacy programs have been decentralized, have had multiple providers and sources of funds, have been adapted to each region (but with some central coordination), and have focused on social groups more than individuals. For example, Taojiang County in Hunan Province has reduced its illiteracy rate to less than 5 percent by a combination of prevention (by improved elementary education and reduction of drop outs), eradication (by adult literacy education) and upgrading (by postliteracy activities). During the 1980s, substantial improvements in the rural standard of living have discouraged some adults from literacy education as a diversion from making more money but have encouraged others as a means of doing so. In contrast with India, China has achieved a low rate of population growth, but the controls have been less rigid for Han Chinese in rural areas and for ethnic minorities out of respect for their customs. Contacts with adult educators in other countries through UNESCO and International Council on Adult Education activities have been mutually beneficial, and additional international cooperation has been advocated. Recent national conferences of Chinese adult educators have recommended improvements in organization and administration, encouragement of participation, use of full-time and part-time teachers, recognition of success, and use of comprehensive approaches. This example illustrates a combination of decentralized local planning and regional adaptation within central guidelines and general coordination. It also shows a more collective approach in which local groups of people have encouraged each other to achieve community goals—in contrast with a more individualized orientation in literacy programs in Western industrialized countries.

Canada

Adult basic education and societal factors influencing it in Canada have been more similar to those in the United States than in the countries from which the earlier examples have been taken. Similarities include illiteracy rates, performance by young adults on literacy tests from the National Assessment of Educational Progress, and greater illiteracy for older, rural, and native peoples. Basic education for recent immigrants has also been a growing challenge in Canada. Although adult illiteracy has not been viewed as a major problem, there has been growing recognition that in a technological society the threshold of functional basic education should be equivalent to secondary education and that illiteracy is associated with personal and societal problems such as poverty and illness. In a highly educated country, illiterate adults feel stigmatized, a situation that discourages many from seeking help (Southam, 1987; Taylor and Draper, 1989; Thomas, 1983).

Canadian adult basic education is provided by various organizations, public and private, large and small, recent and long standing. The 1977 recipient of a UNESCO medal for meritorious work in literacy and basic education, Frontier College, has adapted its laborer-teacher model to work with volunteers in urban areas (Charters and Hilton, 1989; Thomas, 1983). Another example of urban adult basic education depends on collaboration among providers in the East End of Toronto (Gaber-Katz and Watson, 1991; Taylor and Draper, 1989; Resource A, Gaber-Katz). The community-based approach is responsive to undereducated adults in densely populated, low-income neighborhoods, who have shown a preference for small-scale participatory programs. The intended benefits include increased literacy not only for individual self-expression but also for social and political empowerment to solve local neighborhood problems. Collaboration by the school and the library has supported efforts by program staff to recruit and work with volunteers as well as participants from the neighborhood. Participants have also helped produce educational materials. In this community-based approach, staff members provide staff development for tutors to encourage learner-centered methods and growth for tutors. Drawing both participants and tutors from the neighborhood has encouraged involvement and relevance.

A quite different Canadian approach is found in the work of World Literacy of Canada (WLC), which was begun in 1955 by four Canadians who were inspired by two Americans engaged in adult literacy work abroad. One of the Americans was Frank Laubach, of each-one-teach-one fame, and the other was Welthy Fisher, who began Literacy House in India at the urging of Gandhi. As a non-government association, WLC began by providing support for Literacy House, it then broadened its support to include community-based, nonformal basic education for poor adults in other developing countries where there were good prospects that the WLC and local organizations combined could sustain an effective literacy program. More recently, WLC has assisted related educational efforts in Canada. It has received matching funds from the Canadian International Development Agency. The WLC approach is very collaborative, and education has been its main activity for the benefit of illiterate adults, the staff members and volunteers who work with them, and members of the WLC association and donors who support the program (Gaber-Katz and Watson, 1991; Resource A, Draper).

These and other adult basic education programs in Canada have been shaped by various societal influences. One has been a growing federal financial role tied to vocational and economic development, where the responsibility for actually conducting education rests with the provinces and local communities. Another is the growing recognition that a broadened view of lifelong learning is essential for economic productivity and an equitable government. Also, although there are graduate programs for adult education practitioners in various provinces (there are large ones in Ontario and British Columbia), staff development remains a widespread concern. Commonwealth ties and the Canadian International Development Agency of the federal government have promoted an international perspective on adult education. As in the United States, pluralistic provision and funding of adult education have retarded the type of comprehensive planning that has occurred in Sweden (Taylor and Draper, 1989; Thomas, 1983).

Strategic Planning

The foregoing review of societal influences on local adult basic education programs suggests several implications for strategic planning. These pertain to goals, participants, staff, stakeholders, and contingencies. In addition to usual planning attention to internal provider purposes, strengths, and weaknesses, a cross-national perspective on planning can strengthen attention to external societal threats and opportunities such as economic conditions and government priorities.

Goals

Program goals and intended outcomes for participants are based on assumptions by staff and policy makers regarding the nature of the problem addressed by literacy education and appropriate responses to it (Arnove and Graff, 1987; Bhola, 1988; Charnley and Jones, 1979). Government influence is apparent in the examples from the United States, Sweden, and Saudi Arabia. Given the American tradition of extreme emphasis on individualism, it may not be surprising that popular commentaries on the illiteracy problem in the United States focus on adult illiteracy as "causing" social problems such as poverty, crime, and unemployment (Chisman, 1989; Chisman and Associates, 1990). This individualistic emphasis reflects U.S. cultural beliefs. With this definition of the problem, recommended programs tend to be remedial efforts to promote personal change that will presumably enable individuals to advance economically. It is further assumed that if many undereducated adults achieve such personal progress, social problems such as poverty, unemployment, crime, illness, hunger, and homelessness will be reduced. In practice, many participants are satisfied with their educational progress, and improved self-esteem is a major outcome (passing the GED exam is associated with higher earnings); however, the main benefits are not occupational (Beder, 1991).

By contrast, some experts on adult basic education make quite different assumptions about the nature of the illiteracy problem and appropriate solutions (Bhola, 1987; Clemson, 1985; Mpogolo, 1984, Nji and Nji, 1985; Odunuga, 1984; Okeem, 1982; Omolewa, 1984). They agree that individual performance and societal problems are connected but do not place the main emphasis on individual deficiencies and remediation. They sometimes view such approaches as blaming the victim and suggest that nonparticipation by undereducated adults reflects their recognition that illiteracy is less a cause than a symptom of powerful socio-economic forces that cause their plight. This difference in assumptions is illustrated in the contrasting assessments of adult basic education in India (Wagner and Puchner, 1992). Thus, part of the educational effort should address ways to transform social, political, and economic arrangements, using participatory approaches such as group, organization, and community development. This approach was used in the Toronto, Canada, example. Within the framework of structural transformations that emphasize economic development and not just productivity, adults can gain confidence that progress is possible and that opportunities are available; as a result, they have a better chance to become empowered through broad programs of personal and social development (Beder, 1991; Fingeret and Jurmo, 1989; Harman, 1987).

Participation

One strategic planning issue for a local provider is therefore whether the main program goal should be remedial, adaptive, or transformative. This planning decision depends in part on beliefs about potential participants, about the multiple reasons they attend, and about what explains low participation rates and high attrition rates. Part of what must be taken into account is the delayed gratification expected of predominantly working-class participants, compared with the more immediate rewards for middle-class participants in most adult education programs. Furthermore, conditions of poverty that affect many illiterate adults serve as major deterrents to participation, as is illustrated by the examples from India and Saudi Arabia. Adults may develop a sense of alienation from the majority culture and lack of optimism about advancement, depending in part on whether they feel enveloped by a culture of poverty or whether they feel connected with various subcultures through affiliations with family, community, religious institutions, voluntary associations, enterprises, or ethnic traditions. Situational and especially attitudinal deterrents should be reduced to attract nonparticipants. Underrepresentation of women in some countries and of men in U.S. basic education programs calls for explanations and perhaps corrective policies. Strategic planning can identify connections between characteristics of potential participants and the intended program benefits (passing of a GED high school equivalency exam, access to educational opportunities, job training activities, and existence of employment opportunities). The positive role of peers is apparent in the examples from Australia, China, and Canada.

Staffing

Staffing for adult basic education poses a crucial challenge for strategic planning. One of the most widespread criticisms of adult basic education and literacy programs is overreliance on volunteers and part-time staff. The West Virginia library and the Irish programs mainly depended on volunteers. Both volunteer and part-time roles make valuable contributions; these staff members may be more committed, develop rapport with participants, add program flexibility, and act as a subsidy. However, there are problems related to costs, recruitment and supervision, program instability, and depth that full-time staff members can help solve. A major weakness in the Saudi Arabian example was heavy reliance on school teachers. Strategic planning should explore optimal staffing patterns in relation to availability of potential staff and incentives to attract and retain a satisfactory mix of able staff and volunteers. The Australian and Canadian examples illustrate methods of staff development. In some U.S. programs, well-trained volunteer tutors provide much-needed intensity and support on which participants come to depend, but if tutors reach the limits of their training and are unable to help participants progress, the result can be frustration, tutor attrition, feelings of abandonment, and participant attrition.

Stakeholders

Strategic planning typically includes identification of major stakeholders to benefit from their ideas and support. For adult basic education, it is generally easier to involve those who are in some way close to the program (staff, participants, and representatives of organizations that refer new participants or place graduates) than those who are more distant (policy makers, mass media contacts, and funders). The examples from India and Saudi Arabia show inadequate cooperation, in contrast with the examples from Ireland, Australia, China, and Canada. Strategic planning can help in several ways to involve more distant stakeholders. Special workplace, community, or family literacy projects can include advisory committees composed of a broad range of interested people, a practice that can buttress strategic planning. Although it may be more difficult to involve state or national policy makers and funders in local strategic planning, a state plan that reflects federal guidelines (like the one in California) can provide a framework for planning and cooperation. Although aspects of these broader plans may not seem entirely satisfactory, they do create a starting point for cooperating with other local providers covered by the state plan to propose modifications, even including revised legislation and guidelines or increased appropriations. Such concerted efforts should also address societal conditions that contribute to illiteracy from a lifelong learning perspective (Beder, 1991). Most state plans are revised every year or two. Annual reports from local programs provide for accountability but also can be used to interpret needed changes, which findings from program evaluation can support. Through such efforts and efforts such as Project Literacy U.S., local providers working in concert can help raise understanding of the importance of adult education programs to the public, policy makers, and even powerful elites not already committed to them. The importance of comprehensive approaches can be seen in the Indian programs. Strategic planning can provide a more persuasive basis for proactive efforts to increase program priority in the face of competing demands from other users of scarce resources.

Local literacy consortia and councils can greatly increase the impact of adult basic education, but there are also impediments to cooperation. Collaboration can accomplish joint needs assessment and contextual analysis, resource sharing, combined staff development, and concerted public information campaigns. Impediments to cooperation include distinctive approaches, preference for separate images and jurisdictions, and an uneven extent of cooperation.

Leaders of local providers have long struggled with an inadequate resource base, annual fluctuations, and uncertainty that undermines planning and implementation. Collaboration can enhance stability. Heavy reliance on short-term, unpredictable funding is an impediment to planning, as well as an issue for planning to address.

Contingencies

Strategic planning for a local provider includes attention to the specific contingencies in the service area (Bhola, 1988). The strategy of informed pluralism entails understanding of programs of related providers in the service area; the goal is to seek cooperation when it is appropriate and beneficial. Program specialization for various segments of illiterate adults is especially important. Local contingencies include demographic trends, relations with providers of other adult education programs, and employment opportunities. The Indian example illustrates pessimism; the Irish example, stigma, as local contingencies that reflect widespread attitudes affecting participation. Worker ownership of the West Virginia steel plant is such a local contingency. By including people associated with the related activities in the planning process, along with information about their activities, program leaders can strengthen program resources, coordination, quality, and responsiveness. The standardization and rigidity of preparatory education should be avoided in the interests of the vitality and flexibility that allow adult basic education to be pluralistic and responsive (Beder, 1991). As noted in several of the examples, use of educational technology sometimes provides a vehicle for collaboration to gain economies of scale and reduce unit costs. Cooperation costs money and time, but the benefits are sometimes well worth the investment. The importance of favorable economic conditions is apparent in the examples from Sweden, Australia, and Saudi Arabia. Strategic planning can help identify especially beneficial opportunities for cooperation and support.

Leadership for adult basic education involves planning issues related to other types of educational programs for adults covered in subsequent chapters. Included are rural development, minorities, cultural programs, community problem solving, and health education.

4

Programs for Cultural Minorities

Conflict between cultural minorities and the dominant cultural majority is a hot issue in the United States and in many other countries. Although there are important distinctions between subcultures in developing and in industrialized countries, a comparative perspective can help adult education practitioners assist people in underdeveloped regions and neighborhoods in the United States.

Minority Subcultures

The 1990 U.S. census reports document the increasing size and diversity of subcultures, which contribute to the turbulent context for planning adult education programs for cultural minorities. Leaders of such programs confront a dilemma regarding agency mission in a pluralistic society, one that is shared by their counterparts in other countries that have received many immigrants (such as Canada, Israel, and Australia) and in countries composed of diverse subcultures (such as Nigeria, the former Soviet Union, and the former Yugoslavia). The dilemma concerns the balance between an assimilationist educational mission (designed to resocialize adults from diverse cultural backgrounds to fit into the patterns of the cultural majority), and a cultural pluralistic mission (intended to help individuals preserve their distinctive cultural traditions, which may enrich and change the majority culture). Regardless of the mission that is chosen, program leaders confront political, economic, and social crosscurrents contributing to the complexity of their program context.

Cultural diversity in the United States is even greater than it appears on the surface. As in other countries composed largely of immigrants and their descendants, immigration and national origin have been major sources of minority subcultures, but not the only sources. Other characteristics that help identify minority subcultures include language, religion, affluence, gender, ethnicity, age, region, and handicap or disability. Minorities are usually defined in relation to the majority culture, which reflects cultural power or dominance more than proportion of the total population. (The term *minority subculture* refers to a segment of the total national population that may have high or low prestige or intrinsic value.) The distinctiveness of each subculture reflects shared cultural values and characteristics. The experience of minority group members depends to some extent on pluralistic acceptance by the members of the majority or dominant culture, which can range from hegemony and cultural imperialism all the way to respect for individual rights and freedoms, acceptance of diversity and language rights, and assurance of equal opportunities. There is great potential for conflict when minority group pressure for change confronts resistance from the majority culture, and this can greatly affect educational programs for minorities. The fabric of society remains intact in part because most people are associated with multiple subcultures so that solidarity arising from some (such as religious affiliation, regional location, gender, or age) may somewhat offset divisiveness resulting from other subcultural differences (such as those related to ethnicity, language, unemployment, or socioeconomic status). However, people tend to associate with people similar to themselves.

In the United States, immigration continues to be a major source of cultural diversity. The immigrant experience consists of an extended dual-culture transitional period between leaving the former culture and beginning to function satisfactorily in the new culture; this is a time when many immigrants feel that they are between cultures with the full benefits of neither. Discrimination can extend this condition for generations. Strategic planning of adult education for cultural minorities can help practitioners go beyond general stereotypes and instead recognize the variety within each subculture. For example, within all Hispanic or Asian immigrants, there are important differences related to country of origin, familiarity with American language and customs, and conditions under which they departed from their native lands. Educational programs can recognize major cultural differences, such as those between expatriate intellectuals from Chile versus illegal aliens from Central America, or Japanese executives versus Hmong hill people. Though not immigrants, Native Americans can be from more than one hundred tribal nations.

For immigrants and native-born minorities, the size of the subculture is only one consideration. Another is relative status and acceptance in relation to people in the majority culture. Majority and minority status refers mainly to relative power. Thus, adult education programs for cultural minorities can address quite different goals, such as assimilation into majority culture, resistance to assimilation by preserving the subculture, and transcultural efforts that entail pluralistic reconciliation among various subcultures in relation to a less dominant majority culture. The conflict and change that occurs is the result of both the assertiveness of minorities and societal influences. Some influences are produced by economic and political conditions such as unemployment rates and political power. Other influences have to do with policies and practices, such as equal opportunity procedures and immigration quotas. The high proportions of emigrants to the United States from Asia and Latin America during the 1970s and 1980s, compared with high proportions of emigrants from Europe between the 1930s and 1960s, reflect differing legislative ceilings based on national origins, as well as problems in various countries that stimulated emigration.

A distinctive feature of adult education for members of diverse minority subcultures is that they have shared values as they deal with economic conditions, social change, and international influences. As program leaders respond to minority aspirations, strategic planning can help clarify program goals, generate support by participants' friends and family members, and sometimes cope with resistance by powerful elites. Because subsidy is necessary, government policy and financial support is important to help participants achieve self-sufficiency and make the transition to adult education generally. This chapter explores how an understanding of cultural minorities might contribute to agency planning and leadership (it does not discuss inclusion of multicultural content in adult education courses).

Adult education for cultural minorities and subcultures of all kinds can also pursue a comprehensive transcultural strategy. Such a strategy accepts multicultural interdependence and recognizes conflict among subcultures as a problem that requires attention by the entire society, not just members of a subculture. Strategic planning for such comprehensive adult education programs include objectives that enhance performance in both the subculture and the majority culture, as well as objectives for growth by members of the majority culture and for bridges between preparatory and continuing education. The following examples and overviews from the United States and other countries suggest ways to strengthen strategic planning through attention to societal influences. The examples and rationale focus mainly on four planning themes. One is the importance of an agency leadership that emphasizes goal clarification and staff development. A second theme is the cultural values of potential participants and the impact of social change on their educational participation. A third is the influence of government priorities that are affected by international events as well as economic conditions. The fourth theme is the importance of local contingencies and agency collaboration. The concluding section of the chapter suggests some implications for strategic planning related to these ideas and other societal influences.

Immigrant Education

For more than three decades, U.S. international relations in Southeast Asia and the 1980 Refugee Act have created a flow of refugees and emigrants who must be served by U.S. immigrant education programs for adults. A few years ago, about two-thirds of legal immigrants who entered the United States were from Southeast Asia. An example of a refugee education program occurred between 1979 and 1986 in a middle-class suburban city of 60,000 people an hour's drive from a large midwestern city. The suburban city had a Southeast Asian refugee population of about 3,000 people and was designated an affected area. The local Young Woman's Christian Association (YWCA) served as the provider of a refugee education program for adults. The main program goal was to help refugees become self-sufficient productive members of American society as soon as possible through instruction in vocational English as a second language, vocational education, and adjustments regarding work, family, and community for adult refugees and their families. This short-term goal emphasized early employment to minimize government support. By 1986, more than 2,400 of the 3,000 refugees had been employed, and about thirty people a month were being placed in jobs.

In 1979, the YWCA director of community services received funding for her refugee education proposal from the state refugee office. Her community services office served as the main provider agency and conducted instruction in English as a second language (ESL), but she received cooperation from the YWCA as the parent organization and from other organizations in the community. The YWCA contributed planning, coordination, in-kind assistance, and a positive image in the service area from its previous ESL programs. This was the only refugee education program within a forty-mile radius. External collaboration included working with enterprises to set program objectives and arrange job placement for those completing the program and cooperating with educational institutions to furnish vocational education instruction. The program director provided effective leadership to maintain cooperation from a network of stakeholders. An investment in staff time and money was made to aid volunteer tutors so that staff effort would be cost beneficial. Over the years, some of the staff development activities originally provided by the YWCA were assumed by external organizations such as educational institutions and professional associations.

Toward the end of the program period, those completing the program were perceived as desirable community members and workers. Originally, some local residents had been apprehensive that the YWCA was sponsoring an influx of refugees who would become a community problem. The director worked with her staff and people associated with the broader refugee program in a community education effort to help many local groups understand that each refugee family in the community was church sponsored, that indeed additional housing and social services were needed, and that there would be benefits as well as costs to the community. This effort, combined with program success, resulted in high community acceptance and cooperation.

There were multiple influences on participation. The early wave of refugees who took part in the beginning had more educational preparation in Asia than the second wave. This initial higher literacy level (including some exposure to English) contributed to progress by refugees in the first wave but created unrealistic expectations for refugees in the second wave. The general literacy levels and job skills of both groups were low for U.S. requirements, however. Their optimism about anticipated benefits encouraged them to make difficult role changes and adjustments to a new culture. The comprehensiveness of the program and the success in the community of those completing the program reflected both individual and societal aspects of personal and economic development. Local economic conditions allowed employment opportunities for successful participants, and some started their own enterprises.

Government policies and financial support were very influential in achieving these results. Federal and state governments have set a high priority on educational and other means to assist refugees with supportive policies and finances. In addition to providing the YWCA with substantial external funding, the state refugee office allowed desirable flexibility and established time limits on support for each refugee family that urged everyone to make rapid progress toward self-sufficiency. Toward the end of the program period, there were reductions in external support, which curtailed related services; the YWCA sustained these services by using volunteers (Resource A, L. Knox).

This example illustrates strategic planning that includes major stakeholders related to work and family roles of refugees; general community support; and contributions by enterprises, educational institutions, social service agencies, state government, and volunteers. Program relevance and participant progress reflect a focus on functional workplace literacy for survival and self-sufficiency, along with a holistic concern for all roles of family members and the difficult adjustments they confront (which result from both international and local change). This comprehensive approach was in contrast with some programs that focused narrowly on teaching English as a second language.

Other U.S. Programs

Immigrant education is but a part of a great variety of educational programs for adults from various subcultures. In addition to immigrants, there are native-born minorities such as blacks and Native American Indians, adults who are developmentally disabled or handicapped, and many other less-advantaged subcultures related to socio-economic status, age, gender, or place of residence. The League of Women Voters has sponsored educational activities for the subculture of women, designed to increase political power. This section provides an overview of adult education programs by various providers for some of these subpopulations, including comments on major societal influences that have implications for strategic planning. Given the diversity of subpopulations and educational needs, it is understandable that there is also a great range of adult education programs and providers to serve adults from minority cultures. The examples focus on programs that were most relevant to subculture concerns; of course, adults from these subcultures mainly select programs that seem pertinent to them from among the many available.

Immigrants

Immigrant education has been conducted by various providers and has been aimed at many objectives. ESL, vocational education, and other programs for immigrants and other adults from minority subcultures have been provided by various organizations in addition to the YWCA: public schools, community colleges, community-based organizations, and voluntary associations and sometimes enterprises, religious institutions, libraries, correctional institutions, and proprietary schools. A central issue regarding ESL programs has been the inadequate supply in relation to the large and growing demand. The 1980s matched the former record of 8.7 million immigrants who arrived in the United States during the first decade of the century. About five million U.S. residents currently lack minimal English proficiency. During the next decade, about half of the people who enter the work force will be recent immigrants. Unfortunately, current ESL programs are serving only a small proportion of the immigrants, and in some communities people must wait one to two years. Planning should address expanding a pluralistic system of providers with special attention to able full-time instructors (Chisman and Associates, 1990; Merriam and Cunningham, 1989, chap. 37). Most immigrant education programs have addressed objectives in addition to ESL, such as basic education and vocational education, but the typical goal in these and most other programs for cultural minorities has been to help participants progress within the majority culture. Seldom has the goal been structural change in the majority culture or syncretism (in which both minority and majority cultures change and are enriched). Strategic planning typically confronts minimal efforts with an assimilation rationale.

Disabled

A large, diverse, and neglected subculture consists of developmentally disabled adults who may have such handicaps as impaired vision or hearing, learning disabilities, or physical disabilities such as being confined to a wheelchair. The field of special education that serves developmentally disabled learners has concentrated on preadults, and adult education has neglected learners with developmental disabilities. With few exceptions, the adult education programs that have been responsive to handicapped learners have reduced barriers by providing wheelchair-accessible classrooms, sound amplification, and Braille or recorded books. Because disabilities differ greatly, program adaptations must be specific to type of handicap. Even more than for the general population that participates in adult education, learner self-esteem has been important as both cause and effect of participation, and increased self-esteem has contributed to higher goal setting (Merriam and Cunningham, 1989, chap. 45).

Minorities

Native-born minorities include various subcultures in which members have experienced discrimination that has affected motivation, educational participation, and opportunities to apply new learnings. Native American adult education has been affected by federal legislation and program support so that planning has tended to be political. In addition, there has been great variation among states and localities regarding the social, health, political, and economic conditions of Native Americans and the assistance and cooperation that have been given (Cassara, 1990). Participation rates have been low.

Another program has been nonformal education for minority entrepreneurs (Merriam and Cunningham, 1989, chap. 44; Mescon, 1987). During the 1980s, the Entrepreneurial Institute—a South Florida training and development consortium composed of five colleges and universities, county government, and the private sector—was formed to encourage minority economic development and help existing minority-owned small businesses to survive. Competitive pressures and lack of expertise had caused high rates of failure, and during the 1980s the failure rate increased dramatically for small businesses owned by minorities and nonminorities alike. In spite of increasing minority interest in business ownership, there was lack of growth, in black-owned businesses especially. Therefore, the educational institutions associated with the institute each arranged for low-fee short courses offered during evenings or weekends and provided ongoing technical assistance to specific small businesses on practical matters likely to promote survival. Between 1983 and 1986, an initial five courses a year increased to thirty, and more than one thousand minority business people participated. In a follow-up evaluation, 96 percent of the respondents said that the courses had helped them develop their business plans, almost 70 percent said that the courses helped them get into business, 34 percent said that they started a business after taking courses, and an additional 52 percent planned to start a business within six months. In 1986, a presentation based on this unusual partnership between government, the private sector, and higher education institutions was made to people from public and private sectors in the United Kingdom interested in adapting the institute approach for minorities there.

The Entrepreneurial Institute approach had several features with implications for strategic planning. One was a clear focus on a local special population whose detailed characteristics and educational needs could be considered in program development (in this case black adults in South Florida whose success in starting small businesses had been less than for other subpopulations). A second feature was collaboration among government, private sector, and educational institutions, with each partner making distinctive contributions. A third was a combination of learning activities, which included accessible short courses and follow-up technical services. A fourth was evaluation for program improvement and justification. A fifth feature was inclusion of major stakeholders in the strategic planning process.

Strategic planning can help adult education leaders understand the range of cultural minorities in the service area and to decide which should have priority, given agency mission and resources. Within and among subpopulations (such as immigrants, native-born minorities, the disabled, and many other less-advantaged subcultures), there is much variation. Strategic planning can suggest methods and procedures that are responsive to distinctive values and traditions that characterize members of those subpopulations that an agency decides to serve. Contextual analysis can alert leaders to societal influences on the selected subpopulations and to the existence of providers likely to serve other subpopulations, so that referrals can be made.

Australian Adult Education Programs

Australia shares with the United States and Canada several characteristics that have influenced adult education in general and programs for cultural minorities especially. These characteristics include British colonial roots, an indigenous population prior to British colonization, high levels of immigration from various countries over the years, ethnic diversity, and a federal constitution that divides responsibility between federal and state or provincial governments. Each country has a rich variety of public and private educational programs for adults. This section on Australia begins with an example of adult education for immigrants, followed by a brief review of societal influences on immigrant education policies and programs, an example of adult education for aboriginals, and comments on adult education in the country generally.

Immigrants

An example of the nationwide Adult Migrant Education Program for non-English-speaking immigrants is the program provided by the Northern Territory Open College of Technical and Further Education, based in Darwin (Resource A, McGrath). The free program consists of full-time day and part-time evening courses, workplace literacy courses, distance learning arrangements, and tutorial assistance. The focus is on English as a second language, but some attention is given to other aspects of adjustment to a new culture, such as vocational education and counseling services. The anticipated benefits of the program are great enough that family and friends of new arrivals encourage early participation. Because of the collaborative nature of the program, there is a joint commonwealth-states committee for national planning and a state consultative committee to promote planning and cooperation within each state. The continued arrival of non-English-speaking immigrants has stimulated improved national policy and support for this program, which has been financed nationally and operated locally. Research and evaluation studies have contributed to planning and staff development.

This program in the Northern Territory and similar ones throughout Australia contrast with the approach to immigrant education that existed following World War II. Prior to 1945, immigration was mainly from Britain, Ireland, and northern Europe, with the exception of the gold-rush era between the 1840s and 1890s, which brought many Chinese to Australia. Because most of these new Australians were English speaking and from a similar cultural tradition, immigrant education was minimal. Immigration was encouraged during periods of economic expansion and halted during depressions. Concern about the tyranny of distance—distance from friends and allies—emphasized increasing the European population to promote security and development. Since 1945, Britain has remained the largest source of immigrants, but they have been joined by large numbers from Eastern Europe, from the Mediterranean, and—increasingly since the 1970s—from Southeast Asia. There have been conflicting opinions about immigration over the years. In 1947, 57 percent of respondents to a Gallup poll opposed Australian participation in a plan to resettle homeless Jews, but Australia accepted more in relation to population size than any country other than Palestine.

Prior to the 1970s, individual immigrants were expected to assume the main responsibility for rapid and inconspicuous assimilation, and little migrant education or assistance was provided, other than a little preembarkation or ship board orientation. Chain migration helped assimilation, as men arrived first, became established, and then sent for their families. Refugee families from Southeast Asia needed more assistance. The 1978 Galbally report and related legislation provided a main turning point toward greater government responsibility for immigrant education and services and acceptance of a multicultural society. National economic goals continued to encourage immigration to fill open entry-level jobs. The major influx of refugees from Southeast Asia coincided with the shift toward greater acceptance of multicultural diversity, which the mass media helped to explore. However, the prolonged and widespread economic recession since the mid 1970s has restricted immigration education efforts due to inflation, unemployment, and limited tax funds.

The Federal Commonwealth Adult Migrant Education Program included both on-arrival language and orientation programs and services and ongoing educational activities designed to prepare immigrants to make the bridge to the range of adult education offerings for the general public. Included were a variety of general and specific English language courses offered full and part time, distance learning offerings, workplace literacy programs, and home tutoring arrangements. Some programs were bilingual and encouraged immigrants to preserve their own culture, in contrast with the earlier assimilationist policy. In addition to counseling services for immigrants, attention was given to cultural awareness by professionals who dealt with immigrants and to public understanding. During the mid 1980s, conflict related to the program revolved around the effect of budget cuts on earlier policy support for multiculturalism (Duke, Rudnik, and Davis, 1986).

Aboriginals

Of course, immigrants are not the only cultural minorities in Australia. Prominent among the indigenous minorities are the aboriginal people with their varied traditions. They were the first immigrants, coming from Southeast Asia over forty thousand years ago. In 1788, when the first European settlers arrived, an estimated 350,000 aboriginal people spoke two hundred languages. Currently, they number less than 200,000 (about 1 percent of the Australian population), and only fifty of the native languages are actively used. The following examples describe but two of the many adult education programs for aboriginal people.

A nongovernment aboriginal management training and cultural institute based in Sydney conducted an aboriginal village management training program. The institute used a community development approach with five components: (1) preworkshop community visits regarding needs assessment, content preferences, and participant selection; (2) on-campus workshops in Sydney on management topics, combined with field visits to accelerate social development; (3) off-campus workshops as practical laboratories on specific topics; (4) inter-community visits to observe and analyze management of specific community activities such as housing or enterprise development by aboriginal people; and (5) follow-up visits to assist participants and to brief on-site personnel so as to facilitate improved practices.

Social change was a major influence on this program to enhance the proficiencies of aboriginal people who were assuming increased management responsibilities in local government and village councils. Prior to a change of government in 1972, it had been generally assumed that surviving aboriginals would either be absorbed or remain in separate isolated locations unconnected to the majority culture. It then became legal to establish aboriginal community organizations, and subsequent policies to encourage greater self-management forced role changes on many local people who were interested but unprepared to assist in improving community management. There were a number of societal influences on the program and participants. One was geographic isolation from other aboriginal communities, as well as distance from the institute in Sydney. Other influences included low literacy levels by participants, for whom English was a foreign language; different and ethnically traditional ways of thinking about management; health problems; and lack of local facilities.

The program approach emphasized sharing and collaboration. Each-one-teach-one procedures for participants had a multiplier benefit for other local people. The collaborative approach between whites in the institute and aboriginal people in the local communities was responsive, fluid, and sensitive to aboriginal culture. Participants helped develop materials, and participants and staff learned from each other, a process that was an important source of staff development (Resource A, McNamara).

This and most other aboriginal adult education programs have been conducted by nonaboriginals (Willis, 1986). An exception is the Tranby Aboriginal Cooperative College, founded in 1958, which was and remains the only major aboriginal-controlled general education center in New South Wales. Throughout the major issue has been colonialism, dependency, resistance, liberation, struggle, and self-determination (Tennant, 1991, chap. 6). The minority culture seeks self-determination through use of mainstream institutions. This drive has been part of a recent trend that has affected adult education generally and has increased government support for greater access and participation in education, employment, and community life by minority subcultures.

One goal for aboriginals and immigrants has been to prepare them to use all types of adult education opportunities, including programs by colleges of technical and further education, enterprises, trade unions, and universities and colleges. Unfortunately, economic restructuring during the past decade or more has contributed to reductions in university support for adult education. Other program areas have been rural adult education, distance education, University of the Third Age programs for elders, and programs by voluntary associations. A basic tension has evolved between adult education providers and policy makers who emphasize utilitarian outcomes that benefit enterprises and minimize dislocations related to economic, political, and social change. In the process, traditional distinctions between postsecondary education providers have dissolved, community adult education centers have grown and become politicized, and adult education staff members have become more professional (Tennant, 1991).

These examples of adult education for cultural minorities in Australia reflect some broad societal influences to be considered in strategic planning. Included are social change, increased priority and commitment to a multicultural society, impact of economic conditions and allocation of resources for programs that require subsidy, and importance of collaborative approaches. Such influences were reflected in a November 1991 report by the Commonwealth of Australia Senate Standing Committee on Employment, Education, and Training entitled *Come In, Cinderella: The Emergence of Adult and Community Education*. The report contained thirty recommendations to strengthen many aspects of adult education, including policy making, funding, collaboration, adult education research and staff development, access, reporting, support services, and attention to select populations such as elders, disabled, and inmates. Implementation of these recommendations tends to be affected by the past accomplishments and current image of existing programs (Duke, 1984a; Smith, 1986; Tennant, 1991).

Other Countries

Similar societal influences have affected adult education for cultural minorities in other countries. In some countries with high immigration rates (for example, Israel and Canada), national policies and programs have supported immigrant education, which is not the case in many countries with low rates of immigration. However, even in countries without native peoples and high immigration rates, there have been adult education programs for "guest workers" and their families and even for nationals working abroad.

Israel

A distinctive example of immigrant education was the Tehila adult education program, used in the 1980s for black Ethiopian Jews coming to Israel. This wave of immigration was one of many during this century and was assigned high government priority as the gathering of exiles into one people after two thousand years. Early Jewish immigrants were predominantly from Europe; more recent immigrants have been predominantly from developing countries in the Middle East, South Asia, and North Africa. Adult education programs were revised to reflect these changing characteristics of participants, mainly declining levels of education and familiarity with modern society. With the leadership of the Department of Adult Education, the Israeli government subsidized local Tehila programs operated by many organizations to teach immigrants basic education, including Hebrew and Jewish and Israeli culture, to accelerate the process of integration into a pluralistic society.

A predecessor of the Tehila was the Ulpan, an intensive residential education program in which adults who typically had some education before they emigrated spent about five months immersed in learning Hebrew. Middle Eastern immigrants with little education usually went to work at simple jobs or raised their children in new development villages, where they gradually learned the language and customs. Since 1977, eighty Tehila centers have been established to serve mainly middle-aged women from Middle Eastern origins who had basically adjusted to the language and culture and wanted further literacy education.

By contrast, the Ethiopian immigrants experienced great trauma leaving their country and had quite different backgrounds than earlier immigrants. Accordingly, the Tehila programs for them were modified. Sixty-five percent of the Ethiopian immigrants were illiterate, and many lacked preconditions to literacy, such as familiarity with western culture, beliefs, and gestures upon which Tehila instructors had depended. As a result, program length was increased to two years, instructors learned some of the participants' Amharic language, and the early content was focused on adjustment, language, and even interaction with talkative Israelis (in contrast with the Ethiopian custom of saving words). Staff development contributed to program modification, and staff and participants learned from each other. The Ethiopian learners were highly motivated, and many continued beyond the Tehila program to various other educational offerings. Fortunately, the Tehila programs for Ethiopians were generously financed with the help of American Jewish contributors (Grebelsky and Tokatli, 1983; Resource A, Tokatli).

The Tehila programs have been only one type of adult education available to Israelis, who live in a society composed of Jews, Muslims, Christians, Druze, and atheists from many national and ethnic origins (Giladi and Reed, 1985; Israeli, 1978). Another type of program for a large indigenous minority has been Arabic adult education. Recent conflicts between Arabic and Jewish residents of Israel, which reflect long-term regional tensions, have disrupted Arabic adult education programs, which a decade earlier were promoting advancement for participants and increased mutual understanding among Arabs and Jews. Program content and process drew on Arabic traditions of family and village life but also modernization and mobility. There was even a program in East Jerusalem for teaching both Hebrew and Arabic that contributed to an atmosphere of mutual learning among Arabs and Jews (Grebelsky and Tokatli, 1983; Israeli, 1980). The recent damage to such programs demonstrates the powerful impact of political and religious conflict in the region. Local educational progress seems unlikely without greater regional understanding.

Canada

As noted earlier, along with Australia and the United States, Canada is a large pluralistic country with adult education programs for both immigrants and indigenous minorities and with an even longer and stronger tradition of multiculturalism. Since World War II, earlier restrictions on Asian immigration have given way to a heavy influx of newcomers from Asia, increasingly from Hong Kong. In 1987, only 24 percent of annual Canadian immigrants were from Europe and the United States, compared with 95 percent thirty years earlier. This shift has been especially prominent in British Columbia, in which province the first Chinese-born lieutenant governor was named several years ago. The prospect of Chinese absorption of Hong Kong in 1997 has contributed to the flow of people and funds to Canada, especially to Vancouver and Toronto. Although most immigrants confront substantial adjustments, the affluence and English facility of some Hong Kong migrants in Canada provide a marked contrast with Ethiopian migrants in Israel.

An interesting example of adult education for an indigenous minority is provided by programs for French-speaking residents of the province of Ontario (Roberts, 1982; Taylor and Draper, 1989; Thomas, 1983). Part of the explanation for the fact that one-quarter of adults in Ontario were functionally illiterate (as defined by less than the equivalent of nine years of schooling), was the high illiteracy rates for Francophone Ontarians. The disparities between Francophone (French-speaking) and Anglophone (English-speaking) residents of the province in the 1980s were produced by at least three influences: the preparatory education system, isolation, and underfunding of responsive adult education. For almost a century, the government funded common schools in both English and French. In 1912, Regulation 17 drastically limited use of the French language in Ontario schools. For most of this century, the result was an imposed educational system that discouraged many Francophone Ontarians from achieving functional literacy. Isolation of Francophone adults resulted from geographic separation in French-speaking areas, conflict between Roman Catholic Francophones and Anglophones (who were predominantly Protestant and Irish Catholic), and restricted economic conditions due in part to the limited education. Lack of adult education opportunities prior to the late 1980s reflected absence of libraries and community development traditions in Francophone areas. Since then, Francophone Ontarians have gained full access to government services in French, and community literacy programs for Francophones have been established. Minority status, economic difficulties, scattered locations, and bilingual young people attracted to greater opportunities in the majority culture are likely to be continuing impediments to broad multicultural education.

Netherlands

Many European countries have received refugees during the past decade or two and have developed adult education programs for immigrants, with an emphasis on language acquisition (Johnson, 1984). One case is the Language School for Refugees in the Netherlands, provided since 1982 by a refugee assistance society and supported by government reimbursement for participants who complete the program. The program is located in the large international port city of Rotterdam, where the highest unemployment rate in the Netherlands compounds the problem of accommodating immigrants from various countries, including Iran, Poland, Turkey, Zaire, and the Eritrea district of Ethiopia. After a few years, the number of participants tripled, and more than half completed the program. Program content and procedures have dealt with the trauma many participants experienced fleeing their country and seeking asylum in the Netherlands. In addition to language acquisition, topics include basic tasks to function in a new culture. A basic staff is supplemented by volunteers (Resource A, Stark [a]).

Germany

Some European adult education programs for guest workers and their families reflect differential supply and demand for workers from country to country. For example, during the 1970s and 1980s, the expanding economy of the former West Germany created unmet demand for workers, which encouraged guest workers from countries with an oversupply (such as Turkey and Yugoslavia). In addition to adult education for guest workers, programs were also provided for their family members after they had been in Germany for some years and wanted help in preparation for work and life there. Such programs were neglected during the 1970s but began in the 1980s. An example of one is an educational program to help Turkish women in Germany achieve greater vocational and social integration, in which their aspirations fit program goals but are in conflict with their family traditions (Resource A, Meyder). Another approach to adult education for guest workers was provided a decade or more ago by Yugoslavian programs for Yugoslavs working in other countries, especially Germany

Strategic Planning

There are some distinctive features of planning educational programs for adults from minority subcultures. The features pertain to staff leadership, participation, public policy, economic conditions, and collaboration.

Leadership

Even more than for other types of adult education, staff leadership is a crucial but weak link in the chain of components that lead to successful programs for cultural minorities. There are several reasons why staffing is unsatisfactory. A major challenge for strategic planning is to specify essential proficiencies of program staff and volunteers, then to attract and retain people possessing them, and then to provide them assistance to enable them to perform satisfactorily. Realistic specification of staff proficiencies seldom occurs. Expectations for staff members and volunteers tend to be high. Cultural pluralism and empowerment of members of minority subcultures are attractive goals, but resistance to change by members of the majority culture can be powerful. Against these high expectations, strategic planning should compare the supply of able, well-prepared people interested in largely part-time or volunteer roles with only short-term commitments (given the largely intangible incentives for doing this work).

In the professional literature on this topic, there are repeated complaints about staff shortages, dissatisfaction, and attrition (Cassara, 1990; Chisman and Associates, 1990; Merriam and Cunningham, 1989, chap. 37). Inclusion of staff members and volunteers from the minority culture has obvious benefits, but these people tend to be in short supply or just overlooked, and most adult education programs for minority subcultures depend on staff from the majority culture (as indicated in most of the examples in this chapter). A major but often overlooked asset of the people who plan and conduct such adult education programs has been their ideological commitment. Staff and volunteer development provides a major way to enhance the proficiencies of available people, and effective in-service activities can also serve as incentives. A strategic planning goal is to obtain satisfactory staff and volunteer performance to achieve desirable program outcomes. This objective requires attention to intended outcomes, staff proficiencies, available incentives and rewards, staff development activities, and availability of able applicants. The assimilationist goals in the examples from Germany and the Netherlands contrast with the more pluralistic goals in the examples from the United States (YWCA), Australia, and Canada. Program breadth is demonstrated in the two examples from Australia and those from the United States (YWCA) and the Netherlands. Strategic planning should therefore include several categories of stakeholders, including staff members, policy makers,

and providers of in-service education. A desirable planning outcome should be congruence among intended outcomes, staff roles
and abilities, and incentives.

Participation

A fundamental societal influence on adult education for members
of many minority subcultures has been sweeping social change that
creates a turbulent context for such programs. The urgency of responsive programs has been especially apparent during periods of
high immigration, such as Ethiopians to Israel or Asian and Hispanic migrants to the United States. However, discontent within
indigenous subcultures sometimes boils over, as evidenced by riots
by U.S. blacks during the 1960s, and in 1992, separatist moves in
Francophone Canada, and uprisings by Palestinians in Israel and
Slovenians and Croatians in the former Yugoslavia. Regional discontent contributed to the U.S. civil war and to regional strife in
many countries, including China, Nigeria, India, and the former
Soviet Union. The stance of adult educators tends to be reactive—
developing programs once there are legislation and appropriations.
The Tehila example from Israel reflects program modification for
a different clientele. Strategic planning should help adult education
leaders early recognize emerging trends and build policy support for
timely programs. A multicultural perspective can provide a rationale for obtaining a broad base of stakeholder support.

Adult education for cultural minorities confronts a basic dilemma that strategic planning should address. The dilemma is between national unity (often based on a majority culture) and
acceptance of diversity and equality of opportunity for one or more
subcultures. Syncretism and other multicultural perspectives seek to
balance desirable features of unity (political solidarity, social cooperation, economic strength, and interdependence) with those of diversity (democracy, equity, nondiscrimination, and preservation of
subcultural traditions). In principle, such a balance might seem
readily attainable. In practice, differences in power and values between majority and minority cultures often lead to conflict. The
German example of education for Turkish women indicates the
influence of traditional family values. A majority of the population

may or may not identify with the majority culture, which usually includes the dominant political and economic power. Minority subcultures generally have less power and status. They often seek greater equality of opportunity and respect for their cultural traditions. Adult education can respond to any aspect of this dilemma. Strategic planning can help an agency decide which aspect to address.

As several examples in this chapter illustrate, there has been a trend in some countries away from assimilation of subcultures by a dominant culture toward increased acceptance of multicultural diversity. When there is widespread acceptance of a majority culture, the pressure on minority subcultures to conform can be pervasive and powerful. Adult education for minorities that is restricted to literacy and basic education in effect promotes assimilation and reinforces the status quo of the majority culture. At the activist end of the continuum, adult education can promote solidarity and resolve within a subculture on behalf of radical structural change to reduce or eliminate the hegemony and oppression of the dominant culture. Between these two extremes, there are various policies that adult education could follow, including bilingual, bicultural programs that accept both minority and majority cultures, emancipatory education to raise consciousness within minority subcultures regarding influences of the majority culture, and multicultural programs designed to resolve conflicts and promote sharing and interdependence among majority and minority cultures (Cassara, 1990). The multiple subcultures with which most adults are associated can contribute to multicultural understanding of the interdependence of subcultures and thus of syncretism. Solidarity regarding religion or region may mitigate divisiveness and perhaps exploitation related to social class or ethnic tradition. One function of strategic planning should be to recognize such options and their implications, so that there is understanding and commitment to the policy adopted by the provider agency, along with the capability to implement it effectively. Participant involvement in planning is especially important.

The dilemma described earlier can become especially difficult to resolve when educator and learner values differ. For example, some adult educators subscribe to emancipatory education, with its emphasis on critical thinking, recognition of assumptions, analysis of psychological and societal constraints, and other aspects of transformative learning (Mezirow, 1991). By contrast, learners from some subcultures have values that emphasize tradition and group solidarity instead of individual freedom and change. An example is the Hmong people from rural Southeast Asia, who have a predominantly oral tradition (Cassara, 1990; Merriam and Cunningham, 1989). There is a risk that emancipatory education would undermine such a subculture. Instead of counteracting cultural imperialism, a program might inadvertently promote it. Education for cultural minorities can focus on goals for individuals or for members of a subculture.

Policy

The examples in this chapter show some of the ways in which government policy regarding immigration and indigenous minorities can greatly influence adult education. Government business and labor policy may either favor immigration for purposes of humanitarian relief or economic growth or oppose it to protect cultural traditions or employment opportunities. Few Americans advocate unrestricted immigration, but quotas arise from value judgments; and as immigrant characteristics change from wave to wave, there is a major impact on adult immigrant education programs. Likewise, policies regarding subcultures within a country are reflected in actual equality of opportunity for all minorities. In a multicultural democratic society that respects differences, adult education programs can be responsive to the diversity of traditions and aspirations within each subculture in ways that enrich all people in an interdependent society. In societies in which social stratification is a major problem, strategic planning for adult education should explore policy options to help members of the majority culture understand that discrimination and exploitation is a problem that affects all. This approach can be difficult for provider agencies that depend on support from the majority culture, but the foregoing examples demonstrate that it can occur. Inclusion of educational programs aimed at policy makers and public understanding—not just at members of minority subcultures—suggests a comparably broad range of educational program opportunities and stakeholder involvement in strategic planning. Planning and forecasting should also provide early identification of trends that constitute threats or opportunities for a provider.

Many adult education programs for cultural minorities have been remedial efforts to assimilate learners into at least some aspects of majority culture. This has typically been the case when immigrant education programs have been mainly to teach the new language and programs for domestic minorities have been mainly to teach basic literacy and entry-level vocational skills. Multicultural approaches generally include attention to bilingual and bicultural content; bridge courses to prepare participants to use general adult education offerings; self-esteem; and family, political, and occupational roles and opportunities. Follow-up and supportive services can also contribute to empowerment. Supportive public policy was reflected in examples from the United States, Australia, Israel, and Canada. An even more comprehensive approach that recognizes interdependence among cultures would be educational programs directed both at public understanding and at people in professional and social service roles whose responsiveness can promote multiculturalism. For such a comprehensive approach to succeed, strategic planning should explore which providers might best contribute, along with arrangements for cooperation.

Economic Conditions

One of the most powerful and intractable societal influences on adult education for cultural minorities is economic conditions. Most such programs depend heavily on external subsidy because participants are usually unable to pay for much of program costs. Economic conditions are especially influential because they affect many aspects of society. To state the situation positively, in general economic prosperity encourages immigration and upward mobility; reduces unemployment and accelerates occupational advancement; improves standard of living, enables adults to pay some of the educational costs, and increases their optimism regarding doing so; encourages enterprises to support and reward educational participation; increases tax and private funds available for program subsidy; and allows greater program offerings and reducing waiting lists. Favorable economic conditions were reflected in examples from the United States, Canada, and Germany. Because adult education programs for cultural minorities have been especially susceptible to irregular support and underfunding, strategic planning should not be daunted by pervasive economic and financial influences but should seek ways to diversify and increase financial support. This task usually entails trying to convince people from the majority culture why such support is in their interest.

Collaboration

Broadening the support base is part of the reason for strategic planning. The range of stakeholders that should be involved in planning, as well as desirable collaborative arrangements, depends on local contingencies. Such contingencies include provider purposes and resources, the programs of other providers in the service area, local economic conditions, and the extent of conflict between the majority culture and local subcultures. The Canadian examples from Ontario and Alberta illustrate differing contingencies. Stakeholders to consider are potential participants, program staffs, policy makers and funders, enterprises, and related social service agencies. For comprehensive approaches, additional stakeholders may be necessary to reach the general public and related professionals. In addition to such a broad base of cooperation, specific arrangements for collaboration may be required. Collaborative arrangements involve substantial time and resources to establish and sustain; as stated previously, they also have both advantages (complementarity, resource sharing) and disadvantages (time for coordination, conflicting expectations), so they should be used selectively (Cervero, 1988). Strategic planning with regard to collaboration should consider the distinctive contributions that each partner should make, along with costs and benefits.

In addition to the foregoing planning issues, adult education for cultural minorities relates to program areas covered in other chapters, such as basic education, rural development, corrections, elders, and especially community problem solving. The chapter on continuing professional education is relevant to those interested in securing professional assistance for minorities.

5

Distance Education

Vision is especially important for distance education leadership because agency functioning depends on the commitment of multiple stakeholders to high standards and resource acquisition to achieve educational goals. Supportive government, the parent organization, and related organizations can be crucial because of the expense of educational technology. Responsiveness to the need for participant access and choice can increase enrollments and reduce unit costs. Strategic planning and implementation can help balance attention between both program quality and access for learners and contributions by other stakeholders.

Features of Distance Education

Although some of the terminology and technology is new, for more than a century basic concepts and procedures of distance education (such as correspondence study and external degrees) have been fundamental to some types of adult education (Houle, 1973; Keegan, 1986; Rumble and Harry, 1982). Distance education means that there is an agency that provides education and evaluation, using educational media for two way communication of content between a learner and an instructor who are separated during at least most of the teaching-learning transaction (Duning, Van Kekerix, and Zaborowsky, 1992; Holmberg, 1989; Keegan, 1986; Moore, 1990; Rumble and Harry, 1982; Verduin and Clark, 1991). Technology helps link individual learners with learning resources. Strategic planning can assist leaders of such distance education providers in strengthening linkages and in addressing societal influences on program functioning.

Many adults have participated in distance education (in contrast with face-to-face instruction) because it has fitted their preferred learning style or because it has enabled them to reduce barriers of distance or conflicting commitments. In addition to fairly independent learning procedures that participants prefer or are willing to accept, they expect assistance. Distance education procedures increase their access to learning resources and their choice of how and when they would learn. Adult participation in distance education has been encouraged by growing societal acceptance of close connections between living and learning throughout adulthood (MacKenzie, Postgate, and Scupham, 1975).

Various media can be used singly and in combination to link participants with learning resources, including people and materials. Print media (such as syllabi and readings) have been the mainstay of correspondence study, are used with other media, and are familiar, convenient, portable, flexible, and inexpensive. Audio media have included audiotapes, phonograph records, the radio, and educational telephone conference. Video media include broadcast and cable television by aerial and satellite broadcasts and videocassettes. Computers can be used in various ways, including simulations, instruction assistance and management, and interactive video disks (Duning, Van Kekerix, and Zaborowski, 1992, chap. 4; MacKenzie, Postgate, and Scupham, 1975; Merriam and Cunningham, 1989, chap. 46; Niemi and Gooler, 1987, chap. 3; and Verduin and Clark, 1991, chap. 6). Effective use of expensive educational technology calls for strategic planning.

Estimated worldwide annual use of distance education in recent years has been about ten million people. Estimated annual U.S. distance education enrollments in recent years have included about four million in proprietary schools accredited by the National Home Study Council, more than half a million in military correspondence schools, and about 200,000 in higher education telecourses and video conferences for college credit. In the United Kingdom, annual open university enrollments have been more than

60,000. In China, the TV university accounts for a large portion of higher education enrollments.

Distance education is provided under various organizational arrangements. Sometimes an external degree organization grants higher education degrees and course credits based on experiential and other forms of learning completed elsewhere. A second arrangement is similar but is sponsored by public or private educational institutions that provide at least some of the instruction. A third type includes most of the major academic providers of distance education in the United States—the conventional colleges and universities that offer a combination of resident instruction, extension courses, and distance education courses and degrees. A fourth type is consortia of institutions that share costs and programs to provide more comprehensive and coordinated offerings. Examples of this arrangement are the Association for Media-Based Continuing Education for Engineers and the National Technological University, which each consist of a consortium of engineering schools that furnishes television courses at university campuses and industrial locations. A fifth type is the institution organized specifically for teaching at a distance, such as the Open University in Britain or Athabasca University in Canada. A sixth arrangement is the organization that develops educational media for use by other providers but offers little direct assistance to participants. Some enterprises have distance education arrangements that parallel one of the foregoing types; but the courses are for people who work in the enterprise, and credits and degrees are seldom involved. A distinctive characteristic of any one or combination of these arrangements is the expense of educational technology and development of course materials, which when divided among an increasing number of participants allows reduction of unit costs. Similar efficiencies occur in relation to group size for face-to-face instruction, but the large initial costs and very large numbers of potential learners who could be served by distance education programs make collaborative or other such arrangements especially attractive (Keegan, 1986; Merriam and Cunningham, 1989, chap. 17; Verduin and Clark, 1991, chap. 3). Strategic planning can help organizations select and modify organizational arrangements.

Some of these features of distance education influence organizational relations, such as with the parent organization or with government. Offering through distance education the same courses and degrees available through resident instruction in an educational institution can raise many policy, procedural, and jurisdictional questions related to goals, quality, costs, articulation, responsibility, image, and coordination. Such organizational dynamics can injure residential preparatory education programs (such as poor-quality distance education that damages institutional image) and can negatively affect distance education programs for adults (such as unreasonable and unnecessary constraints on distance education to avoid needed reform of the resident instruction program). Under favorable conditions, these dynamics can strengthen the continuum of education and promote lifelong learning. Strategic planning can help a distance education provider understand the strengths and weaknesses of current organizational arrangements and select aspects to be improved to achieve provider and parent organization purposes with the support of stakeholders (Duning, Van Kekerix, and Zaborowski, 1992, chaps. 3, 5, and 12; Houle, 1973; MacKenzie, Postgate, and Scupham, 1975; Woudstra and Powell, 1989).

Strategic planning extends beyond analysis of organizational relationships to consider future mission and societal influences. Government contributions are generally in the form of coordination and costs. For example, satellite transmission footprints (reception areas) do not conform to state or national boundaries, and so raise jurisdictional disputes. Investments in some educational technology (such as a broadcast educational television network or educational telephone network) can be so great that government-funded distance education providers may be urged to combine efforts in a cost-and-use-sharing consortium (Keegan, 1986; MacKenzie, Postgate, and Scupham, 1975, chap. 12).

A crucial issue is quality. There is long-standing evidence that adults who complete distance education programs are more able and achieve better than average resident instruction students. However, instances of programs with low quality and high attrition rates have tarnished the image of some correspondence education providers, a factor in the decision to change the name to distance education in recent decades. A growing volume of research and evaluation study reports document that well-designed distance education programs can achieve outcomes that are as good or better than face-to-face forms of education for adults and costs can be lower (Bates and Robinson, 1977; Duning, Van Kekerix and Zaborowski, 1992, chap. 9; Holmberg, 1989, chap. 4; Keegan, 1986, chap. 13; MacKenzie, Postgate, and Scupham, 1975, chap. 14; Verduin and Clark, 1991, chap. 5). Strategic planning can use such evidence of effectiveness to plan and buttress local evaluation studies for justification of goals and resources as well as program improvement.

The following examples and rationale address five themes related to strategic planning. The broadest theme is the importance of agency leadership that includes attention to vision, goals, agency functioning, relations with the parent organization, and staffing. A second theme is participation, which is affected by educational technology and cultural values. A third is collaboration, and a fourth is resource acquisition. The fifth theme is concerned with societal influences and trends, such as economic conditions and public policy. The chapter concludes with implications for strategic planning.

University Distance Education

A fairly typical example of U.S. university distance education over the years is the School of Continuing Studies Program in Independent Study by Correspondence at Indiana University. Begun in 1912, the almost four hundred distance education courses offered in 1987 paralleled the content of on-campus Indiana University courses. Enrollments had tripled during the previous decade to ten thousand participants in credit courses and one thousand in noncredit, compared with a long-term trend of 10 percent annual increase. The full-time administrative, counseling, and support staff numbered about thirty-five, with about two hundred people who devoted part time to course preparation, instruction, and evaluation. These part-time instructors wanted to work in distance education because of the flexibility that educational technology allowed, the connection to the university for instructors from the community who were not full-time faculty members, and the supplementary income policy for full-time faculty members who did distance teaching.

Participants were encouraged by many features of distance education. Instruction involved an instructor, study guide, readings, and periodic exams and sometimes audiotapes, videotapes, or broadcast television. Each lesson included the study guides, which listed questions and assignments; supplementary materials; written assignments; self-assessments or exams to be graded; and feedback from the instructor. Recent enrollment increases largely reflected the addition of a General Studies Degree Program, which allowed degree completion by distance education without having to take on-campus courses; it also permitted use of standard proficiency tests, evaluation of experiential learning, and transfer of credits earned at other institutions. Counseling for independent study participants and toll-free telephone lines to talk with instructors also helped. Distance education technology and procedures created the flexibility and convenience to fit study into participants' schedule and life-style. The university provided some state financial support for the independent study program, and all participants paid the same tuition and fees as state residents. A generally satisfactory economy and competition for highly educated staff members encouraged enterprises to recognize those who gained further education by advancement and reimbursement of educational costs. Staff members recognized these benefits and were also encouraged to participate in the distance education program by recognition of discrepancies between their current and desired educational levels; they also understood that new content and role changes resulted in obsolescence and the need for updates or new knowledge for enhanced proficiency. In general, participation was due to interest and access.

Program planning drew on many sources of information, including conclusions from needs assessments, evaluation, and research studies; reactions from participants, instructors, and course authors; initiatives from program administrators; and periodic self-study combined with external reviews. University support for the independent study program included some financial subsidy and acceptance of distance education as part of the outreach mission. The foregoing categories of stakeholders illustrate those who should be included in strategic planning (Resource A, DiSilvestro).

Other U.S. Programs

As indicated earlier, various types of distance education providers in the United States evolved during the past century; these types were the product of both the pluralistic societal context and arrangements for most types of adult education. The preceding example of independent study by correspondence at Indiana University is one of more than seventy university distance education providers that together serve more than a quarter-million participants annually. Some community colleges (in locations such as Chicago, Miami, and southern California) have made innovative use of educational technology for distance education in their densely populated service areas. There were about five hundred proprietary home study schools, which account for the largest share of U.S. distance education. Many large, high-tech enterprises include distance education as part of their staff development and have expanded their use of educational technology greatly during the 1980s. In 1982, 70 percent of Fortune 500 enterprises were using audio teleconference instruction, 23 percent computer teleconferencing, and 21 percent video conferences. By 1987, 40 percent used videoconferences. For each type of provider, consortial and backstopping arrangements have evolved to develop materials and promote their use by many providers. Examples include the National University Teleconference Network (NUTN) (based at Oklahoma State University at Stillwater), business video conference networks (which increased from two in 1982 to more than forty in 1987), and the Public Service Satellite consortium, composed of professional associations and other organizations that regularly employ various forms of telecommunications in their continuing education programs. Some joint arrangements (such as National Technological University and the Adult Learning Service of Public Broadcasting) have arranged to produce educational materials for various types of providers (Moore, 1990).

The following discussion briefly suggests the functioning of some contrasting distance education providers, which has implications for strategic planning.

External Degrees

The first examples are several similar external degree programs that consist of distance education only; they have no full-time faculty or resident students. In the late 1960s, Empire State College began one such program for adults throughout New York State, using ideas and staff from Goddard College in the adjoining state of Vermont. Empire State College emphasized student initiative in designing individualized programs of study to meet degree requirements; the program offered several modes of study and arrangements to demonstrate achievement. Major elements of the program included regional learning centers and faculty members who helped students develop individualized study plans, established degree requirements, and used learning contracts (MacKenzie, Postgate, and Scupham, 1975).

The Regents College Degrees (RCD) program in New York State is an external degree program created in 1970. In 1990, it offered associate and bachelor's degrees in liberal arts, business, and nursing. After one decade, more than 35,0000 people had enrolled, of whom 21,000 continued to enroll. By 1990, more than 46,000 people had graduated, and more than 8,000 enrolled each year. This distance education program grew out of the state's Regents College Examinations program, which began in the early 1960s and now offers tests in more than fifty content areas. In 1976, the tests were made available through more than two hundred testing centers nationwide and at military bases around the world. The tests were prepared by more than five thousand faculty members from public higher education institutions in the state who acted as consultants to the examination program. The quality of this program is demonstrated by the fact that half of its graduates went on for further higher education, mostly at conventional institutions.

Two years after the regents program began, the adjoining state of New Jersey started a very similar Thomas A. Edison College under a cooperative arrangement with RCD to reduce duplication and costs by sharing faculty contributions and exams. In 1990, Edison College enrolled 7,300 students taught by two hundred part-time faculty members; more than 5,000 had graduated over the eighteen years of the program's existence. Within its degree requirements, Edison has used many ways to evaluate outside learning to grant credit equivalency. Included are its own proficiency examination programs, other examination programs (such as American College Testing and that of the Department of Defense), exams based on twenty-seven telecourses on videocassette, transfer of college credits, and assessment of prior learning.

Through the Defense Activity for Non-Traditional Education Support (DANTES), the U.S. military services have standard ways to assess voluntary learning by military personnel through exams for credit in about fifty academic and technical fields. DANTES also administers various external proficiency and achievement tests to military personnel and has published an *Independent Study Catalog and Guide to External Degree Programs* to help them enroll in secondary and postsecondary distance and external degree programs. With a voluntary military, provision of educational opportunities during peacetime has been a major recruitment incentive.

Stephens College in Columbia, Missouri, was one of the original twenty-five founding institutions of the University Without Walls (UWW) arrangement in 1971. The current Stephens College Without Walls (SCWW) distance education program requires 120 semester hours of credit for a bachelor of arts degree (of which at least 21 must be completed with Stephens College faculty members following successful completion of a seminar). The remaining study can be achieved through independent study, weekend seminars, and intensive or conventional courses. Other credits could be earned in various ways, including from courses by other UWW institutions. Unlike the first four examples, Stephens College has provided some of the teaching for the SCWW program. Early SCWW graduates reported that completion of the degree was beneficial at work, about half went on for further studies, and only 14 percent experienced difficulty with acceptance for further study because of their external degree. A planning issue is the contribution of evaluation procedures and instruction provided by the awarding institution on acceptance of external degrees earned through distance education.

Continuing Education

As stated previously, most academic distance education in the United States is furnished by conventional continuing higher education providers. The universities with the largest college credit and non-credit enrollments are Indiana University, Brigham Young University (Utah), Pennsylvania State University, University of Minnesota, Ohio University, California State University at Sacramento, Purdue University (Indiana), University of Florida, and University of Wisconsin. Although Wisconsin has provided correspondence courses and four external degrees, most of its distance education has been noncredit continuing professional education, much of it provided by educational telephone networks and other forms of educational technology pioneered there. Penn State has extensive credit and noncredit distance education offerings, including correspondence study, educational television, and other educational media to supplement course-based instruction by full- and part-time faculty members offered at 250 locations. It is possible to complete a bachelor's degree entirely by independent study. A consortium composed of Penn State and the state's Educational Communication System has used thirty-one cable television outlets to reach the homes of over 700,000 cable television subscribers. In 1985, Penn State pioneered use of compressed video for instruction that reduced transmission costs, which can be a major expense of distance education.

Consortia

Another type is consortial provision, in which a number of cooperating organizations share the costs of producing compatible programs that they accept to meet their requirements, thus reducing costs and increasing opportunities. Between 1974 and 1982, the ill-fated University of Mid America (UMA) existed as a consortium of eleven universities in seven midwestern states. UMA experienced many problems associated with such consortial efforts. Among these were ambiguity of purpose, high costs of television-series production mainly controlled by the production center, insufficient attention to utilization, control over awarding of credit by individual institutions (UMA did not grant degrees or award credit), and thus inability to sustain a high level of subsidy. The result was that UMA was terminated (Millard, 1991).

Networks

A more successful consortium has been the National Technological University (NTU), formed in 1984 and composed of twenty-four prominent engineering schools. As noted earlier, NTU evolved to provide televised credit courses from the Association for Media-Based Continuing Education for Engineers, which had started a decade earlier and continues to provide noncredit programs and shared the same satellite network. Each year NTU has broadcast more than five thousand hours of credit and noncredit courses to sites in over one hundred enterprises around the United States. From its headquarters at Colorado State University, NTU arranges for courses that are designed and reviewed by interinstitutional faculty committees and produced at member institutions. Master's degrees in five engineering specialties can be earned totally through NTU. This evolutionary process—which has depended on cooperation from the range of universities producing programs and the enterprises utilizing them—shows many desirable features of strategic planning to be emulated by other distance education consortia (Verduin and Clark, 1991, chap. 3).

Oklahoma Network

During the 1980s, the Oklahoma State Regents for Higher Education—with support from the state, the W. K. Kellogg Foundation, and several Oklahoma foundations and in concert with the state's higher education institutions and libraries—undertook an ambitious project to expand telecommunications as a basic ingredient to a strengthened, comprehensive network of continuing higher education, including distance education. A major and integral part of the project was development of a telecommunications, data, and instructional system that included televised instruction, computer networks, extension of a microwave system, and fiber-optic linkage that encompassed almost the entire state; this comprehensive network was sometimes connected with the nationwide NUTN mentioned earlier. The resulting comprehensive and multipurpose educational utility was more than any one institution could have developed alone and included various forms of distance education for both preparatory and continuing higher education, fifty-two Educational Information Centers around the state at libraries, and Cooperative Extension Service offices that helped adults clarify their occupational and educational goals and discover relevant educational opportunities.

As an educational utility coordinated by the regents, an informal network was established to encourage cooperation among many continuing education providers in the state. Instead of diminishing institutional responsibilities, the project encouraged administrators and faculty and staff members to exert leadership and engage in planning to use the telecommunications capability to serve educational purposes. Including information transmission among state agencies as part of the telecommunications capability increased policy and financial support from state government. The strategic planning approach greatly reduced the typical technical, policy, and attitudinal deterrents to use of educational technology. The project demonstrates that when educational goals are paramount, an educational utility can enhance educational quality and faculty contributions and satisfaction and not undermine them (Millard, 1991; Niemi and Gooler, 1987, chap. 7). However, centralized planning can create resistance.

The Oklahoma Network is similar to the International Consortium at the University of Maryland and an increasing number of consortial arrangements for distance education in which learners work mainly with able faculty and staff from one institution who plan, develop, use, and improve the educational process and materials. The consortium enhanced the educational resources and political support that each provider received. Nevertheless, such collaboration sometimes has problems, such as unequal contributions, different administrative procedures, and dissatisfaction with educational methods and materials from other providers (Verduin and Clark, 1991).

Types of Media

Each form of educational technology, used separately or as part of integrated information systems, has had distinctive benefits and limitations that have implications for planning distance education. Print was the earliest form of educational technology. Although tested procedures for its use in correspondence study over the years have been rejected by new distance education projects trying to shed the home study image, print media have been important to most successful distance education programs. Guidelines have evolved for selection and preparation of readings and study guides that promote achievement, interaction with the instructor, learner initiatives, and use of questions for guided conversation or inquiry. Print media have the advantages of being inexpensive and flexible but the disadvantages of requiring sufficient literacy and interest.

Television in many forms has expanded adult education availability and access in recent decades. A Corporation for Public Broadcasting survey reported that one-third of U.S. higher education institutions conducted 10,500 telecourses in 1986 that served 400,000 participants. Forms of television use have included broadcast, narrowcast-cable, and videocassette by educational institutions and enterprises and for public dissemination. Though most use of television has been one way and relatively expensive, it can be used interactively in combination with other media and methods; this approach helps to personalize and make more flexible a medium with great visual power.

Audio media, such as radio, audio recordings, and teleconferencing, are also used for distance education and have both distinctive benefits and limitations. Compared to television and computers, audio media are inexpensive, widespread, portable, and easy to operate. As opposed to printed materials, voices can convey enthusiasm, and people can listen while doing something else, such as traveling by car. Broadcast radio can reach large audiences inexpensively with timely and popular topics, but it is limited with respect to complex topics and specialized audiences. Audio recordings (such as phonograph records, audiocassettes, and compact disks) are more permanent and interruptible media that allow repetition and use with small audiences. Audio teleconferencing allows three or more people to interact, and an audio bridge allows discussion to occur at many sites, which may also be connected by electronic blackboards or slow-scan television to transmit visuals.

Teleconferencing allows greater interaction but is more expensive than radio or audio recordings.

Computer simulations and other forms of computer-based education have helped distance education to become more interactive. Ways of utilizing computers for instruction in distance education vary greatly. One example is the University of Mississippi's use of computers to enrich correspondence courses. In another instance, hospitals and professional organizations have for years offered physicians opportunities for problem-based learning using computers. In the mid 1980s, about half of the large (Fortune 500) enterprises were employing computer-assisted instruction in their staff development activities.

As helpful as each type of media has been when used separately, it has been more desirable to have an integrated approach in for distance education. There are many benefits: each medium contributes its special strength, effectiveness is maximized and costs minimized, learners gain access to enormous and specialized information resources, participants learn in ways that fit their preferred learning styles, and learners interact with each other if they want. Guidelines for providing integrated educational technology systems as part of distance education recommend using technology systems to achieve educational goals, adapting them to local contingencies, combining human intermediaries and technology, and helping learners use educational technology (Duning, Van Kekerix, and Zaborowski, 1992, chaps. 1, 2, 7, and 10; Garrison, 1989; Niemi and Gooler, 1987). Symbiotic relationships between libraries and distance education can also be strengthened (Burge, Snow, and Howard, 1989).

Although most of the foregoing examples of distance education are from continuing higher education programs for adults with fairly high levels of formal education, educational technology has broadened the audiences for distance education. Other programs are aimed at adult basic education, correctional education, and occupational education. For audiences with low levels of education, electronic media have the advantages of oral communication and of privacy. For purposes of strategic planning, it is important that distance education leaders understand the distinctive features of audiences, media, provider arrangements, and especially those systemic combinations of people and technology that make distance education effective in achieving educational goals. There are ample examples where such synergistic planning has been lacking, resulting in expensive technology being underutilized or technology becoming a driving force that distorted educational goals (Duning, Van Kekerix, and Zaborowski, 1992).

Adult Education in Canada

This section begins with examples of distance education for adults in Canada's two westernmost provinces, British Columbia and Alberta. It is followed by some additional examples and analysis of distance education in Canada and concludes with a brief overview of adult education in the country; this will indicate the context of distance education and the background for Canadian approaches to additional types of adult education discussed in other chapters.

British Columbia and Alberta

British Columbia, the westernmost province, has a population of about 2.75 million thinly spread over a very large area (mostly tree-covered mountain ranges and vast northern river valleys). This situation makes travel difficult and distance education desirable. Aside from metropolitan Vancouver with 1.1 million people and metropolitan Victoria with 130,000 people, only three communities have more than 50,000 population, and the northern half of the province has fewer than 50,000 people. The University of Victoria began distance education through correspondence study for social workers in 1978, and the same year the university began to use the Hermes communication satellite (which in 1979 was employed to downlink a distance education credit course on teaching to five community colleges throughout the province). Use of satellite space allocated to the province by the federal government was coordinated by the British Columbia Institute of Technology.

The two other public universities in the province, the University of British Columbia and Simon Fraser University, had engaged in various forms of distance education over the years and were also expanding their use of electronic media. In addition, the province supported a Correspondence Education Branch, which was originally for secondary school students but which later included some adult education. An Open Learning Institute (OLI) was established by the province in 1978 to provide adult basic education, vocational education programs, and courses leading to undergraduate degrees in liberal arts and sciences. In 1980, the provincial government formed the Knowledge Network of the West (KNW) to provide an overarching telecommunications system for distance education by satellite and cable transmission, to be used by the several providers. In 1981, KNW moved from the studio at British Columbia Institute of Technology to its fully equipped television studio located at the University of British Columbia, which included a toll-free telephone line for distance education participants.

To augment the coordinated technology, in 1984 the government of British Columbia formed a provincial Open Universities Consortium to bring together the provinces' three universities, OLI, and KNW to pool their academic resources, coordinate distance education programming, and assure transfer of credit among institutions. The consortium was subsequently expanded as an Open Learning Authority to include university, college, and general programming sectors. To reduce the problem of inadequate library materials in remote locations, the University of Victoria expanded its off-campus library service (Infoline) to allow distance education participants free search, request, and shipment of course-related materials. OLI arranged a similar service with the Simon Fraser library. OLI expanded from transmission of television courses to inclusion of computer-assisted learning, live interactive television, and teleconferencing. By 1985, it was serving about 17,000 participants annually. In 1985–86, the University of Victoria had over three thousand registrations in credit and degree and certificate programs alone.

The strong policy and financial role of the provincial government in creating a complex, integrated provincial telecommunications network to serve multiple providers and program areas has been a major influence on the evolution of distance education in British Columbia. New technological capability (such as the communication satellite) has stimulated this development, along with a very sparse population in most of a very large province aside from a few large cities along the southern border. Detailed policies and plans have also been influenced by the cooperating provider institutions, which were pressured by the provincial government to work through a consortial arrangement. Leadership has reflected the high value placed on educational access and quality. Increasing mastery of technology and programming by provider staff members have contributed greatly to quality, public confidence, and learner participation. In this approach, the consortium has not become a university and embraced instructional system design (as has the independent Athabasca University in the neighboring province of Alberta), but the cooperating providers have retained faculty functions (Shale, 1987). The pent-up demand by adult learners has been reflected in rapidly increasing enrollments, has stimulated provider and government progress, and has been sustained by anticipated benefits, the value placed on education, and appreciation of access provided by technology. Participation rates per capita in distance education have been greater than for some developing countries with hundreds of thousands in enrollments but huge populations. It is the confluence of such influences that strategic planning seeks to understand, anticipate, and reflect in the vision and cooperation of multiple stakeholders (Mugridge and Kaufman, 1986; Resource A, Haughey).

The two decades of evolution of Athabasca University as an independent and exclusively distance education institution provides an intriguing counterpoint to the Open Universities Consortium, especially regarding strategic planning issues such as emerging technology, political influences, economic conditions, and institutional relations. Before Athabasca University (AU) was begun in 1970, the relatively affluent province of Alberta had three public universities, the original institution located in Edmonton (University of Alberta) and recent additions in Calgary (1966) and Lethbridge (1967). The first president of Athabasca University (AU) had been the province's deputy minister of education since 1966 and was a major advocate of the university's creation, which occurred during the last of the thirty-six-year Social Credit party rule in the province. This ended with a Conservative party upset in 1971, creating some uncertainty about the future of AU. Located in rented "factory outlet" facilities in an industrial park in St. Albert, a suburb northwest of Edmonton, AU was created to address surging demand for undergraduate education, when concern about the growth and diversity of the University of Alberta across the river was at its height.

In its early months, the new Conservative government halted planning for AU (postsecondary enrollments had declined that year); however, the small staff doggedly persisted, and in 1972 the provincial government approved a pilot project. Especially in the early years, AU was characterized by insecurity about its future, great political involvement, a strong but vague sense of mission, and staff determination to succeed despite it all. At the outset, course delivery was mainly self-paced correspondence study, supplemented by a telephone tutor for each course; over the years, various media and methods were added (for example, instructor-paced teleconferences and limited use of radio, television, and audio- and videotapes). AU emphasized open admissions, personalized learning, credit coordination, interdisciplinary studies, and exploration of new but cost/effective delivery systems. AU governance was by the Governing Council, which served in the capacity of board, senate, and faculty council.

In 1977, AU published criteria for selection of its future permanent site. One central requirement was institutional autonomy, but it was assumed that AU would be located near Edmonton (for accessibility to printing and communication facilities) and near to the University of Alberta (which provided library and computing services and especially academic staff, many of whom assisted part-time as AU course writers or tutors). Thus, it came as a shock to the AU president and council chair when with only a half-hour's notice on March 5, 1980, the provincial government announced that AU would be relocated to Athabasca, a tiny village with a population of about 1,800, located almost a hundred miles north of Edmonton. The AU president and a council member resigned in protest. With the possible exceptions of provincial government officials, who could say that they moved some state agencies out of Edmonton, and the owners of the land on which the new AU building was constructed, few people benefited from this move. The higher education external degree students located throughout Alberta and other provinces did not, and only a handful lived in the northern half of the province. More than half the staff refused to move and resigned. Without the hidden subsidy of easy access to resources in the Edmonton area and with additional transportation expenses, costs rose. The move was no boon to the village of Athabasca; there were no resident students, and only a small staff lived there (many commuted from Edmonton), so the increased costs for expanded village services and facilities related to AU probably outweighed economic benefits to the village.

Financial support from the province has been constrained by the economic downturn since the 1970s. Nevertheless, during the early 1980s, AU course enrollments more than doubled in a five-year period. In its first two decades, AU received an initially high and consistent level of government financial support, but cost-of-living increases lagged behind inflation. Fortunately, AU was able to obtain external funds, especially from telecommunications enterprises, to support program initiatives that allowed it to diversify and strengthen offerings. The combination of educational technology and staff leadership produced a good solid distance education program. Although it lacked some of the high-profile, innovative, high-technology delivery systems of other distance education providers, it evolved an approach that was attractive and readily emulated by other organizations venturing into distance education. The AU staff combined traditional academics with nontraditional instructional design. The move to the village of Athabasca and the related evolution of union collective bargaining resulted in some organizational shift away from a nontraditional integrated approach to planning and provision of distance education courses (Mugridge and Kaufman, 1986; Rumble and Harry, 1982, chap. 2).

Strategic planning and implementation concepts and procedures can contribute to staff development, flexibility, and responsiveness to the shaping influences of potential participants and other providers. The resulting broad perspective can offset an inordinate focus on small internal questions. Instead, it can bring the relevance of the external context into the provider organization to increase linkage and competitive position. It is especially important to enhance the influence of staff members associated with both the program and external stakeholders, especially participants. In the mid 1980s, when AU was facing impending provincial cutbacks, the staff

used planning to respond with a strategy designed to restrict participant flexibility in order to reduce provider costs by expanding
support by cooperating organizations to increase rates of participant
progress and completion. Greater cooperation with local organizations was appreciated by participants and by the provincial government, which valued service to rural areas. The result was increased
enrollments and improved participant performance without increased costs (Murgatroyd, 1990; Woudstra and Powell, 1989).

This discussion of distance education providers illustrates a
few of the many approaches that have been taken and the contextual
influences that have affected them. Beginning in the early 1970s, a
trend toward open universities based on distance education technology was increasingly evident in other countries. There was the
Open University in Britain (1969), Everyman's University in Israel
(1974), TV universities in China (1978), Open University in the
Netherlands (1981), and University of the Air in Japan (1983). International conferences and publications promoted exchange of information about goals, procedures, approaches, results, and
rationales that helped new providers learn from those with greater
experience.

This valuable international exchange of information among
practitioners has enriched the planning of distance education. Approaches to university-based distance education have differed in
some fundamental ways, such as whether degrees have been granted
by an independent open university (such as the United Kingdom's
Open University or AU) or by the parent institution (such as the
Indiana University example). Sometimes an instructional system
design approach has been used (such as in the British Open University or AU); sometimes a faculty-centered approach is employed
in which major decisions were made less explicitly. High-quality
programs can be provided by the various approaches, but each has
distinct features related to characteristics and numbers of participants served, costs and benefits, and governance arrangements
(Shale, 1987). Comparative perspectives have enriched strategic
planning for distance education and helped leaders select an approach that fits their context. Extensive use of distance education
by enterprises and other provider organizations creates additional
variations with implications for strategic planning.

As a further indication of the expansion of distance education around the world and the value of international cooperation and exchange of information among providers, in 1988 a Commonwealth of Learning organization was formed, based in Vancouver and composed of representatives from forty-eight countries engaged in distance education (Garrison, 1989; Holmberg, 1989; Mugridge and Kaufman, 1986). The goals of the Commonwealth of Learning (COL) have been to promote sharing and creation of distance education materials for use in the member countries; to strengthen staff development, information exchange, and collaborative research and evaluation; and to assist distance education providers to improve student services and transfer of credit among member institutions. COL activities include a newsletter and other publications, international conferences, and joint international projects.

For more than a century, many distance education programs for adults have been offered throughout Canada, and there are now more than twenty. From the introduction of Queens University correspondence courses in 1889 (soon after inexpensive, generalized postal services began), through the start of university-extension radio lectures and the Farm Radio Forum in the 1920s (as radio became available, followed by television in the 1950s and computers and satellites in the 1970s), various distance education providers have functioned within provinces. For example, in Alberta, in addition to AU, the Southern Alberta Institute of Technology has offered some courses via computer-managed learning used for authoring, student assessment and feedback, and student records; computers have also been employed to manage various home study materials such as texts, workbooks, kits, audio and videotapes, and telephone tutorial assistance. Distance education approaches, providers, and program offerings have varied from province to province. In addition to the large, sparsely populated western provinces such as Alberta and British Columbia, various providers have also been active in Quebec and Ontario. The technology employed has included communications satellites, telecourses, audio teleconferencing, computer-based distance education, and optical disk technology. Seven essential ingredients that have been identified for successful distance education in Canada regardless of specific educational technology are responsiveness to learners, program quality, technical system reliability, reasonable cost and accessibility, interactive components, student support arrangements, and institutional commitment (Mugridge and Kaufman, 1986). For distance education providers that are agencies of higher education institutions, relations with the parent organization have been a crucial influence on planning, implementation, and agency functioning (Burge, 1988; Garrison, 1989; Mugridge and Kaufman, 1986; Wagner, 1988).

Distance education providers have functioned within a rich environment of educational opportunities for adults that prepare for, accompany, and follow up on distance education activities. Similar to the United States, adult education programs are pluralistic (Bates and Robinson, 1977). National programs include naturalization programs for immigrants, vocational retraining for the unemployed, basic education for illiterates, educational programs for military personnel, and nationwide satellite arrangements for provincial distance education efforts. Most other adult education activities occur under exclusively provincial or local auspices and are based in educational institutions, enterprises, religious institutions, libraries, labor unions, penal institutions, community agencies, and voluntary associations.

Quebec and Alberta

Roberts (1982) provides an insightful analysis of contrasting provincial cultures on adult education in Quebec and Alberta that is useful for understanding regional differences in Canada, as well as the types of societal influences that strategic planning can address in any country. The regional ideology of Quebec reflects its heritage as the traditional francophone (French speaking) province in central Canada. The social development of the province has been affected by the French tradition, influence of the Roman Catholic church, and a strong rural outlook along with contributions of the two large cities of Montreal and Quebec City. The relatively centralized democratic socialist government of Quebec has resisted federal incursions into adult education in the province (throughout fluctuations in separatist pressures) and has developed general policies and comprehensive plans for coordinating various types of adult education in the province, with an emphasis on social development.

By contrast, the regional ideology of Alberta is a product of its more recent anglophone (English speaking) tradition in an affluent western province. Agriculture and oil dominate the economic base. The culture is marked by rapid change, private enterprise (with an emphasis on individualism), personal development, and economic criteria for judging adult education plans and achievements. The two provinces have similar government ministries and departments. Adult education providers and programs are more pluralistic, diverse, and independent in Alberta, especially the large urban areas of Edmonton and Calgary, than in Quebec. Government support for adult education has emphasized supplementing other providers, especially in rural areas, as illustrated by Athabasca University. Extensive informal contact among adult education practitioners in the province encourages cooperation.

In Quebec, federally funded but locally operated manpower training programs have tended to have broader objectives than in Alberta, where the emphasis has been on productivity. Rural adult education has been similar in the two provinces, with attention given to quality of life as well as agricultural production and marketing. Yet in Quebec, it has reflected long-standing government resistance to farm organizations, combined with syndicalist traditions for diversified agriculture dependent on local markets. In Alberta, farmers were organized and politically powerful beginning in the 1920s and 1930s, and their agricultural markets have become more international. With respect to adult education for native peoples, in Alberta there has been a resource development emphasis; in Quebec, a more wide-ranging program stresses traditional native pursuits, entry to mainstream occupations, and greater autonomy for native peoples to conduct their own programs. Adult illiteracy and basic education programs to address it have been more extensive in Quebec than in Alberta.

In both provinces, labor unions have provided educational programs for their officials. Higher unemployment and lower income levels in Quebec have contributed to greater labor union strength and militancy there, which have resulted in more funds available for workers' education and broader social and political educational objectives. In Alberta, there has been less concerted effort by adult education practitioners to lobby legislatures or government offices. In Quebec, commission proposals for cooperative planning have received support but also criticism (as an inordinately centralized approach that reflects the traditional French influence).

Because distance education providers use technology that may require cooperation and serve participants from many provinces, attention to pluralism and ideology within and across provinces has often been even more important for distance education leaders than for leaders of many types of agencies with local service areas. Strategic planning should clarify the niche that a new or expanding distance education provider can fill and the main societal influences likely to help and hinder its efforts.

Other Countries

As noted earlier, distance education for adults has evolved rapidly in recent decades in many countries around the world, with more than ten million participants annually in undergraduate and graduate college credit courses (Verduin and Clark, 1991). The following examples describe approaches taken, societal influences experienced, and implications for strategic planning. The examples are from China, Australia, Sweden, Norway, the former Soviet Union, Britain, the Netherlands, Germany, Israel, Nigeria, Ghana, and Latin America.

People's Republic of China

In China, traditional use of standard exams for assessing educational and occupational progress, overcrowding of higher education institutions, media development, and demand by adults for further education opportunities combined to stimulate a great expansion of distance education during the 1980s. Three resources contributed to this expansion: broadcasting, correspondence study, and new examinations. Established in 1979, Chinese Central Television and Broadcasting University (CCTBU) qualifies as the largest educational institution in the world by virtue of annual enrollments exceeding a half-million in the late 1980s. Each year, CCTBU offers more than 150 basic courses, plus many specialty courses in nineteen fields such as liberal arts, economics, science, and engineering. Educational provision and assistance have been decentralized; thirty-nine provincial providers maintain a total of almost six hundred local instructional branches that make available an aggregate of twenty thousand sections. Educational institutions have constructed more than three hundred transmission stations, more than nine hundred receiving stations, and more than fifteen thousand video rooms. Because participants are typically employed and CCTBU offers in-service courses, placement of graduates has not been an issue; however, if the economy does not expand sufficiently to absorb them in the future, it could become a long-term problem. All participants pass a national standardized entrance exam. CCTBU effectiveness and flexibility have been restricted by limited television transmission time, course coverage, and cost.

Some higher education institutions in China served as many as thirty times more students through correspondence study as full-time resident students a decade ago (following the cultural revolution), but this extreme emphasis declined thereafter. Most correspondence instructors teach part-time in addition to their regular teaching in the institution. A continuing challenge to providers has been to maintain a satisfactory ratio of instructors to participants.

Building on the centuries-old tradition of standard exams for civil service selection, China created an educational examination system for self-study during the 1980s. This program combined national exams with guided self-study to achieve government economic modernization goals. During the decade, more than ten million people participated, and a half-million passed examinations and received specialist diplomas. Beginning in 1981 with pilot projects in four locations, the examination system was established in twenty-nine provinces by 1985. The following year secondary education exams started, and by 1988 national regulations were established for higher education exams for self-study.

These three ingredients (broadcasting, correspondence, and examinations) and other resources for distance education could be used individually or in combination. National exams provide quality control and allow flexibility in the ways that adults acquired proficiencies. Several features of traditional higher education institutions have influenced development of distance education in China. These are the prestige and vehicle of higher education completion for career advancement, the elite and theoretical orientation of traditional higher education programs restricted to young people, and the inability of higher education institutions to serve all of the people who wanted to attend.

Government policy in support of distance education has reflected social change, economic reform, and international influences. Distance education costs much less and has fewer restrictions on enrollments than traditional education (in addition to participants studying part time while working in enterprises); these factors allow it to accommodate large numbers of part-time students (Rumble and Harry, 1982, chap. 5; Wang, Lin, Sun, and Fang, 1988, chaps. 9, 11, and 12; Zhu, 1991). Of special interest for strategic planning of distance education in other countries is use of high government commitment but limited financial resources in drawing upon resources such as examinations, broadcasting, and correspondence study in an effort to accelerate adult education provision to achieve national economic development objectives.

Australia

Differing from China in several respects, Australia is an example of a longer and more gradual evolution of distance education provision. Early university provision of distance education (beginning with the University of Queensland at Brisbane since 1911 and the University of New England at Armidale since 1955) was characterized by regular faculty courses used for external students from large, sparsely populated areas. This integrated model assured comparable offerings, standards, and achievement for resident and external students. However, it lacked cost advantage and responsiveness to special needs of external students (MacKenzie, Postgate, and Scupham, 1975; Rumble and Harry, 1982). During the late 1980s, the Commonwealth Tertiary Education Commission reviewed distance education provision as part of administrative reorganization by a new national government. During the previous two decades, tertiary distance education providers had increased from six to thirty. This proliferation partly reflected state, not national, establishment of higher education institutions, which during the 1970s expanded distance education offerings to adults to compensate for dwindling enrollments on campus by young full-time students. The commission concluded that some programs were unsatisfactory, and consequently six providers (some consortia) were designated, increased funding was provided, a working party on standards was initiated, and the National Distance Education Conference was begun to provide a national forum for planning and consultation (Johnson, 1991).

Earlier efforts to strengthen distance education in Australia included use of educational technology (including computers), encouragement of professional collaboration, use of telephone and audiotapes to make participation more interactive, and use of counseling and educational brokering (especially to benefit less-advantaged participants). The pioneering educational brokering provided by the Regional Learning Service in Syracuse, New York, was an influence on similar arrangements at Deakin University in Australia (Castro, Stirzaker, Northcott, and Basch, 1986; Gough and Coltman, 1979; Livingston, 1987). Some of the distance education support services that have evolved in Australia are the types of services that distance education leaders in China also wanted to strengthen.

Sweden

Sweden has many similarities with Australia, regarding features of distance education. Some of these are decentralized arrangements as supplementary ways to increase access for adults to existing universities and long-standing public policy commitment to use distance education to increase equity for adults in sparsely populated regions of the country or remote from university towns. Distance education and resident courses have had similar content, readings, and exams. In addition to geography and priority, social and population change that has reduced higher education enrollments and appropriations has also affected funding for distance education. During the 1980s in Sweden, distance education courses were produced by the Swedish Educational Broadcasting Company (SEBC) through

higher education institutions that also provided audiotapes, telephone study guidance, and face-to-face meetings. By 1988, SEBC
had produced about five hundred courses, which each year enrolled
about fifteen thousand participants. For the courses supported by
television broadcasts, only about 2 percent of the people who viewed
the series enrolled for course credit. SEBC has produced each course
in cooperation with at least one university, which has approved the
curriculum and prepared the examinations. A correspondence institute has prepared the study guides. Courses have also included radio
programs, written assignments, suggested advanced readings, and a
manual for study circle discussion. Some SEBC courses have served
as the basis for study circle courses. Topics for SEBC courses have
ranged from history of ideas to labor law, computer literacy, and
new enterprises (Swedish Educational Broadcasting Company,
1988). As a result, distance education courses have used a combination of broadcasts, publications, and individual and group contact
on which various organizations collaborated.

Participation has been affected by social change that has
made further education desirable (because of occupational and educational benefits) and distance educational feasible. Participants
have expressed satisfaction with the quality of their educational
experience, especially the flexibility that reduced time and location
barriers related to work and family responsibilities and the contribution of telephone and other technology that allowed interaction
and feedback (Resource A, Willen).

Norway

The adjacent Scandinavian country of Norway is like Sweden in
many respects but different in that the rural population is more
concentrated in towns served by district peoples' colleges, which
result in their collaboration over the smaller number of available
distance education courses. Norwegian influences on efforts to increase access through distance education can be seen in the work of
the Norwegian Correspondence School (NKS). Founded in 1914 and
reorganized in 1976 as a private business management correspondence school (with some tax funds subsidy), NKS has had about
90,000 active participants annually, out of a Norwegian population

of about four million people. Based in Oslo with a staff of forty, NKS has worked with about four hundred professionals from various fields who have served part time as correspondence study tutors and collaborated with other organizations for materials and examinations. NKS has developed and continually revised course materials and provided orientation materials for tutors, along with optional weekend staff development conferences (which only a few tutors have attended).

Like all other Norwegian correspondence courses, the government Royal Ministry of Education approves all NKS courses and provides some subsidy funds so that the fees paid by participants are reduced. NKS has contracted with district people's colleges, which in turn have selected, hired, and supervised the tutors. Eighty percent of the classes that most distance education participants attend once a week (to supplement the correspondence study lessons) are offered by the people's colleges. The remaining courses are offered by other voluntary study organizations. Although the local contact between college and tutors is beneficial, tutor performance has varied greatly, and NKS would have preferred more direct connections with tutors. Other collaborating organizations have included the National Institute of Technology, which served as an independent examiner, and the Association of Norwegian Engineers, which cosponsored one of the program areas for its members and provided related instructional materials (Resource A, Aksjoberg). This example demonstrates the relationships between geography, local adult education providers, and collaborating organizations for distance education, including some advantages and disadvantages (Nordhaug, 1983, 1991).

Soviet Union

The former Soviet Union has had a long history of distance education. It began in 1926, with a considerable expansion following World War II, followed by regulation under the 1958 Education Reform Act. In addition to eleven distance teaching universities (emphasizing technical fields such as engineering, agriculture, and finance) identified in the early 1960s, most traditional universities offered some distance education courses. In 1979, about 40 percent of total university enrollments nationwide were in distance or evening courses. Although there was some use of educational technology for distance education, uniformity was emphasized for distance and traditional courses regarding content, materials, and comparability of diplomas. Arrangements were made for release time, paid leave, and compatible work assignments so that workers could combine productive work and successful studies (MacKenzie, Postgate, and Scupham, 1975; Rumble and Harry, 1982).

United Kingdom

One of the best-known distance education providers has been the U.K. Open University (UKOU). This institution was established in 1969 and had a heavy emphasis on broadcast television at the planning stage. As a separate distance education institution, UKOU contrasts with the collaborative examples from China, Australia, Sweden, Norway, and the Soviet Union. The UKOU has been called the product of a particular time and place (Titmus, 1981). In a 1963 campaign speech, Harold Wilson proposed a university of the air; this proposal was the result of the 1963 Robbins report on the need to expand higher education opportunities, especially for working-class adults, at a time when there was growing use of educational television and discussion of its future. When the Labour party won the 1964 general election, Wilson became prime minister and appointed one of his ministers, Ms. Jennie Lee, to realize the idea, along with Lord Perry as the first vice-chancellor of UKOU. By the time that students began to enroll, political and educational realities had changed, the UKOU became an independent university. The founding of UKOU reflected the commitment and influence of a few politicians. Charles Wedemeyer's pioneering of articulated instructional media for distance education at the University of Wisconsin between 1963 and 1966 led to his invitation in 1968 to advise on design of UKOU. In the early years, government funding covered almost 90 percent of the costs. No qualifications were required for admission, but resources allowed enrolling about half of the applicants. Coordinated course texts and supplementary broadcasts were prepared by teams composed of professors, instructional designers, educational technologists, and BBC producers. UKOU benefited from part-time assistance from professors and experts from other U.K. universities and organizations.

By the early 1980s, after a decade of operation, UKOU annually enrolled about 65,000 undergraduate participants, and by 1984 more than 69,000 had earned a bachelor's degree there. Courses were prepared by teams, attrition was at an acceptable level, total costs per student were less than half of traditional universities, and UKOU had a positive image among participants, enterprises, and other educational institutions. As with other British universities, the UKOU is mainly supported by government funds, but in the early 1980s student fees increased (which restricted participation by adults with limited resources); in the 1980s, a UKOU degree cost a student considerably more than part-time enrollment at a traditional university. Over the years, there has been a shift away from the planned reliance on broadcast television toward more emphasis on interaction with tutors and other participants at study centers, in self-help groups, and through telephone tutoring. This shift reflects participant preferences, a largely urban population able to attend study centers, resistance of traditional higher education to part-time study, various providers of noncredit adult education, and expansion of UKOU courses without corresponding increase of broadcast time.

The great success of UKOU has enhanced the image of distance education. It also contributed to changing the name of the International Council for Correspondence Education in 1982 to the International Council of Distance Education. During the 1970s, it stimulated the creation in other countries of more than ten similar degree-granting distance education universities with full degree programs, composed of sophisticated courses, educational technology, and evaluation procedures (Garrison, 1989; Holmberg, 1989; Moore, 1990; Rumble and Harry, 1982; Titmus, 1981; Verduin and Clark, 1991).

Netherlands

A similar distance education open university was established in the Netherlands in 1981. The Netherlands and Britain share somewhat similar histories regarding correspondence education for adults dating back more than a century. In each country, the expansion of distance education since World War II was the result of increased demand unmet by higher education institutions. Provider accreditation evolved in the forms of the Correspondence College Standards Association in Britain and the Foundation for Inspection of Education by Correspondence in the Netherlands. In each country, accreditation criteria included qualified instructional staff, sound and current course content, evaluation, methods conducive to participant success, and agency management (Curzon, 1977).

By the late 1970s, there were more than forty accredited correspondence schools in the Netherlands, four of which accounted for 95 percent of the enrollments. Four guidelines for program excellence were quality standards, state responsibility, government financial support similar to compulsory education, and equal opportunities for all. In 1984, the Open University of the Netherlands (OUN) admitted its first participants as an open admission, independent, degree-granting institution similar to UKOU. However, it has relied on the thirteen other universities in the country for course development. OUN instructors have focused on guiding the learning process instead of transmission of information. During its first two years, OUN enrolled more than 35,000 participants for an average of two problem-oriented courses. These combined the features of traditional university and higher vocational education studies. This progress occurred in spite of a premature start that left course authors too little time to prepare materials, inclusion of too many course areas and tasks in the early years, tensions between the academic and business sides of OUN, and a government crisis that resulted in reducing the projected government budget by half and raising participant fees. In the mid 1980s, OUN initiated a pilot effort of home-based, interactive, computer-managed distance education that included simulations and communication with tutors and other participants. Although there was initial competition with traditional universities, OUN has sought to increase cooperatioon (van Enckevort and Leibrandt, 1987). The Netherlands programs are revealing of international influences as well as relations with government and traditional universities.

Germany

An example from Germany shows another collaborative approach. Since 1966, the Courses by Radio department at the German Institute for Distance Studies (GIDS) at the University of Tübingen has cooperated with other organizations in the provision of a multimedia distance education program composed of radio broadcasts, study guides, examinations, and study groups. Course areas have covered a wide variety of academic fields and general topics of interest to teachers, the public, and students. Provider staff members are from the cooperating organizations, which are represented equally on the planning committee. GIDS provides expert consultants, prepares study guides, and arranges for exams and participant opinionnaires. Six public radio stations produce and edit each series of thirty one-hour broadcasts. Participating public higher education institutions contribute expertise to assure that course content and examinations meet the standards for college credit. The six state Education Departments are responsible for exams and recognition of certificates. The six state adult education associations arrange for optional evening courses through their local adult education centers, which in turn cooperate with local adult religious education programs. The GIDS office in Frankfurt arranges for registration and exams.

Program finance has also been cooperative. Federal and state funds take care of GIDS expenses for Courses by Radio. The radio station's public service contribution absorbs radio program production costs, including honoraria for presenters. Participants pay a course fee, which covers the expense of study guides and exam scoring. The adult education centers charge a small fee for participation in optional study groups; this pays for administrative costs and honoraria for discussion leaders. In the late 1980s, more than 90 percent of participants said that they were satisfied with the program, attrition was less than 10 percent, and nearly 25 percent passed the exam and received a certificiate (Resource A, Schmoock).

Another institution, the Distance Teaching University (DTU), was founded in 1975 in the German state of North Rhine Westphalia but serves adult part-time students throughout Germany. In contrast with GIDS, in 1981 all 1,200 DTU courses were print based, of which only forty used supplementary audiocassettes, and fifteen offered optional videotapes. The DTU (Fernuniversität) mission and success in serving mostly working adults (who devoted about thirty-five hours a week to work and about twenty to study) confronted some resistance from traditional higher education. Partly as a result, the DTU evolved organizational arrangements similar to traditional universities and emphasized faculty roles more than large course development teams. Sets of print materials traditional in German universities were stressed, with less emphasis on student support services, although there were study centers and computerized systems for assistance. The DTU received help from centers for developing distance education audiovisual materials and for distance education research (Rumble and Harry, 1982, chap. 5).

Israel

In 1976, when Everyman's University (EU) enrolled its first students, it joined seven traditional universities in Israel. Entry is open at EU; no formal entry qualification is required other than basic literacy and some preparatory courses for some subjects. Most of the teaching is through correspondence materials, supplemented by face-to-face instruction in regional study centers, and radio programs (some of which are available on audiocassettes). In 1980, EU was approved to award the B.A. degree, and most of the part-time EU tutors had full-time academic positions at traditional institutions. Foundation subsidy during the first five years was replaced by government subsidy. Student fees at EU are about 60 percent of student fees at traditional Israeli universities (Gross, 1978; MacKenzie, Postgate, and Scupham, 1975; Rumble and Harry, 1982, chap. 6).

Developed and Developing Countries

The preceding examples illustrate some of the approaches taken by higher education–based distance education. Even the independent providers (such as AU, UKOU, and EU) have depended on much interorganizational cooperation, and collaborative providers (such as the examples from Australia, Sweden, the former Soviet Union, and Germany) have relied on planning and contributions by multiple stakeholders. Most of the examples are from technologically advanced countries in which basic economic and political conditions, along with a technological infrastructure (such as reliable telephone, electricity, and mail service), are assumed. In some developing countries, the lack of such conditions and other negative societal influences have been major impediments to distance education. Some of these are unsatisfactory mass communications (such as broadcasting, printing, and mail); shortage of trained distance educators; insufficient acceptance of distance education (self-directed study) within family, community, and government; and inadequate language fluency. In addition, there have been social, political, and economic reasons why distance education has failed to fulfill its promise of greatly increased educational opportunities in developing countries. Some of these reasons are primary use by the more highly educated; unemployment, competition for jobs, and "diploma disease" (unhealthy emphasis on certificates) among the more highly educated; and rural-urban migration, which partly reflects questionable modernization and development models from more technologically advanced countries, combined with inadequate strategic planning in the developing countries (Arger, 1985; Cory, 1980; Edstrom, 1970; Gunther and Theroux, 1977; Nyirenda, 1982; Stroud and others, 1982). Even use of educational radio to serve undereducated adults in developing countries can be improved if used in conjunction with study centers staffed by discussion leaders who relate well to participants and other local community members and also provide feedback to increase program relevance (Nwaerondu and Thompson, 1987).

Nigeria. Economic conditions can also be a major influence on the success of distance education, as illustrated during the 1980s in Nigeria by the University of Lagos's Correspondence and Open Studies Institute (COSIT). With an expanding population now about 100 million, the West African country of Nigeria became independent in 1960 but continued the educational patterns inherited from the U.K. colonial period. COSIT was established twelve years after the University of Lagos in 1962, which was located in the main commercial, political, and educational city in Nigeria. By

1984, Nigeria had twenty-six universities, twenty-six polytechnics and fifty-five colleges of education. Support for COSIT's distance education programs reflected high priority and prestige associated with university education, combined with geographic barriers that made distance education attractive to adults in remote areas.

The severe economic depression during the 1980s affected COSIT in many ways. Government retrenchment included cancellation of study leaves for the large number of people who worked for the government, which drove civil servants who wanted further education to correspondence study, which they could pursue concurrently with work. If the government had expanded instead of reduced financial support, COSIT could have increased enrollments to compensate for cancellation of study leaves. Instead, the government removed the restriction on charging tuition for COSIT courses, which allowed expansion of offerings but discouraged people with the least ability or willingness to pay, especially in a deteriorating economy. Participation was also affected by other positive and negative factors: anticipated benefits (such as improved status and career advancement), evidence of desirable outcomes from past participants, attitudes of family members and friends, program image, social change, population increase, and poor economic conditions (such as inflation and unemployment of college graduates). Previously, COSIT graduates had experienced desirable occupational advancement. In addition to their direct impact on COSIT, poor economic conditions adversely affected the other contributing organizations (such as mail delivery and other educational institutions that provided study centers for group meetings to accompany radio broadcasts and mailed correspondence materials).

Economic conditions also reduced the COSIT staff's opportunities for career mobility, which along with bonuses received for distance teaching had contributed to staff stability. Staffing was also affected by use of educational technology and by staff development activities provided for the instructors (Resource A, J. Okedara (a)).

Ghana. One widespread and effective application of distance education in many developing countries has been the in-service education of school teachers. (This was an early emphasis in UKOU and EU.) Among the influences on the provision of upgrading, refresher, and specialist courses in developing countries have been severe teacher shortages, participant ability and motivation, and concurrent study and work, which benefits schools, teachers, and their students. However, sometimes other influences (such as poor economic conditions and political ideology) have been major deterrents. For example, in the mid 1980s, these two influences undermined a modular in-service teacher education program (TEP) developed by the University of Ghana's Institute of Adult Education, which began its correspondence education program in 1970. The modular TEP was administered through the Teacher Education Division of the Ghana Education Service, which was highly centralized with insufficient local cooperation. Because of a severe teacher shortage, the TEP was intended for untrained elementary school teachers who studied part time for their first two years as full-time teachers in rural schools and then were able to study full time to complete their degree. The distance education modules were on topics that complemented their early teaching experiences and prepared them for full-time study. This approach used distance education methods to reduce spatial barriers and allow the teachers and their students to benefit from the outset of their teaching. Like programs in other countries with British colonial roots, the original TEP plan was patterned on U.K. external degree procedures, and it continued to receive subsidy from the U.K. Overseas Development Administration (in the form of funds) and British Council (in the form of personnel). However, national values in Ghana resisted continuation of TEP, so when poor economic conditions reduced tax funds, the government reduced TEP staff. A possible solution that was considered was collaboration with local or regional institutions that could contribute to development of instructional materials and provision of local study groups (Resource A, Ansere).

Latin America. A number of Latin American countries have developed distance teaching universities in recent decades. One is Venezuela's Universidad Nacional Abierta (UNA). Venezuela is mainly an agricultural country with an internal economy; however, the oil industry, which provided more than 90 percent of exports and two-thirds of the fiscal reserve in 1980, has added an international economic ingredient. During the 1970s, government plans to diversify the economy and increase productivity were being slowed by lack of educated human resources. In spite of an increase from 6 to 15 percent of young people enrolled in traditional higher education institutions, costs were rising. UNA was established in 1977 to collaborate with other organizations to expand and democratize educational opportunities that would be comparable to other institutions but would cost less. Degree programs were provided in fields such as administration, education, engineering, and mathematics. Preparation of course content and materials was by full-time UNA academic staff in conjunction with external academic consultants and writers. By 1980, they began using a computer-assisted, guided-learning system, providing students individualized instant feedback, adapted from one developed at Pennsylvania State University. Improved economies of scale for all of UNA depended on increased course enrollments. It was observed that student dependency retarded the self-discipline required for successful use of distance education. Other problem areas identified in 1980 included the need to find (1) a balance between unique arrangements for distance teaching and sufficient similarity with other universities and (2) a satisfactory equilibrium between academic standards and enrollments that would allow UNA to be cost-efficient (Rumble, 1985; Rumble and Harry, 1982, chap. 10).

Also in 1977, Costa Rica established a distance teaching university (UNED). The 1973 census had reported that only 5 percent of the population had graduated from secondary school and an estimated 30 percent of the adult population was functionally illiterate. In 1978, the traditional state universities admitted only half the qualified applicants. UNED was created to accommodate through distance education those people who could not enroll in the traditional universities for economic, social, or geographic reasons (Rumble and Harry, 1982, chap. 4).

Strategic Planning

The foregoing approaches to distance education briefly suggest implications for strategic planning. This concluding section elaborates on those implications by reviewing nine planning themes that distance education leaders in any context should consider. The themes are shared vision, agency functioning, parent organization relations, staffing, educational technology, collaboration, resources, societal influences, and trends.

Vision

A fundamental feature of leadership generally is stakeholder commitment to shared goals. Distance education leaders confront some special challenges as they seek to achieve and maintain a shared vision among their stakeholders in the context of their service area and country. Participation and support by those involved (such as participants, staff, and policy makers) reflect their image of the quality of the distance education provider's programs and benefits. Strategic planning should enable leaders to make a convincing case about program excellence and anticipated benefits. Planning process and conclusions can contribute to total quality management commitment and criteria, which include attention to course standards, content, responsive opportunities for learner interaction, student support services, instructional staff, and evaluation procedures. Dependence on complex technological and organizational support requires scrutiny of additional features of agency functioning such as technical reliability, parent organization commitment, agency administration, and cost-benefit procedures. Program goals and anticipated benefits are the product of values (such as equity and access for various subpopulations and acceptance of distance education as comparable to traditional residential programs). The importance of having such vision at the outset is apparent in the examples from New York State, Oklahoma, Alberta, Britain, Costa Rica, and Venezuela. Strategic planning should help leaders discover the values of stakeholders and evidence to validate program quality. Fortunately, there is increasing research and evaluation evidence that distance education programs can be at least as effective as traditional programs (Verduin and Clark, 1991). Strategic planning and program evaluation can help assess and strengthen specific distance education provider programs (Duning, Van Kekerix, and Zaborowski, 1992, chaps. 2 and 4).

Agency Functioning

Leadership and planning entail more than vision and goals; they also require a systems view of many aspects of management so that agency functioning results in goal achievement. Strategic planning should help distance education leaders strengthen linkages among various stakeholders so that each experiences mutually beneficial exchanges that contribute to progress toward agency mission (Keegan, 1986, chap. 11; Woudstra and Powell, 1989). For example, planning conclusions regarding subpopulations of participants should enable agency administrators to develop and market high-quality, responsive, and accessible programs. The programs described earlier indicate the various ways in which agency leaders have sought to promote positive agency functioning. Attention to program quality and its evaluation can also help to enhance the centrality of distance education within the mission of the parent organization and major funders (Rumble and Harry, 1982, chaps. 11 and 12). Among the five or six types of distance education providers, each has distinctive strengths and limitations (Garrison, 1989; Keegan, 1986, chap. 8; Verduin and Clark, 1991). Strategic planning can position the provider agency in this broader context, suggest the niche that it can best fill at successive stages of the organizational cycle, and assess the supplementary contributions required from other organizations (Duning, Van Kekerix, and Zaborowski, 1992, chap. 5; Kimberly, Miles, and Associates, 1980).

Parent Organization

Several administrative contributions to agency functioning pertain especially to relations with the parent organization (enterprise or educational institution). Except independent institutions such as AU, OUN, Everyman's University, and UKOU, most providers must take these relations into account. They include governance arrangements, policies, financial support, and specification of jurisdictions in which agency and parent organization can make separate or joint decisions. (An example of a jurisdiction is the right to approve course content and grant degrees. Institutions vary greatly in the ability of the agency to make or influence such decisions.) The parent institutions approved degree requirements at Indiana University, Stephens College, University of Victoria (Canada), and University of New England (Australia). Past leadership efforts by distance education agencies have sought to increase their importance within the parent organization. The place of these agencies have been influenced by enrollment trends for traditional resident students and openness of traditional universities to nontraditional approaches. Including external stakeholders with power in the service area in strategic planning can strengthen leadership on behalf of distance education. This is especially important when a major conclusion of strategic planning is that external influences (legislation, funding, technology, and collaboration) are crucial. Agency functioning and program quality are affected by trends and issues important to the parent organization, which vary with organizational type and mission. Arrangements for instructional design illustrate accommodation to specific contingencies related to the parent organization (Duning, Van Kekerix, and Zaborowski, 1992, chaps. 8, 9, and 12).

Staffing

Planning is especially important for distance education because it entails coordination of the contributions of various specialists, including tutors, authors, course designers, educational technology specialists, and coordinators. Attention to human networks is essential for a balanced perspective on technology in relation to purposes and learners. In many distance education programs, assistance is provided by full-time faculty members from other institutions (New York State, New Jersey, Britain, Netherlands). In DANTES and NTU, the faculty members came from the cooperating institutions. In China, distance education compensated for shortages of qualified faculty members. The potential for conflict is great when content experts, course designers and media staff (members such as television producers and directors) each want to have the final word. Distance education providers have been stimulated to use educational technology as it becomes available. Each form of educational technology has advantages and disadvantages to be considered as leaders decide which combination of media will best achieve agency goals. Educational leadership involves consideration of criteria such as fit with local contingencies, use of special strengths of each medium, ways to maximize effectiveness and minimize costs, and assistance to participants in using technology and obtaining information in ways that fit their preferred learning styles. Some expensive types of educational technology (such as broadcast television) may require large numbers of participants in order to be cost effective. Incentives and staff development that emphasizes teamwork are two crucial ways in which distance education leaders can attract and develop able staff members who will work in concert in highly interdependent roles. These two aspects warrant high priority regarding planning and leadership. Strategic planning should identify the main staffing issues and increase commitment and ability to address them (Duning, Van Kekerix, and Zaborowski, 1992, chap. 1).

Technology

The diversity and physical separation of distance education participants from provider staff make strategic planning crucial if programs are to be responsive. It is especially important in countries with sparsely populated areas, such as Canada, Australia, Sweden, Norway, and the former Soviet Union. Attention to access has been evident over the years, but there has been less focus on equity and impact. The very use of educational technology that has done much to increase access has been a major barrier to many potential participants who lacked the self-direction to persist until they achieved their goals. As with market research, strategic planning can analyze the diversity of potential participants that a provider seeks to serve in relation to agency goals and resources; it can also specify major segments of participants based on their characteristics, outlook, and activities. The resulting conclusions can then be used to combine media and related services for each segment of participants so that a provider is likely to attract and retain them until they successfully achieve their goals. Pertinent clientele information includes educational level, extent of self-direction, encouragement from change events and associates, learner needs and deterrents, and perception of program quality and feasibility in relation to alternative educational opportunities. Television was used in NTU, China, and

Sweden. It became less central as UKOU was implemented. Radio was not so extensively employed in Germany, and a low-tech approach was used in AU. In Oklahoma, many forms of technology were used. Strategic planning can draw on information about responsiveness and impact of approaches by other providers to strengthen program development procedures, with special attention to vision, scanning, quality, and service area that the technology should serve (Duning, Van Kekerix, and Zaborowski, 1992, chaps. 4 and 7). A comparative perspective should help distance education leaders adapt ideas and practices from other providers to fit the contingencies of their local agency and their environment's cultural values. The combination of exams and self-directed learning was central in the examples from New York, DANTES, and China. In Ghana, government ideology helped to terminate the program.

Collaboration

Because distance education tends to be especially dependent on interorganizational cooperation, strategic planning should clarify major goals, arrangements, benefits, and problems associated with collaboration. Few distance education providers possess all of the resources and capabilities that they require, so one purpose of strategic planning is to identify sources of and obtain cooperation from other essential organizations. For one provider, desired collaboration may be sharing expensive educational technology (British Columbia), for another it may entail a source of specialized part-time faculty expertise (New York, New Jersey, former Soviet Union, UKOU, Netherlands), and for a third a cooperating organization may provide local tutors and discussion leaders. Potential arrangements include formal consortia, contractual arrangements with suppliers, informal resource sharing, and contacts through associations. In the Soviet Union, enterprises provided assistance. In DANTES and Stephens, assistance came from cooperating institutions. AU lost a hidden subsidy when it moved. Such cooperative transactions are more likely to be successful if there is a mutually beneficial exchange that results in empowerment and support. Strategic planning should involve stakeholders in the process of creating partnerships characterized by common goals, complementary contributions, and shared benefits. Planning should also seek to reduce typical impediments to collaboration such as inequitable contributions, incompatible procedures, and dissatisfaction with instructional materials developed elsewhere. Information about opportunities for cooperation can be useful (Duning, Van Kekerix, and Zaborowski, 1992, chap. 10).

Resources

One reason for interorganizational cooperation is to obtain required resources, which for distance education based on sophisticated educational technology can be extensive and complex. Strategic planning should help distance education leaders identify and obtain such resources from multiple sources. Such planning should also clarify the financial transformation cycle in which agency image and goals help attract resources enabling people to plan and conduct programs of sufficient benefit to justify costs. Resources have many forms and sources: participant fees, government funds, parent organization hidden subsidy, public service time, in-kind contributions by cosponsors, venture capital from funders, and time by volunteers. Oklahoma received foundation grants. Strategic planning should help leaders make such transactions cost beneficial for both the distance education provider and each of the people or organizations that provide important resources. Diversification is important because economic conditions affect government funds and other sources of support. Budgeting helps achieve fiscal stability in relation to mission and contingencies (Duning, Van Kekerix, and Zaborowski, 1992, chap. 6).

Societal Influences

Strategic planning can also help distance education leaders to go beyond the evident contextual influences such as geographic barriers and broader adult education opportunities. Such planning should also enable leaders to recognize and address more remote societal influences that tend to be taken for granted, such as economic conditions, political priorities, social change, and cultural values. These affect more tangible decisions (legislation, appropriations, regulations, and media coverage). For example, conclusions regarding societal influences can be used in decisions and rationales for external support, including diversified support from multiple sources. Such planning and support are especially important for reaching underserved adults (Duning, Van Kekerix, and Zaborowski, 1992, chap. 11).

Trends

Leadership needs a perspective on an evolving agency that includes understanding of past trends that helped shape the current organizational culture and resources. Leadership also requires a shared vision of desirable future directions that takes into account contextual threats and opportunities. Leaders involve stakeholders in strategic planning to help create the future. Environmental scanning is one way to identify emerging trends relevant to the agency. Scanners use a taxonomy to prepare abstracts of selected reports and publications and then identify a manageable number of themes and implications for future agency directions. In the process, scanners and other stakeholders also gain proficiency and commitment. Political support was crucial for the initiation of UKOU. In Australia, a government review reduced the number of distance education providers. By understanding the distance education provider as an open-learning, multimedia system, leaders can both *refine pertinent standards of quality* (such as attention to access, interaction, and equity) and *strengthen the process of ongoing agency renewal* by helping stakeholders contribute to both goal definition and achievement. Such understanding is fundamental to strategic leadership. Pilot projects and persistence in planning and implementation enable leaders to assess the feasibility of potential directions, to minimize risks, and to evolve gradually; the process entails attention to environmental threats and opportunities as well as to agency strengths and weaknesses (Duning, Van Kekerix, and Zaborowski, 1992, chaps. 3, 5, and 7).

Leadership in distance education benefits from themes central to several other chapters. Distance education helps overcome problems of distance that confront rural adults. It has been used especially for staff development by enterprises (especially large enterprises with multiple locations) and for part-time study in educational institutions. Continuing professional education participants have sufficient educational background and incentives for participation that allow them to progress better in distance education activities than adults with less formal education. Distance education procedures have also been used effectively in correctional education.

6

Staff Development

One of the largest and fastest growing types of educational programs for adults in the United States has been the education and training activities that all types of enterprises provide for the people who work in them. These programs are also referred to as staff development and human resource development. Such enterprises include both private sector business and industry and public sector government agencies, as well as military service, hospitals, and schools. Annual aggregate budget estimates for staff development provided by all enterprises range beyond $100 billion. Planning, coordination, and some of the instruction are furnished by people who work in an education and training department in larger enterprises or by a person with personnel responsibilities in some smaller enterprises. However, most instruction is supplied by other people who work in the enterprise (especially supervisors), supplemented by outside experts. In recent years, staff development has been increasingly viewed as part of a broader human resource development function and the enterprise as a learning organization. Training and development staff members perform multiple roles (such as program administrator, instructor, evaluator, needs analyst, and media specialist), and multiple proficiencies have been identified for each role (McLagen, 1989). A special challenge to leaders of staff development is to be responsive to individual career advancement while advancing organization development and productivity in a rapidly changing environment.

179

Although all people who work in an enterprise might participate in staff development activities, in practice the extent of involvement has tended to increase with level of status and expertise. Members with the highest education receive the most training. In some types of enterprises (such as electronics and pharmaceutical manufacturers), training is also provided to customers, and in some types (such as community agencies and youth-servicing organizations) training is given to volunteers as well. Organizational development activities (such as quality circles) focus on teams of people who work in interdependent roles and emphasize content such as communication, cooperation, team building, conflict resolution, and ways to increase productivity.

Planning and leadership for enterprise staff development has been affected by both broad societal influences and local organizational contingencies (Carnevale and Johnston, 1989). Especially in the private sector, staff development has felt the impact of economic conditions, technological change, and competition from other enterprises (Kairamo, 1989). When a paper mill is computerized or a stock brokerage firm experiences a sharp drop in the stock market, there are major changes in the work and training. Effective staff development has been responsive to changes that affect the total enterprise, which in turn influences the mission, resources, and priority of the department that coordinates staff development. Because strong staff development has been integral to enterprise planning, supervision, and human resource selection and development, organizational culture has been influential. Most staff development departments address a range of organizational and personal goals, such as increased productivity and career advancement, based on mastery of both theoretical and practical knowledge (Kairamo, 1989). Professional associations, labor unions, and training consulting firms have provided additional educational opportunities, and many enterprises offer tuition reimbursement for part-time study at educational institutions. Some enterprises have more formal collaborative arrangements, such as for use of television courses prepared by university engineering colleges mainly for manufacturing enterprises to serve their engineers and technical personnel. Strategic planning for staff development gives special attention to influences from the parent enterprise as well as from the dynamic external environment in which the enterprise functions.

The leadership and image of the training and development function promotes individual career advancement; even more, they reflect enterprise values, standards, and productivity. Quality improvement approaches recognize the influence of teamwork among work associates for increasing productivity. Strategic planning analyzes opportunities and threats in the turbulent societal context, which influences the enterprise and human resource development activities. Such societal influences include technological change, economic conditions, political climate, occupational supply and demand, cultural values, competition, and international relations.

Paper Mill Computerization

In-service education in enterprises has served many purposes, including orienting new staff members to standard operating procedures, remediating substandard performance, rewarding excellent performance, and facilitating organizational change. An example of the latter purpose is training and development related to computerization of paper mills (Zuboff, 1988). Prior to computerization, traditional paper mill managers and operators functioned in an action-centered oral culture, in which staff members thought about the present flow of action with little time devoted to deliberate reflection. Crucial knowledge was indigenous, arose from accumulated experience, and was difficult to codify. Much of staff development consisted of coaching and on-the-job training. Patterns of organizational life, such as relations between managers and operators, influenced introduction of computers, and computerization influenced organizational life.

Computerization sometimes undermined understandings associated with action-centered performance in an oral culture and introduced new meanings associated with explicit textual knowledge and a shift of knowledge and authority to the computer system. Dependence on written computer text introduced new ways of thinking and increased the distance between knower (employee) and known (information). Compared with implicit authority of managers and tacit knowledge of operators before computerization, afterwards there was more abstract and reflective reasoning based on symbolic mastery and explicitly constructed meanings. Computerization brought many changes including increased pace of change, fewer staff members, decline in social exchange, disruption of role identity, and a shift from individual to team cooperation and problem solving based on shared data. Computerization also made the organization more transparent, increased the intellectual content of work, and reduced former distinctions between manager and operator roles.

Prior to computerization, transcendent enterprise values and specialized education gave managers authority, and resultant private knowledge gave managers power and control, which helped maintain distance from operators. Computerization increased and changed interaction between managers and operators by challenging managerial authority, status differentials, and unilateral surveillance. The most dramatic shift related to successful computerization was that managers moved from directing performance to directing learning. After the transition, when a paper mill was computerized and functioning well, it became apparent that technology was not enough for organizational change and that staff development was essential. Early in the transition, training and development had been underused because the demands and potential power of computerization were underestimated. With experience, it became clearer that systematic learning was necessary for crucial changes in meaning, commitment, and performance. It also became evident that staff development to enhance decision making by operators produced major cost savings and that staff members learned in different ways and at different rates. Training and development for all staff members reduced distinctions between roles and statuses and increased responsiveness to quality of work life (Zuboff, 1988). Aside from some of the specifics associated with staff development during a transition to computerized paper mills, this example illustrates organizational and societal influences on strategic planning for enterprise training and development.

The following cases and rationale focus mainly on three chapter themes that pertain to strategic planning. One is leadership of the staff development function. This includes attention to local contingencies that affect the organizational unit of the enterprise that coordinates training and development. Also included in this theme are educational goals and values, relations with the enterprise, participation by enterprise members, and educational outcomes. A second theme has to do with more remote societal influences (economic conditions, technological and other trends, and international relations). The third theme is collaboration with other organizations, such as associations, unions, and educational institutions. The chapter concludes with implications for strategic planning.

Other U.S. Programs

Training and development to help enterprise personnel adapt to technical change have been small but important aspects of staff development by all types of U.S. enterprises. In this largest and fastest growing segment of the broad adult education field, there has been great variety in types of enterprises, program areas, and educational methods to help staff members learn and apply new learnings. In addition to the foregoing example from a manufacturer, this section describes staff development in a labor union, financial institution, school system, investment company, hospital, university, and business, each of which shows distinctive organizational and societal influences that have implications for strategic planning. Of course, staff development occurs in all other types of public and private enterprises such as retail sales, government agencies, and the military service.

Program Areas and Planning

As indicated earlier, all but the smallest enterprises have been the main providers of training and development for their staff members, with additional contributions by labor unions, professional and trade associations, and educational institutions. The extent of participation has also been greater for people with higher levels of status and responsibility than for employees in jobs at lower-skill levels. The former category includes people in all types of managerial and supervisory roles and professionals such as engineers, scientists, teachers, and health professionals. Other program areas directed mainly at the remainder of staff members may consist of workplace literacy, sales training, office skills, and technical training. Some programs serve a broad cross section of staff members and are aimed at organizational development, communication and human relations, career development, and international training. Educational methods encompass many used by other providers, such as instruction that takes place in courses, workshops, and seminars. However, some methods are distinctive as they occur in enterprise settings. Some of these are on-the-job training, self-directed learning, meetings, team building, simulations (role playing, case analysis, simulations using computers), and audiovisual methods (Bard, Bell, Stephen, and Webster, 1987; Craig, 1987; Eurich, 1985; Lieberman and Miller, 1979; Lusterman, 1985; Marsick, 1988a; Nadler, 1984).

Labor Unions

Labor unions have made distinctive contributions to staff development, in part because their workers' education programs serve their members. Union membership is traditionally composed of nonmanagement staff members in lower-paid jobs; however, in recent decades, it has included middle-class workers. Most workers' education includes preparation for union leadership (collective bargaining, union management, labor history), but especially larger and stronger unions also provide vocational, basic skills, and general education in their workers' education offerings. Various forms of collaboration—labor education associations, labor colleges, the interuniversity labor education committee, study leaves, and government retraining programs—have been used to strengthen workers' education. Recent societal influences on workers' education include automation, unemployment, workplace democracy, and the relative power of labor unions in the working and middle class (Hopkins, 1985; Levine, 1975; Mire, 1956).

Strategic planning for enterprise staff development should include attention to internal strengths, weaknesses, and characteristics related to type and size of enterprise and staff composition and to typical program areas and educational methods. Labor union contributions to staff development should also be considered. Top management support is especially important (Nadler and Wiggs, 1986). Planning is essential in relation to external opportunities and threats for the organizational and societal context in which a staff development department functions. The following examples from various types of enterprises illustrates distinctive patterns of external influences and implications for strategic planning.

Financial Institutions

In 1979, an institute was started by a national trade association of financial institutions to provide individualized distance learning activities for staff members of affiliated local institutions. During the next seven years, the institute director achieved steady increases in numbers of participants and in staff (to nine people) and an annual budget exceeding $1 million. The distance education self-study materials were used by individual staff members and were sometimes part of staff development activities coordinated by relatively small local financial institutions or their state association. The core institute staff arranged for external consultants to develop the educational materials. The institute functioned on a cost-recovery basis from fees paid by participants.

Among the various societal influences on participation were national economic conditions during the 1980s, turbulence and changing practices within the several types of financial institutions, technological change (such as computerization of records), and increasing competition for able personnel generally and especially for women, who were going into a greater variety of jobs than a decade or two earlier. Additional influences included a positive image of continuing education, employee recognition of benefits from participation, and encouragement by work associates. Some nonparticipants preferred face-to-face instruction.

Each local financial institution had a training officer, who in small institutions worked on educational activities part time along with personnel functions; in large institutions, the officer was assisted by additional training staff members. Institute distance education courses, with their use of correspondence study lessons and tests supplemented videotapes, served as a high-quality, low-cost, and self-paced method that local institution and staff members used as a part of their total in-service education activities.

As the parent organization of the institute, the association contributed to its policy, planning, and staffing. Another part of the association—one twice as large as the institute—provided staff development activities in the form of meetings and conferences. Negative organizational influences on institute finance and staffing included competition with the conference program for funds and lack of complete management support. Institute staff members credited their own continuing education activities with making major contributions to their planning and effectiveness. This program demonstrates the influence of economic conditions, technological change, and relations with the parent organization and local financial institutions that strategic planning should address (Resource A, Knox (d)).

Schools

As opposed to the self-study programs provided by the institute for individual staff members in relatively small local financial institutions, staff development programs for elementary and secondary school teachers have tended to be related to the functioning of a local school system in which there are many teachers who perform similar roles. Planning staff development for teachers has been largely by school administrators, with increasing contributions by the teachers themselves. Societal influences have included frequent national reports that criticized public school programs, stability in the numbers of school students and teachers compared with earlier growth (which had resulted in many teachers aging in place), and increased occupational choice for many young women who would formerly have entered teaching. During the past decade, there has been growing dissatisfaction with traditional in-service education for teachers and increasing research and writing about ways to make staff development more effective for teacher career advancement and student achievement. Previously, staff development in many school districts was characterized by in-service days arranged by administrators, perfunctory classroom visits by supervisors, and accumulation of college course credits for higher placement on the salary schedule.

By contrast, the following example reflects desirable features of teacher staff development in an individual public school within a larger district and state in which additional educational opportunities were available. Major features of the staff development effort were assumption of major responsibility for professional growth by teachers themselves and a carefully designed and comprehensive approach that considered teacher career stage, organizational culture of the school, and impact of in-service activities on student activities and achievement (Fullan, 1990). This approach was similar to quality improvement in other settings (Berwick, Godfrey, and Roessner, 1990).

Comprehensive staff development (including career-long formal and nonformal learning activities) helped teachers and administrators who planned in-service activities to differentiate for successive career stages (Joyce, Bennett, and Rolhelser-Bennett, 1990). Some beginning teachers were seen as energetic and interested in innovation. The large majority of participants in required in-service sessions were accomplished master teachers who continued to progress on their own, and others characterized as adequate followers dependent on context and expectations. Another stage consisted of reticent teachers (who were withdrawn and sometimes obstructionist individuals who often spent more energy resisting change than improving) and teachers preparing for retirement. Effective staff development activities sometimes managed to move teachers who were withdrawn and passive about in-service activities into a career renewal stage.

The norms and culture of a school system have been influential on the vitality of staff development, as shown in the differing degrees of teacher motivation to participate in staff development activities; interest in participation is greater when peers are enthusiastic about innovation and growth and less in a school where peers resist change.

As in the helping professions generally, a major criterion for success of teacher staff development has been impact on student achievement, but it has been difficult to evaluate this influence because in-service activity is but one of many influences on achievement. As a result, such programs stress intermediary characteristics of teaching and learning that staff development could enhance and that are likely to increase achievement. Emphasis has been given to teachers' sense of efficacy, high but realistic expectations for student performance, a supportive classroom climate for learning, teachers waiting after asking questions, and especially a large amount of student time spent on learning tasks.

A long-standing but recently refined form of staff development associated with improved teacher performance is clinical supervision; the supervisor and teacher discuss a class session to be observed by the supervisor who notes teacher and student behavior, which they discuss later with a view to planning future instructional activities. This association between performance, feedback, and improvement has also been demonstrated regarding microteaching. The benefits of clinical supervision depend on satisfactory working relationships between supervisor and teacher. In such programs, many teachers perceived postobservation conferences as unproductive and supervisors as artificial and threatening. By contrast, successful conferences encouraged teachers to engage in productive innovation and goal setting. Peer coaching is a similar procedure in which experienced teachers observe each other's classrooms and then discuss observations with varying degrees of feedback. Program evaluation demonstrated that coaching resulted in improved teaching and student performance.

The main conclusion from studies of teacher staff development with regard to strategic planning was that leadership should address the process systematically to include teachers as learners, classroom dynamics, and school improvement to strengthen student engagement and achievement (Fullan, 1990; Joyce and Showers, 1988; Joyce, Bennett, and Rolhelser-Bennett, 1990). Unlike computerization of a paper mill, economic conditions and technological change were minor influences on teacher in-service education, compared with major influences such as public perceptions of educational quality, changes in staff intake and turnover, and shared planning of staff development by teachers and administrators in a school system culture characterized as supportive of innovation and growth (Menges and Mathis, 1988). Similar conclusions emerged in Britain, Australia, and Canada (Daresh, 1987).

An Investment House

In another instance, an abrupt economic change triggered a need for staff development and a collaborative program response. People who follow the U.S. stock market may remember October 10, 1987, as the day that the Dow Jones industrial average fell 508 points to 1738.74—a one-day loss of 22.6 percent on record-shattering volume. This event was shocking to the thousand brokers associated with an established investment firm with a hundred offices in various states. This firm was traditionally supportive of employees and their families as reflected in support for education, counseling, and community services. A team of university experts on coping with stress approached the investment firm to propose an educational program to help the brokers and their families deal with the crisis.

Many customers felt shock and stress and sometimes blamed the stockbroker for their losses; and brokers paid on a straight commission basis were concerned about their family finances as well as customer well-being. Brokers have been characterized as competitive and independent; many assessed their personal worth by their income, so their self-esteem suffered. Many had never done other types of work and felt ill prepared to change careers, another source of stress.

The university's proposal went to the chief executive officer of the investment firm, who was concerned about cost cutting as a result of the crash. This individual referred the proposal to a conservative advisory group of branch managers, who enthusiastically endorsed it. The university team's first major discussion of the proposal within the investment firm was with the vice president for personnel, who was supportive and passed the proposal to the training director. The training director was initially resistant because he questioned its importance and believed that it was being forced on him by top managers at a time when they were cutting his budget and staff. A long meeting with the university team convinced the training director of its merit, and he was extremely supportive afterwards.

In the collaborative educational program that followed, the consultants met with local managers, brokers, and their spouses to assess needs and plan educational activities. There were several positive influences on the program: the dramatic event that precipitated it and forced major adjustments, the experience that brokers have dealing with fairly high stress levels and interpreting such dynamics, and initial support by management and training staff. Negative influences included cost cutting by the investment firm, which reduced the training department, personnel shifts, and further delegation of program responsibility to someone lower in the training department with less interest in the program. Implications of this example for strategic planning include the impact of a major event, importance of management support, difficulties with collaborative programs, and the tendency for enterprises to reduce training budgets during periods of financial downturn when increased staff development might seem desirable (Resource A, Knox (e)).

Hospitals

Hospitals also have staff development activities for nurses and other health care personnel (O'Connor, 1986). External influences on planning can be seen in a recent modification of a program for intensive care unit (ICU) nurses in a medium-sized hospital; the ICU staff and supervisor there were very supportive of improved staff development. The new program was an individualized competency-based orientation for new (and some experienced) nurses, in which preceptors guided active learning by participants who wanted to be users of knowledge, not just recipients. The coordinator worked with a planning committee, and the preceptors were volunteers. The coordinator held a workshop and provided a manual for preceptors who developed individual learning plans. Weekly meetings between preceptor and learner reviewed progress and plans and evaluated achievement using the competency statements selected and developed for the learning plans. Societal influences included the severe nursing shortage, constant change in the technology used in ICUs, and lack of familiarity with ICU practice by recent graduates and nurses from other specialties. The program met the nursing care standard of the Joint Commission for Accreditation of Hospitals. The coordinator found it helpful to discuss this shift from a series of traditional sessions to the more efficient and effective individualized competency-based orientation with her counterparts in nearby hospitals who were considering similar modifications.

For teaching hospitals affiliated with medical colleges, staff development can become even more complex, especially when the goal is to involve a diverse range of stakeholders in a broad effort to improve the functioning of the entire organization. Two decades ago, an external consultant worked with a medical college dean and the director of the affiliated teaching hospital to guide future-oriented strategic planning and organizational development (Weisbord, 1987, chap. 12). The consultant discussed how external influences affected internal relationships. (A recent study had concluded that most internal changes in higher education reflected external influences.) Major changes were occurring in higher education, including shrinking research funds, cost containment pressures, shortages of primary-care professionals, competition among specialties for resources, and conflict between college and hospital regarding their respective missions. Internal conflict between professors and administrators, as well as between college and hospital, made cooperation difficult. The consultant organized planning committees, each composed of all major categories of stakeholders. The consultant role helped them reduce past disagreements regarding mission, organization, and resources and arrive at agreements on structure and function that served the institution well for the next decade or two. This organizational development approach used planning to improve quality. Weisbord (1987) concludes that this classic case continues to illuminate crucial relations between change, planning, and staff development.

Workplace Basic Skills

A contrasting example is basic skills education for entry-level staff in business and industry. Basic skills include functional workplace literacy and numeracy, along with prevocational education to prepare workers for occupational tasks and further job-related education. With increasing public awareness of problems related to adult illiteracy and recognition by the chief executive officers of major enterprises regarding growing shortages of qualified entry-level staff, some enterprises are beginning to provide remedial basic skills education. In 1987, such programs were provided by 20 percent of enterprises with more than fifty staff members and 30 percent of enterprises with more than ten thousand staff members. The growing gap between job requirements and skill levels of applicants has occurred because job requirements (including basic reading and math) has been rising while the numbers of new workers and their preparation have been declining. A result has been to increase staff development provided for all workers, not mainly for those who already had the most formal education. One feature of effective basic skills education has been a strong connection with actual job performance, which enhances motivation and application. Another has been collaboration with other enterprises and with labor unions and educational institutions, an especially important factor for smaller enterprises, which usually lack resources to provide programs on their own. Government support of workplace literacy has also helped. In some enterprises, educational advisors have assisted staff members in selecting and pursuing basic skills education likely to benefit them (Carnevale, Gainer, and Meltzer, 1990; Chisman and Associates, 1990, chap. 7; Lee, 1988). Basic skills education has helped enterprises to compensate for inadequately prepared new entry-level staff members.

Action Learning

Most participants in adult education generally want to use what they learn, but this fact has been especially so in staff development. As adult education providers, enterprise training and development departments have been unusually well positioned to emphasize application because of their concern for both staff development and enterprise productivity. One approach that emphasizes application has been action learning (Marsick, 1987; Marsick and Watkins, 1990; Pedler, 1983). Action learning projects are generally planned and implemented by one staff member or a small group of them, and the goals are improved performance at individual, group, organizational, or occupational levels. By focusing on a desirable improvement related to enterprise functioning, the staff member engaged in an action learning project involves other staff members who have a stake in the improvement. As a result, learning and action become complementary parts of the process. Over the years, similar concepts and procedures have been termed *action research, organizational development, action science,* and *participatory research.* All share some basic ideas, such as active participation by learners including diagnosis of current performance and content, attention to desirability of goals, planning and evaluation of learning activities and impact on organization, explicit attention to application, and seminar sessions to help action learners reflect on the process (Argyris, Putnam, and Smith, 1985; Beaudin, 1986; Carnevale, Gainer, and Meltzer, 1990; Craig, 1987; Goldstein and Associates, 1989; Pedler, 1983; Silberman, 1990). Strategic planning can identify situations in which action learning projects may be especially beneficial.

International Management

The concluding example in this section on staff development in the United States focuses on cross-cultural understandings, which have been especially important for the increasing number of staff members in enterprises with international dealings and even in domestic enterprises in which managers contend with contrasting subcultures. Studies of international differences in organizational values and behavior have implications for both management and training (Adler, 1986; Bellah and others, 1985; Hofstede, 1980). American cultural orientations have been characterized as individualistic, private, and action oriented in the present or near future; other cultural orientations place greater value on group solidarity, public concerns, being (not doing), and past traditions. There are also differences in the ways that status is assigned and uncertainty is approached. Staff development activities have been increasingly provided to help staff members understand and deal effectively with cultural differences, both internationally and for domestic subcultures.

The discussion of staff development in U.S. enterprises is indicative of the even greater diversity of programs and influences that exist in practice. Economic conditions were a pervasive influence, dramatic in the case of the program on stress reduction for stockbrokers, more gradual in other programs (such as for the staff of local financial institutions or of multinational enterprises). Technological change was particularly influential in some programs (for example, in paper mills, financial institutions, nursing, medical school, action learning projects, and even brokerage houses (to the extent that computerization contributes to fluctuations in the stock market). Supply and demand for personnel to work in enterprises affected the priority for staff development, with shortages having apparent consequences for financial institutions, nursing, and workplace literacy programs. Collaboration in staff development took various forms, such as planning for the program for stockbrokers, assistance for workplace literacy, cooperation for organizational change in the medical college and action learning examples, and preparation of educational materials by outside experts for the financial distance education program. In the United States, staff development has depended heavily on the effort of individual enterprises, compared with Sweden where public policy supports supplementary contributions, especially for less-educated workers. Relations with the remainder of the enterprise and the priority for staff development were very influential in all examples, with great variation in the extent to which such relationships helped or hindered. Interpersonal relations, such as between managers and staff members, were one specific aspect (as seen especially in the programs for paper mills, teachers, nurses, and the medical college staff). Almost all examples emphasized active learner engagement in planning and implementing staff development activities. Self-directed learning has long been recognized as important for staff development for professionals but more recently has been accepted as important for most staff members. The major educational outcomes in the programs discussed varied from individual benefits for financial institution staff members and stockbrokers to organizational benefits in the programs for paper mills, teachers, nurses, the medical college, and action learning. There has been a general trend away from enhancing individual expertise toward internally oriented organizational development and greater attention to social change as reflected in quality improvement and global competition.

Adult Education in Yugoslavia

Many of the foregoing themes regarding staff development were also prominent in the distinctive context of education for self-management provided collaboratively by enterprises and workers' universities in the former Yugoslavia composed of six republics. Since World War II, political and economic conditions in Yugoslavia have been major societal influences on the evolution of these unique educational programs. The initial example in this section is from Vojvodina, an autonomous province in the north of the Republic of Serbia in the former Yugoslavia. It is followed by an overview of various types of adult education providers and programs in the former Yugoslavia, along with comments on societal influences and implications for strategic planning.

In 1988, the workers' university in Novi Sad, the main city in Vojvodina, employed 140 staff members full time with another 500 part-time staff members who provided various adult education programs for people working in 120 enterprises that employed more than 100,000 people. Twenty-five smaller workers' universities that each typically employed fewer than ten people were located in all of the population centers in Vojvodina. (Similar exclusively adult education institutions, such as the nondegree credit programs of U.S. community colleges, were found throughout all six republics and two provinces of Yugoslavia.) Half of Vojvodina's population was associated with the very productive agricultural sector, but Vojvodina also had a diversified economic base with substantial industry. Its 1986 Law on Education referred to education for self-management as one program area of workers' universities in collaboration with enterprises. Other program areas included preparation for taking examinations at elementary, secondary, and advanced levels; languages; and cultural, practical, vocational, health, and family life education. (During the past forty years in all six of the former republics, workers' universities declined in numbers and enrollments but increased in size and contributed greatly to educational advancement of the adult population. Program emphasis shifted from popular education for reconstruction following World War II, to various balances between vocational and sociopolitical education, to more comprehensive offerings in recent years, but with the emphasis on vocational education due to an increasing reliance on cost-recovery financing. A continuing challenge was the attraction of able instructors in technical areas (Bertsch and Persons, 1980; Husen and Postlethwaite, 1985; Resource A, Oljaca).

In 1987, education for self-management constituted about half of the enrollments in the Novi Sad workers' university, and these collaborative programs were an important part of staff development in the enterprises in the region. During the 1950s, when there was strong government control, the concept of self-management mainly reflected workers councils' influence on economic decision making. The concept spread to other sectors, including election to offices at community and republic levels, as reflected in the 1974 Yugoslav constitution. The essence of social self-management was that workers participated extensively in decision making in major work units with minimal government intervention; it was similar to workplace democracy by labor unions or decentralized management of cooperatives in the United States. After 1978, there was a worsening of the Yugoslav economy and declining interest in self-management; there was also dispute regarding the causal relationships between them (Soljan, 1985; Resource A, Oljaca).

Like other examples in this book where people gained influence on important decisions, the introduction of self-management in Yugoslavia in enterprises and then in other community organizations stimulated some adults to engage in adult education to prepare them to make sound decisions, including attention to human values and societal influences. Labor unions were a major source of funding for education for self-management and of program planning. Enterprises and individual participants made smaller contributions, as staff from the workers' university worked with all three (unions, enterprises, and participants) in joint program planning. Course content included most topics related to self-management, such as decision making, interpersonal relations, enterprise management, delegation systems, strategic directions for economic development, distribution of income, and economic and societal influences. Methods emphasized group discussion and analysis of issues. Program evaluation findings helped make the offerings responsive to participants, labor unions, and enterprises.

As previously stated, the major influence on adult education in Yugoslavia in the past was economic conditions. In the 1950s and 1960s, ideological commitment to restructuring was a social and political influence. During periods of economic prosperity, funds were forthcoming from labor unions, enterprises, and the government, and workers were motivated to participate. During periods of economic decline, resource allocation also declined, and there was a shift in workers' universities toward cost-recovery vocational education programs (Resource A, Oljaca).

Education for self-management was only one program area in workers' universities, and these were but one type of provider of educational programs for adults. The remainder of this section provides an overview of the extensive variety of such programs that evolved during the past forty years in the former Yugoslavia, along with highlights of major societal influences on them that have implications for strategic planning.

There have been four broad categories of adult education providers in Yugoslavia. One was the loose network of people's and workers' universities. They provided a great range of educational and cultural programs in addition to self-management, including functional literacy, civil defense, vocational education, home economics, arts, languages, media, and cultural events. Local cultural centers provided similar programs. A second category was composed of the adult education activities of elementary, secondary, and higher education. Participation trends in such programs since World War II reflected rising levels of formal education in the general population (compared with a relatively low initial level), reform of secondary education to include vocational education, deterioration of economic and social conditions for more than a decade, and reduced prospects of occupational advancement based on increased educational level. Education reforms during the 1970s, which placed responsibility for school-related adult education under the formal educational institutions, resulted in some constraints on adult education. A third category included staff development activities provided directly by enterprises for workers, organized especially within major sections of larger enterprises. Many medium-sized enterprises had professionally prepared training officers to provide leadership, and larger enterprises had entire departments for staff development. The fourth category consisted of the remaining providers, such as federal military service, local police and civil defense, and social and political organizations. Content was predominantly on self-management and leadership development (Sol-jan, 1985).

Adult education was powerfully shaped by Yugoslavia's pluralistic history. In recent years, frequent newspaper accounts of conflict between the federal government and the republics and provinces composing the country refer to long-standing differences in history, language, religion, and ethnic traditions. The founding of Yugoslavia as a monarchy following World War I combined areas that had previously been independent states but for centuries had been controlled by the Austro-Hungarian Empire in the north or the Ottoman Turkish empire in the south. For thousands of years, the tension between Eastern Europe and the Orthodox church on the one hand and Western Europe and the Roman Catholic church on the other was epitomized by the Balkan situation and especially the areas that became Yugoslavia. Islam was an additional influence under the Ottoman empire. As occurred in other countries in other parts of the world created from diverse nationalities, a dominant issue has been unity versus diversity.

Although Yugoslavia became a socialist federation following World War II and was initially aligned with the Soviet Union and Eastern Europe, it soon became a leader among nonaligned nations and developed ties with both East and West. A few program areas like education for the military and political education were for the entire country and emphasized solidarity and shared values. From the outset, however, responsibility for education, like other political, economic, and social concerns, to a lesser extent, was decentralized to republics, provinces, and local communities. This approach increased responsiveness to local concerns but decreased attention to countrywide solidarity and cooperation. Self-management was useful locally but gave little attention to federal interdependence. During several decades following World War II, there was great progress in adult education. Most workers' universities were established then, and adult literacy efforts helped reduce illiteracy from almost 50 percent to about 15 percent (mainly older adults). University study for people who worked in adult education was more advanced than in most countries and contributed greatly to theory and practice. Constitutional changes and legislation during the 1970s consolidated past progress and optimism regarding benefits from adult education. However, as we have seen, deteriorating economic and political conditions during the past decade or more undermined support from government, labor unions, enterprises, and other major stakeholders (Bron, 1985; Charters and Associates, 1981, pp. 79-85; Krajnc and Mrmak, 1978; Organization for Economic Cooperation and Development, 1981; Savićević, 1970; 1981; Soljan, 1985; Tonković, 1985).

The strategic planning issue that the Yugoslav experience dramatizes is the extent to which adult education can assist the integration of quite different cultural traditions or at the very least counteract disintegration. Recent events have demonstrated the depth of cultural differences. In Yugoslavia, federal influences toward integration were mainly political, which tended to be resisted at the republic and provincial levels where the main economic and cultural influences were felt (a situation contributing to separatism instead of solidarity). Most adult education also occurred at republic and local levels. It appears that adult education contributed more to progressive decentralization and reinforcement of subcultures than to countrywide unity. Early optimism and support for adult education were certainly high, but social, economic, and political differences became increasingly powerful (Bron, 1985). The separation of former Yugoslav republics as separate nation states happened with such animosity and violence that people and communities, as well as adult education programs, were destroyed. The long-range implications for adult education remain unclear. A planning question for staff development and most other types of adult education is how to proceed when there are major subcultural differences. This issue has surfaced in recent years in the United States and other countries in the form of racial and labor conflict.

Other Countries

Varying societal and organizational influences on enterprise staff development can be seen in other countries as well. This section contains examples from Sweden, Germany, the United Kingdom, China, Australia, and Japan, which provide additional perspectives and implications for strategic planning.

Sweden

Sweden has been at the forefront of policy and financial support for all types of adult education, including staff development by enterprises. Recent policy reviews have been aimed at improving the balance between public and private investment in adult education for work. In the past, government subsidies for occupational adult education were somewhat independent of enterprise investment in staff development. In seeking to improve links between work and learning, combinations have been explored between educational leave and assistance; occupational education provided by educational institutions, unions, and associations; and various collaborative and customized programs. Labor unions have both supported adult education policies and provided programs.

Enterprise staff development has been the most rapidly expanding and has become the largest segment of the adult education field, but extent of provision has varied with economic conditions. To provide an idea of scale, total annual government expenditures for all forms of education have been about the equivalent of $10 billion, of which about 10 percent was allocated to all forms of adult education. By contrast, enterprises' annual expenditures for staff development were equivalent to about 35 percent of total education expenditures. Each year, about half the adult population participates in some form of adult education, about half occupational. Staff development participation by staff members with higher levels of education is more than twice that by those with lower levels of education, thus increasing disparities. Equity and democracy have been basic values of government policy for support of general and occupational adult education, with special attention to adults with less education, those who are older, immigrants, and rural residents.

National adult education policy has been more comprehensive than in other countries. Recently, the national parliament made changes to increase the responsiveness of staff development to labor market changes and to encourage cooperation between enterprises and educational institutions. Swedish emphasis on labor market education has been the reverse of many other industrialized countries, with Sweden directing 70 percent of allocations to preventive staff development activities and only 30 percent to remedial financial assistance to the unemployed. Recent discussions of adult learning rights have included considerations of educational leave, which has been available since 1975, along with emerging issues. For example, Swedish enterprises have made extensive use of technology, and adult education has been employed to help minimize its adverse labor market impact, which tends to be greatest for unskilled and semiskilled workers. Methods have included worker participation in decision making (self-management), renewal funds set aside from enterprise profits, and cooperation among government, enterprises, and educational institutions. Staff development content includes problem solving, communications, and computer literacy.

Achievement of increased cooperation among stakeholders for more comprehensive attention to staff development has entailed collaboration, programs commissioned by enterprises from educational institutions, and financial contributions by government, enterprises, and participants. There have been multiple influences on staff development: a generally satisfactory economy, specific spending constraints, increased labor force participation by women, emerging relations with the European Community (EC), other international influences, levels of prior education, size of enterprise, available program alternatives, admissions requirements, and other barriers that affect adult education participation more directly.

Recent exploration of policy alternatives regarding occupational adult education have considered various combinations of public sector and enterprise contributions. A promising alternative is the concept of a learning enterprise in which comprehensive policies of government, enterprises, and educational institutions give attention to economic development and job design, as well as collaboration, educational leave, and time for studies, as an inherent part of a job. The concept of workplaces as both productive and learning enterprises fits well with the evolution of Swedish adult education policy as promoting an educative society (Blair, 1985; Abrahamsson, 1990c; Abrahamsson, Hultinger, and Svenningsson, 1990; Charnley, 1975; O'Toole, 1983; Resource A: Abrahamsson; Thang (b)). This concept of the learning enterprise has many implications for strategic planning to strengthen staff development in the United States.

Action learning for managers with international responsibilities provides an excellent example of a staff development approach initiated in Britain and adapted for use in Sweden (as well as other countries). Managers engage in action learning to refine their personal models of leadership through combinations of actual projects, seminars, personal reflection, and exchange of perspectives with peers and experts. The goal is to help managers become holistic strategic thinkers who use judgment in problem finding, solution implementation, and decision making; in these self-renewing learning enterprises, staff members assume mutual responsibility for creation and achievement of goals. Participants in action learning projects use questions to alternate between action situations and knowledge resources. The action learning process has evolved differently in Britain, the United States, Sweden, and Japan to reflect each societal context. It has been especially valuable to help managers with international responsibilities to appreciate cross-national differences in the influence of organizational and national culture on work and education (Marsick and Cederholm, 1988; Marsick and Watkins, 1990, chap. 3; Revans, 1971, 1982). This comparative perspective can be especially valuable for strategic planning.

Germany

In Blair's analysis (1985), differences among Sweden, Germany, and Britain emerge regarding use of staff development and other means to deal with technological change. Of the three countries, Sweden has made the greatest use of adult education and other preventive measures to minimize negative societal impacts of technology, whereas Germany has had the most extensive programs to promote diffusion of new technologies. Germany has made extensive use of apprenticeships for entry-level, nonprofessional workers. Technology and employment have been major political issues and have likely become more so since reunification, which has increased economic agitation and dislocation.

Technological change, a satisfactory economy, and international competition contributed to priority for a major staff development division for professional staff in the European branches of a German multinational enterprise (Resource A, Kilgenstein). Full-time, twelve-week courses were provided for more than four thousand professionals to strengthen their ability for long-term planning. Their participation was encouraged by anticipated career advancement and positive comments by past participants. The enterprise provided full funding, and all instructors were regular higher education faculty members whose work was a supplementary activity. In other enterprises, coaching by an adult educator was combined with assistance by content experts from the enterprise to strengthen staff development through this team effort (Reischmann, 1990).

United Kingdom

In contrast with Sweden and Germany, Britain has had a less developed national strategy for helping the work force deal with technological change. Unemployment has been the highest of the three, much higher than in Sweden; the manufacturing sector has been declining, and economic conditions have been major political issues (Blair, 1985; Moon, Webber, and Richardson, 1986). Government support for staff development has emphasized retraining for higher-status personnel and for the unemployed. Staff development by enterprises and contributions by educational institutions has tended to be fairly independent, in part reflecting the slow shift from general toward vocational adult education (Todd, 1984).

All three countries share with the United States concerns about technology and staff development that warrant exchange. Of interest to all are minimizing labor market impact of technology, gaps between preparation of unemployed people and higher requirements for unfilled positions, special dislocations of midcareer blue collar workers, computer-related training for the work force, and strengthening of management development (Blair, 1985; Farnham, 1987; Further Education Unit, 1986; Russell, 1984). These are important issues for strategic planning.

People's Republic of China

Staff development for enterprises in China provides several contrasts with that in America and Europe. Since 1976, the end of the cultural revolution, the People's Republic of China has been engaged in economic and social reconstruction that has greatly influenced enterprise staff development. In the late 1970s, the four modernizations of industry, technology, military, and agriculture helped initiate the reconstruction, which was accelerated by the opening to the West. During the past fifteen years, there have been concerted efforts to combine work and learning, and staff development by enterprises has been a major part of the effort.

Before that, "iron rice bowl" assurances of a job for life because of the lack of a market system discouraged high-quality production in enterprises and adult education to achieve it. Traditional Chinese values and practices also contributed to resistance to change related to staff development, including lack of reform of enterprise personnel practices. Traditional beliefs helped sustain a separation between formal education degrees, exams, status, and work, including staff development. The ideological emphasis during the cultural revolution set back education generally, and the aftermath was shortages of qualified workers, educated people, and experts to serve as instructors in staff development and other types of adult education. The abrupt changes in direction—from the isolationism of the local economic development of the Great Leap Forward and the class politics of the cultural revolution, to the four modernizations and increased international contacts since then— have made many Chinese reluctant to take risks. The backwardness of the economy, which was partially created by the backwardness of the formal educational system, was in conflict with ambitious national development goals. The formal educational system was then unable to absorb the surge in demand, which encouraged the development of a parallel adult education system at all levels (an important part of which was provided by enterprises). Graduates from the adult education providers were considered equivalent to their counterparts in traditional educational institutions.

The foregoing trends help account for dramatic increases in the priority and extent of adult education during the 1980s and the importance of planning and leadership during a period of rapid, large-scale expansion. Enterprises carried a major responsibility for expansion of staff development because they contained learners, experts, and resources. Because of socialistic ideology, enterprises were not only workplaces but also provided social services for workers. Larger enterprises developed workers' universities; these furnished opportunities for workers to obtain entire elementary, secondary, and higher education degrees; vocational and professional education normally associated with staff development; and even preparatory education schools for family members. Since the majority of small and medium enterprises lacked the capacity to conduct such extensive staff development activities, they shifted the responsibility to other providers and to TV universities and distance learning activities to help adults engage in self-directed study to pass examinations. These developments reflected great optimism about the positive contribution of education to economic development. As traditional higher education graduates began to exceed the capacity of the economic system to absorb them, enterprises were encouraged to reduce their provision of continuing higher education and to emphasize other aspects of adult vocational education and nondegree studies. In the early stages of allowing private work, education began to be viewed less as a source of status than as a potential tool to increase prosperity, and it is unclear whether recent restrictions on private work will affect adult vocational education.

A major source of resources for staff development was an early government provision for enterprises to allocate 1.5 percent of total wages to support workers' education. In this and other ways, enterprises were encouraged to invest in staff development to help workers use new technology and contribute to modernization and economic development. Close connections between enterprises and workers' universities and other adult education providers assisted workers who were fortunate enough to attend to bring work problems to the classroom and solutions back to the workplace. The extent of investment in internal and external staff development was somewhat associated with the level of technology in an enterprise (Hunter and Keehn, 1985; Lei, 1985; Risler, 1987; Rongshu, 1987; Wright, 1985; Zeng, Li, and Wu, 1988; Resource A, Liu). Staff development for Chinese managers included cross-national perspectives (Lindsay and Dempsey, 1985). Workplace application has been a crucial outcome of staff development.

Australia

There is increasing interest in Australia in competency standards and recognition of enterprise-based education. The commonwealth government recently introduced a training guarantee levy that required all enterprises with a payroll over $200,000 to spend at least 1 percent of their payroll on structured staff development and training (this percentage was to rise over time to 3 percent). In 1992, each state had its own training board that dealt with numerous private training organizations. These 144 organizations, referred to as Industry Training Advisory Bodies (ITABs), have been autonomous organizations with representatives from government, enterprises, and employees. The ITABs have been partially funded by the commonwealth, and their activities will be the focus of the new Australian National Training Authority.

Japan

The concluding example, staff development in Japan, is distinctive in several respects. Japan was one of the group of seven industrialized countries, very competitive technologically, which pioneered use of Deming's ideas about employing staff development procedures such as quality circles to achieve quality improvement goals. Japan was well advanced over the United States in this respect. At the same time, Japan shares many Asian cultural values with China, including emphasis on group solidarity versus the individualism of the West, lifetime employment practices in large enterprises (which account for about 25 percent of the work force), and advancement and pay based mainly on seniority. Thus, the emphasis of staff development is on long-term enterprise productivity instead of on individual advancement, which reduces staff resistance to technology due to fear of displacement. Small and medium enterprises without the capability for extensive internal staff development used government adult vocational education institutes and sometimes the staff development programs of larger enterprises (similar to staff development provided by the large U.S. accounting firms for members of smaller firms). However, social and economic changes resulted in recent gradual changes in the employment system that emphasized merit for promotion more than previously.

Reportedly, high-tech enterprises spent .5 percent of total sales for staff development, and staff members devoted about eight hours a week to staff development, half on enterprise time and half on personal time. Extensive and varied staff development has evolved that reflects the Japanese cultural context, including emphasis on teamwork, job rotation, cross training, career paths, and in general long-term productivity and competitive position of enterprises. Recent attention has been given to creativity and to staff development for smaller enterprises that did not benefit from some of the foregoing features of large enterprises (Hanaoka, 1986; Oshima and Yamada, 1985; Saha, 1987; Warner, 1985). Generally, there has been less collaboration on staff development by enterprises and higher education institutions than in the United States.

Trends

At this point, it might be helpful to review briefly major themes in staff development internationally, especially some comparative perspectives from Europe. The powerful shaping influence of each national political and economic context on staff development by enterprises is generally acknowledged. However, when distinctive features are addressed, staff development leaders have been able to adapt concepts and procedures from other countries to their own cultural context. This approach has become increasingly desirable and likely with the growing internationalization of enterprises, as shown in the increased economic integration of many nations in the European Community beginning in 1992, changing relations between Eastern and Western Europe, the increase in emerging multinational economic communities, and the growth of multinational enterprises. Comparative perspectives are also fostered by regional collaboration within countries by enterprises, labor unions and professional associations, government, and educational institutions.

Widespread influences have included adapting to technological changes and encouraging innovations, new products and services, and even creation of new enterprises. Leadership for staff development should also address broad economic and social problems that result from major changes (such as "deskilling," displacement of low-skilled workers, and the roles of enterprises, government, and educational institutions with respect to unemployment, especially when it is long term), and assistance to young, entry-level staff members. Relations between government and unions can influence staff development; fragmented labor unions in India weakened support for workers' education, in contrast with strong cooperation between government and unions on behalf of workers' education in Canada (Hopkins, 1985). Collaboration and distinctive roles among providers of staff development are related to most of the foregoing themes. An emerging idea is use of staff development for organizational development using action or participatory research procedures to address assumptions and structural changes in enterprises and work roles (Argyris, Putnam, and Smith, 1985; Bogard, 1989; Craig, 1987, chap. 40; Merriam and Cunningham, 1989, chap. 32; Reason and Rowan, 1981; Steedman, 1984).

Strategic Planning

The very large and expanding amount of staff development provided by all types of enterprises in the United States makes planning for this segment of the adult education field very important. Because each enterprise can plan quite independently, there is great variation regarding planning goals and procedures, and it is difficult to suggest *uniform* guidelines for strategic planning for staff development. However, responsiveness to a rapidly changing environment makes such planning especially important. In this concluding section, it is assumed that people with leadership responsibilities for staff development engage major stakeholders in a process likely to produce desired changes in the staff development department and related aspects in ways that fit enterprise goals and local contingencies. The section addresses a number of issues and influences that suggest important challenges and tasks that staff development leaders should consider. The issues pertain to local contingencies, cultural values, economic conditions, technological change, international influences, collaboration, and desired outcomes.

Contingencies

Each *enterprise* has an organizational culture composed of the traditions and values that shape its mission and contributions in pursuit of that mission. Each adult education *provider* also develops a distinctive organizational culture. Unlike providers associated with educational institutions that serve external clients, staff development departments are parts of the enterprise in which the learners work, and they share an organizational culture. Although this shared context can compound conflict between a staff development department and its enterprise, when there is substantial agreement the common organizational culture allows great coordination of program planning and implementation and application to achieve results. Both operating units and training departments influence staff development budgets. Thus, in addition to societal influences, strategic planning for staff development should include major organizational influences and local contingencies.

Some of the major trends in enterprise organization and environment that are relevant to staff development are shifts from stability to turbulence, from a national to an international focus, from output to productivity, from centralization to decentralization, from individuals to teams, and from independence to social accountability (Kairamo, 1989, part 5). Many of the examples in this chapter refer to contingencies that entail adaptation to new work requirements. In the paper mills, computerization changed both operator and supervisor roles. In the schools, clinical supervision and peer coaching emerged as individualized methods of staff development. In the two hospital examples, there were personnel shortages. In the Chinese example, traditional universities were unable to absorb the surge in demand and respond to national modernization goals, so adult education providers were able to perform a parallel function for part-time students.

An important feature of each enterprise that affects its staff development is the type of products and services it provides and the position that the enterprise occupies within its industry or type of activity. Implications for staff development become apparent when considering contrasts between an enterprise such as a government agency or private corporation with a monopoly and one with a small market share in a very technical and competitive field and turbulent environment. In the latter instance, market niche and time pressure are likely to be more influential on staff development plans than in the former. As the examples in this chapter indicate, another influential local contingency is the size of the enterprise. Small enterprises without the resources to provide a full range of staff development activities may have to rely on regional arrangements, such as services by outside adult education providers (educational institutions and even consortial arrangements) for strategic planning and program offerings. For example, many small enterprises could arrange for centralized environmental scanning or needs assessments services to be provided for each staff development officer or department to use to guide their internal programming (similar to local newspaper use of a national news service).

Perhaps the most crucial influence of the enterprise on the staff development function is the relative priority given to training and development, as reflected in policies, allocation of resources, cooperation, and beliefs about the contribution of staff development to enterprise productivity and quality (Mackenzie, 1991). This is why it is very important for staff development strategic planning to represent the main constituencies within the parent organization so that the program focuses on benefits highly valued by the enterprise. This approach places a premium on building and maintaining supportive relations within the parent organization.

Another contingency has to do with the relative extent of training and development provided to various categories of staff members and the forms of assistance provided. This contingency includes supply and demand in the labor force pools from which the enterprise recruits for each staff category (Kairamo, 1989). It also includes the extent of self-directed learning by participants that seems desirable and feasible, along with attention to equity and organizational development. Quality improvement approaches emphasize system appraisal and teamwork. These are issues to be considered in strategic planning. A similar contingency pertains to sources and roles of people who plan and conduct staff development activities. Sources include full-time educators in a staff development department, enterprise staff members (such as supervisors who devote part time to training and development), and outside experts. Staff development resources are both bought and sold by enterprises. A basic goal of strategic planning is to achieve satisfactory contributions to staff development by enterprise staff to achieve a high-quality program that strengthens enterprise support and recognition (Cooley and Thompson, 1986; Nadler and Wiggs, 1986, chap. 9).

Effective leaders of staff development are likely to be alert to such local contingencies and internal strengths and weaknesses as a result of informal associations with other enterprise personnel, as well as conclusions gained from strategic planning. The *formal* planning process tends to be even more important in order to recognize *external* trends and issues, such as national cultural values, economic conditions and trends, technological change, and international influences.

Values

National cultural values can be seen in both implicit and explicit choices made regarding such matters as democratic participation in social and political decision making, emphasis on individual versus group performance, equality of opportunity for subcultures, commitment to lifelong learning, attractiveness of technological development, and acceptance of dislocation of workers. Influential cultural values that were demonstrated in the examples discussed in this chapter include individual advancement in the association of financial institutions; income as a criterion of occupational worth for the stockbrokers; self-management in the Yugoslav workers' university; democracy, equality, and minimizing of technological dislocation in Sweden; and solidarity and seniority in Japan. Strategic planning can consider current legislation and other policies to reflect in staff development activities, but it can also address proposed policies and legislation to be initiated and supported in proactive efforts to improve the climate for the enterprise in general and the staff development function in particular (Walker, 1983). Some educational activities may even be aimed at policy makers.

Economic Factors

The examples in this chapter illustrate the various ways in which economic trends and conditions powerfully influence enterprises and their staff development functions. In addition to influencing the resources that the enterprise acquires and its allocation of resources to staff development, economic, social, and political conditions affect many aspects of training and development. Favorable conditions (such as political stability, economic growth, and satisfactory opportunities for subcultures) have ramifications for many aspects of the societal context of the enterprise, including the staff development function. These might include cooperation from other organizations and an accepted belief that benefits from further education exceed the costs—as illustrated by the examples from Sweden, Germany, and Japan. Economic conditions in the foregoing examples caused unemployment, which affected the labor unions; the drop in the market for stockbrokers; gradual internationalization of enterprises for some managers; worsening of the economy in spite of a diversified economic base in Novi Sad, Yugoslavia; and declining manufacturing, contributing to increasing unemployment in Britain. The challenge to strategic planning is to identify a manageable number of useful social, political, and economic indicators to specify current conditions and identify emerging trends (Campbell, 1982; Johnston, 1987; Riche, 1988; Thoursonjones, 1986; Ward, 1984). Some of these indicators are used by effective enterprise managers, who should make the information available to staff development leaders.

Technological Influences

Enterprises vary greatly in the extent to which they are affected by technological changes. For some, there is little impact of technology beyond its impact on the general society. By contrast, in some enterprises (such as those engaged in manufacturing electronics or pharmaceuticals), technological changes can be swift and sweeping. In such enterprises, strategic planning for staff development depends on monitoring at least the projections of emerging technological trends made by the parent enterprise and using the conclusions to plan responsive activities to both prepare for and facilitate adjustments. Technological change was a major influence on staff development in many of the examples, including the paper mill, labor union, intensive care unit, teaching hospital, action learning programs, Sweden, Germany, and Japan. Educational technology (audio and videotapes, computer simulations) can serve staff development, which can both help achieve adjustments to technology and explore desirability and implications of possible changes.

International Impact

For an increasing number of enterprises, one societal influence is international. In addition to multinational enterprises, many enterprises have a growing number of suppliers and customers from other countries (Cerna, 1987; Corvalen, 1977; McAllister, 1987; Mutahaba, 1986; Organization for Economic Cooperation and Development, 1985). Thus, in addition to global competition for the enterprise, there are direct international influences on staff development, such as helping managers and other personnel work effectively with people from various national and cultural backgrounds. The implications of international influences differed in our examples, such as a comparative perspective for international management, relations with the EC for Sweden, adaptation of action learning procedures in four countries (Britain, the United States, Sweden, and Japan), and competition in Germany. The emergence of regional common markets in Europe, North America, and other parts of the world are likely to accelerate such global influences on staff development. As more enterprises become multinational, national preparatory education requirements may become restrictions, and staff development should give increased attention to enhancement of instructor performance, increased teamwork within the enterprise, and long-term planning (Kairamo, 1989).

Collaboration

It is not easy to identify emerging economic, social, and technological trends either domestically or internationally because there are multiple indicators and interpretation can be ambiguous. For example, instead of a threat to staff development, a downturn in one part of an enterprise can serve as an opportunity for education and innovation to create new products or even new enterprises. A benefit of strategic planning is broadening the perspective on contributions by staff development. Part of a broader view can be new forms of collaboration between an enterprise's staff development department and other providers or supporters of adult education: educational institutions, labor unions, associations, government agencies, and consulting firms. Especially for smaller enterprises, such assistance and cooperative arrangements may constitute the main portion of staff development. Large enterprises decide which aspects of staff development are best provided internally and which are best contracted for from outside. The examples regarding stockbrokers, the teaching hospital, workplace literacy, action learning, and the role of Yugoslav workers' universities in helping enterprises with self-management illustrate the variety of situations that can result in collaboration. By including people from cooperating organizations in the strategic planning process, staff development departments can strengthen current collaboration and discover new opportunities. However, planning should consider costs as well as benefits of collaboration. With impending labor shortages in Europe, increased cooperation between enterprises and educational institutions seems desirable.

Outcomes

The foregoing planning issues have focused on influences and program functioning. This concluding one considers desirable outcomes. Staff development can seek to produce changes of quite different types and scope. Examples of contrasting outcomes include passing an exam (China), improving individual performance (financial institution), increasing work team productivity (hospital, Japan), accelerating career advancement (Germany), and guiding innovation in the enterprise (action learning, Sweden). Long-term benefits deserve special attention. The school teacher program showed an emphasis on intermediate outcome measures (sense of efficacy, high expectations, supportive climate, large amount of time spent on task) that should lead to improved achievement but also the importance of recognition of several categories of teachers. Strategic planning stakeholders and procedures will vary with intended outcomes, especially if there is an effort to offset at least partially some broad social problem or subcultural conflict. The likelihood of enterprise staff development producing major organizational or social change can be increased by synergistic comprehensive programs. The Swedish exploration of learning enterprises suggests one approach. In countries with a postindustrial information society, distinctions between work and learning are becoming blurred, and most staff members at all status levels are knowledge workers who need to understand why as well as how. Organization development approaches (action learning projects, participatory research) promote such concern for goals as well as procedures (Argyris, Putnam, and Smith, 1985; Bard, Bell, Stephen, and Webster, 1987; Marsick, 1987; Mouton and Blake, 1984; Nadler, 1984; Silberman, 1990). For some changes, staff development for policy makers is essential. Strategic planning that includes major stakeholders is crucial for such comprehensive staff development.

Several other chapters contain ideas related to staff development. For enterprises that include professionals as staff members, there are direct connections to continuing professional education, aside from programs for managers. Workplace literacy combines attention to basic education and staff members of an enterprise who participate. Enterprises are major users of the educational technology that is also used in distance education. For enterprises with minority subcultures, related issues can be common to both. And finally, one form of cooperation among providers is encouragement of staff members to participate part time in adult education offered by educational institutions, often with tuition reimbursement by the enterprise.

7

Correctional
Education

Education of prisoners may seem remote to most practitioners, but correctional education has provocative implications for adult education leaders in other program areas. There are some distinctive features of correctional education. These pertain to characteristics of adults in prisons and jails, the evolution of correctional education, and the educational goals for purposes of rehabilitation in the context of the organizational culture of penal institutions. Some of the issues that are highlighted in educational programs for incarcerated adults have surprising implications for adult education leadership in many other settings, especially regarding obtaining support for program goals by stakeholders from the parent organization and public policy makers. Also, there are many ways in which prison education parallels adult education outside.

Features of Correctional Education

In the United States, federal and state prisons are intended for convicted offenders with sentences more than one year, whereas local city and county jails are meant for convicts with shorter sentences and for people being held before trial and sentencing. Some offenders are supervised in community settings under conditions of probation, parole, and transition services. In 1991, about 2.5 million U.S. adults were under some form of correctional supervision. Thus correctional education extends beyond prison walls, but the focus of this chapter is on penal institutions and the prison context.

The number of inmates in U.S. *federal* prisons almost doubled between the early 1970s and the late 1980s to around fifty thousand. This increase occurred during a period when there was a small population increase, including in young men who are the main clientele for penal institutions; increases thus reflect greater reported crime and especially use of punishment to fight crime rather than a larger general population. Federal prisons constitute a small part of the seven hundred prisons in the United States, and together all prisons confine about a half-million adults. The nearly 3,500 local jails have an average daily population of about another quarter-million. The remainder are under other forms of correctional supervision, such as parole. The total constitutes more than 1.2 percent of the American adult population; for males, the proportion is more than 2 percent. The mostly male population of the federal and state prisons consists disproportionately of unemployed, undereducated, minorities, and learning-handicapped people, although there are many exceptions who are highly educated and have held responsible positions. More than 80 percent did not complete secondary school, between 60 and 80 percent have been classified as functionally illiterate, and fewer than 10 percent can pass a standardized achievement test at grade-12 level (Merriam and Cunningham, 1989, pp. 356, 357).

The punishment and custodial orientation of the general public and of penal institution security staff helps account for the low priority for education and rehabilitation, to the extent that correctional education is provided for less than 12 percent of the total prison population, and only one in five local jails has any form of education for inmates. Initiative for improvement of correctional education depends mainly on leadership by correctional education staff from the prison and cooperating organizations. Low priority has been the result of little value on rehabilitation by custodial staff and the general public. Compounding influences have been underfunding and overcrowding of inmate populations.

Although scattered examples of correctional education by prison staff, chaplains, and religious volunteers have occurred since the first penitentiaries, contemporary tax-supported correctional education has been evolving for more than a century. In 1847, New York State took the early lead by mandating the provision of correctional education in all institutions. About 1870, the reformatory movement began in Elmira, New York, which emphasized educational and vocational programming along with indeterminate prison sentences. Since World War II, federal legislation in support of adult basic education, vocational education, and job retraining has helped finance correctional education, along with increased state support in many states. Probation and early release have been combined with education. Unfortunately, the unprecedented increase in incarcerated offenders has strained prison budgets, a situation that in turn has reduced the extent and variety of correctional education programs, in spite of increased support for adult education.

In general, correctional education is for self-help to counteract antisocial behavior through general and vocational education; the intent is thus to equip people under correctional supervision to be responsible community members. Widespread goals are to enhance inmates' vocational and general abilities, to provide inmates with opportunities to change behavior and values, to reduce recidivism, to provide passive control of inmate behavior, to support functioning of the penal institution, and to undergird institutional work assignments. The public, policy makers, and prison officials have generally been unwilling to provide sufficient support for correctional education, in the face of competing priorities. In response to U.S. opinion polls, most of the public seems supportive of secondary and vocational education for prisoners, but not higher education opportunities. Ironically, some of the most innovative prison education programs have been provided by higher education institutions.

Perhaps the most severe problem that confronts correctional educators is the organizational culture of the penal institution. The fact that about 90 percent of the people under correctional supervision participate in no correctional education reflects the low priority by prisons and prisoners for education and for rehabilitation generally. Security dominates the practices of guards and most other people who work in correctional institutions, which tend to be overcrowded, underfinanced and understaffed. Prisons have been characterized as total institutions, in which authoritarian regimes seek to control many aspects of the lives of dependent inmates. One obvious result is isolation of inmates from family, friends, and the external society. When these features of prison life are combined with tyranny from the inmate subculture and sometimes participation in a criminal subculture prior to incarceration, the result can be that many released inmates are even less likely to function with a socially acceptable sense of morality than before their imprisonment. These results are reflected in recidivism rates (repeated arrest and conviction) of between 50 and 70 percent for parolees who were rearrested for new crimes within six years. It is a major challenge to correctional educators to achieve desirable results, given limited resources and strong countervailing forces (Bell and others, 1979; Duguid, 1989, 1990; Merriam and Cunningham, 1989, chap. 27; Morin, 1981; Sutton, 1992). In this chapter, these edited volumes based on reports by many contributors are cited frequently because they constitute major recent and comprehensive overviews of correctional education.

The following examples and rationale address three main themes important for strategic planning. The first is leadership in relation to societal values, educational goals, and outcomes. Various stakeholders have contradictory expectations. Four contrasting approaches are presented. A second theme addresses additional aspects of agency culture, functioning, and contingencies, including relations with the larger penal institution, educational participation by inmates, educational technology, and staff development. A central issue is tension between prison security and correctional education. The third theme includes more remote influences, such as government and public priorities and collaboration, especially with educational institutions. The concluding section of the chapter summarizes these and other influences and their implications for strategic planning of correctional education.

Ross Correctional Institution

The Ross Correctional Institution, located in Chillicothe, Ohio, has served as a complex for men eighteen to fifty years of age, composed of a medium security compound for 1,450 inmates and a minimum security honor camp for 250 inmates. Operated by the Ohio Department of Rehabilitation and Correction, Ross demonstrates the evolution of the Ohio Plan for Productive Prisons developed in 1987.

This plan proposed to confine adult offenders in safe, secure, humane institutions with a correctional program characterized by a combination of training, work, and education—an approach based on a training, industry, and education (TIE) concept. This concept was developed at a 1985 conference in Chicago that brought together staff members from both correctional education and prison industry to formulate shared goals and partnerships. The Ohio plan emphasized work assignments for inmates linked to training and education.

At Ross and all other state prisons that implemented the Ohio plan approach to the TIE concept, there are several distinctive features. Each prison job and work assignment has clearly defined job descriptions and specified requirements for education and training. All work assignments include similar characteristics: real-world job duties, emphasis on productivity, job performance evaluations, focus on pride and purpose, pay incentives and disincentives, career ladders, suitable rewards, job involvement, work ethics, and training-education-job linkage. All inmates were required to work, and if they lacked qualifications for a better job, training and education were available. Functional literacy is top priority; inmates with less than sixth-grade reading level on a standardized test are required to complete ninety days of basic education, and further attendance is voluntary. A deputy warden in each institution coordinates all TIE functions and related departments. A job coordinator at each institution coordinates inmate assessment, counseling, job listings, and work records.

In addition to the adult basic educational program, there is individual and small-group peer literacy tutoring, vocational education in five trades, high school equivalency (GED) and high school courses, and opportunities to earn college credits toward associate or bachelor's degrees in business or human services. When inmates enter the reception center, they take tests assessing basic skills and general aptitudes, which are included in an inmate employment portfolio that also includes pertinent civilian information and pre-prison and prison education, training, and employment information that accompanies the inmate on each institutional transfer. This portfolio of information, along with job counseling, is used for making job and educational placements. Prerelease programs serve inmates during the six weeks before release to help the transition from prison to community; topics cover job readiness, completion of employment portfolios, and job placement in cooperation with the Ohio Bureau of Employment Services. Some postrelease educational assistance is also provided. From entry to release, work in the prison industry, vocational training, and general education makes complementary contributions to a comprehensive rehabilitation effort (Duguid, 1990).

Other U.S. Programs

The foregoing example of the Ohio Plan program at Ross, based on the TIE concept, is a promising exception to the general problem of correctional education in the United States, where about 90 percent of inmates receive no educational assistance. One outcome used to assess the effectiveness of corrections is low recidivism. It is therefore discouraging that the recidivism rate for U.S. parolees has been more than 50 percent, and one recent study found that 69 percent of 11,300 parolees in twenty-two states were rearrested for more than 36,000 new serious crimes within six years of release (Duguid, 1990, pp. 113–128).

Work

In recent years, correctional educators and others interested in penal reform have emphasized reconciliation and rehabilitation, in contrast with the long-standing reliance on retribution and punishment. This emphasis on rehabilitation has given increased attention to attitudes instead of focusing mainly on performance. One goal of correctional education has been to help inmates develop a socially acceptable sense of morality so they can function responsibly in the community. Correctional educators have long recognized that it is difficult to train for freedom in captivity, and that education alone can not resocialize inmates. Correctional education has been affected by public opinion, laws, prison staff, and reactions of inmates to their prison environment. Within this comprehensive societal framework, correctional education seeks resocialization for reintegration into society by merging educational activities with improved work, family, and community life. The Ross example of the TIE concept of corrections for productive work emphasized the occupational role. The following example stresses the family member role.

Family

The Eastern New York Correctional Facility (called Eastern), located in Napanoch, a rural area of the Hudson River valley about a two-hour drive north of New York City, is one of more than fifty prisons operated by the New York State Department of Correctional Services. Eastern consists of a maximum security facility for almost 1,000 prisoners and a medium security annex for about 150 prisoners, all men. The concept of an educational group for incarcerated fathers was proposed in 1985 by a faculty member from the nearby campus of the State University of New York at New Paltz. In 1987, after the recently expanded Family Services Office at Eastern received two members of the Fathers Rights Association of New York for an exploratory meeting about establishing a support group for imprisoned fathers, support for a fathers group increased. Later that year, a speaker from Prison Families of New York conducted a seminar for inmates on issues of concern to incarcerated fathers, the participants asked to meet again, and three weeks later the Fathers Group began to meet regularly.

The rationale for the Fathers Group was that strengthening the father-child bond would help the father improve in prison and become a more active and effective father and role model after release. The program aim was to provide imprisoned fathers with knowledge about parenting and child development and to provide a support group to help participants cope with family concerns. Consciousness-raising discussion of family-related issues addressed values and moral aspects of parenting. Inmate interest was high, and there was a long list of fathers who wanted to participate in the three components (mutual support meetings, monthly educational seminar sessions, and a certified parent education course). The support meetings aim to improve the self-esteem of participants through increased understanding of both their capabilities and limitations as incarcerated parents; discussion of responsibilities of parenthood, ways to improve parent-child communications, and effects of parental incarceration on children; and analysis of sex roles and related issues in contemporary society. A special concern is the infrequent and difficult process of visits by family members and ways to make visits constructive experiences. The ten-week parent education course topics includes family relationships and stress, child development and care, parental influences on children (such as alcohol and drug abuse, discipline versus punishment, and child abuse, as well as positive influences of parental behavior on children). The three program components help participants deal with deterioration of relationships with their children during confinement and prepare inmates to assume positive parental roles after their release.

Program success reflect cooperation between prisoner initiatives and Family Services assistance that results in a cost-effective program and participant commitment. Plans for the future include a reference library with books and videotapes based on previous program sessions, and a follow-up survey to evaluate the program components and the results when the fathers are released and returned to their families.

Community Focus

By contrast with the examples of correctional education related to work and family, the following educational program addressed community issues and citizen roles in ways that were relevant to the prison experience and postrelease functioning. In 1988, several public issues discussion groups were started at Central Correctional Institution (Central), operated by the Georgia Department of Corrections, in Macon, eighty-five miles south of Atlanta. A variety of educational activities were available at Central, including individualized basic education, secondary and vocational education courses, and higher education courses provided by nearby colleges.

Most prison education consists of fairly solitary remedial activities similar in content and methods to preparatory education missed earlier. By contrast, Central houses more than five hundred inmates on four acres of land, so there was high social density and group pressure on individuals, which makes their use of limited discretionary time valuable. In this desolate environment, inmates experience the pains of imprisonment, including loss of liberty, autonomy, security, goods, services, and heterosexual relationships. Traditional prison education provides insufficient opportunities to interact freely and speak with and listen to others in a positive social environment that can provide some sense of power and help them examine their own values and beliefs.

To combat these problems, the public issues study groups use materials and procedures from the National Issues Forum (NIF) developed by the Domestic Policy Association with support from the Kettering Foundation. NIF was modeled after participant-centered and -led Swedish study circles in which small groups of friends or associates read background materials and then meet for in-depth democratic discussion of current social issues, with a group member as discussion leader. Intended outcomes of NIF participation at Central include exchange of views, expressions of opinions, exercise of leadership, development of critical thinking, promotion of trust, tolerance for diversity, experience of democracy, and development of a sense of community in a hostile place. NIF readings consist of brief, focused, easy-to-read nonbiased booklets, each of which effectively explains the salient details of a public issue such as crime or education that is discussed during ten two-hour weekly sessions.

Participation in NIF study groups provides inmates with rare opportunities for constructive exchange of ideas as a temporary escape from the absolute authority of the prison administration. Democratic participation did not occur at the outset. Initially, there was little respect or tolerance for others' ideas, as most members focused on differences instead of shared views. Segregated from society, rejected and stigmatized, the inmates felt alienated. The NIF experience allows them to project themselves into discussion of issues related to their families, communities, and country. As they communicate with each other during the weeks, they discover that they share values that shape their positions on issues, and this experience reduces feelings of alienation. After initial anarchy, distrust, and displays of egotism, trust and tolerance slowly develop, and members begin to identify with each other and to define reality, issues, and solutions collectively.

The structured but flexible interdisciplinary learning environment and process of the small study group helps participants understand how adults learn. As democratic discussion enables participants to replace physical encounters with verbal ones, they begin to speak freely and frankly, without fear of physical reprisal. In the study groups, inmates become both student and teacher by exercising independent thinking and talking, which helps reduce feelings of alienation, inadequacy, and powerlessness and enhances feelings of self-worth. Follow-up interviews with participants indicated that many reported reductions in feelings of alienation, isolation, idleness, and mental decay in prison and increased feelings of connection with important issues in the outside world. Furthermore, the analytical abilities developed through discussion of issues could serve as prerequisites for many jobs after release. Though the correctional educators were convinced that NIF participation contributed to trust, respect, tolerance, and friendships, too little time had elapsed since participants' release for the educators to determine whether the program would influence criminal behavior and recidivism (Duguid, 1990).

Mandatory Programs

Throughout all U.S. jails and prisons, the 10 or 15 percent of inmates who receive correctional education participate in various programs that reflect differing influences and views of desirable program purposes and procedures. Some policies have been controversial. An example is mandatory basic education in federal prisons started in 1982. The policy included achievement testing for inmates, with required basic education enrollment for ninety days for inmates who scored below sixth-grade level. Each federal prison was to restrict inmate advancement to prison industry jobs and wage levels until inmates met the sixth-grade standard, was to monitor participant progress, and was to have an appropriate system of incentives and rewards for satisfactory progress and completion. In 1986, the standard was raised to eighth-grade equivalency. There was little resistance from inmates and staff. Participation in such programs increased greatly. Between 1981 and 1986, the average daily inmate population in federal prisons increased by 54 percent, while basic education completions increased 327 percent. This success was created by the incentive provided by connecting educational achievement with advancement in wages and promotions. It also reflected the introduction of computer-based education in federal prisons during that period, which allowed correctional educators to serve expanded numbers of participants. Some states also adopted mandatory education in their prisons.

Volunteerism

By contrast, some correctional educators have emphasized volunteerism and peer tutoring in adult basic education in an effort to minimize external requirements and emphasize intrinsic motivation. In many instances, initiatives for educational activities that inmates helped plan and conduct have come from cosponsoring organizations from outside the prison (such as associations and educational institutions). Sometimes such collaborative relationships have been mutually beneficial, such as projects aimed at high-risk students of concern to local school systems as well as prisons. Some correctional education programs have been targeted at handicapped inmates, some of whom have been included in mandatory basic education programs that previously they would not have attended. In recent years, correctional education for female offenders has been increased so that it would be more comparable to that for male offenders. Other major issues have been improved staff development and transitional services (Duguid, 1989, 1990; Merriam and Cunningham, 1989, chap. 27; Sutton, 1992).

In general, the distribution and types of correctional education vary greatly in the United States. Most inmates in all types of correctional institutions receive no correctional education each year. This lack of provision and participation reflects a range of situational and personal influences. Major situational influences include negative attitudes toward inmates and correctional education by the general public, policy makers, and prison staff, combined with increases in prison populations that produced overcrowding and underfunding. Major personal influences included low educational levels, minority background, irregular employment history, and negative views of self and society that discourage some inmates from participation in available educational programs. Most correctional education programs for the few inmates who participate has been characterized as remedial basic and vocational education with content and methods similar to elementary and secondary education but with individualized procedures that minimize inmate interaction. The main examples in this section describe unusual efforts to relate correctional education to outside roles in work, family, and community; to improve the motivation of participants; to help prisoners apply what they learn to their later civilian life; and to reduce recidivism rates.

Correctional Education in Canada

Educational programs for Canadian inmates have also been varied across provinces and types of penal institutions. A distinctive and exemplary approach evolved in British Columbia during the 1970s and 1980s in which educational institutions conducted programs for inmates. This effort began in 1972, when the University of Victoria conducted a pilot correctional education program at the British Columbia Penitentiary and Matsqui Institution, and by 1973 the program was formalized by a contract between the university and the Canadian Penitentiary Service. More recently, Simon Fraser University began a similar prison education program through its Institute for the Humanities.

The correctional education programs in British Columbia have been distinctive in several respects. The main feature was that these university-based programs sought to create an alternative educative community within the correctional institution, quite separate from the prison system. Inmates completed courses to earn an entire B.A. degree, with objectives comparable to the on-campus degree. The goal was to increase constructive social engagement in prison and after release and to decrease recidivism. This alternative community approach contrasts with typical correctional education approaches tied to case management, financial incentives, and parole that constitute extensions of the prison system. These inmates were similar in many ways to their counterparts in the outside community except that they had been convicted of committing a crime and were enduring a restrictive prison experience. Many inmates developed feelings of rejection, suspicion, and cynicism about prison-based educational activities.

The university thus sought to create a community in the prison comparable to the experience that students might enjoy outside as responsible members of a just democratic society. In their student role, inmates explored influences on their behavior. Instructional staff composed of carefully selected, full-time faculty members from the university and part-time adjunct faculty members—who were neither part of nor aloof from the prison world—served as straight role models. The B.A. course content emphasized history and the social sciences and was used to help inmates progress in their cognitive development (problem solving, choosing, and decision making, especially related to life changes), moral development (strengthening a socially acceptable sense of morality), and development of self-esteem (many inmates felt like failures, even as criminals, by virtue of having been caught!).

Experience in this alternative educative community sharpens contrasts between the participants' student role, their role as a prisoner in an authoritarian total institution, and various roles prior to imprisonment. As students, inmates experience the democratic climate of courses and pursue action learning projects that help them internalize functioning as community members. More advanced inmates also serve as teaching assistants for credit courses and teach noncredit courses for other inmates. For the more advanced inmates able and willing to pursue a university B.A. program, the benefits from participating in this alternative educative community include a sense of responsibility that might help them to function well in the outside community after their release (Duguid, 1980, 1987, 1989, pp. 61–78; 1990).

Other noteworthy correctional education programs have occurred in other provinces for different inmate populations. From Saskatchewan came a rationale for literacy-council use of inmates as volunteer tutors in prisons. Procedures for recruiting and orienting inmate tutors and for providing them with supervision, preservice, and in-service education parallel approaches used by usual literacy councils, which also helps to develop an educative community for inmates with low levels of formal education (Duguid, 1989). Another approach to basic education in a Saskatchewan prison (begun in 1984 and evaluated in 1988) uses educational television to provide a program in the Prince Albert High-Maximum Security Unit—a unit so secure that inmates are allowed contact with neither the teacher nor each other. The program consists of broadcasts of closed-circuit videotapes into cells and one-to-one tutorials with protective glass between inmate and teacher. Participant achievement and satisfaction are high in this basic education program, which was rated highly by an evaluator and by correctional educators elsewhere; the main criticism was that such distance education use of educational technology could further compound a dehumanizing isolation unless compensatory forms of discourse and communication were provided (Duguid, 1990).

Other Countries

Worldwide, millions of people have been imprisoned under many kinds of conditions. In Europe alone, more than a third of a million are in penal institutions at any one time. The extent and type of correctional education reflect the national and prison context. However, a central issue in recent years for many correctional educators, especially those in Europe and North America, has been standards for education and treatment of prisoners. Consensus regarding this issue is evident in the report *Education in Prison,* adopted on November 13, 1989, by the Committee of Ministers of the Council of Europe. The report affirmed the fundamental right of inmates to educational opportunities (especially because a high proportion have very little successful educational experience) and emphasized that correctional education assisted both individual and society and facilitated the return of the prisoners to the community. Recommended standards included access for all prisoners to a wide range of learning opportunities to develop the whole person through library access and educational programs related to vocational, cultural, and social education to enable inmates to function in prison and after their return to the community. Standards also pertained to administrative and financial support from prison systems so that educational staff and methods were effective and prisoners were not penalized but were encouraged to participate in effective education; this would be provided in cooperation with

outside adult education providers and continued after release. Such
standards were reflected in resolutions regarding education and
treatment of prisoners adopted on December 14, 1990, by the United
Nations General Assembly. The rationale for the standards recognized widespread tensions between correctional education and security concerns of prison regimes and urged that prison education
emulate and cooperate with the best of voluntary adult education
in the outside community, while recognizing negative features of
inmates' life experience and prison conditions (Council of Europe,
1989; Sutton, 1992).

This consensus is the result of broader trends and agreement
on personal and social influences on crime, expectations regarding
imprisonment, and treatment of prisoners. Correctional educators
from various countries, especially Canada, Netherlands, and Scandinavian countries, have helped to focus attention on the complex
interplay of economic and political conditions, the legal system,
public opinion regarding punishment and rehabilitation of inmates, and management of prisons (Council of Europe, 1989;
Morin, 1981). Sutton's (1992) report on basic education in prisons
assembles information about correctional education in developing
countries that has been difficult to obtain. Low educational levels
have been characteristic of inmates in many countries.

United Kingdom

The evolving basis for and practice of correctional education can be
seen in the United Kingdom since 1948, when local education authorities assumed responsibility for provision of educational activities in prisons. Two issues persisted: the balance between punishment and rehabilitation and the question of whether freedom could
be trained for in captivity. Outside provision of educational opportunities resulted in significant increases in correctional education—
from token support prior to 1948 to recent annual expenditures of
about 2 percent of the total prison budget. This figure allowed for
four hundred full-time education staff members and about three
thousand part-time teachers, including lecturers and tutors from
universities and voluntary associations. Yet tensions between education and security persisted. The educational approach shifted

from rehabilitation within the prison context, to educational opportunities in preparation for release, to adjustments of both education and prison conditions to promote resocialization in the context of normalization in a reality prison. Availability of open university distance education courses that employed educational technology constituted a major new resource for correctional education, but actual access by inmates depended greatly on conditions in each prison. Access also reflected public and prison staff attitudes as well as inmate educational level and motivation. As in Canada and the United States, provision of correctional education by higher education institutions benefited inmates with higher levels of educational attainment more than functionally illiterate prisoners. Since 1990, there have been new initiatives by the U.K. Home Office Prisons Department, including sentence planning (Duguid, 1989, 1990; Sutton, 1992).

Republic of Ireland

Correctional education in various countries illustrates some different approaches and societal influences with implications for strategic planning. For example, prison education in Ireland has been affected by major themes in Council of Europe recommendations, especially the desirability of following adult education purposes and procedures used in the outside community. Such features include voluntary participation, individualized instruction, and attention to learner experience. This approach has entailed local flexibility to allow individual teacher initiative to include inmates in the process of making program development decisions. Also, correctional education has had substantial priority in relation to other prison activities, with most of it taking place during the normal working day and about half of the inmates voluntarily taking part in educational activities. This approach contrasts with North American trends, such as mandatory basic education and a heavy emphasis on employment training (Duguid, 1990).

Norway

Correctional education in Norway reflects the small and scattered but homogeneous population. The prisons are small—only six have more than 100 inmates, and twenty-five prisons have fewer than 40 inmates. Most inmates in local prisons serve very short sentences. Small prison size and short sentences deter provision of educational opportunities. However, during the 1970s, correctional education increased dramatically, from 20 inmates who studied full time to 280. This total in the late 1970s was about 10 percent of all inmates, and almost twice as many participated part time. A widespread characteristic of inmates was lack of education: a third had not completed compulsory schooling, many had low basic skills, and many had negative attitudes toward school and themselves as students. A goal of correctional education was to provide experience with success to encourage further education in prison and after release. Inmates did have positive attitudes toward their prison education (which contrasted with their negative attitudes toward being in prison and toward the security staff), a reaction that reflected the responsiveness of correctional education activities and staff. As conditions after release (especially unemployment and drinking) were also a problem, correctional educators explored educational and living arrangements before and after release that would improve rehabilitation, such as semiliberty before parole for work or study in special or regular adult education programs in the community and regional halfway houses to provide transitional care. Another approach was provision of library services and educational activities in the prison by educational providers from the community (Duguid, 1990).

Australia

Correctional education in Australia shares with Norway problems of distance and sparse population, which contribute to limited educational opportunities in small prisons and postrelease transitions for inmates far from home. Vocational education has been a top priority, but such programs have confronted barriers related to competition with labor unions, lack of up-to-date technology, and shifting market trends. Limitations in vocational education and restrictions on prison jobs (so that they were not in competition with union labor outside) constrained inmates' employability after release. Educational programs for inmates have been increasingly strengthened by collaboration with regional colleges of technical and further education (Duguid, 1990).

Tanzania

Vocational education is also a major emphasis for correctional education in Tanzania, within an overall national policy of education for self-reliance that stresses relevance, application, critical thinking, and cooperation. Correctional education has been similar to programs in other educational institutions and has sought to prepare people for low, medium, and high technologies and generally balanced community and national development. Prison education has included not only inmates but also prison staff members who receive continuing education in special programs in all types of educational areas, depending on the staff member's specialty. In provision of education related to both individual and societal needs, staff development has paralleled the programs provided to inmates to emphasize the supportive role of all prison staff members for achievement of correctional education objectives (Duguid, 1990; Sutton, 1992).

Strategic Planning

Improvements in correctional education directly depend on leadership by correctional educators. Without such leadership, initiatives are unlikely from any other source—not from the general public, policy makers, prison administrators, or staff from educational institutions in the outside community. Strategic planning can increase support from these sources. Such planning should address themes related to stakeholders, collaboration goals, and organizational culture.

Stakeholders

As we have seen, in spite of the increasing burden of the criminal justice and prison system spawned by societal problems (such as poverty, unemployment, substance abuse, and illiteracy) and expansion of support for correctional education in recent decades, rehabilitation of prisoners continues to receive low priority. Occupational education has generally been emphasized (as seen in examples such as Ross (Ohio), Australia, and Tanzania. However, there have also been other priorities: parenting skills in Eastern (New York) and community focus in Central (Georgia) and British Columbia. Leadership by correctional educators should address the implicit values of potential stakeholders as an essential condition of support. Standards for correctional education (such as those recommended by the Council of Europe and endorsed by the United Nations) can also contribute to the rationale used to increase stakeholder support.

In-service education for correctional educators and closely related prison staff tends to be neglected and can be best strengthened by linking it closely to educational and strategic planning activities for other stakeholders, especially inmates, prison staff, and policy makers. Such staff development is an investment that can contribute to improved performance in current roles, career enhancement, and vision regarding desirable future directions to broaden the base of leadership. This was illustrated in the Tanzania example. Sound staff development both enables and benefits from strategic planning activities (Duguid, 1990; Merriam and Cunningham, 1989; Sutton, 1992).

There are additional stakeholders whose collaboration in provision of correctional education and contribution to strategic planning are important to strengthening program resources, process, and outcomes. One category reflects public policy regarding prisons and jails and correctional education in particular. Included are federal, state, and local legislators and public administrators who recommend, approve, and implement legislation related to penal institutions. The influential role of the Canadian Penitentiary Service was shown in the British Columbia approach. It is important that such authorization, appropriations, and administrative policies reflect an understanding of the basis for investments in correctional education and of the conditions under which it is likely to provide satisfactory personal and societal benefits. Mandatory basic education in U.S. federal prisons has been such an issue. As indicated in the examples from Tanzania and Ireland, national policy support and international standards strengthen correctional education. The Australian example illustrates the lack of such support when labor unions resisted inmate preparation for jobs after release. It also helps to have general public understanding and support, which according to survey responses is stronger for basic education than for higher education opportunities. Priorities for correctional education are also based on beliefs regarding humane treatment of prisoners. In recent decades, there has been increasing collaboration in correctional education by outside organizations, especially higher education institutions but also school systems and voluntary associations. Involvement in strategic planning by stakeholders from all of these external organizations can enrich plans and strengthen cooperation in their implementation (Duguid, 1989, 1990; Merriam and Cunningham, 1989; Sutton, 1992).

Culture

The organizational culture of the parent institution in which correctional education occurs powerfully influences the contingencies that program leaders seek to address, so it deserves special attention in strategic planning. This organizational culture partly reflects inmate characteristics: type of crime committed, length of sentence, educational level, self-concept, and occupational abilities. Such characteristics contribute to the personal side of the equation that influences the motivation of inmates to participate in correctional education and their postrelease application of what they learn. Examples of organizational values include the "just society" educational program in British Columbia, educational requirements for work assignments in Ross, respect for other people's values in Central, flexibility and respect for inmate experience in Ireland, and cooperation and self-reliance in Tanzania. The other side of the equation reveals organizational characteristics: size, location, staff orientation toward purposes and procedures, and extent of overcrowding and underfunding (which can result in an institutional environment that is punishing, isolating, and desolate or one that emphasizes rehabilitation and reconciliation). Influences of organizational culture are seen in the connections made between correctional education and prison industry work at Ross, barriers to family contact at Eastern, insulation from authority at Central, and the Irish example in which individualized voluntary opportunities mainly assisted inmates with higher levels of education. Other organizational influences have to do with whether educational opportunities are available, whether participation is mandatory or voluntary, and whether instructors have the latitude to be responsive and include inmates in the decisions made about program development. The combination of these personal and situational influences affect the percentage of inmates who participate in correctional education (Duguid, 1989; Morin, 1981; Sutton, 1992). Educational technology has both advantages and disadvantages for correctional education. The benefits include individualized provision of specialized content for inmates at times and locations where their schedules and security precautions allow. This advantage was illustrated by video use in the Prince Albert maximum security prison and by open university courses in British prisons with low educational budgets. The main disadvantage is that educational technology can further isolate inmates from human interaction; it thus calls for compensatory socialization and complementary opportunities for participation in an educational community or supportive reference group (Duguid, 1990). Strategic planning that involves stakeholders from correctional education and from the prison can address issues related to both education and security, inmates and staff.

Collaboration

Educators unfamiliar with corrections may be surprised at the many similarities between correctional education and adult education in general. Situational influences that are intensified by the prison as a total institution have counterparts in the outside community that may be taken for granted and go unnoticed. In recent decades, correctional educators have been urged to emulate the best of adult education. Guidelines for adult vocational education in the larger society are echoed in efforts to increase cooperation between correctional education and prison industries and to prepare inmates to succeed in available civilian jobs after release. Collaboration was important to many of the programs described, including Eastern, British Columbia, Britain, Norway, and Australia. Critical thinking, decision making, transformative learning, and a socially acceptable sense of morality are desirable outcomes in both prison and community settings.

In addition to outside courses for inmates (that occur in some countries such as Finland, Denmark, Canada, and the United States), external organizations can cooperate with correctional education programs in various ways. Staff development activities can be strengthened for both regular staff members (Ireland, Netherlands), and peer tutors (Canada, Colombia, Mali). Materials and assistance can be provided for activities such as discussion groups, newsletters, reading clubs, and libraries (Czechoslovakia, Portugal, United Kingdom). Tests can be developed for individualized assessment (Australia, Canada, United States). Follow-up educational opportunities can be provided after release (Sutton, 1992).

Goals

Intended outcomes and program objectives provide a crucial reference point for strategic planning. Attention to postrelease activities and circumstances included not only efforts to reduce recidivism but also external conditions likely to deter rehabilitation, such as unemployment and substance abuse (Sutton, 1992). The Ross, Eastern, and Central programs that emphasized postrelease success were in contrast to the Australian example (which included little training for outside occupations) and the Norwegian example (which sought to improve attitudes, but after release very negative conditions prevailed).

Four contrasting approaches to correctional education have emerged in various times and locations. The earliest assumed that imprisonment should provide a lesson, as reflected in the names of these institutions, which were based on terms such as *repent* (penitentiary), *correct* (correctional institution), and *reform* (reformatory). A secondary approach assumed that the isolation, security, and punishment features of the prison would be the inevitable context. However, correctional education would provide educational opportunities with content and methods similar to the preparatory education that inmates missed earlier; when they were released, they could apply what they learned. This basic remedial and vocational education approach tended to be undermined by inmate cynicism and authoritarian prison regimes oriented strongly toward security and punishment. A third approach was the reality prison designed to help inmates cope constructively with the prison culture and circumstances (with educators and security staff working together) in the belief that prisoners able to do so successfully would eventually function better on the outside. The fourth was the creation by an external provider of an alternative community, designed to help inmates perform as responsible members of a just, democratic, educational community. As demonstrated in the British Columbia program, such an approach is aligned neither with the prison regime nor the inmate culture but seeks to resocialize prisoners through participation in educational decision making and enabling advanced inmates to serve as teaching assistants in credit courses and to teach noncredit courses. Strategic planning should enable correctional educators to select or develop a rationale for an approach that fits their values and circumstances and to gain understanding and support from relevant stakeholders.

The themes in several other chapters relate to correctional education. Part-time study is sometimes provided by educational institutions in correctional institutions. Basic education and literacy are major curriculum areas in correctional education because of the high proportions of illiterates. Prisons contain a disproportionate number of minority adults. Distance education use of educational technology has been very useful given the contingencies in some correctional institutions.

8

Cultural Programs

Cultural programs are aimed at both personal search for meaning and shared cultural values. A rich diversity of educational activities by adults can be subsumed within a broad rubric of cultural, general, or liberal education for adults. Such programs are nonoccupational. Most combine study, discussion, and reflection to extract insights from cultural traditions that can enrich individual consciousness. Topics from the arts and humanities tend to predominate and stress spiritual values, appreciation of esthetic and cultural traditions, respect for other people, and experiencing of a holistic sense of self in a social and physical context. Attention is given to various life roles: family member, volunteer, citizen, user of leisure, and member of a religious institution. However, the emphasis usually transcends life roles and applications, such as occupation. Unlike specialized programs described in the other chapters, all adults are potential participants in cultural adult education programs.

Scope of Cultural Education

Although the learning scope of cultural education activities and intended outcomes tend to be personal (such as heightened consciousness and sense of social mission), leadership and program advocacy in this area have been crucial because cultural adult education programs have seldom survived on the basis of cost recovery from participant fees. They have depended on champions who articulated a program vision and obtained external resources and program subsidy. Within each program area of cultural adult education, there has been attention to both self-actualization and interdependence, and content has often been drawn from ancient traditions or from new-age ideas and in some instances has blended the two.

Attention to value judgments, morals, and ethics is prevalent in cultural education programs, and the spiritual search is an avowed goal of many educational activities for adults provided by religious institutions, interfaith consortia, and small private and local organizations interested in meditation and spirituality. Another multidisciplinary program area is family-life education, including marriage enrichment, parent education, and intergenerational programs. Rationales for adult religious and family education, concentrating on personal growth and interdependence, have been enriched in recent years by feminist literature.

Another program area makes the case for cultural education and study of the liberal arts and sciences (touched on in Chapter Two on part-time study in educational institutions), including history, philosophy, the arts, languages, literature, and science as general education (Jones, 1988). This adult education is also provided by libraries, museums, arts organizations, and the media (such as public radio and television). Science education for the general public manifests itself in programs on ecology, environment, conservation, and outdoor education.

Another holistic program area with both global and local aspects is world affairs education (Styler, 1984, part 5). Other programs have focused on sensitivity training or on critical thinking. Thus, cultural education ranges from analysis of traditional texts to experiential learning from inner spiritual journeys. The focus may be on traditional content or the process of inquiry, but in the diverse program areas subsumed in cultural education, concern with personal search and value judgments is widespread. Strategic planning confronts some special challenges regarding provision of these educational opportunities for adults and attention to contextual influences that affect the personal journey. This is the special challenge for leadership in the diverse programs falling into the category of cultural education.

Several themes important for leadership and strategic planning can be identified in the following examples and rationale regarding cultural adult education. One theme is the provider agency mission, goals, and approach, which depend on both agency contingencies and cultural values. A second is participant interests, which result from trends and change. A third is government and community priority for programs that seldom succeed on a cost-recovery basis and entail some forms of subsidy. A fourth and related theme is acquisition of resources, including collaboration as a form of resource sharing.

National Issues Forum

Given the diversity of the cultural adult education programs with which it is grouped, the National Issues Forum (NIF) is quite distinctive in some respects but shares with many nonoccupational programs several characteristics, such as value issues, multiple perspectives, and personal benefits. The following example occurred during the 1980s in Grand Rapids, located in southwest Michigan. The local convener organization of the NIF program was the Grand Rapids Junior College (GRJC), in cooperation with the nearby Gerald Ford Presidential Museum and Library and other local organizations. As in other U.S. cities where NIF programs have been sponsored by organizations such as schools, universities, libraries, and organizations such as the League of Women Voters, the program was based on materials and guidelines provided nationally by the NIF with support from the Kettering Foundation and the Public Agenda Foundation. The NIF materials included issues booklets with readings for each topic, a guide for local conveners, discussion guides, and questionnaires. A version of the issues booklet was prepared with similar content but with a lower level of reading difficulty.

The nationwide NIF goal is to provide a deliberative forum for local citizens to discuss and better understand controversial issues related to topics such as taxes, social security, schools, agriculture, federal deficits, welfare, health costs, environmental protection, and crime. The main emphasis is on individual development and collective judgments. As adults discuss various facts and viewpoints, they come away with increased understanding, a way to participate in informed decisions, and a deepened sense of social values. A related goal is to convey citizens' informed conclusions to policy makers and the general public. Local conveners are able to decide how they want to use NIF materials and procedures along with their preferred program emphasis.

After the first few years, during which the Grand Rapids Junior College (GRJC) sponsored a few forums, a volunteer coordinator began a vigorous collaborative approach with other community organizations. During the third and fourth years, five or six organizations conducted about fifteen programs, which attracted about six hundred to eight hundred people. In addition to the junior college and the presidential library, the organizations included colleges, senior citizens groups, the League of Women Voters, a library, and the Urban League (an association to achieve social progress for black people). The cooperating organizations contributed volunteer time, facilities, member participation, and contact with policy makers.

Small study circles that met for three to five sessions to discuss each topic were added to the large public forum format, mass media were used to inform a larger audience about the issues, and at the end of the series a hundred people met in the Ford Library auditorium in a forum to report their conclusions. The volunteer coordinator worked with a steering committee composed of people from cooperating organizations and interested forum participants. Although the college president, other staff members, and the library director were generally supportive of the NIF program and provided in-kind free use of space and some staff support, the forums and study circles were planned and conducted quite independently under the direction of the volunteer coordinator.

Substantial resources flowed into the NIF program, but very little was in the form of money. The contribution of NIF to its local programs was mainly materials subsidized by the Kettering Foundation. Participants paid their own expenses to attend conferences and workshops for which program costs were subsidized. The $3 charge for each issue book was usually paid by learners, but increasingly the college provided books without charge. There were not any personnel costs because all staff were unpaid volunteers, and co-sponsor staff who helped with the NIF program did so as an in-kind contribution.

The president of the Kettering Foundation was committed to increasing the level of what he called "civic literacy" so that citizens would be better informed about domestic policy issues. This atti-tude had contributed to the formation of the NIF to stimulate and guide the provision of local programs. The president had earlier headed a university and had then served as a federal cabinet officer concerned with domestic issues in the Ford administration. His work influenced former presidents Ford and Carter and other prom-inent government leaders to participate in early NIF president li-brary conferences.

The Grand Rapids NIF coordinator who started after the first few years was approaching retirement as an executive in a local company. He attended the second NIF conference held at the L. B. Johnson Presidential Library in Austin, Texas, as a community representative on the GRJC steering committee for the NIF. This was a very moving experience for him. Talking with NIF staff and consultants, program coordinators from other cities, and dignitaries there to hear the report of NIF conclusions to public policy makers (such as former U.S. secretaries of state and defense) resulted in a commitment to devote some of his retirement time to NIF. The president of the college and the director of the Ford Library asked him to serve as the new NIF coordinator, and he agreed. The pro-gram expanded greatly in the subsequent few years. This commit-ment of time, talent, and a vision of what an NIF program could contribute resulted in increased program quality, while expanding the number of organizations and participants. There is some uncer-tainty about continuity when a transition is made to his successor.

The rapid expansion of NIF programs in local communities around the United States during the 1980s, including the program in Grand Rapids, reflected the initiative of the NIF, Kettering, and staff from the Public Agenda Foundation, who helped develop the NIF idea and rationale, conducted survey research on societal trends and issues, and wrote the annual issue booklets. Others who pro-vided national leadership for NIF were a consultant who had coordinated the American Issues Forum during the U.S. bicentennial celebration and the director of the Center for the Study of Citizenship at Syracuse University.

Their efforts were affected by general societal trends. Generally held beliefs during the 1950s regarding progress, science, and resources were shaken during the 1960s with the rise of pluralistic views about fundamental value choices related to foreign policy, natural resources, and alternative life-styles. By the 1970s, the world was shrinking even further, and it was becoming even more difficult to make choices about major issues: civil rights, abortion, defense policies, equal rights, and drug abuse. Some positive influences were local and specific to Grand Rapids, Michigan. Certainly the location there of the Ford Library had an impact. The lack of a major university in Grand Rapids may have made it easier for GRJC to take the lead in this project. Good working relationships between the GRJC dean and an NIF staff associated contributed to early local involvement in planning and initiation of an NIF program. The few local adult education programs on public responsibility meant that local people with such interests had few alternatives available. In recent decades, a growing reliance on cost-recovery financing of continuing education programs based on participant fees has increased the proportion of work-related programs and decreased the proportion of nonoccupational programs that typically require subsidy.

There were also some negative influences. In an age when citizens are urged to "think globally and act locally" national policy issues tend to seem remote to many adults, who may feel uncertain what to do differently after they increased their awareness and understanding of social issues. This is particularly the case for many citizens who lack confidence that they could influence public policies. Other efforts to involve local citizens in discussions of important public issues have waxed and waned. Examples have included the adult education for public responsibility programs of the Fund for Adult Education in the 1950s and early 1960s, the Great Books Program, and the Foreign Policy Association's Great Decisions discussion groups and forums. The same types of adults tend to participate in all of these programs—people with relatively high levels of formal education and social concern. Citizens with a sense of political efficacy and connection with the power structure seem to enjoy discussing policy issues. Although some working-class and minority adults participated in NIF programs connected with prisons and literacy programs, many people who felt powerless and estranged tended to want a more action orientation. Even a snow storm can be an influence, such as one that cancelled an NIF forum in Grand Rapids (Resource A, Knox (f)).

Other U.S. Programs

The National Issues Forum is but one type of cultural education program. Although it shared with most other types of cultural adult education an emphasis on holistic personal development, multidisciplinary content, limited financial support, and reliance on volunteer leadership, it was unusual in that it had a Kettering Foundation subsidy. The following overview indicates the variety of other types of cultural adult education programs and suggests challenges for strategic planning of such nonoccupational programs for which it is assumed that the benefits are mainly personal. Programs concentrate on religious and spiritual issues, marriage and family, women's concerns, the library and the museum, the arts, mass media, public issues, and human relations.

Religion

A range of organizations have provided adult education activities related to religious faith, spiritual experience, and moral development. The specific program purposes and activities are very diverse; they may be intended to help people understand and practice their religious traditions, to facilitate dialogue with other members of a faith community, to promote their moral development, and to encourage translation of personal convictions into their choices in daily life. In-service education is important for the clergy and lay leaders who plan and conduct adult religious education because of the twin challenges they confront as they guide members on their faith journey. One challenge focuses on the members' dialogue and active search for meaning from the precepts and examples of their religious tradition reflected in most of the adult religious education materials. The second challenge has to do with empowerment of members to live their faith in the complex realities they confront. Local congregations vary greatly in the percentage of members who participate in adult religious education in the course of a year. In some communities, voluntary associations and consortia of religious institutions conduct interfaith educational programs. In addition, in many communities, various organizations and associations sponsor educational activities on spirituality and meditation based on Eastern and Western traditions to enable adults to pursue the inner journey toward lower stress and higher consciousness (Elias, 1986; Goldman, 1975; Harman, 1988; Merriam and Cunningham, 1989, chap. 30; Simmons, 1988; Stokes, 1983; Vogel, 1991).

Family

With their historic emphasis on strengthening families, it is understandable that religious institutions have provided family-life education programs, as have the Cooperative Extension Service (CES), public schools, the YMCA-YWCA, social agencies, and voluntary associations. For example, religious institutions provide marriage enrichment programs to help couples with good marriages improve mutual understanding, communication, and cooperation. CES family-life education programs have been varied; they have concentrated on parenting, nutrition, and (recently) youth at risk. The other providers have offered adult education opportunities on parenting, family planning, and issues such as hunger and homelessness. Some programs have been intergenerational for children, parents, and sometimes grandparents (Harman and Brim, 1980). Many of the most effective family-life education programs have focused on selected aspects but have done so within a holistic context of the entire family unit functioning within a broader societal setting. They have also analyzed trends and issues from a multidisciplinary perspective.

Women

Several features of adult education programs designed especially for women help illuminate dynamics related to general education, in part because women are now predominant in most types of general education programs. When social trends between World War II and the early 1960s are compared with those of the subsequent three decades that gave rise to the women's movement, dramatic shifts in women's roles, consciousness, and adult education participation become clear. Interrelated aspects of social change have included urbanization and mobility, family planning and reduced numbers of children in middle-class families, increased divorce, and greater proportions of women working outside the home. Some of these women are heads of households and displaced homemakers, and their growing numbers, especially of minority women, are reflected in the rising percentage of families headed by women that are living in poverty. The growth of higher education women's studies programs and special continuing education for women have added to a growing knowledge base regarding relevant issues from diverse disciplines such as religion, history, philosophy, literature, psychology, sociology, nutrition, and health. Women's changing roles in family, work, community, and education have affected relationships between men and women and resulted in declining sex-role stereotypes and increasingly androgynous characteristics shared by men and women. In contrast with the equal proportions of adult men and women who participated in all types of educational programs in the early 1960s (Johnstone and Rivera, 1965) and the preponderance of male participants earlier, women have predominated during the past three decades (as reflected in the statistics on part-time study by returning students in higher education). The interest of women in consciousness raising and empowerment has been accompanied by increased attention to their ways of knowing—broadened emphasis on social, emotional, intuitive, spiritual, and holistic insights relevant to general education (Belenky, Clinchy, Goldberger, and Tarule, 1986; Lewis, 1988; Merriam and Cunningham, 1989, chap. 42).

Library

In the past, adult services in support of self-directed study for cultural education purposes have been an important function of public libraries; these activities have included readers' advisories and book-based discussion groups. Unfortunately, these services have declined, and there has been general retrenchment in library financial support in recent decades. During the 1960s and 1970s, however, many public libraries expanded outreach efforts to go beyond their traditional middle-class patrons and serve less-advantaged adults to a greater extent. During the 1980s, federal funds assisted some libraries to expand literacy-related services for adult new readers. W. K. Kellogg Foundation funds helped some libraries develop community-based learning and information centers located in public libraries. Along with access to library collections of books, periodicals, and media, such services enabled interested adults to continue their general education by selecting materials from various sources to pursue their personal interests. These efforts reflected initiatives of local staff and volunteers because a widespread, persistent issue has been the acquisition of sufficient resources and commitment to extend beyond service to traditional library patrons through special outreach programs (Heim and Wallace, 1990; Merriam and Cunningham, 1989, chap. 28).

Museum

Nearly five thousand museums in the United States contain collections and exhibits that constitute a rich resource for cultural adult education. These art, history, and science museums differ greatly in size, purpose, and collection; the adult learners who visit vary in sophistication: and their learning activities range from casual to sustained. Electronic technology such as audio tours, computer simulations, and videotapes have been used increasingly to augment collection-based experiential learning and discovery in museum education activities for adults that include tours, lectures, study groups, and in-depth courses on site and in the field. Distinctive examples include visiting reconstructed historic communities, engaging in discovery as part of a scientific expedition, and participating in art courses. In addition to appreciation, such in-depth and sustained learning activities help participants understand their own creativity and that of the artists, historians, and scientists who made the collections possible. Museum educators have given increasing attention to responsiveness to special populations like cultural minorities and intergenerational family groups (Collins, 1981; Commission on Museums for a New Century, 1984; Merriam and Cunningham, 1989, chap. 28).

Arts

In addition to art museums, adult education in the arts has been furnished by all types of educational institutions and by associations and organizations associated with art, writing, music, and the other arts (such as dance, theater, and film). Distinctive programs combine study and discussion with firsthand experience in performances or studio and architectural tours so that artists and their works can speak for themselves (Jones, 1988).

Media

Arts and cultural programming by the mass media, such as on public radio and television, has increased access and appreciation for a large audience. In addition to performing arts, public television has broadcast outstanding science education programs for the public. Broadcasting has provided a resource for increased understanding of various public issues, including history in the making, world affairs, and environmental issues. Some of these programs have been used either live or on tape by educational institutions and other adult education providers, thus enabling adults to discuss and analyze the trends, issues, and implications. Some associations, such as the Foreign Policy Association, the League of Women Voters, and the National Issues Forum described earlier, have used such combinations of media and discussion to increase the local relevance of sometimes remote issues. Telephone call-in programs and teleconferencing have been used to increase interaction (Chamberlain, 1980; Gueulette, 1982; Merriam and Cunningham, 1989, chap. 34).

Human Relations

Many cultural adult education programs have given attention to human relations as process and outcomes. In addition to guidelines for improving discussion leadership and participation, some pro-

grams have focused on experiential learning and applied group
dynamics laboratories for sensitivity training (Benne and others,
1975; Bradford, 1974). The intended outcomes of some adult education programs have been improved human relations in the participants' various life roles through participation in educational
activities that vary greatly in their relative emphasis on knowledge,
attitudes, and skills. It has been anticipated that personal change
would lead to social change.

Ways of Knowing

The foregoing examples of cultural adult education programs in
the United States suggest the following implications for strategic
planning. There are many ways of knowing (Belenky, Clinchy,
Goldberger, and Tarule, 1986). Occupational and other adult education programs to achieve instrumental outcomes typically emphasize empirically tested, organized knowledge. By contrast,
additional ways of knowing can be achieved by various cultural
adult programs such as women's studies and adult education in the
arts, human relations, religion, and spirituality. Although adult
education often has both personal and societal benefits, cultural
adult education emphasizes transcendent values that enrich personal search for meaning. This connection between the global and
local can be seen in programs on public issues and the arts, combining mass media and small-group discussion, family-life education, and educational programs by libraries, museums, and
religious institutions. Although benefits and outcomes are important in all adult education, cultural programs stress mastery of multidisciplinary content to appreciate the active process of creative and
spiritual search for meaning. This emphasis on transcendent value
issues and choices occurs especially in programs such as spirituality, human relations, women's studies, arts, and public issues.

Because cultural adult education programs generally lack
participant reimbursement by enterprises related to occupational
and economic advancement, subsidy for educational technology,
materials development, and staff support are usually required in the
form of volunteer assistance, foundation grants, and collaboration.
Attention to program support was evident in the interfaith, family-

life, arts, public issues, museum, library, and mass media programs discussed. Strategic planning for general adult education should encourage creative search for meaning through use of various ways of knowing, exploration of transcendent values, and connections between global and local concerns and program support.

Soviet Adult Education

This section provides an overview of educational programs for adults as they functioned during the 1980s in the former Union of Soviet Socialist Republics before it was superseded in late 1991 by the Commonwealth of Independent States. The section begins with a major example of cultural adult education that was briefly discussed in Chapter One; Znanie was an all-union society devoted to popular adult education in science, the arts, and public issues. Znanie also provided work-related adult education for people in scientific occupations and agriculture, but the focus of this case example is on cultural adult education. The section then briefly reviews other types of adult education in the former Soviet Union during the 1980s and concludes with some comments on implications for strategic planning of adult education in the new commonwealth during the early 1990s.

Znanie offered one of the largest adult education programs in the former Soviet Union. During the 1980s, Znanie was a voluntary society with a membership of more than three million scientists, engineers, higher education faculty members, school teachers, and experts from various scientific and cultural fields (artists, musicians, writers, and film makers). Each year, nearly 400,000 scientists and other experts taught in the people's universities, many on a volunteer basis. Znanie had general responsibility for people's universities but also worked through other organizations—museums, libraries, planetariums, mass media, and its own publishing house. Its educational programs for adults were provided in the various republics and provinces of the Soviet Union. The organization's creation in 1947 consolidated previous popular science education programs. The Communist party and government had great influence on program emphasis, especially political education.

The most recent constitution of the former Soviet Union

gave public organizations a wider scope for displaying initiative in tackling tasks related to the development of the individual and promotion of the people's educational and cultural standards as specified by the Communist party. On June 19, 1972, the Znanie Society was awarded the Order of Lenin by the presidium of the USSR Supreme Soviet in appreciation of its dedicated work in disseminating political and scientific knowledge and "educating" the people in a communist spirit.

The Znanie Society was a powerful mass organization. The congress of the society, which was convened every five years, was its supreme body. During periods between the congresses, the society was governed by its board, which elected a presidium. The presidium of the board appointed an executive bureau to organize educational activities and work with councils composed of leading scientists, lecturers, and methods experts. The people's universities had local public councils, and these local councils were governed by a central council. Znanie provided training for its lecturers in nearly 100,000 seminars each year. Most of the people who conducted programs were volunteers, but some received small honoraria or incentives. Znanie was especially interested in lecture goers who wanted help in satisfying their personal needs, such as broadening their horizons, solving everyday life problems, and educating their children. Millions of adults attended lectures and courses, and tens of millions obtained publications each year. Their participation in general education activities was encouraged by their personal values, solidarity with associates, and anticipated benefits.

Participants paid very small fees (which recovered about 10 percent of direct costs), and their enterprises and organizations paid directly most of the remainder of direct costs. The main income and expenditures were related to lecture series, and the second largest budget category was for publishing.

There were several positive influences on Znanie's progress. Znanie's international ties were wide and varied. It closely cooperated with the societies for propagating scientific knowledge in the socialist states and maintained useful contacts with scientific and educational organizations in a number of countries. The Znanie Publishing House and the editorial boards of the society's five journals also maintained business relations with their counterparts abroad. Every year, hundreds of Znanie lecturers traveled abroad, and the society played host to visitors from other countries. Such international contacts promoted mutual exchange of information about economic, scientific, technical, and cultural progress and about methods of disseminating knowledge.

The ninth congress of Znanie occurred in 1987. Responding to the transition then occurring in the nation, the congress confronted fundamental rethinking of approaches to activities of the society. The congress stated that Znanie should be striving to assist in the carrying out of a course of action to accelerate the socioeconomic development of the country, the revolutionary reconstruction (*perestroika*) of all spheres of life in Soviet society, and the affirmation of an atmosphere of openness (*glasnost*). Measures were taken so that the work of organizations of the society would correspond to specific features of the current stage of social development and to the inquiries and interests of the Soviet people.

Yet several influences made it difficult for Znanie to be effective. The offerings of the society were not fully utilized. Some lecturers failed to satisfy the listeners because they lagged substantially behind the level of contemporary knowledge achieved in practice (Resource A, Fishevski).

The remainder of this section provides a brief overview of the majority of Znanie activities that were for occupational and economic purposes and of the many other providers and programs of general and occupational adult education. Because this overview provides background information for examples of Soviet adult education in other chapters, it covers both general and occupational programs. Although the foregoing Znanie case example focused on cultural education, actually the majority of the offerings were work related, especially regarding science, engineering, and agriculture. During the 1980s, in addition to Znanie, there were many other providers of various types of adult education.

Contemporary Russian adult education partly reflects programs and societal influences both since the October 1917 revolution and before. During the eighteenth and nineteenth centuries, adult education consisted mainly of cultural education by the Russian orthodox church and vocational education by the government. As the twentieth century approached, less than one-fifth of the adult population was even literate. Beginning in the 1890s, V. I. Lenin and his wife N. K. Krupskaya were active in study circles related to the workers' movement. After the 1917 revolution, Lenin issued a decree (in 1919) on eliminating illiteracy for all people between the ages of eight and fifty. Because of his commitment to strengthening the link between labor and education, a new system of adult education was initiated that encompassed workers' universities, political education schools, adult basic education programs, libraries, museums, and cultural centers.

Following World War II, illiteracy had been largely eliminated, and the two main program areas of general and vocational education were furnished by two types of providers: educational institutions and a parallel out-of-school system (such as Znanie and people's universities). A major emphasis was on provision of universal opportunities for secondary education, especially for young workers. For both secondary and postsecondary education, most educational institutions (in addition to full-time studies for young people) offered evening and correspondence courses (that allowed adults to study without leaving their jobs), and enterprises allowed paid leaves for preparation to take major examinations. The Soviet government relied on adult education to advance its ideological, economic, and social goals—such as to promote national identity, to minimize the influence of religion, to improve the status of women, to increase economic productivity, and to enrich cultural activities and use of leisure time.

Communist party policies, government regulations, and financial support shaped most of adult education offerings. Occupational adult education was provided by enterprises, labor unions, and educational institutions. In the early 1980s, 47,000 people's universities enrolled about thirteen million people annually in programs similar to noncredit public community college offerings in the United States. They had no entrance requirements or completion exams that restricted access to educational counseling and occupational and general education courses, but some participants used such activities to prepare for exams related to other educational institutions (which if they passed gave them higher occupational status). The military made available extensive training to its personnel (Allison, 1987; Segal, 1988). General education activities were provided by many organizations: libraries, museums, theaters, and cultural centers. After decades of neglect, there has been growing emphasis since the 1960s on adult education research and formal preparation of adult education staff and volunteers (Lee, 1986; Onushkin and Tonkonogaya, 1984; Vladislavlev, 1979, 1980).

During the 1980s, Soviet adult education reflected many influences, including topography, climate, centralized government, ethnic and national diversity, policy support, an unsatisfactory economy, less than 30 percent of the population concerned with organized religion, growing domestic dissatisfaction, and a political transformation in many respects more major than the 1917 revolution (Charters and Associates, 1981, chap. 3; Wells and Goetz, 1987). Especially during the later 1980s, poor economic conditions reached crisis proportions, reflected in declines in gross national product, agricultural output, trade with the West, and trade with socialist-bloc countries (related to greater independence in Eastern Europe) and increases in the budget deficit, national debt, inflation, poverty (especially in the central Asian republics), and crime rates (related to shortages, declining living standards, and alienation of the young). The political reconstruction and increased openness were related to economic conditions, to growing dissatisfaction with centralized planning and control, and especially to long-standing nationalistic ethnic tensions within and among republics. A result in late 1991 was the dissolution of the Soviet Union and the emergence of a Commonwealth of Independent States composed of most of the former republics. Before its dissolution, the area of the Soviet Union was twice that of the United States (the Russian Republic has three-quarters of the area of the Soviet Union) but only 17 percent more population; much of the northern and eastern regions were sparsely populated. Although Russian was the official language, the nation contained more than 170 ethnic groups speaking more than 130 languages, and the constitution provided for education in one's native language. Adult education reflected these geographic conditions and the pluralism that resulted, by both accommodating local conditions and promoting all-union solidarity.

By the early 1990s, the sweeping economic, social, and political changes were affecting adult education in many ways. Programs were influenced by declining resources due to inflation and

loss of subsidy, diversion of attention to other priorities, focusing of
some adult education activities on urgent aspects of the transformation, and international assistance. For example, adult education providers in the United States and other Western countries collaborated
with counterparts in the Russian Republic and other republics in the
commonwealth and with some of the newly independent Central
and Eastern European countries to adapt instructional materials;
these were related to engineering and management for use in continuing education activities to help guide the development of free
market economies and increase modernization and productivity of
industry. Znanie continued to evolve as a vehicle for adult education
to help people cope with the massive changes they confronted. As
a result of recent developments, concepts and procedures for U.S.
programs may have increasing relevance as decentralization and
democratization occur in the new commonwealth, in Central and
Eastern Europe, and in other parts of the world.

Other Countries

This section provides an overview of cultural adult education programs during the 1980s indicating distinctive program features
and societal influences in countries in various parts of the world.
The examples are taken from Czechoslovakia, Sweden, Australia,
Germany, Italy, Ireland, United Kingdom, Canada, and Japan.
This overview suggests some additional implications for strategic
planning.

Czechoslovakia

In Czechoslovakia, the House of Culture (especially in smaller communities) has been the main provider of cultural adult education
similar in many respects to comparable institutions in socialist
countries in Eastern Europe, the former Soviet Union, and some
Asian countries (Skalka and Livecka, 1977). The following example
of a House of Culture occurred in a town of eight thousand inhabitants in the central Bohemia district of Czechoslovakia during the
mid 1980s, before the country became independent of the Soviet

Union and more open to the West. The House of Culture was financed and controlled by the government, as were the library and the socialist academy, which also provided general adult education activities. Adult education and cultural activities were also offered by voluntary associations and hobby clubs and by local organizations that provided musical and recreational activities.

The agency staff consisted of a former librarian who served as director, nine other full-time employees on her staff, and between five and ten part-time lecturers at any one time for specific courses. They tended to be dedicated, because they worked there despite low salaries. As a member of the town council, the director coordinated program offerings for the town and surrounding villages and dealt with the ministry of culture, tasks that entailed much bureaucratic paperwork. The agency was fully financed by a state budget, which the director had to follow, and public lectures were free; but there were low fees for courses, study tours recovered half the costs, and concerts yielded a surplus that was half as much as the government subsidy (though this surplus had to be returned to the government). During the winter and spring of 1988, the educational activities consisted of lectures on health and family life; courses on languages, photography, drama, and typewriting; and study tours, concerts, art exhibits, film forums, and performing arts activities.

Program success depended greatly on the part-time staff and volunteers who did the teaching. These individuals relied almost entirely on lectures, and (as is the case for many providers in the United States and other countries) no staff development was furnished to help them use more active learning opportunities. In less than a year, aggregate attendance totaled more than nine thousand, but some people participated in several activities. About one-third of local inhabitants attended some House of Culture activity annually, but they were mostly brief performances. Only 5 percent of local adults attended lectures, and only 1 percent attended longer courses; moreover, the House of Culture was the only provider of adult education programs in this course format. Recommendations to improve general adult education programs included decentralization of decision making, provision of furniture appropriate for adults, a revolving fund to allow expenses to fluctuate with income, and assistance and financial incentives to encourage instructors to use more active methods of teaching and learning (Resource A, Hartl).

An update from a revisit to this small community by the case author in 1992 reveals the political, economic, and social changes that have occurred there in recent years. The most evident one has been the opening of many new stores for consumer goods and services, although 80 percent of enterprises remain government-owned, awaiting privatization. Adult education and cultural institutions have changed more slowly. The library and House of Culture (renamed the Culture Center) remain the only government-supported adult education institutions in town. Although no private adult education institutions have been created (as occurred in Prague and in other large cities), small organizations have begun conducting their own programs for which there was a market. Hobby clubs arrange programs for their members, travel agencies conduct tours, and private organizations organize concerts. The Culture Center staff has been reduced to three, language teachers work longer hours with more students, participant fees and staff salaries remain low, and the local government has continued to provide some financial support. International exchange of art exhibits has increased. With the loss of many programs and staff members, the center has begun renting space to outside groups, the income from which has become the main source of subsidy and enabled the center staff to improve the heating system, open a bistro, build a local radio station and recording studio, and plan new programs. The recent separation of Slovakia and the Czech lands will be a further influence.

Sweden

Study circles have been the most widespread and well-known format among the many cultural adult education opportunities in Sweden. During the 1980s, about one million persons (not quite two-thirds women) participated in a total of more than 300,000 study circles annually, out of an adult population of barely six million. Almost all study circles are coordinated by about ten educational associations, some of which conduct other types of general adult education programs. These provider associations have been in existence for fifty years or more in conjunction with the temperance movement, religious denominations, political parties, and labor unions. Content emphasis of local lay-led study circles has changed over the years but includes school subjects, languages, history, literature, arts, and public issues. Guidelines emphasize democracy, liberation, cooperation, printed study materials, societal benefits, and learner participation in setting up lectures and planning activities. Building on U.S. and European antecedents before the turn of the century, study circles have been refined and expanded by Sweden more than any other country. Government support has increased over the years because of strong commitment to this form of general adult education as a part of national policy to increase equity and access to such opportunities regardless of place of residence, age, and level of formal education. This policy has been achieved using independent associations as social movements with decentralized program responsibility to serve many and varied learners, about 90 percent government subsidy, and guidelines that allow the associations great latitude for responsive programming. This combination of strong governmental policy and financial support, decentralized initiatives by the independent associations and local organizers, and cohesive national traditions and values has contributed to distinctive and successful programs (Blid, 1989; Oliver, 1987; Sundqvist, 1983–84).

Australia

Study discussion groups have occurred in other countries, including Australia, but have not been so dominant a form. The following four brief examples of cultural adult education in Australia include study discussion, experiential education, and networking. For four decades, the discussion program department of the Council of Adult Education (CAE) for the state of Victoria, based in Melbourne, has supported a home-based general adult education program in the state, which in recent years has annually served almost eight thousand participants in more than seven hundred study discussion groups. In 1987, the program had 1,200 titles from which each group could select for their monthly discussion topic. The content included social issues, international affairs, literature, biography, travel, religion, film, art, and music. Each month, a group receives a box through the mail that contains fifteen books, fifteen study guides, and supplementary materials. Program leadership is provided by volunteer local organizers and discussion leaders and by CAE staff in Melbourne. With very few resources, the staff receive and replenish and mail these book boxes to groups, upgrade materials, use technology for distance education and processing materials, and encourage interchange among local groups. Low participant fees encourage participation but restrict CAE staff support. Shipping costs are one-third of fee income. Some government technical and further education (TAFE) funds subsidize CAE staff in the department. Initiating, planning, and sustaining this program reflects CAE leadership, but societal influences also affect it. Distance education learners tend to be invisible to the parent organization and to the government. Over the decades, more adult education by other providers has become available locally. About 95 percent of the participants have been women who because of remote location, limited finances, young children, or old age appreciate the program content and arrangements. Employed women are typically served by other programs (Resource A, Dow).

Another Australian example is the Women's Access Program (WAP). This consists of short courses held in several population centers to serve women in the largely rural area (a fifty-kilometer radius around Albury on the border of the state of Victoria and New South Wales in southeast Australia). In contrast to the preceding statewide distance education program, which has gradually come to be dominated by women, WAP was created in about 1983 to provide outreach study groups for women only: full-time homemakers and women working part time who were little involved in TAFE education programs. This program of the local Continuing Education Center (CEC) focuses on consciousness raising and increased access to education for women with the greatest educational need through multidisciplinary courses. Participation has been encouraged by anticipated benefits and low fees (the staff preferred no participant fees), but this approach has restricted funds for materials and staff salaries. Child care and transportation assistance are provided. The women's movement and changing roles of women affect TAFE priority and appropriations for women's programs, CEC initiatives, and women's receptivity to adult education about women's issues. The CEC planning approach emphasizes various ways of knowing, cooperation, and decentralization. A restricted budget and low honoraria make it difficult to attract staff (Resource A, LaNauze).

A third example of cultural adult education is marriage enrichment workshops, patterned on similar programs begun in other countries during the 1960s. These were introduced in Australia in 1978 and expanded (especially in eastern Australia) nationally to the extent that the first marriage enrichment conference was held in Sydney in 1987. The association that has supported programs and provided leadership preparation for the couples who conduct local workshops is Couples of Marriage Enrichment Australia (CMEA), based in the state of Queensland in northeast Australia. CMEA has benefited from growing interest in family-life education, the impetus from experience in other countries, and a positive image of marriage enrichment. Collaboration has mainly come from religious institutions and community groups with a commitment to improving family life. The workshops have three formats: a full residential retreat from Friday evening through Sunday afternoon (which is most desirable and effective, but most expensive), miniretreats from Friday evening through Saturday (which are less expensive because couples sleep at their own homes Friday night and bring their Saturday lunch), and growth groups that meet for twelve two-hour weekly sessions. The purposes and reported benefits of marriage enrichment (ME) workshops have been to enable couples to make good marriages better by recognizing the importance of working on their marriage, improving communication, seeing differences as means for growth, and dealing positively with conflict. CMEA has provided leadership development for couples who complete ME workshops and then serve as volunteer group organizers and leaders (many of whom are people from the helping professions and their spouse). Low fees and costs have encouraged participation but restrict funds for publicity and assistance. Also, many couples are reluctant to spend money and time on private concerns about marriage. Societal influences on participation include trends that affect families (urbanization, mobility, two careers, women's movement), increasing attention to interpersonal relations (such as for men and for management roles), optimism that conflict can lead to growth, belief in potential program benefits based on positive comments by past participants, and recognition of the multiplier effect of benefits for other family members (Resource A, Kerr).

The fourth Australian example is the collaborative approach of a community information center of Carringbush Library, in Richmond, Victoria. The library collaborates with adult education providers related to other organizations and educational institutions in the region, which contributes to a positive image and visibility and encourages participation. Social and technological change was reflected in trends and issues. These stimulated information seeking, affected the flow into the community of immigrants who wanted assistance, and heightened interest and the sense of anticipated benefits by local residents. The library administrator assists those involved in gaining a vision of the library as a community information center, obtaining government appropriations and grants to finance adult education and outreach activities, and using technology, staff, and volunteers. Contributors to strategic planning include the reference and local history librarian, community arts officer, adult literacy coordinator, town planner, town clerk, recreation officer, and people from many groups: library users, adult activity participants, and people interested in local history. Impending state reductions in appropriations for libraries were a potential negative influence (Resource A, Letcher).

These are but a few examples from the many cultural adult education programs in Australia over the years. Providers throughout Australia include community adult education centers, neighborhood houses, the Workers' Education Association, and evening colleges. The University of Sydney has provided study group opportunities for more than fifty years (Davis, 1980; Tennant, 1991).

Germany

The following brief discussion of four cultural adult education programs in Germany illustrate some additional program features and societal influences that have implications for strategic planning. An example of a folk school (VHS) during the late 1980s was the municipal Adult Education Center (AEC), which began in 1947 in Herrenberg in the state of Baden-Württemberg and served a suburban area of about sixty thousand people near Stuttgart. Within the federal system, education legislation and appropriations were at the state (not national) level. AEC income sources were approximately 11 percent from the state, 12 percent from the district, 34 percent from the city, and 41 percent from participant fees. Aside from about half that was work related, the main content areas for AEC general adult education courses and seminars (for leisure study and discussion of issues) were political science, history, law, education, philosophy, psychology, fine arts, crafts, music, literature, geography, natural science, language, homemaking, health, study tours, senior citizens, and a program for people from other countries (including guest workers and refugees). Planning is by the full-time staff and an advisory committee composed of members of the city council and administration and representatives of religious, educational, and cultural institutions. Instructors (many recruited from among the large numbers of unemployed teachers) also contribute to planning. Instruction tends to be learner centered, uses educational technology, but lacks a learning center for individualized study. Staff development is provided. Increasing demand resulted in an annual growth rate of about 12 percent. Influences include strong interest in social and political issues, increasing free time, a favorable program image, growing interest in foreign languages, increasing government subsidy, and staff commitment to balanced offerings that include general education (Resource A, Werner).

The second German example is the State Center for Political Education. This organization serves the entire state of Baden-Württemberg and was created in 1972 to consolidate the work of several organizations formed after 1945 to promote democratic recovery and encourage pluralism. All funds are from the state government, and programs are free to participants. Half of the programs are cosponsored by organizations such as religious institutions and local adult education centers. Policy is set by center trustees, and consultants supplemented staff for planning and conducting specific programs. Participants include individuals and groups, and efforts to reach adults who are the least active politically sometimes results in two-day programs that are held in town marketplaces. Statewide, about eight hundred events are held annually for a total of about 36,000 people (Resource A, Schiele). Center-related programs constitute one of the few concerted political education efforts by a liberal democratic government (Styler, 1984, part 5).

A third German example of cultural adult education is a unique Women's Museum in Wiesbaden, Hessen, begun in 1984 and sponsored by the feminist Women's Workshop Center for Communication and Education. Planning and implementation is the responsibility of the museum staff, composed of three full-time and one part-time staff members and fourteen volunteers. The exhibits and museum education activities are aimed at general education; understanding and valuing women's contributions; and helping women learn about their own being in the world. Evolving and interactive exhibits encourage visiting women to change and add items that help them understand their and other women's lives. Thus, women themselves are the starting point of collections of the legacies of their lives and objects of their daily experience (household items, photographs, decorations, art works, writings, and documents). Annual activities include about five exhibitions, nine seminars, and one hundred group gallery tours for a total of about twelve thousand visitors. Women find out about activities from semiannual announcements of coming programs, along with press coverage, posters, and flyers for individual activities. Financial support is from state and city funds, contributions, and entrance and participant fees. A major influence has been consciousness raising from the international women's movement since the 1960s (Resource A, Engels and Klein).

The fourth German example is adult religious education provided by the Catholic Educational Organization (CEO), founded in 1972 in the predominantly rural region of Rottweil, about one hundred kilometers southwest of Stuttgart. The fundamental program purpose is to enable interested adults to use many ways of knowing to explore and reflect on important questions and issues related to various areas of life. Content areas include public issues (such as schools or politics), religious questions, personal topics (such as family life, health), and creativity and the arts. The CEO offers some cultural adult education programs directly, assists about fifty Catholic church congregations in the region to strengthen their educational activities, and serves as liaison for cooperation with other adult education providers in the region: the Lutheran Church, the Folk School Adult Education Center, the Historical Society, and the Health Office. Planning is provided by a general assembly from congregations and related organizations that meets occasionally to set broad policies and select an executive committee for three-year terms; the committee works with the two paid CEO administrators who work with local paid and volunteer instructors and community leaders. Each congregation also has an adult education planning committee. Staff development for instructors and volunteers is an important but difficult staff role. Sources of funds for the CEO budget include participant fees, the Catholic diocese, and state and local government (Resource A, Muller).

Italy

An Italian program shows how a library can extend cultural education opportunities to underserved and largely blue collar adults. Beginning in 1984, faculty members and students from the Department of Adult Education at the University of Florence have worked with the region of Tuscany (which during the previous fifteen years had started 287 public libraries) and the nearby community of Castelfiorentino (which was interested in broadening its library patrons to include more underserved adults). In response to an inquiry from these two levels of government, the university helped them engage in strategic planning. This included identification of a wide range of voluntary associations and segments of the library service area and cooperation with a cross section of people in planning activities to broaden the diversity of patrons. As a result, the librarian trains people from each association to conduct guided library tours for their members, arranges for free television broadcast time for associations, trains volunteers to respond to afternoon telephone calls regarding health and welfare services, arranges for outreach reference and readers' advisory services, organizes a reading and discussion group for homemakers, publishes a calendar of community events, and publishes a quarterly publication written by local residents and provides journalism courses to help them to do so. In these ways, the library and university collaboration enables blue collar adults who have not used library services to enhance their cultural education as a means to empowerment and enriched quality of life (Resource A, Federighi).

Republic of Ireland

Preservation of a traditional language can serve cultural education purposes. An example from the Department of Education of the National Broadcasting Service (RTE) in Ireland demonstrates the valuable contribution mass media can make and the importance of cooperation from other adult education providers. During the early 1980s, RTE initiated a series entitled *Now and Then* to promote at least occasional use of the Irish language (Gaelic) throughout the country. Two major program objectives were to demonstrate how easy it was to speak and understand Gaelic (because English had become the predominant language especially in urban areas) and to encourage use of accessible audiotapes and easy-to-read publications to reinforce learning for television viewers and radio listeners. Basic principles and various uses of spoken Gaelic were illustrated by well-known personalities using contemporary life situations. Active participation by viewers was encouraged by distance learning methods like radio and television broadcasts, telephone call-in programs, course readings and tapes, community learning groups and tutorials, and feedback. There was no fee or formal registration for the broadcast series, although books and audiotapes were sold; RTE paid most of the broadcast expenses. Interested community groups were able to arrange for tutors and meeting places for group discussion. A follow-up evaluation reported that many adults participated and improved their ability to understand and speak Gaelic. They requested greater creativity in television broadcasts, match between broadcasts and resource materials, and opportunities for feedback to RTE. The series ceased after a few years. It was recommended that in addition to greater broadcaster support and subsidy, collaboration by other providers was essential for learner assistance and support services (Resource A, MacMahon).

The foregoing examples from Czechoslovakia, Sweden, Germany, Italy, and Ireland reflect a historic European tradition of adult education for life that now not only *includes* cultural adult education but in the past was *mainly* nonoccupational adult education. Landmark programs included the Danish folk schools, people and culture offerings in France, and the Workers' Education Association in Britain. This tradition of liberal adult education provided much of the rationale for general adult education today (Charters and Hilton, 1989, chaps. 3, 5, and 8; Kairamo, 1989).

United Kingdom

In Britain especially, rising national concern about economic productivity during the 1980s greatly shifted priorities away from cultural adult education and toward adult education for specialized vocational competence (similar shifts began during the early 1990s in Sweden). Declining government priority and support for cultural adult education have been especially challenging to programs related to cultural development through the arts, including visual arts, writing, music, and community theater. These can be especially valuable vehicles for understanding fundamental themes of human existence in various subcultures and parts of the world. Recommendations for strengthening adult education for cultural development (particularly the arts) to enrich perception include attention to various providers and responsiveness to subcultural interests in contrast with an elitist focus on unicultural approaches from the past. The 1975 Alexander report on adult education in Scotland emphasized individuality, resource use, a pluralist society, and education for change. In spite of negligible improvements in policy and financial support, local adult education providers have managed to increase responsiveness to less advantaged adults (Corner, 1990; Jones, 1988; Jones and Chadwick, 1981; Styler, 1984).

Canada

The combination of government support and independent initiatives to provide cultural adult education has also been evident in Canada. Frontier College was a landmark nongovernmental program to serve less-advantaged adults with general education (Charters and Hilton, 1989, chap. 6). An example of government-supported cultural adult education was provided by the public library in cooperation with the public school in North York near

Toronto, Ontario (Merriam and Cunningham, 1989, chap. 28). Distinctively Canadian features have been apparent in these and many other cultural adult education programs that tend to reflect international and domestic multicultural viewpoints (Selman and Dampier, 1991).

Japan

In Japan, cultural adult education has been a major part of social and cultural education (Komada, 1977). National legislation in 1949 and 1959 established and strengthened citizens' public halls supported by local government to promote cultural enhancement for all citizens. During the 1980s, there were more than seventeen thousand citizens' public halls that provided social education, which included intergenerational programs on social change and family relationships. Cultural education was also provided by libraries and museums and through educational broadcasting (including the University of the Air in metropolitan Tokyo); women's studies were furnished by the National Women's Education Center. In addition, about four hundred centers that feature many cultural adult education offerings are offered by newspaper publishers, department stores, and broadcasting companies and serve about 400,000 adults annually in spite of high fees. Topics include languages, religion, philosophy, literature, history, cooking, fine arts, health, and psychology. Societal influences include increased income and leisure time (Moro'oka, 1987).

Strategic Planning

The concluding section summarizes the societal influences and implications for strategic planning suggested by the preceding cultural adult education programs. The implications are grouped in themes according to agency mission, societal priorities, responses to change, diversified resources, provider collaboration, and leadership. For each theme, agency planning initiatives are suggested in response to societal threats and opportunities to strengthen cultural adult education in order to better serve adult learners. In general, planners should be responsive to national and community influences that are important for their own program and its benefits for adult learners.

Mission

Each provider agency has an implicit mission shaped by tradition, educational resources, typical clientele, and policy guidelines. Although some landmark cultural adult education programs (such as folk schools, study circles, and workers' education associations) have established distinctive program images and agency missions, cultural adult education is often diffuse, a situation that calls for explicit attention to the rationale for this type of program. When cultural adult education activities are the main offerings of a provider such as a museum, religious institution, or arts organization, then the purposes and resources of the parent organization help establish the image and priority for the cultural education offerings. However, when the provider is part of an educational institution or private organization that offers both specialized occupational education and cultural education opportunities for adults, strategic planning may be especially important to increase understanding of and support for cultural education programming. In the foregoing examples, the U.S. museums interpreted their collections for special populations; Znanie emphasized cultural, political, and scientific topics; the German women's museum focused on understanding women's experience; and the Italian library sought to include blue collar adults.

The rationale for cultural education content and benefits can be clarified and communicated by strategic planning. Agency rationales for cultural education reflect both traditional and emerging sources of inspiration. Traditional sources in Western countries have emphasized arts and humanities as subject matter rich in content related to societal values to preserve and transmit national culture; in some instances, these subjects have helped to reconstruct traditional myths and practices that had suffered neglect or cultural imperialism so that current practices could be understood in historical perspective. (Examples include Danish folk schools, Swedish study circles, and the Irish-language series on television). Emerging sources of inspiration in Western countries come from new-age beliefs from Eastern and developing countries that emphasize consciousness raising and the inner journey to gain a more holistic sense of interdependent self. Social change can result from widespread personal change. (Examples include women's studies, marriage enrichment, and spirituality programs such as meditation.) Compared to most specialized occupational adult education, cultural education typically draws from multidisciplinary content to explore various ways of knowing, especially related to attitudes and values (Byrne, 1987; Inglis and Bassett, 1988). In both developing and industrialized countries, political education can enable an enlightened public to make participatory democracy work by discussing choices and reducing conflict through exploration of disagreements in peaceful ways (Styler, 1984). Strategic planning can help leaders be open to such varied ways of knowing and to distinctive local events and resources that should play a part in shaping the provider mission. These include museum collections and (for educational institutions) both faculty expertise and experts from the community interested in part-time teaching.

The clientele most readily attracted to cultural adult education programs are well-educated, middle-class individuals, whose education and experience contribute to their interest and confidence. Leaders of many cultural education programs seek to broaden their clientele to include more working-class adults. Strategies to accomplish this objective can be seen in the examples from Sweden, the former Soviet Union, Czechoslovakia, Australia, Italy, Scotland, and Canada. Success usually requires deliberate attention to subsidy, access, decentralization, relevance, and participation.

Priority

In most of the instances in which cultural adult education programs served a larger proportion of working-class adults, this broadened clientele was the result of explicit priority and public demand. Usually, government policy and financial support provided subsidy funds and encouraged provision of resources and assistance from other sources. These facts are evident in the examples from the former Soviet Union, Czechoslovakia, Sweden, Australia, Germany, Italy, Ireland, Britain, and Japan, where the typical rationale emphasized equity and access for all interested adults, not just those able to pay the full costs. These examples also illustrate the competition that cultural adult education faces from other public priorities: economic development and health and welfare services. Strategic planning should help policy makers appreciate the contribution that cultural adult education makes to that informed and articulate public essential to a democratic society and to individual development (Bhola, 1988; Hall and Stock, 1985; Simmons, 1980; Thompson, 1983).

Change

Planning should especially help strengthen a broad base of public support for such values by increasing understanding of the potential contribution of cultural adult education for dealing with major social trends and issues. This role seems especially important given the declining trend for adult political education. The example of German political education initiated in the aftermath of World War II shows both a high degree of support and the unusual conditions that led to it. However, public support for cultural adult education usually comes about because of concern over domestic trends and issues such as immigration, ethnic conflict, women's roles, aging, urbanization, taxes, health, crime, environmental pollution, leisure time, and economic conditions. In remote regions (as in the former Soviet Union, Sweden, and Australia) access is especially important. In addition to economic policy choices to be discussed in cultural adult education programs, economic conditions affect the ability of government, enterprises, providers, and participants to pay program costs. Increasing leisure allows more adults to consider cultural education topics. In a shrinking world, there are also international trends and issues that are being increasingly recognized as relevant. Strategic planning can help leaders to understand societal influences and to develop responsive programs: for example, intergenerational educational programs (as in Sweden and Japan), when rapid social change requires adjustments by young and old; and multicultural educational programs (as in Australia and Canada), when ethnic tensions call for both preserving distinct traditions and promoting mutual understanding and solidarity. Attracting hard-to-reach adults entails provision of accessible and relevant programs that are responsive to their concerns and life style, and strategic planning can improve the fit between program offerings and participant characteristics in part by attention to the broader societal context in which both function. Cultural education can pave the way for increased freedom (Styler, 1984).

Resources

Perhaps the most persistent and widespread challenge to leaders of cultural adult education has been acquisition of resources for program subsidy. During earlier decades, when occupational and cultural adult education programs were usually subsidized based on a commitment to compensatory education for immigrants, rural, or working-class adults, a larger proportion of offerings was for cultural education purposes; in recent years, economic development has become the main program rationale. As previously noted, this shift has occurred in the United Kingdom and in Sweden, as well as in the United States. For occupational adult education in the United States, enterprise reimbursement allows many adult education providers to finance their programs based on cost recovery from participant fees. This practice has contributed to shrinkage of non-occupational cultural education programs. Strategic planning can help program leaders broaden program support, because (as illustrated especially by several of the German examples) a basic strategy is diversification of funding so that no one source finds the charges prohibitive. As shown especially in several of the Australian examples, very low fees may encourage participation but restrict funds for materials and staff support. Widespread sources of subsidy include use of volunteers, collaboration (such as the Italian university assistance to a library), and private foundation grants (such as Kettering support of the National Issues Forum and Kellogg support of Community Information Centers in the United States). Government was a major source in Czechoslovakia and the former Soviet Union. Involvement of people associated with such external resources in the strategic planning process can increase their understanding and support.

Collaboration

Strategic planning can particularly promote collaboration. When provider resources are inadequate, one strategy is to broaden co-sponsorship, as illustrated by the Grand Rapids National Issues Forum in the United States and the Carringbush Library in Australia. Sometimes there is an obvious main provider of a type of cultural education program, as we saw in selected examples from the former Soviet Union (Znanie), Czechoslovakia (House of Culture), Sweden (study circles), and Germany (political education). However, it is generally the case that cultural adult education providers need to use collaborative planning and resource sharing as a way to increase program vitality and continuity. Especially (as in examples from Australia, Ireland, and Japan) when media and technology are components, collaboration can increase access and impact, but programs usually require subsidy (Saxena and Sachdeva, 1985). Cultural adult education leaders who are familiar with program strategies in other countries can use that understanding to adapt practices and rationale to fit their own context. For example, the cultural education offerings of the Japanese publisher may seem unique until we recognize the extent to which cultural education offerings of some urban U.S. universities are financed on a cost-recovery basis.

Leadership

Use of each of the foregoing implications for strategic planning depends on the caliber and vision of the cultural adult education staff and volunteers. A prime challenge to leaders is to attract and develop people who will plan and conduct effective programs. Sometimes, as in the example of the German VHS adult education center, large numbers of unemployed teachers provide a rich pool of applicants, but usually selection and development of able staff are major tasks. In spite of examples of effective staff development in the religious adult education program in Germany and the library outreach program in Italy, there is general complaint about inadequate attention to this domain. Staff development can be part of strategic planning by the provider agency that deepens the commitment to balanced and high-quality cultural education offerings intended to increase equity and access for underserved adults. This commitment is seen in the examples of U.S. religious education, Swedish study circles, Australian and Italian library programs, and German religious education. A crucial ingredient in these programs' success has been leaders who championed a particular vision and acquisition of resources. Strategic planning can help attract, develop, and empower such champions.

The themes in this chapter relate especially to similar ones in several other chapters. For example, the chapter on elder education indicates how increasing numbers of well-educated older adults are raising demand for programs on history, philosophy, religion, the arts, and public issues as elders reflect on trends and issues from past generations and consider implications for future generations. The chapter on community problem solving emphasizes collective action to address public issues, and the current chapter stresses the individual enlightenment that enables adults to take wise action. The chapter on part-time study in educational institutions encompasses support for cultural as well as specialist education.

9

Continuing
Professional Education

Successful educational programs for professionals are shaped by various influences, including both personal qualities and societal factors. Personal qualities include ability, performance, and potential influence on other people. Societal factors consist of new knowledge gained from education and experience, career opportunities, practice standards, multiple continuing education providers, cultural values, and public expectations (Friedson, 1986; Houle, 1980). These societal factors are the influences addressed by strategic planning and implementation.

Scope of Continuing Professional Education

A large and increasing number of people work in occupations at some stage of professionalization. Depending on definition, estimates of the percentage of professionals within the U.S. work force range from 15 to 28 percent (Cervero, 1988). Central to the concept of professional is the process of systematic learning to prepare for the field of practice and to maintain proficiency in a context of changing knowledge base and practice. An adjunct of evolving professional careers is a continuum of preparatory and continuing education to enable practitioners to progress from novice to expert. An important part of this systematic learning is self-directed, in addition to participation in formal education supplied by educational institutions and nonformal education furnished at the workplace, by professional associations, and by other providers (Houle, 1980).

Continuing professional education is closely associated with both role performance and the organizational and societal context in which practice occurs. Because professional role performance is recognized as important to society, there is growing interest in performance standards and accountability (Cervero, Azzaretto, and Associates, 1990; Cervero and Scanlan, 1985). Thus, strategic planning of continuing professional education should consider not only combinations of knowledge and experience to maintain proficiency, but also contextual influences such as the impact of professional performance on an increasingly informed public and relations between continuing education providers.

Contextual influences on the development of medical expertise are considered in a recent research report by a team of scholars from the Netherlands and Canada (Schmidt, Norman, and Boshuizen, 1990). North American studies of expertise indicate similar dynamics in various professional fields (Chi, Glaser, and Farr, 1989). In their cognitive science rationale for development of medical expertise, Schmidt, Norman and Boshuizen conclude that movement from novice to expert involves a combination of knowledge and experience relevant to each clinical problem. Experienced clinicians increasingly use indigenous knowledge from experiential learning to create their own cognitive structures called illness scripts; these include scientific generalizations about causes of symptoms but even more are based on recollections of prototypical and actual patients and the context in which illness occurred. In contrast to novices with limited clinical experience, who tend to use elaborate pathophysical causal models of disease for problem solving, experts learn to compress information into fewer high-level concepts that helps them focus on pertinent knowledge. They then combine that understanding with illness scripts derived from clinical experience, with memorable patients who personified the clinical problem and its solution. Furthermore, under the time pressure of actual clinical conditions, experts are able to recall more pertinent knowledge than novices. As novices become more expert, then, their clinical reasoning becomes more holistic and takes into account more situational influences on the problem and its solution. This approach is similar to Sternberg's (1988) triarchic theory of intelligence, composed of knowledge acquisition, performance, and metacomponents (to plan, monitor, and evaluate problem solving). One of the many implications for planning continuing professional education programs (that tend to emphasize updates on new knowledge) is the importance of helping professionals reflect on both public and personal knowledge in relation to performance and evolving expertise. Metacomponents of problem solving have many aspects that are similar to learning to learn—which includes planning, monitoring, and evaluating one's own learning activities (Smith and Associates, 1990). The foregoing rationale also parallels the development of expertise by adult education leaders who combine practical experience with organized knowledge and metacognition.

As indicated earlier, professional performance and related continuing education have occurred as an open system in which situational influences are important and outputs affect inputs. In this dynamic external environment, many changes have implications for planning continuing education. Included are career transitions, organized knowledge, indigenous knowledge, economic conditions, supply and demand for professionals, circumstances affecting the clients of professionals, interprofessional relations, and societal expectations (influencing relicensure requirements and malpractice legislation) (Houle, 1980). Professional performance typically has an impact on clients directly and other people indirectly. In most professions, clients are also affected by other influences—illness, peers, and economic conditions—so it is often difficult to attribute benefits or harm that clients experience from professional performance, let alone from continuing professional education intended to enhance that performance. As clients become more knowledgeable consumers of professional services, they should become better able to judge the quality of performance.

In spite of scattered mandatory continuing professional education requirements that require minimum numbers of hours of participation every few years, participation in specific activities is usually voluntary. With multiple providers of continuing professional education, professionals have many alternatives from which to choose. The resulting demand has shaped offerings; some are oversubscribed early, and others are canceled due to low enrollments. Image of likely program benefits and costs is thus a major influence. Provider planning committees can consider the enrollment economy along with trends in the field and provider mission and resources as decisions are made regarding program offerings. Because most continuing professional education programs in the United States are financed exclusively or mainly on a cost-recovery basis from participant fees, enrollments greatly influence budgets, and staffing of people to plan and conduct programs is on a part-time or short-term basis.

There have been four major types of providers of continuing professional education. They are educational institutions (especially university professional schools), professional associations, the enterprises where professionals work, and independent providers (such as consulting firms). Each type of provider has distinctive strengths and weaknesses. Most programs are conducted by a single provider, and in many instances such arrangements are very satisfactory. However, sometimes collaboration has enabled two or more providers to offer a more effective program than any one of them is likely to conduct alone. The combination of many providers of continuing education and collaborative arrangements has greatly affected programs and planning for professionals (Merriam and Cunningham, 1989, chap. 39; Queeney, 1990). The following continuing professional education programs in the United States and other countries reveal major societal influences on program purposes and participants, with special attention to collaboration and implications for strategic planning to strengthen such programs.

The examples and rationale address several themes that were important for planning continuing professional education. One is participation by highly educated professionals, who are influenced both by the continuum of preparatory and continuing professional education and by technological and other societal trends during their careers. A second theme is multiple stakeholders, with attention to goals and linkage. Aspects of this theme pertain to outcomes, including continuing education as only one influence on professional performance and multiple beneficiaries of improved performance. A third theme is collaborative arrangements among various stakeholders, including interprofessional education to address issues relevant to various fields, international influences, and resource acquisition to support continuing professional education.

Continuing Medical Education

Most professionals in the United States have engaged in continuing education programs and self-study projects. Such participation arises from personal backgrounds and attitudes that contribute to their efforts to achieve higher levels of expertise. In addition, educational activity is affected by situational influences such as work demands, career advancement opportunities, encouragement or discouragement by peers, and availability of educational opportunities. Similar societal influences also have an impact on providers of continuing professional education as they plan and conduct programs. The following example of continuing education for physicians illustrates how societal influences affect programs and suggests implications for strategic planning.

Physicians' decisions to participate and persist in continuing medical education activities and apply what they learn are shaped by various situational influences, some of which could be addressed by strategic planning (Fox, Mazmanian, and Putnam, 1989; Knox, 1990). These influences include extent of change in the field of practice, extent of role change and career advancement, cost containment pressures, work and family demands, practice arrangements and consultation with peers, level of affluence, access to educational opportunities, and an occupational tradition of valuing career-long learning. Continuing education leaders who have understood such situational sources of encouragement and discouragement of participation have been able to plan more responsive and accessible programs than those who have not. Planning for specific programs could include contextual analysis, a marketing mix to address situational influences as well as interest in content, and provision of educational programs for occupational teams when organizational development was a goal.

Many primary-care physicians develop personalized professional development strategies composed of a sequence of educational activities from different sources (Green, Grosswald, Suter, and Walthall, 1984; Knox, 1974). For example, a physician might review his or her practice profile to identify a health problem (seriously affecting many current patients) for which the prospect of improved practice seems likely and might then read recent publications on the topic to clarify basic concepts and recent developments in the field. Because local specialists on that topic might in the future review malpractice charges, asking them questions might be avoided in favor of attending a distant conference provided by a university or professional association. At the conference on the topic, the physician could attend sessions, ask speakers specific questions, and especially discuss informally with other participants their experience with the health problem and related clinical procedures for purposes of both understanding and confidence. Sometimes encouragement to use a new procedure may be more important than new knowledge. Planners who understand such personalized professional development can consider typical programs and their providers and thus build on other programs.

As indicated earlier, each type of provider of professional education has distinctive capabilities (Cervero, 1988). The hospital at which physicians have practice privileges is one provider. In addition to providing materials, presentations, and discussions on new developments related to practice specialties, hospitals offer organizational development activities for physicians and related health care staff that are focused on an area where the quality of health care can be improved. Practice audits are combined with practice standards in the field to specify areas of improvement to be addressed by targeted continuing education activities for members of the health care team. Practice audit information collected periodically can then be used to monitor improvements in staff performance that reflect the impact of continuing education activities. An understanding of such organizational development activities for hospital staff members can be used for strategic planning purposes not only for personal career development strategies but also for organizational development activities aimed at health care (Berwick, Godfrey, and Roessner, 1990; Payne and others, 1984). Quality improvement efforts encourage such organizational development in all types of enterprises.

Other types of providers of continuing education also have distinctive capabilities. Professional associations concentrate on issues and standards that may be unique to a medical specialty. Independent consultants who provide continuing education for many clients develop comparative perspectives on program content and design that can be used to encourage innovation. University medical colleges include both departments and faculty specialists on medical topics, as well as departments and colleagues in other related parts of the university.

Sometimes provision of continuing education is collaborative, which has implications for strategic planning regarding participation, staffing, and resources. For example, two major tasks for continuing education program administrators are acquisition of resources to pay honoraria for instructors to plan and conduct programs, and recruitment and selection of instructors based on incentives that the administrator can arrange. A major source of instructors for university-provided continuing medical education is medical school faculty members. An important source of participants is physicians who practice in community hospitals in the geographic area from which the university-connected teaching hospital receives referrals of patients. Often, the director of continuing education in a community hospital seeks university cosponsorship of programs held in the community hospital for the convenience of local physicians, with the university director of continuing medical education arranging for professors of medicine to conduct educational activities in the community hospital. These professors' decision to assist reflects commitment to the profession, lifelong learning, and the outreach mission of the university. The decision also demonstrates a recognition that effective provision of such outreach activities is a way to encourage participants to refer patients to the teaching hospital; the professor's research and teaching of medical students and residents depend on these referrals (Knox, 1982b). Continuing education leaders who appreciate the potential of such symbiotic partnerships are alert to promising collaborative relationships.

In many states, there are arrangements to encourage high-quality continuing medical education and cooperation among providers. In the 1960s, the Illinois State Medical Society began planning that led to formation in the 1970s of the Illinois Council on Continuing Medical Education. This organization continues to encourage, assist, and accredit local providers of continuing medical education, as well as to supply handbooks, workshops, and other assistance to continuing education instructors and coordinators.

Many local continuing education providers, such as community hospitals, professional associations, and universities, are accredited to provide programs to serve many of the 25,000 currently licensed physicians in the state. Local continuing medical education provision is coordinated full- or part-time by physicians, nurses, and educators, who also volunteer to serve as members of on-site accreditation visits of continuing education programs. The accreditation process helps reassure physicians that programs by accredited providers are of high quality, assists accredited providers in improving their programs, and helps providers that do not receive approval to identify ways to strengthen their programs. Physicians seldom pay fees for continuing medical education in community hospitals; the costs are borne mainly by the hospital, sometimes with assistance from external organizations such as pharmaceutical companies (Resource A, Pearson and Cervero). External influences that have affected programs include widespread economic pressures on hospitals that threaten their continuing education budgets, mandatory continuing education requirements by state licensing boards or professional associations, concerns about malpractice, the American Medical Association's Physician Recognition Award for voluntary education participation, and increasing expectations of public accountability.

The standards for the Illinois council to judge the quality of local continuing medical education programs come from the Accreditation Council for Continuing Medical Education and its predecessors. This national council is composed of the American Medical Association and other organizations in the medical and hospital fields. The process by which these national standards evolved, the quality elements that composed the standards, and their rationale are described in Green, Grosswald, Suter, and Walthall (1984).

Strategic planning can help leaders select, refine, or develop such standards; recognize and respond to major societal influences; monitor program functioning, including collaborative arrangements; and in general strengthen continuing medical education for the benefit of the participants, their patients, and society. Recent health care standards based on clinical algorithms or heuristics for decision making can also be used to guide continuing medical education planning and evaluation. It is difficult but important to gain agreement on such standards (Davis, Thomson, Oxman, and Haynes, 1992; Landa, 1983).

Other U.S. Programs

The preceding continuing medical education program reflects some special features of the medical profession in the United States. As previously stated, every other professional and quasi-professional occupation has a variety of continuing education activities that also reveal distinctive features of its field. The estimated number of such occupations ranges from fewer than twenty to more than forty. Each field has one or more associations, along with educational institutions. For many occupations, the enterprises or organizations in which professionals work also provide continuing education opportunities. Some fields even have an association or informal group for people who coordinate the programs. During the 1980s, there have been a number of comparative studies of continuing education in various professions (Cervero, 1988; Cervero and Azzaretto, 1990; Houle, 1980; Knox, 1982b; Nowlen, 1988; Queeney, 1990). In each field, continuing education activities reflect the type of knowledge base, impact of social change, relationship to clients, and organizational arrangements in which practice occurs.

Houle (1980) identifies five basic settings of professional practice. One is the entrepreneurial setting, such as dentistry, in which practitioners individually or in partnership provide direct service to clients. A second is the collective setting, such as a school system or social work agency; here practitioners from one or more professions furnish mutually facilitative services and engage in collective action. A third is the hierarchical setting, such as administration; in this situation, organizational dynamics and interpersonal relations are central concerns. A fourth is the adjunct setting, such as an attorney in an enterprise in which a practitioner advises or assists other members of the enterprise in isolation from other members of the profession. The fifth is the facilitative setting, such as working in a professional school, voluntary association, or a government bureau. In this case, practitioners have left their typical work in order to advance the profession. A comparative perspective on distinctive features of a profession can enable leaders of continuing professional education to adapt concepts and practices from other professions to enrich the vitality of their fields. There have been few analyses of continuing professional education across professions outside the United States.

Engineering

Engineering shares with medicine the influence of scientific and technological change and the emergence of distinctive specialties (such as mechanical, chemical, civil, and electrical engineering), each with separate professional school departments, major fields of specialized knowledge, examinations, publications, and societies. For years, the Joint Council on Engineering Education promoted exchange among people engaged in continuing education for engineers. Engineers have also shared with physicians substantial ability to learn throughout their careers, based on selection, preparatory education, and work experience. More than other professionals, most of the occupational learning of engineers has been on the job or self-directed. Many work in settings characterized by rapid technological change and competition among enterprises. In addition to personal performance, systematic learning can increase productivity for the enterprise, which can lead to benefits such as career advancement, financial rewards, and recognition. The work roles of engineers and technicians connect them with other people in the enterprise. Self-directed learning activities can be integral to changing work assignments. Learning activities may reflect career stage as well as specific job. Unlike novice engineers, whose learning tends to be oriented toward work assignments and associates within the enterprise, learning by experienced engineers in very responsible positions is often oriented toward peers and experts outside the enterprise. Engineers may also select from alternate career paths, such as higher levels of technical specialization, lateral moves to other specialties, or a change to management responsibilities. For engineers who aspire to management roles, motivation to study continuing management education is often greater than to study continuing engineering education in a technical specialty (Willis, Dubin, and Associates, 1990).

Leaders who coordinate continuing education for engineers on behalf of universities, associations, or enterprises confront some challenges. One pertains to priorities. The urgency of technological change in the field, competitive position of the enterprise, and potential obsolescence for the engineer can create a focus on technical updates and eclipse attention to other important topics for continuing education: environmental impact, ethical dilemmas, and conflicts between individuals and organizations (Cervero, Azzaretto, and Associates, 1990). Another challenge relates to multiple stakeholders in continuing engineering education. In addition to people associated with enterprises, universities, and associations as providers of continuing education, external stakeholders may be beneficiaries (such as engineers' clients), collaborators (such as cosponsors), and supporters (such as government and foundations). Enterprises with more than five hundred staff members typically provide substantial continuing education opportunities internally, whereas enterprises with fewer than fifty staff members depend mainly on sending them to external continuing education provided by associations and educational institutions. Enterprise support for continuing education is also affected by economic conditions. As desirable as it is to support continuing education as an investment in human resource development during periods of economic downturn, in practice these are periods when enterprises reduce training budgets; this reality is a major reason for diversifying financial support for continuing education. Strategic planning allows multiple stakeholders to identify emerging trends and issues related to a vision of the contribution that continuing education can make to practice in order to reduce widespread reliance on reactive updates to offset obsolescence.

Pharmacology

Pharmacology is another professional field affected by scientific change, but it is also one engaged in recent decades in a redefinition of professional role. Professional associations and some university pharmacy schools use continuing education to create a clinical pharmacist role that includes patient education. The planning process includes achieving consensus on major competencies, procedures for accrediting continuing education providers by the Council on Pharmaceutical Education, and development of procedures for self-critical practice review to enable pharmacists to initiate self-managed learning activities closely associated with improvement of professional practice (Cervero, Azzaretto, and Associates, 1990; Queeney, 1990). As with development of computer simulations to enhance diagnostic abilities through continuing medical education, creation of materials and procedures for support of self-managed learning by pharmacists entails large initial investments, which assume extensive use to reduce unit costs. This is another challenge for strategic planning and like investment in facilities for distance education, is a major reason for collaboration.

Teaching

Additional perspective on strategic planning for continuing professional education is gained by consideration of programs for the helping professions—teaching, library science, social work, law, and some aspects of management (Cervero, 1988; Houle, 1980; Knox, 1982b; Nowlen, 1988). Professional development for elementary and secondary school teachers has been typically centered in staff development provided by the school system or regional teachers' centers, in part because of the large numbers of local potential participants; this situation differs for some medical or engineering specialties, which may have only a few members in a local area and rely primarily on regional or national conferences. School-based, in-service education also emphasizes benefits for school programs as well as individual careers. Additional providers of continuing education for school teachers include university and college schools of education, which offer degree credit courses at convenient times and locations, and professional associations, which sponsor state and national conferences and commission reports on professional standards. Continuing education for higher education faculty members has confronted greater individualism and specialization; traditionally, efforts to strengthen the individual's scholarly specialty are the outcome. In recent decades, there has been a movement to include teaching and organizational development as purposes of faculty development offices.

Library Science

In each profession, planning and implementation of local continuing education programs have been shaped not only by widespread economic, political, and social conditions that have affected other professions and the entire society, but also by distinctive local and national features of that profession. For example, planners of continuing education for public librarians have confronted issues related to public library budgetary constraints and population shifts that affect demand and services in the center city, suburbs, and rural areas; at the same time, the numbers of special librarians have expanded rapidly, and they deal with sophisticated technology, such as computerized information-base searches (Horne, 1985). A few decades ago, a Continuing Library Education Network and Exchange (CLENE) developed outside the American Library Association (ALA), mainly because major association support for people who coordinated continuing education for librarians had lower priority than many other issues. As a reflection of rising priority for continuing professional education and of effective leadership, CLENE became part of ALA in later years, and the woman who was the main driving force behind CLENE became president of ALA. Resulting materials and workshops have enriched local and state leadership and planning for continuing library education.

Other Professions

Field-specific influences are also illustrated by continuing education for social workers, attorneys, and managers (Knox, 1982b; Nowlen, 1988). Content and methods of continuing education for social workers have reflected their preoccupation with interpersonal relations. Continuing legal education programs have been overwhelmingly conducted by specialist practitioners and not law professors, as a result of attorneys' preoccupation with new developments (such as tax law) and the practical aspects of lawyering. These areas are perceived as outside the focus of law professors' attention to legal reasoning and precedent. As a result, state and national associations and institutes for continuing legal education conduct a larger portion of continuing education and university law schools a smaller portion than is the case for many professional fields. Managers and executives in business and industry tend to rely mainly on continuing education opportunities outside their enterprises, such as conferences by the American Management Association and executive MBA programs by university business schools. As with senior engineers, external providers are especially attractive because they include interaction with peers in other enterprises and the managers' enterprise typically pay the costs.

The foregoing highlights of continuing education in various professional fields suggests the diversity of societal influences on local programs that strategic planning might address in specific instances. However, several themes emerge from this diversity. Practitioners in each professional field and specialty within it use many sources of expertise (including organized knowledge from formal education and indigenous knowledge from experience) to inform their practice, which should be responsive to particular contingencies. As practitioners progress from novice to expert status, continuing professional education programs should be beyond technical updates on new developments and instead provide more holistic opportunities for practitioners to reflect on their practice. Such reflection should include critical analysis of goals, procedures, and results of current practice in relation to espoused theory and organized knowledge (Schön, 1987). Strategic planning can help leaders gain such a holistic perspective on continuing education; also important is the continuum of professional education, which can be strengthened by consideration of relations among educational institutions (as the main sources of preparatory professional education) and associations and enterprises (as major additional providers of continuing professional education).

Mandatory Continuing Professional Education

The much discussed and widespread issue of mandatory continuing professional education that emerged during the 1970s demonstrates how societal pressures can create responses related to professional fields that may not be beneficial to continuing education or society (Merriam and Cunningham, 1989). Throughout, there has been general agreement that continuing professional education is desirable. The issue has revolved around the nature of the problem to be solved by mandatory continuing education, which relates to the small number of members of a field whose practice is believed to be substandard or unethical. Proponents of mandatory continuing education prefer requiring that a minimum number of hours each year be spent by all members of the field in continuing education activities, in contrast to challenge exams or peer review for members suspected of unsatisfactory performance. Opponents of mandatory continuing professional education have pointed out that such process requirements are unlikely to address public demands for accountability and responsibility by each field that would remove unsatisfactory members from practice. Most members of each field already participate in more hours of continuing education than the minimum, and members whose performance is substandard seem to warrant performance review and disciplinary action; continuing education activities did not assure that they would learn anything that would improve their practice. Strategic planning could encourage inclusion of the public and regulating agencies as serious stakeholders. This issue also raises the question of whether the main purpose of a continuing professional education program is to improve function (helping to maintain the current status of the profession), to cause conflict (seeking to reduce the power differential between professionals and their clients), or to be critical (exploring dialectical relationships between professions and society, with attention to means and ends) (Cervero, 1988).

In most continuing professional education programs, a central issue is the quality of instruction. Program quality has depended heavily on the performance of the people who plan and conduct programs, which is usually a part-time arrangement. As a result, responsibility for selection and supervision of the people who help adults learn rests with program coordinators. A crucial aspect of strategic planning is to enable coordinators to perform well this process of part-time staff selection and development. Innovative coordinators have also pioneered use of interactive television to reach scattered specialists and evaluation to assess program impact. A benefit of a comparative perspective on continuing education in various professional fields and locations is that it becomes easier to recognize generic guidelines for educational leadership, compared with distinctive local features and contingencies when planning specific programs.

Adult Education in Germany

Most of the available information about German educational programs for adults pertains to western Germany. The following example of continuing medical education, which constitutes a very small part of a diverse range of German adult education offerings, indicates several societal influences that planning might address. This section concludes with a brief overview of various types of adult education in Germany as background for German examples in other chapters.

Following both world wars, Germany sought to reduce the concentration of power in the central government by devolution to state (Länder) governments and private organizations and by strengthening of adult education. The national constitution of West Germany granted freedom of occupational and educational choice. One result has been an oversupply of physicians, a situation that has also appeared in urban areas of the United States and some other industrialized countries. For many physicians in general practice, an attractive solution to this problem is to become a specialist, which has higher status and income than general practice. This role change has required acquiring new knowledge, completing clinical hospital training, and passing the specialty licensing exam. European Community agreements on professional practice have promoted consistency.

In one German state, a professional association set the conditions and guidelines for specialty training and exam; the actual continuing medical education and supervised clinical experience was provided by hospitals; and the program plans were made collaboratively by the association and the hospitals. Few funds were entailed, but the hospitals provided the main resources, mainly in the form of in-kind provision of staff time and facilities. Most of the people who planned and conducted the continuing medical education activities were from the hospitals. They were heavily oriented toward supervised clinical practice, but they also used oral examinations of specialized knowledge (Resource A, Renschler). West

Germany was one of the most affluent European countries, a fact that—along with decentralization—contributed to the oversupply of physicians and also to the collaborative program described.

The preceding program was one of many varied types of continuing education for many professional fields. The recent unification of East and West Germany is likely to influence these and most other types of educational programs for adults for some years. About half of all adult education participation takes place in the folk schools, which are adult education centers similar to community colleges and people's universities. An elite and remote university tradition restricts both their provision of adult education and cooperation with folk schools. Enterprise policies that allow short-term educational leave have helped evening folk school programs at the expense of longer-term residential folk school programs. West German enterprises have been the other major provider of educational programs for adults. Another provider has been labor unions, whose cooperation with enterprises and participation in management has resulted in industrial peace; this has both contributed to prosperity and been a beneficiary of it. Other adult education providers consist of religious institutions, municipal evening schools, technical colleges, proprietorial schools, voluntary associations, military forces, political foundations, chambers of commerce and industry, sociocultural centers, libraries, and museums. Programs include credit and noncredit study at educational institutions, television and distance education, occupational retraining, and comprehensive rural education for both agriculture and transition to nonfarm occupations. Adult education for citizenship continues to be a unique program area in Germany and Austria, but one that has not expanded with most other program areas in recent decades. In the public portions of this pluralistic provision of adult education, decentralized local provision has occurred within federal and state legislation, appropriations, and guidelines for official examinations (Reischmann, 1988; Schneider, 1977; Schwier and Piazolo, 1985; Titmus, 1981; Werner, 1986). German adult education has been greatly influenced by past political and military history, and recent economic system and prosperity. It now confronts adjustments to reunification and relations with the European Community.

Other Countries

The following brief overviews of continuing education (mainly for physicians, engineers, and school teachers) each show program features and societal influences that can yield insights useful for strategic planning of continuing professional education in the United States or in other countries.

Soviet Union

In contrast with the very decentralized approach in Germany, the former Soviet Union provided an example of more centralized arrangements. The Central Institute for Advanced Medical Studies had a national role in provision of postgraduate medical studies, in collaboration with other institutes and medical schools in the various republics. The all-union national government fully funded all related activities and was very influential on program policies and coordination. However, the collaboration with institutes and medical schools showed a degree of pluralism. One function of the institute was staff development for the people who conducted continuing medical education activities (Resource A, Vartanian, Orlov, and Nazarova). With the advent of the Commonwealth of Independent States, more pluralistic arrangements are likely to arise. The process by which this change occurs will be of great interest.

Australia

Collaboration is a recurrent theme in many continuing professional education programs. An example from Australia is the two-day Country Pediatric Program provided by the South Australian Postgraduate Medical Education Association. This is based in Adelaide but is held in three population centers about 120 miles north of Adelaide. Australia is a large, sparsely populated country, in which 86 percent of the population lives in urban areas mostly located on the coast. Of the fewer than one-and-one-half million people in the state of South Australia, more than a million live in Adelaide. Repeating a continuing medical education program in three small inland cities has made the program more accessible to pediatricians practicing in those areas.

The association has had a very positive image as a continuing education provider, and successful collaboration with a children's hospital in Adelaide and a national association of general practitioners has produced contributions of leadership, planning, cash and in-kind financial support, and staff assistance to plan, conduct, and coordinate the program. Outstanding specialists have been very willing to volunteer to teach in the program, in part because they expect referrals from participants as a result of effective teaching. Program evaluation has consisted mainly of participants' ratings of their satisfaction with presenters; there is also a brief item on the extent to which their objectives in attending the program have been acheived.

Economic conditions in Australia have affected the program in at least two ways. Income levels for physicians have enabled them to afford the fees, expenses, and time off to attend the program. Economic conditions have allowed a foundation associated with the professional association to subsidize some of the program costs. The moderate registration fees that result from foundation support, volunteer instruction, and contributions by cosponsors encourage participation, along with exposure to new developments in the field to forestall obsolescence and specific benefits to the physicians' practice and patients (Resource A, Duyverman). Between 1987 and 1992, the association's program offerings expanded to eighty. Part of the increase reflects new government provisions for slightly higher remuneration for family physicians who have recently completed continuing medical education programs. Strategic planning in other locations and professional fields can explore potential benefits of collaboration and volunteer teaching by specialists in their areas.

Canada

A similar collaborative effort to keep costs low and provide access to continuing medical education programs for primary-care physicians in a sparsely populated area occurred in Canada (Resource A, Jennett). A continuing education program on early detection of cancer and on office-based practices related to cardiovascular disease was provided for physicians practicing within one hundred miles of Saskatoon in the western province of Saskatchewan. The program was conducted by the Division of Continuing Medical Education of a university college of medicine in collaboration with a hospital and a professional association. Detailed planning was by a committee composed of both professors and practitioners, and program participants actively contributed to program planning decisions.

Efforts to encourage participation included use of educational technology (such as teleconferencing) to increase convenience and access through distance learning program segments, provided at minimum expense. The usual costs associated with learning opportunities were largely avoided through the use of volunteer faculty. Expenditures associated with learning materials were covered by granting agencies. Other positive influences included professional commitment by physicians and public interest in improved medical care. The main negative influence was the difficulty of being away from a demanding rural practice. For some physicians, other negative influences were loss of income or time away from family or recreation activities. A follow-up evaluation six and twelve months after the program concluded that the educational activity affected professional performance at low cost. Six months after the program, participants were performing the recommended practices significantly more than were nonparticipants.

Greece

Similar features are found in continuing medical education activities in Greece offered by the Society for Medical Studies. The society began in 1961 as a major advocate and provider of continuing medical education; it was created by physicians concerned about discrepancies between medical practice in Greece and other countries and who went abroad to continue their education. Over the years, publications, regional seminars, and other activities were aimed especially at rural primary-care physicians, many of whom lacked hospital connections. Because the society had a modest budget, the main support was volunteer time by members who wrote articles and conducted seminar sessions. Although the proportion of physicians who participated was small, the lack of alternatives for rural physicians made the effort important. Negative influences included low morale among physicians, due to a declining standard of living (which reflected economic and political conditions), oversupply of physicians in urban areas, and government policies regarding income reporting and medical records that reduced maintenance of records which might have been used by physicians to help recognize their educational needs. Programs were also provided by associations and hospitals. In 1989, the Athens-based Center for Continuing Medical Education was founded, which was designed to serve especially those of the thirty thousand physicians throughout Greece who practiced in rural areas and did not have hospital affiliations that would have included continuing medical education opportunities. The center also serves many urban physicians. Since 1989, the center has emphasized provision of distance learning programs, commitment to rural physicians, and increased cooperation with similar programs in other countries. In 1991, the center launched expanded use of distance education materials: self-assessment inventories and educational technology such as audiotapes and a television project that used fourteen rural stations in 1992.

In these instances of continuing medical education, various types of organizations took the lead in collaborative arrangements to serve physicians who confronted special deterrents to participation, such as those in rural areas with few programs available. Arrangements included volunteer instruction by specialists, subsidy to keep fees low, and distance education arrangements.

Engineering Education in Other Countries

As stated previously, engineering is another field with a scientific base and even greater attention to technological change. In many countries since the 1970s, there has been increasing priority and demand for continuing engineering education to link new knowledge from various countries to domestic economic development. Because large enterprises typically have extensive educational programs for their staff, a wide-ranging concern has been provision by professional associations and educational institutions of educational opportunities for engineers who work in small- and medium-sized enterprises. Of course, continuing engineering education varies from country to country in ways that reflect the national context. The following examples illustrate some of the influences that have implications for strategic planning.

Norway

In some countries, one or a few providers have been preeminent (Nordhaug, 1983, 1991). This is the case for the Norwegian Institute of Technology in Trondheim, which (as the only major university engineering school provider of continuing engineering education) has established a special niche as a major provider and collaborator based on the special expertise of its faculty. The government has provided policy support but little subsidy for continuing engineering education, so support from enterprises has allowed programs to become increasingly self-sustaining. Programs are conducted by regular institute faculty members (who have come to depend on their overload pay because base salaries have not increased with inflation) and by practicing engineers (who emphasize practical problem solving more than theory). The institute has complemented the Norwegian Society for Professional Engineers, which conducts many two-day programs. The institute has also collaborated with the Norwegian Agency for International Development in continuing education programs for engineers from developing countries. Over a twenty-year period, there were a thousand graduates of these international programs from sixty countries. Program content (paper, power, marine, petroleum) has reflected both institute expertise and application in developing countries. Capacity building for educational institutions in the developing countries has been emphasized by short courses located there, team projects, and the institute staff's conducting projects in cooperating countries (Auganes, 1985; Zhang, Ren, and Ruan, 1989).

Brazil

Brazil's rapid industrial development during the 1960s stimulated expansion of continuing engineering education, which was further encouraged by legislation in 1975 and 1976. Almost all of the programs provided by engineering schools, professional associations, and private organizations have been very traditional and have shown a desire for a comprehensive rationale for improving continuing engineering education. A related assertion is that because of the rapid transformation of world technology, countries will remain underdeveloped unless there are arrangements for technology transfer from more technologically advanced countries. Recent efforts to strengthen programs in Brazil include development of continuing engineering education centers, use of educational technology for distance education, and establishment of an engineering reference library (DeBrito, 1985; Zhang, Ren, and Ruan, 1989, pp. 970–973).

People's Republic of China

China hosted the Fourth World Conference on Continuing Engineering Education in 1989, which yielded a number of English-language reports on various programs in China (Zhang, Ren, and Ruan, 1989). Most of them comment specifically on increasing priority by government, enterprises, and educational institutions on continuing engineering education as decision making has shifted from government to enterprises. The expansion has occurred especially since the mid 1980s nationwide and in special economic zones. The national government has expanded the broad planning framework, and some provincial and local governments have increased financial support (Zhang, Ren, and Ruan, 1989). Improved education has been a major goal, with general collaboration among various providers of continuing engineering education that use a variety of methods. The main providers have been enterprises and universities, with some reports of continuing education associations. Methods have included self-study, reading, study groups, tutors, courses, exams, and conferences. Several providers have used television to compensate for the lack of potential instructors under age fifty due to the cultural revolution, which curtailed education of engineers and everyone else for more than a decade. In general, program priority has increased as modernization has included international relations and decentralization with moves toward a socialist market economy.

Japan

By contrast, the market economy of Japan has long supported continuing engineering education as part of broad human resource development policies to increase productivity of enterprises and enhance the talents of technical personnel. Self-study is expected to enable engineers to deal with technological change, troubleshoot ill-defined problems, and allow the enterprise to be competitive. The lack of contribution by university engineering schools is related to the difficulty in passing the entrance exam, even though the percentage of secondary school graduates who go on to higher education has increased greatly in recent decades. Increased provision of continuing education by engineering schools is due to a preparatory education orientation toward theory, in contrast with enterprise emphasis on practical applications in specific settings. Attention to career paths helps engineers to select from educational opportunities.

The Japanese practice of lifetime employment for about one-quarter of the work force employed in large enterprises fosters retraining, cross training, teamwork, quality circles, job transfer, and rotation. Salary level is less related to ability and performance than to educational level and seniority, an approach that reduces flexibility but encourages supervisors to increase the abilities of subordinates without fear of displacement. Recent shifts have been toward creativity, merit systems, and exchanges among enterprises and abroad (Hanaoka, 1986; Oshima and Yamada, 1985; Saha, 1987).

United Kingdom

Similarities and differences regarding continuing engineering education in Japan and Britain help illuminate societal and organizational influences that have implications for strategic planning (Zhang, Ren, and Ruan, 1989, pp. 867–885). In both countries, comprehensive approaches seem desirable to reduce shortages of engineers; in addition to making use of continuing education, these approaches include increasing the numbers of engineering school graduates, offering more attractive incentives, promoting technicians, reducing turnover, and reducing recruitment difficulties of enterprises. Compared with the United Kingdom, Japan tends to give more attention to planned change, research and development, and future-oriented training through long-term seniority, job rotation, and group staff development. By contrast, Britain has stressed preparation of individuals for immediate technical problem solving and promotion to management instead of advancement in technical specialties. In Japan, in contrast with the U.K., there has been greater emphasis on personnel development by top management and personnel departments; use of project teams related to research, development, and production; assignment and rotation of engineers to projects to develop abilities; and use of the criteria of seniority and ability to promote individuals along specialist career routes comparable in status and salary to managerial progression.

In Britain, government support has consisted mainly of encouraging enterprises to increase continuing engineering education; there has been little or no legislation or direct subsidy. Enterprises have taken the initiative in efforts such as the Professional Industrial and Commercial Updating Program (PICKUP), which was started by the Department of Education and has included some cooperation between universities and enterprises. Economic decline in the United Kingdom has stimulated support for continuing engineering education, and demand has increased—as reflected in a 1982 regulation requiring off-site continuing education before taking the civil engineering final professional exam. In most specialties, engineers have attended programs with time off and financing from the enterprise. Programs have been available from various providers, including associations, enterprises, and higher education institutions. Enterprises are not required to provide continuing education, and some have been concerned that engineers who participate will be more likely to move to another enterprise. Since 1977, higher education institutions have confronted issues of economic survival. In this environment, continuing education has shifted from liberal education toward economic justifications for increased occupational education. Collaboration for continuing engineering education has occurred especially when universities recognized benefits from partnerships with industry. In one region, five higher education institutions and an association have collaborated. The Open University has used various instructional methods, including television and other forms of educational technology for distance education, to provide an M.S. program for practicing engineers with access to laboratories in their enterprises and faculty members from both higher education and industry. The feasibility of such distance education offerings has depended on numbers of participants in relation to obsolescence rate of content to allow acceptable unit costs for courses (Ramsden, 1985; Zhang, Ren, and Ruan, 1989, pp. 645–649, 849–853).

Germany

In the Federal Republic of Germany, most *continuing* engineering education was provided privately (primarily by enterprises for their own engineers), compared with predominant government funding of *preparatory* education. This arrangement may have served engineers in larger enterprises well, but not the unemployed and engineers in smaller enterprises who attended programs provided by professional associations and educational institutions. The continuing education opportunities created by IBM for its engineers and related staff working in Germany illustrate the extensive programs provided by a large multinational enterprise in which education and work were closely connected and had both individual and enterprise benefits. For continuing engineering education in general, varied funding sources were desirable because program offerings were influenced by economic fluctuations, such as those related to the oil crisis in the early 1980s (Scheibl and Bartz, 1986; Zhang, Ren, and Ruan, 1989, pp. 1082–1089).

Netherlands

Government policy can encourage collaboration for industrial innovation. The Netherlands has recognized knowledge as an important resource for innovation, and continuing education as a valuable means for providing it to engineers in small- and medium-sized enterprises, as reflected in a 1979 policy document on innovation. Technology transfer centers have been established to accelerate exchanges in both directions between research and practice. Collaboration has been promoted between enterprises and higher education institutions such as universities and higher technical schools. There has been some government support, but most of the costs have been paid by enterprises and individuals. Practical training has been emphasized, and some student technology transfer projects have led to further cooperation between an enterprise and educational institution. A comprehensive approach includes industrial training for educators (van Meygaard, 1985).

International cooperation related to continuing engineering education in the Netherlands and other European countries seems to be increasing, and more is likely with the onset of the European Community (EC). Although there has been little cooperation among European universities, at least one proposal was made in 1985 for an EC-related office to broker cooperation between higher education institutions, associations, and enterprises for provision of continuing engineering education. Such programs tend to be highly competitive and conducted on a cost-recovery basis, and strong programs that compete well can result from collaboration, as illustrated by a joint effort by Ireland, Jordan, and the United States (Kelly, 1985).

Programs for Teachers

The foregoing examples illustrate societal influences on continuing professional education for high-status occupations with few specialists in a location who confront rapid change. By contrast, the following examples for occupations such as school teachers suggest some additional implications for strategic planning.

Nigeria

Since 1979, a continuing education program for mostly rural school teachers with only an elementary teaching certificate (some of whom teach in the lower grades of Nigerian secondary schools) has been provided by the Institute of Education at the University of Ibadan, founded in 1956 but since 1977 separate from the university department of education. The institute conducts continuing education, applied research, and cooperative projects to strengthen local schools. Since 1976, when the government decided on universal primary education, there have been shortages of certified elementary school teachers. The government provided a special subsidy during the first year of this in-service education program, but since then financial support has been from participant fees, with some subsidy from the institute budget. Enrollments have increased over the years and doubled between 1987 and 1988. The program purpose has been to enable teachers with the basic certificate to attain the next higher certificate and to improve their teaching performance and modernize schools. There is evidence that valuable improvements have occurred. Additional benefits include the higher certificate, which allows admission to higher education, the chance of a prize for academic achievement, and the prospects for increased pay (which has been delayed by economic problems). In addition to improved teaching, program plans are geared toward regional program locations to allow access throughout a large area; they are also aimed at promotion of improvements in the schools through dissemination of new knowledge and changed attitudes toward modernizing elementary education. The parent university has greatly influenced policy, plans, and staffing, which mainly includes faculty members but also some school staff members (Resource A, C. Okedara (b)).

Ghana

A similar program in Ghana was for undereducated rural elementary school teachers (Resource A, Ansere). A distance education approach well served the many uncertified teachers located in rural schools throughout the country but was opposed by the central government because the method had roots in the British colonial period.

Republic of Ireland

Government influence was also central in an example from Ireland. The Health Education Bureau of the national government established high priority for in-service education of secondary school teachers by influencing policy and plans and providing full funding (Resource A, Donoghue). The program reflects collaboration between the bureau and local schools. In addition to bureau priorities, program policies are responsive to increasing public concern about health and feedback from earlier program participants. Staffing decisions are influenced by bureau financial arrangements, but also by local schools and evidence of outcomes. Participation by teachers as students in the program is influenced by anticipated benefits, collaboration with the schools, and some evidence of results.

Greece

In-service education of elementary and secondary school teachers in Greece is related to the fragmented and limited provision of adult education generally, political and economic turmoil, and classical-philosophical versus vocational emphasis in education. Former programs by the government were held in few locations (which discouraged participation) and had centralized priorities (which emphasized transmission of classical knowledge). Recent efforts to implement proposals to reform in-service for teachers by establishment of quasi-independent teacher centers have been delayed by economic and political problems. These centers were to have had government financial support and shared governance by representatives of teachers' unions, schools, and universities (Resource A, Kassotakis). Universities have emphasized classical preparatory education and provided little continuing education, and adult education has been provided by various organizations, such as local adult education centers for literacy education, voluntary associations and private enterprises, vocational education programs similar to community colleges, and to some extent the Orthodox Church, which was a major preserving force during four centuries under the Ottoman empire. Societal influences include strong patriarchal family ties, patron-client loyalties, and fierce independence. During the 1980s, the socialist government somewhat reduced the urban bias that previously depressed rural services. Poor economic conditions and lack of government continuity have been additional deterrents to adult education (Boucouvalas, 1988).

Continuing education for teachers in various countries reveals influences and implications for planning similar to those in

Greece. A fundamental feature is an effort to serve large numbers of geographically dispersed school teachers, who are unable to pay the full program costs; this situation makes government financial support important if difficult to obtain. Public concern about improving education and university collaboration with local schools have helped in-service efforts. Poor economic conditions have been a pervasive hindrance, which makes diversification of program financial support desirable. Recognition of learner benefits encourages participation.

Programs for Other Professions

Examples of continuing education in other professional fields provide additional insights. For instance, there has been a long-standing interest in creating a college for senior police officers in Ireland to supplement and reinforce local staff development for police. Because government was the main source of funds, economic conditions affected external funding. However, the first two phases have been completed at a cost of $23 million. The decision to proceed with the college reflected social change—mainly worsening crime problems—and increased emphasis on human relations, which increased priority for an intensive continuing education program for current senior officers (Resource A, Moran).

An extensive cross-national study of work-related values identifies cultural differences with major implications for continuing education of managers. National differences regarding such cultural characteristics as individualism, avoidance of uncertainty, and power differentials affect management development activities in the context of enterprise and national subcultures. Especially in enterprises with international connections, effective managers seek to understand local contingencies as they promote organizational development to achieve teamwork in support of shared visions. National differences also reflect subcultural differences within the United States. Hofstede (1980) concludes that organizational development programs to stimulate interpersonal openness and feedback, which have been effective in America, have been somewhat less so in Britain, have tended to be dependent on authority in France, are considered a distraction from task achievement in Germany, are felt to be subversive in Latin America, and are considered potentially embarrassing in Japan. These findings underscore the importance of contingency leadership based on understanding of cultural values as an important feature of continuing education of managers who interact with people from various subcultures.

Sometimes it is desirable to begin with a social issue and then attract concerned practitioners from several professions for an inter-professional educational program to address interrelated aspects of the issue. In an Australian example, university continuing educa-tion staff members established a neutral venue for a program on welfare and health care, which served social workers, physicians, nurses, attorneys, police officers, school teachers, and community health workers. Program planning and finance were influenced by the university as the parent organization, by collaboration with various organizations and powerful elites, and by appropriations of government funds, which decreased in part due to worsening eco-nomic conditions (Resource A, McDonnell). Interprofessional edu-cation is also the main purpose of a recently established Center for Interprofessional Studies at the University of Nottingham in the United Kingdom.

Strategic Planning

This concluding section highlights major implications of the pro-grams just discussed for strategic planning. The highlights pertain to the utility of a comparative perspective on participation and on various stakeholders in continuing professional education that is an open system and that sometimes serves best through collaborative approaches.

Participation

In most adult education programs, stakeholders include learners, instructors, and coordinators on behalf of the provider organiza-tions. For continuing professional education, learners can assume major responsibility for educational decision making, and there can be additional stakeholders such as policy makers, people in related occupations, and members of the public to be served. Preparatory education and the nature of professional work make self-directed learning possible and desirable. This fact suggests that strategic planning include holistic consideration of the range of professional education—preparatory education and nonformal acquisition of indigenous knowledge as well as more formal acquisition of organized knowledge—to achieve and maintain expertise. Some professionals have demonstrated their use of such a sequence of learning activities to enhance their proficiencies (Davis, Thomson, Oxman, and Haynes, 1992). A broad view of the continuum of professional education can also be used to encourage and support self-directed learning activities and to improve both preparatory and continuing education.

Participation in continuing professional education is stimulated by various societal trends and conditions. Technological change and modernization in developing countries can be seen in most of the examples from the United States and other countries related to occupations such as medicine, pharmacy, and engineering. Professionals in such occupations respond to both shortages (such as engineers in Britain and Japan) and oversupply (such as urban physicians in Germany and Greece). In contrast with professions composed of dispersed specialists, teaching is an occupation with large numbers of moderate- to low-income professionals who perform similar roles in communities all over the country. Especially in developing countries with many uncertified elementary teachers, the continuing education approach emphasizes individual benefits and methods. Even the programs for Brazilian engineers have stressed individual rewards. There has been some recognition of benefits to school systems, as shown in the U.S. and Nigerian examples. In Nigeria, priority was increased by a government decision on behalf of universal elementary education. In Ireland, growing public concern about law enforcement led to establishment of a long-proposed program for police officers. Internationalization of enterprises has contributed to increased interest in programs on comparative cultural understanding for managers. Strategic planning can help leaders recognize such influences on participation that are salient locally. This recognition can result in identification of categories of potential participants. The examples discussing rural physicians in Australia, Canada, and Greece demonstrate how barriers—such as the difficulty of being away from patients with no one else on call or the lack of hospital connections—encourage use of educational technology and distance education. Public libraries confront shifting patron characteristics and budget problems, while special librarians are dealing with expansion and use of technology. The Japanese engineer example illustrates long-standing support for and connection with career paths, and the program for U.S. primary-care physicians shows sequencing of continuing education activities from various sources. U.S. procedures for mandatory continuing education reflects an attempt to assist professionals whose practice is substandard. The Illinois CME example illustrates use of quality standards for approval of continuing education providers. Strategic planning should help providers recognize and use appropriate standards so that programs will be both of high quality and responsive to participants.

Stakeholders

Strategic planning can also be used to identify and involve representatives of the other stakeholders whose participation in the planning process can improve the plans and their implementation. Stakeholders who provide financial or other forms of support usually have influence on the planning process. It is especially important but difficult to involve stakeholders from related occupations and the public to be served. Such involvement depends on mutually beneficial exchanges. These did occur in interprofessional education programs in Australia, Britain, and the United States.

A comprehensive perspective on program functioning in relation to external influences and benefits can be enhanced by viewing it as an open social system. A systemic approach to planning specifies multiple external influences, with an understanding that continued support depends on satisfactory outcomes. A planning outcome is clarification of the mission of the provider agency. One function of leadership is to communicate such a vision of desired outcomes, so that there is agreement by stakeholders on shared goals. Findings from impact evaluation studies of program outcomes can be used to encourage input by stakeholders.

Successful continuing professional education programs are

shaped by multiple influences. Proximate influences on which a
program depends (such as participants, instructors, and supporting
resources) tend to be represented in the composition of planning
committees. Studies have documented the extent to which the vitality of continuing professional education programs relies on educational leadership that links client systems and resource systems.
There are also more distant influences that include both local contingencies and broader societal influences beyond the service area of
the programs. Strategic planning helps identify such external influences to harness those that help and to deflect those that hinder.
Local contingencies consist of alternative continuing education
providers and opportunities and work-related conditions that affect
professionals' educational needs and use of new learning. Broader
societal influences include rate of change and new knowledge pertinent to professional practice, supply and demand for professionals
in the field, political and economic conditions in the society, and
cultural values like individualism and elitism.

Most continuing professional education planners work in the
context of a provider organization, professional field, and national
setting. A comparative perspective can enrich planning and implementation by alerting leaders to distinctive local contingencies and
alternative approaches to consider. A comparative understanding of
providers includes similarities and differences between the four main
types (associations, enterprises, higher education institutions, and
independent consultants). A comparative view of professions includes five settings (entrepreneurial, collective, hierarchical, adjunct,
and facilitative). One distinctive aspect of an international comparative perspective is the range from technologically advanced to developing countries. The effect of educational program relations on
the field of practice can be to improve function (provide assistance),
to create conflict (challenge goals and practices), or to provide a
critical viewpoint (promote gradual change). Such a comparative
perspective on planning is especially important for the expanding
number of programs that are cosponsored, interprofessional, and
multinational or that involve multiple subcultures. Continuing professional education is one of the most rapidly expanding parts of the
adult education field, so planners should use comparative perspec-

tives to understand influences that help and that hinder program and agency development.

Cooperative perspectives can enrich local strategic planning by suggesting attractive benefits to stakeholders that could promote useful collaboration. The foregoing examples suggest some possibilities. For U.S. engineers, suggestions by potential participants, cosponsors, and supporters can contribute to cooperation among small enterprises, associations, and colleges of engineering. In the Norwegian example, overload pay for faculty members in the only major college of engineering encouraged their cooperation with the professional association on a joint program. In Brazil, government priority fostered collaboration between higher education and professional associations. In China, government support and educational television capability helped to create cooperation between enterprises and higher education institutions. In Britain, government encouragement of enterprises increased their contribution to continuing education, but declining financial support for higher education institutions depressed their assistance. In the Netherlands, the government promoted collaboration between enterprises and higher education institutions (such as through technology transfer centers), and the prospect of EC cooperation was an additional incentive.

Similar societal influences on cooperation occurred for continuing medical education (CME). In the case of the Illinois Council on CME, its accreditation of CME providers (universities, hospitals, associations) was in the interest of program quality, in response to concerns about regulatory agencies, hospital costs, malpractice, and mandatory education. In the former Soviet Union, a centralized institute promoted cooperation with regional medical schools and provided staff development for CME instructors. In the Canadian rural CME example, the medical school worked with hospitals and associations.

There were also multiple stakeholders in collaborative endeavors for teachers. In the U.S. program to improve in-service programs to benefit students, there was cooperation between schools, associations, universities, and teacher centers. The Irish health department responded to public concern and financed in-service education to improve health education in the schools. In the Greek proposal to strengthen teacher centers, public concern, poor economic conditions, and fragmented political turmoil stalled progress. In any country and professional field, the challenge to strategic planning is to identify the main stakeholders and desirable collaboration that will strengthen program goals and quality.

Collaboration

Planners benefit especially from comparative perspectives for purposes of collaboration. Many of the excellent examples in this chapter illustrate influences on and results of various collaborative arrangements. A major theme regarding successful collaboration is complementarity, such as linkage between enterprises and higher education institutions or the importance of association programs to serve smaller enterprises. Complementary contributions are one of three essential conditions of successful collaboration, along with common purposes and shared benefits. Cost sharing for educational technology promotes collaboration, which if successful can lead to other forms of cooperation. In a comprehensive systemic view of continuing professional education, research on the process of planning and implementation is a neglected contribution.

Strategic planning can address acquisition of resources, such as diversification of financial support and combinations of professors and practitioners as instructors. Complementarity was illustrated by the program where professors of medicine offered instruction in community hospitals for physicians who then referred patients to a teaching hospital. Referrals also encouraged specialists to volunteer as instructors in Australia and Greece. Comparative perspectives are especially valuable for planning interprofessional programs, in which differences between several professional fields can be complex, and it is helpful to make major similarities and differences explicit in the interest of shared vision and cooperation. Interprofessional education programs at Ohio State University and at Pennsylvania State University provide contrasting but successful instances in which broader issues such as ethical issues or self-managed professional development promoted cooperation by several professions (Cervero, Azzaretto, and Associates, 1990; Queeney, 1990). Analysis of similarities and differences in continuing education across various professional fields has only been conducted occasionally in the United States. In fact, continuing professional education is usually planned and analyzed only within each separate professional field. However, interprofessional programs, publications, and conferences that include educators from various professional fields can promote a comparative professional perspective unique to the United States.

Although there are some distinctive features of planning continuing professional education programs (related to participants' high levels of education and status and to the sometimes complex relations between programs and stakeholders), the main ideas outlined here are relevant to several other chapters. For example, professionals have availed themselves of distance education opportunities, have been prominent as participants in cultural programs and programs for elders, have been influential in the success of health education activities, and have been criticized as part of the elite establishment in some programs aimed at community problem solving. Continuing professional education concepts and planning procedures are very applicable to all other program areas with regard to in-service education for adult education agency staff members and volunteers who plan and conduct programs. Development of adult education staff (especially instructors) has been repeatedly identified worldwide as a major issue in the field.

10

Education
for Elders

Educational programs for older adults (referred to as elders) have
emerged in recent years. The author's personal teaching experience
during the 1950s in two educational programs for older adults provides a practical introduction to this topic. Back then, few people
would have predicted the subsequent growth of adult education for
elders. One program was the Silver Whistle, an adult education
center and sheltered workshop provided by the Syracuse, New York,
public school adult education division and located in a low-income
neighborhood with a high proportion of older adults; it was open
to interested elders from throughout the city. The average age of
participants was about eighty, and for some of them the "learn to
earn" feature was attractive, because it enabled them to supplement
their retirement income by selling the woodworking and crafts
items they learned to make. The title of the second program, provided by the continuing education division of Syracuse University,
was Preparation for Retirement. However, almost all of the actual
participants were people in the helping professions who worked
with older adults. Similar adult education programs in other parts
of the country also experienced difficulty attracting older adults on
the topic of retirement. During the 1950s and 1960s, few adults over
age sixty participated in adult education.

Trends in Education for Elders

There is a striking contrast between the 1950s and the 1990s regarding the numbers and status of older adults in U.S. society, as well

312

as in adult education. For several centuries after the initial European settlements in North America, the frontier mentality that arose in the New World was largely the product of the younger age distribution in the United States and the lesser reliance on the traditions of elders. Increasingly during this century, more people have been living longer, a situation that has been compounded during the past generation by a declining birth rate.

In addition to the fact that older adults constitute a larger proportion of the U.S. population, there are trends in the characteristics of older adults that have contributed to increased educational participation: improved financial means, younger age at retirement, satisfactory health condition, increased geographic mobility, and residence removed from extended family, and especially increased level of formal education. In addition to these general trends, there is also greater diversity among elders, in part because over the years people become more different from one another.

Along with changing demographics, there have been shifts in cultural values. Rapid technological change has undermined traditional reliance on the personal experience of elders. Geographic dispersion of members of extended families has reduced interdependence and reinforced individualism and the subculture of elders (as exemplified by retirement communities). The longer average length of retirement (because people retire earlier and live longer) has increased political and economic attention to chronic health care, solvency of the Social Security system, and leisure time activities. This value shift has been reflected in moderation of the traditional emphasis on youth in U.S. society and a relative increase in priority for aging-related issues, policies, and programs, including political policies, allocation of economic resources, and increased health and social services.

The emergence of a large aging subculture in a society that previously devalued old people has not only resulted in an improved image of elders in the mass media and increased attention to them in merchandising of goods and services, it has also changed the image of education for older adults. Of course, enough negative attitudes toward these individuals remain that there is some irony in referring to them as *elders,* a term traditionally associated with a select and honored few.

As noted earlier, in the 1950s, there were few educational

programs aimed at older adults, and involvement by elders in other educational programs was very limited. Participation by elders was in part depressed by the much lower average level of formal education that older adults had obtained when they were young, compared with young adults in the 1950s and 1960s. At that time, the stereotype of education for elders was recreation-oriented senior citizens' groups sponsored by community agencies and study circles for older members offered by religious institutions. In the 1990s, there is greater recognition of diversity among older adults and provision of a variety of educational opportunities for them. Large and growing numbers of healthy, affluent, and well educated elders participate not only in educational programs designed for them but in many other types of adult education programs as well, provided by many types of public and private organizations. Unfortunately, much less is currently available for elders with lower levels of education and income. Nevertheless, projections for the next decade or two are that average educational levels of older adults will become comparable to those of the general adult population.

A distinctive requirement of leadership of adult education for elders is to offer program variety and options responsive to the diversity of older adults. Elders are interested in both personal and societal educational benefits. Compared with the past, elders have completed more formal education, have better health, and confront changing family arrangements and cultural values related to age. Program leaders also confront such societal influences as economic conditions, public policy, and multiple adult education providers. Financial subsidy is a persistent issue (Gayfer, 1985; Lumsden, 1985; Merriam and Cunningham, 1989, chap. 40; Peterson, 1983; Pitman, 1984).

The examples and rationale regarding education for elders address four themes that have implications for strategic planning. One is that leadership is especially important in the typically small and informal provider agencies; projection of a clear mission and development of staff and volunteers are thus especially important. A second theme is responsiveness to diverse elders who are affected by social change. A third is the importance of cultural values that affect participants and policy makers. The fourth is the impact of the societal context, such as public policy and economic conditions.

The chapter concludes with implications of these and related themes for strategic planning.

Elderhostel

When Elderhostel began in 1975, 220 people participated. In the early 1990s, Elderhostel programs attracted about a quarter-million older adults annually. However, during the 1960s and early 1970s, efforts to initiate and provide educational programs for older adults met with limited success. In 1962, a retired school teacher initiated and served as director of a mutual aid educational society for retirees called the Institute for Retired Professionals (IRP), which was affiliated with the New School for Social Research, a university in New York City. Members served as instructors as well as learners in the educational offerings and were able to audit regular courses at the university. This pioneering activity spawned similar programs in a few large U.S. cities. Over the years, the director spoke and wrote often about IRP and in 1973 did so at a symposium of the 26th annual meeting of the Gerontological Society in Florida (Hirsch, 1978). That same year, a French university initiated a very similar program called the University of the Third Age. Within a decade, this became one of the most widely emulated educational programs for older adults, with programs throughout the world (Brasseul, 1984; Radcliffe, 1982). Two years after the founding of the French program, Elderhostel began, with dramatic results already noted. All three programs were for active, educated, and fairly affluent elders. A question to consider throughout this chapter is what contributed to the unprecedented growth of University of the Third Age and Elderhostel programs, compared with IRP and other earlier attempts. The answers have implications for strategic planning.

In addition to rapid expansion over seventeen years, Elderhostel has diversified its programs in North America and in countries around the world. Several features remain the same. Domestic programs last one or two weeks, and international programs last two or three weeks. Local educational institutions and other organizations serve as host and provide programs that combine stimulating educational activities and interesting recreational activities, such as sightseeing and cultural events. Aside from travel expense for international programs, costs are modest. In the early 1990s, the annual increase in enrollments was about 15 percent. Recent program innovations have included outdoor adventures (such as white water rafting) and intergenerational programs for grandparents and grandchildren. (Events in the Persian Gulf during 1990 to 1991 resulted in cancellation of programs in the region, but in other times and locations adjustments were made to minimize the effects of turbulence abroad on international programs.)

Cooperating local organizations sponsor programs on topics related to distinctive community resources and interests. For example, in Alaska, a program in Denali Park featured the wildlife and ecology around Mt. McKinley, and the program at Kenai Peninsula College discussed the sea life in Kechemak Bay. In California, a Yosemite Institute program focused on the park; in Hawaii, a program at the Volcano Art Center covered Hawaiian traditions and ecology related to volcanoes. A northern Arizona program was about the Grand Canyon, and a University of Arkansas program featured Ozark mountain folk music. A program of Northwestern State University of Louisiana dealt with the cultures and folklife of that state; in Montana, a Dawson Community College program was on Teddy Roosevelt, who vacationed in that area; in Nebraska, a Chadron State College program was on art related to cowboys. In New Jersey, a Cape May Institute program was about birding. The Sagamore Conference Center in the Adirondacks of northern New York gave a program on literature about those mountains, and the College of Santa Fe in New Mexico had a program on Southwest Indian arts and crafts. Northeastern Oklahoma University offered a course on cowboy culture, and Brigham Young University in Utah had a workshop on genealogy. This selection from the hundreds of local providers and thousands of available courses illustrates the variety in local topics, regions, and types of cooperating organizations. Adult education leaders should consider such potential variety in order to be responsive to the diversity of older adults in their service area.

Many topics, of course, are not local: a Colorado Mountain College course was on writing one's life story; in Delaware, a Wesley College offering included discussing contemporary films with screenwriters; an Eastern Illinois University course was on remembering the Depression; and in Texas, a Baylor University program was on physics and the everyday environment.

During a recent year, moreover, educational programs and study tours for Americans were held in more than thirty-five countries around the world. The following examples provide an idea of topics and locations. In Australia, the University of Queensland course on the Great Barrier Reef included viewing fish by snorkeling and in a semisubmersible; a bicycle tour in Britain visited churches and castles; and in Brazil, those taking a course by the National Institution for Amazon Research visited the Amazon jungle. In China, Hefei Province Institute offered a course on Chinese painting and calligraphy, and in Greece, an Anatolia College course featured locations associated with Alexander the Great. In Israel, an Open University offering analyzed contemporary Israeli society; a Louvre museum course was on French art in Paris; and a Free University of Berlin course was on the many faces of Berlin over the years. In Kenya, the U.S. International University–Nairobi included a safari to the Masai Mara National Reserve, and one of the language schools in Cuernavaca, Mexico, offered an immersion course in Spanish. The growing popularity of Elderhostel international programs reflects the attractiveness of local cooperating organizations and the interests, financial ability, and in some cases the stamina of the participating elders. Leaders with a comparative perspective can more readily cooperate with international cosponsors.

Other U.S. Programs

The August–September 1991 issue of *Modern Maturity,* the magazine of the American Association of Retired Persons (now the largest membership organization in the United States), featured a cover article on older adults going back to school. The story provided an overview of available opportunities and included human interest stories about these people's experiences, tips on doing so successfully, identification of helpful resources, suggestions about auditing and tuition waivers for continuing education courses, and a listing of universities with free or low-fee audit arrangements for people over age sixty or sixty-five. In addition to educational institutions, educational opportunities were available from libraries, museums, associations, religious institutions, private businesses, community agencies, and study tours and in the form of self-study books. The article included information on special programs for elders but emphasized older adults participating in other educational programs.

A major societal influence on education for older adults has been the set of policies and practices related to retirement. Over the years, legislation and practices by enterprises related to mandatory or preferred retirement age have reflected economic conditions and unemployment problems, such as lowering the retirement age to make jobs available for unemployed youth and raising the retirement age when there were labor shortages and social security retirement costs became burdensome. Large numbers of retirees create a demand for educational opportunities by people with time, ability to pay, and interest in largely nonvocational topics. Retirement has also prompted provision of preretirement educational programs beginning several generations ago. Enterprises have been major providers of preretirement education for their employees, but programs have also been provided by educational institutions and other organizations. Typical programs have been brief and informational, often the equivalent of a day or two, on topics such as retirement planning, financial benefits, and procedures for leaving the enterprise. Very few people about to retire have participated (often about 5 percent), and those who have are disproportionately people with higher levels of education, income, and occupational prestige. People forced to retire because of mandatory retirement ages may be angry, a situation that can discourage participation.

In addition to Elderhostel and preretirement programs, there are other programs for older adults, such as the senior centers that include adult education along with recreational activities, meals, and social services. These more comprehensive and inexpensive offerings attract more low-income elders than programs such as Elderhostel. As noted earlier, some religious institutions provide educational programs aimed at older members, but many elders prefer to participate in educational activities for adults of all ages. Some of them even avoid age-graded programs. Choosing from all adult education programs increases greatly the number of available providers, programs, and topics. This choice is especially appropriate because contrary to the false and narrow stereotype of older adults, as noted, diversity increases as people become older; therefore, program options should be greater, not fewer.

As policy makers and program administrators seek to provide differentiated and responsive educational opportunities, attention should be given to the interplay of personal and situational factors that facilitate and act as barriers to participation. Many such influences encourage participation if they are above a threshold that motivates such a decision and discourage it if they are below. Examples of personal influences include health condition, learning ability, educational level, and financial means. Situational influences include program information, available transportation, educational counseling, affordable program fees, accessible times and locations, and attractive topics and methods. Many adult education activities are scheduled in the evenings when classrooms, instructors, and working adults are available. Yet this timing is unsatisfactory for many older adults for whom evening hours are periods of low energy and high risk compared with midday. A great variety of noncredit, nonvocational programs should be provided to be responsive to the range of older learners. Included are practical subjects related to coping—health, nutrition, finances, home repairs, and crime prevention. Other topics should consider public issues and expressive concerns, such as arts, philosophy, spirituality, religion, history, genealogy, and public affairs. The crucial implication for strategic planning is that individual elders vary greatly and that a great variety of educational opportunities should be available to be responsive to the older population (Kasworm, 1983; Merriam and Cunningham, 1989; Manheimer, 1984; Okun, 1982; Peterson, 1983).

Another situational influence has been societal norms and expectations regarding characteristics, needs, and preferences of older adults. More specifically, young people have assumed that the main concerns of older adults relate to death when actually they relate to finances and avoidance of dependency. A benefit of intergenerational programs has been improved understanding. As the number of retirees increases, along with their power as voters and consumers, they are likely to receive increased attention, including their roles as learners. Strategic planning should focus on the match between subpopulations of elders and educational opportunities, with special attention to the undeserved and to the societal as well as personal benefits from educational programs for older adults. A widespread rationale for public subsidy of such programs is that because many elders have limited ability to pay full costs, their programs should be subsidized. (Fee-waiver programs on a space-available basis may entail only marginal costs.) Because they have been taxpayers for many years, they may now feel they deserve such benefits. Elders' programs do not fit the usual economic rationale of occupational education, but it is less expensive to provide educational programs with preventative benefits than to bear the costs of remedial and custodial services due to unnecessary dependency.

Adult Education in China

Educational programs for older adults have been a very small part of adult education in China. An overview of the total scope of adult education at the end of this section provides a background for Chinese examples in other chapters. Analysis of elder education reveals international and domestic societal influences that have implications for strategic planning. Ten years after University of the Third Age was initiated in France, the first "university" for the aged in China was started in September 1983 by Shandong Red Cross in Jinan, the provincial capital. By the end of 1985, there were seventy-three such institutions in various provinces with a total enrollment of over forty thousand (Resource A, Dong and Zhu (a)). Three years later, there were five hundred such institutions for older adults, more than twenty in the national capital of Beijing.

The first one established in Beijing in 1984 was the fifth in the country. This and each of the other institutions reflected the local clientele and leadership. This institution, located in the Hai Dian District of northwest Beijing where there were many higher education institutions, began with a few hundred participants and was financially unstable. By 1989, there were twenty-two classes serving about eight hundred participants, the minimum age was fifty, and there were no other entrance requirements. Most participants are in their sixties. Many intellectuals live in the district, and half of the participants have university degrees. The president is a well-known artist, and program specialties include painting, calligraphy, planting flowers, and writing Chinese history. In contrast with this emphasis on the arts and also exercise for good health, similar institutions in other districts offer programs on cooking, sewing, and current affairs that are also open to older adults from throughout the city. In the Hai Dian District institution, participants attend once a week for four-month terms, and there is a two-year certificate for basic study. In 1989, about twenty part-time teachers typically taught one course each and received small honoraria to cover transportation and to pay for correcting homework assignments. Most of them are retired college teachers or experts. Participants pay small fees, and there is some government subsidy. In response to growing demand, the central location provides teaching plans and coordination for five financially independent outreach centers in the district that enroll an additional five hundred participants.

These universities furnish age-graded programs similar to those of University of the Third Age and Elderhostel, but they and other organizations also produce print and audiovisual materials for use by other elders. Additional organizations also provide reading and discussion groups, programs on preventive health and recreation, and opportunities to view TV university programs. Many educational programs have upper age limits that prevent retirees from participating, a restriction contributing to demand for the remaining programs. In urban areas, retirement ages typically range between fifty-five and sixty, with women retiring younger than men. Retirement is sometimes delayed in occupations with shortages. There were glowing testimonials about personal benefits by participants. Education for elders also benefits society, such as by helping retired engineers and other specialists establish consulting services or using them to settle disputes. Planning of such programs in any country should consider both personal and societal benefits.

Various societal influences have affected educational programs for elders in China. A major and pervasive influence has been the cultural value of thousands of years of respect for older adults, which has resulted in family, economic, political, and social power. In addition, high educational achievement has been a major source of status. Most older adults have received little formal education, and they participate less in educational activities in retirement than the more highly educated. With a population of more than one billion and a relatively early retirement age, China has many unemployed older adults. Especially for the 80 percent of the people who live in rural areas, the main responsibility for care of the aged has rested with the family, with assistance by enterprises and government. Some enterprises pay small educational fees for retirees unable to afford them. In the future, family responsibility for elders may change with smaller family size, increased mobility and urban residence, reduction in centrality of the extended family, and increased social services.

After the ten-year chaos from 1966 to 1976, when many educational programs including adult education came to a standstill, the emphasis has been on rebuilding, modernization, and especially economic development. Since 1977, pent-up demand has strained formal education institutions and contributed to high priorities for work-related adult education. As part of the Chinese decentralized way of dealing with a large population, financing of education for elders has been based on small participant fees, assistance by social forces (associations) and enterprises, and modest subsidy by local and national government. An emerging trend pertains to the contributions of education to the transfer of power from older to middle-aged adults (Wang, Lin, Sun, and Fang, 1988; McCormick, 1984; Payne, 1987; Schulz and Davis-Friedman, 1987; Sher, 1984; Resource A, Dong and Zhu (a)).

As noted earlier, education for elders has been a small part of the entire scope of adult education, which has had an occupational emphasis and often an upper age limit of forty. Educational opportunities for adults of all ages have been offered by many types of providers, with many of the credit and degree offerings loosely structured to parallel the formal preparatory education institutions that provide elementary, secondary, and higher education for younger, full-time students. The formal and the adult education systems have had similar enrollments, and students under forty can transfer in either direction. The adult education system has been less expensive. An early priority area was literacy and basic education, to which various providers have contributed to reduce widespread illiteracy following 1949 and again since 1977. Adult secondary and vocational schools, provided by counties, enterprises, and other organizations, have created postliteracy opportunities beyond mastery of two thousand characters in urban settings (or fifteen hundred characters in rural settings due to the more limited basic vocabulary required). Continuing higher education has also been furnished by various organizations. Aside from adult education providers, such as universities for the aged or workers' universities that sponsor many programs below the higher education level, there are postsecondary adult education providers whose offerings go beyond secondary school–level programs. Because of the long tradition of official exams associated with formal education and civil service, such providers have had great latitude in the ways in which adults could prepare to pass the exams. Some (such as open and evening universities and higher education credit courses by workers' universities) are similar to formal residential education institutions. Distance education opportunities for adults have also expanded in recent decades (such as correspondence, self-study, and especially the TV university in many metropolitan areas, which accounts for one-third of all university credit enrollments).

One reason for participation in continuing higher education programs in China has been occupational advancement. A major provider of adult vocational education has been workers' education programs and workers' universities. Some of them associated with larger enterprises provide credit and noncredit vocational and professional education for members of the enterprise (and sometimes family members) that includes offerings at the elementary, secondary, and higher education level. A goal of adult occupational education has been to relate learning closely to work in contrast with traditional preparatory education that has emphasized general education. Rural adult education programs, for the 80 percent of the population who are peasants engaged in agriculture and the expanding proportion of rural adults engaged in nonagricultural occupations, have been provided by various organizations, including township schools and higher education institutions for farmers. Additional adult education opportunities have also been furnished by social education programs, cultural centers, staff development institutions for teachers, labor unions, mass organizations, and special schools for cadres (officials) and managers. Government at all levels assists parts of this decentralized pluralistic system of adult education with policies, some financial support, and monitoring.

The array of providers and programs highlighted in the foregoing overview were largely developed or revived since 1977. They have dramatically increased the extent of adult education participation and reflect a range of interrelated societal influences. In addition to suggesting the context in which education for elders functions, various societal influences should be considered in strategic planning. Government legislation and other policies have given adult education high priority to help achieve modernization of agriculture, industry, defense, and technology. Recent blending of socialist commodity and planned economy has created additional challenges for adult education. The combination of urgent time pressure, limited resources, and emphasis on economic development helps account for an upper age limit for many adult education programs. Shortages of qualified workers (even to serve as adult education instructors), together with limited resources, have contributed to an emphasis on adult education by larger enterprises, which have the capacity to provide resources, release time for workers, and placement of graduates. Many small enterprises have relied on separate adult education providers, which were not seen as competitive with formal education institutions until they began to experience difficulty placing graduates in jobs.

For most workers, government and enterprise policies have restricted geographic mobility; these policies were a major influence for many years when the disparity was widening between level of living in urban and rural areas. Career paths and occupational education for adults were influenced by limited job mobility, status associated with the work group more than the individual position, and waiting lists for some adult education programs. Strong extended family power and traditions, especially in rural areas, resisted some government policies (including adult education and family planning), but recent trends toward greater equality have encouraged educational participation by women. Ideology and peer pressure in rural neighborhoods and urban work sites have also increased individual conformity to societal expectations (such as participation in literacy education) so as not to embarrass the work unit. Other cultural values that have fostered educational participation include status associated with educational attainment (as previously stated) and emphasis on order and harmony to the extent that these values encourage adults to explore ways to achieve desired goals without disturbing the system. Some values may discourage educational activity, such as avoiding individualism, sharing credit and blame, and (especially since the 1966–1977 time of chaos) being reluctant to take risks. Cross-cutting status differences have contributed to solidarity. A byproduct of recent sweeping changes in China may be value changes that will affect adult education, such as increased emphasis on personal versus societal progress (Duke, 1984b, 1987; Hunter and Keehn, 1985; Sidel, 1982; Wang, Lin, Sun, and Fang, 1988; Resource A, Dong and Zhu (b)).

Strategic planning can help local adult education providers set priorities during turbulent transition periods that reflect individual, provider, and societal expectations. For some industries and regions, adult education institutes have been established that help technical and managerial personnel gain proficiency for leadership in their specialty, but with international perspectives. Recent reports include recommendations to strengthen attention to nonvocational, cultural, and personal enrichment programs. After more than a decade of emphasis on economic development, planning rationales can help providers modify and broaden program offerings.

Other Countries

This section is an overview of education for elders in various countries around the world to illustrate distinctive societal influences on programs from country to country that have implications for strategic planning. Japan shares with China traditions of respect for elders and family interdependence. However, as is well known, during the past half-century, a homogenous Japanese society has experienced substantial urbanization and westernization.

Japan

As part of post–World War II reconstruction and democratization of education in Japan, citizen public halls (Kominkan) have emerged as major providers of social education for adults. Other adult education providers include libraries, museums, women's organizations, universities, and enterprises. In 1983, there were 164 municipal learning centers and twenty-seven college-level institutes for elders in Japan. During the 1980s, the Munakata city board of education started a citizens' learning network, similar to the Learning Exchange pioneered in Evanston, Illinois, during the 1960s (Farmer, Knox, and Farmer, 1977; Frischkopf and Braun, 1981; Heffernan, 1981; Miura, 1984; Resource A, Miwa). The network was responsive to both older residents and newcomers in this commuter community who wanted an increased sense of community and were willing to help. However, the traditional Japanese value of modesty discouraged people from volunteering as instructors. To remedy this, a neighborhood nomination system was used. One of the first Japanese universities for elders was founded in 1969 in the city of Kakogama in a former agricultural college. This shift in facilities use from agriculture to aging symbolizes major shifts in Japanese society. Older adults study general education, health, gardening, and leadership for elder education; radio, and correspondence study options have increased (Resource A, Fukuchi).

India

In India, attention to elder education has been more recent, with the first national seminar on preretirement planning taking place in 1985. With India's large and expanding population, much of adult education has been aimed at young adults, as reflected in financial constraints that led to an upper age limit of thirty-five for the adult literacy program. Such age limits have been challenged, and inclusion of elders as both learners and instructors has been urged (Adiseshiah, 1985).

France

As noted earlier, it was the University of the Third Age that began a strikingly rapid international diffusion of such programs. Early programs were typically offered by educational societies without entrance or grading requirements. These were affiliated with higher education institutions, were designed to serve active and able society members who were between the second age of middle-life responsibilities for work and family and the fourth age of decline due to illness and extreme old age. Third-age adults were sometimes referred to as the young old. Program participants were usually concerned with teaching and governance as well as learning and social interaction. Both the sponsoring society and the institution benefited from the partnership. The University of the Third Age was responsive to its members and arranged with the institution for classroom space, courses (which they could audit), and faculty members (to assist them). Over the years, the institution has gained increased understanding of older adults and broadened its clientele of students and potential benefactors. The initial diffusion was mainly to French-speaking countries, but within a few years similar programs began in many countries. Most European countries have developed various elder education programs, in addition to the University of the Third Age and preretirement education, to serve their aging population. Societal influences have included increasing numbers of older adults, decreasing retirement age, few educational opportunities, and many able elders to provide program leadership.

United Kingdom

When the University of the Third Age crossed the channel and was transplanted in British soil, there was increased independence from higher education institutions. There was an anti-authoritarian emphasis of the national league that evolved as a confederation of independent local self-help groups that function much as in other countries, except without an institutional affiliation. Economic conditions in Britain during recent decades have contributed to unemployment, early retirement, and erosion of social services, so University of the Third Age societies have served as rallying places to discuss and seek new roles for elders to transcend their unsatisfactory plight. Their spread has occurred especially in middle-sized communities with enough interested elders but without the many educational opportunities available in metropolitan areas. Other elder education resources in the United Kingdom include scattered preretirement programs, media provision of public information, health education, and access to varied educational programs for adults of all ages (Coleman, 1983; Drews, 1981; Glendenning, 1976;

Midwinter, 1983–1984, 1984a, 1984b; Morris, 1984). Recent pertinent developments include associations like Age Concern, the Pre-Retirement Association of Great Britain, the Association of Educational Gerontology, and the British *Journal of Educational Gerontology*.

Germany

The variety of educational possibilities available to older adults in the German lander (state) of North Rhine-Westphalia is illustrated by a recent report on thirteen programs (Buschmeyer, 1991). Since 1975, University of the Third Age educational programs have been provided by an increasing number of German universities, and in recent years most universities in North Rhine-Westphalia have made courses available to older adults. Dortmund University has offered various programs and accepted older adults in regular courses, encouraged by faculty members in various fields who were interested in aging. Since 1979, Dortmund University has participated in a project entitled "Between Working Life and Retirement," which has been supported since 1984 by the lander Ministry of Urban Development, Housing, and Transport. The project has focused on regional problems such as long-term unemployment and early retirement and has initiated and fostered more than a hundred community-based self-help groups that foster self-organized educational activities for older adults. Aside from university offerings, the 1991 report describes other programs, such as church-sponsored courses on life after retirement, a distance education course, a series on dialogue between the generations sponsored by an adult education center, and elder education programs by labor unions and political parties.

Australia

Since the introduction of the University of the Third Age to Melbourne, Australia, in 1984, it has spread rapidly so that by 1990 there were seventy independent local societies that served about ten thousand elders. Rapid growth reflects earlier retirements, lack of responsive programs, and a community-based approach with various local cosponsors. Volunteer tutors allow low fees, but programs mainly serve middle-class, better-educated adults, twice as many women as men, and those interested in both education and social interaction. A series of studies on these programs in Australia provides detailed conclusions about participants, 90 percent of whom reported that the experience was very beneficial (Swindell, 1988, 1990a, 1990b; Resource A, Swindell). Other elder education programs developed since the late 1970s (which have been by various providers) have depended on volunteers and received diversified financial support; many were initiated and sustained by a person with vision and commitment.

Israel

Over the years, Israel has developed many adult education programs, some of which serve many elders or are aimed at retirees. Haifa University provides special programs for retirees, and the Martin Buber Center of the Hebrew University in Jerusalem coordinates an intergenerational program for mixed generations that allows people over age fifty to enroll in standard university courses with full-time students. Those who choose to enroll emphasize intellectual interests and pursuit of philosophical and religious questions as reasons for participation, with little attention to social interaction. This emphasis reflects an aging trend and the high degree of interest by retired people between fifty and seventy years of age who arrived from Europe before 1949 and now pursue studies they might have taken earlier if they had the opportunity (Glanz, 1984, 1985; Glanz and Tabory, 1985).

Ghana and Argentina

In various African countries, education for elders has had low priority in spite of widespread concern about insufficient nutrition education programs for the elderly poor. An intergenerational program by the Institute of Adult Education at the University of Ghana illustrates efforts to enable elders to share understandings about oral history, folk customs, and traditional crafts with young adults. Resulting materials are used to enrich adult literacy pro-

grams (International Council on Adult Education, 1985). Folklore
was a topic in which half the participants were elders in one adult
education program in Argentina, in contrast with most programs
in Latin America that attract few elders (Hernandez, 1984; Resource
A, Hernandez (b)). In some countries, older women have participated in leadership training to work in community development
programs; they study topics such as women's rights, duties, and
civic responsibilities; interpersonal relations; family health; and
women and economic activities.

Strategic Planning

The foregoing examples of education for elders in various national
settings identify major societal influences. This concluding section
suggests implications for strategic planning that leaders of elder
education programs might consider as they work with stakeholders
in their local programs. Ideas and practices from other national
settings must be adapted to fit a local context, and adaptation is
more likely to be successful if someone associated with the planning
in one country is familiar with program and societal context in the
other country. In the process of comparative analysis, it is important to recognize that similarities tend to be general and differences
tend to be specific. The planning issues addressed in this section
include change, staff, learners, audiences, context, providers, values,
economy, and policy (International Council on Adult Education,
1985; Merriam and Cunningham, 1989; Nusberg, Gibson, and
Peace, 1984).

Change

There are many faces of change that contribute to the importance
of planning. Technology can help increase the proportion of retirees in society. Medical technology can influence family planning,
infant mortality, and health conditions that reduce the proportion
of children and increase the proportion of elders. Agricultural technology can allow a small proportion of the population to take care
of production and increase the proportion of elders and other people who live in urban areas with a greater variety of available ed-

ucational and other programs. Postindustrial technology can accelerate the premium on knowledge, rate of obsolescence, unemployment rates, decline in retirement age, devaluation of contributions by older workers, and increases in retirees. The rapid diffusion of elder education programs such as Elderhostel and University of the Third Age reflect both technological advances (such as transportation and media) and social changes (such as increasing numbers of healthy, affluent, and educated elders combined with insufficient educational opportunities). The effects of more well-educated elders can be seen in the examples from America, France, and Israel. Educational technology can influence elder education, especially when joined with opportunities for discussion and interaction (such as videotapes and discussion or computer simulation–based case analysis). Strategic planning can identify relevant emerging trends so that responsive educational programs can be provided.

Staff

The volunteers and staff who plan and conduct elder education programs are the main resource upon which program success depends. Strategic planning by staff members and other stakeholders contributes to commitment, contributions, and staff development. Thus, the planning process is as important as the completed plans, as it contributes to innovation, coordination, and advocacy. Leadership on behalf of elder education entails forward-looking vision and encouragement of contributions to goal achievement, both of which are intended results of strategic planning. A distinctive feature of elder education is the largely untapped potential of older volunteers who can both help plan and conduct current programs and also attract underserved elders. Elder volunteers were prominent in the examples from the United States, China, Japan, France, and Australia. As with adult education worldwide, staff and volunteer development is one of the major inadequacies of elder education. Fortunately, there are many resources in America for staff development that planning can identify: people associated with providers, state and national associations of adult educators, publications related to elder education, resource centers, and university departments that include adult education and educational gerontology. Cosponsors supplied instructors in the U.S. examples of Elderhostel and preretirement education by enterprises and in the Israeli program.

Learners

Planning should especially address the characteristics of elders themselves. In the past, the few elders in adult education programs were predominantly middle class. Now the trend is toward increasing proportions of elders who are healthy, affluent, well-educated, and geographically mobile; thus, this traditional clientele interested in self-directed learning about general education topics, auditing standard courses, taking study tours, and participating in mutual aid societies should increase. They were the main participants in many U.S. programs and in the examples from China, France, Britain, and Israel. With their many and interdependent roles, they are likely to be active members of an emerging educative society. With the large, growing, and diverse population of older adults in the United States, increased attention should also be given to serving the major subpopulations. Their growing numbers and subsequent political and economic power help attract the attention of policy makers. In the pluralistic U.S. society, there are many subcultures to which elder education can be responsive and which local planning can identify. An illustrative subpopulation may be moderately educated elders interested in age-integrated programs on cultural topics and in age-segregated programs on coping with difficulties of later life (Strom, 1988). A specialized subpopulation may be people with negative attitudes toward forced retirement who resist preretirement education. Another may be adults with little formal education interested in programs that mainly use oral communication to learn about topics related to special interests and to survival concerns. Senior centers have attracted more of such adults. Some programs may relate to the transfer of power across generations. Fortunately, there has been a great expansion of organized knowledge from research (and indigenous knowledge from adult educators) about older adults that strategic planning can use for responsive programming.

Audiences

For most educational programs for elders, the intended benefits are individual and expressive, so self-directed and casual programs seem appropriate. However, sometimes broader organizational, community, or societal changes call for concerted educational efforts with multiple audiences, including elders and people in interdependent roles such as family members and friends, helping professionals, and policy makers. Examples include multigenerational programs, community development projects, and organizational development activities aimed at policy makers within agencies providing adult education who can modify program information, transportation arrangements, fee levels, and counseling assistance to be more responsive to elders. Strategic planning can help forge creative partnerships for planning and implementation of such comprehensive programs aimed at multiple audiences.

Context

Planning can help leaders in this field innovate and adapt programs to local trends and contextual influences. Such situational influences consist of economic conditions, population density, neighborhood educational level, and available educational providers and resources. Also included are supportive cultural and social services, as well as competing activities, such as mass media and recreational activities. Local trends and events may be population shifts, educational reforms, and attractive innovations from elsewhere. The combinations of such trends and local conditions help explain the rapid spread of Elderhostel and University of the Third Age, in contrast to the Institute for Retired Professionals.

Providers

A major societal influence that strategic planning for a provider should address is the existence of diverse and independent other providers, a situation that reflects the pluralistic U.S. social system. Leaders for elder education should be able to deal with this complexity and diversity. There are both governmental and nongovernmental organizations that function at local, regional, state, national, and international levels. Providers may be independent (such as Elderhostel), parts of educational institutions (such as community colleges and universities as reflected in the examples from the United States and Israel), or other organizations (such as enterprises, public halls, or religious institutions). Together, they provide all types of adult education opportunities on all topics, both age segregated and age integrated. Understanding such providers can enable elder education leaders to reduce needless duplication and engage in collaboration in those few instances in which this is the most effective way to provide programs that address unmet needs and gaps in service.

Values

Planning includes value judgments, such as selection of desirable goals, clientele groups, and program features. Policies and priorities reflect such values as social justice, family solidarity, respect for elders, lifelong learning, and assertiveness and interdependence. Traditions reflect values and may help or hinder strategic planning. In many traditional cultures such as China and Ghana (and in some U.S. subcultures), respect for elders and their experience benefits older adults, which has not been the case in the youth-oriented U.S. culture generally. Comparative perspectives illuminate ways to combine seemingly disparate values, such as Confucian and socialist ideas in China or self-help and social welfare in other countries. Such understandings are especially valuable during transition periods such as currently confront elders in the United States, Europe, China, India, and Japan. This transition is reflected in questioning the upper age limit on literacy programs in India. Planning comprehensive programs for multiple audiences is especially important during periods of change when resistance is typical. Program images also arise from values, and the attractiveness of a provider's image affects the ease with which stakeholder cooperation is won and maintained. Values are especially central to transformative learning activities that entail consciousness raising about their condition and aspirations and during the program development process.

Economy

Economic conditions have a particularly strong effect on elder education programs, which usually require subsidy (either financial or by extensive use of volunteers). Economic productivity is valued in many nations, especially in the mixed socialist-capitalist systems of China, Commonwealth of Independent States, and Eastern Europe. Within many countries, educational opportunities and arrangements are associated with enterprise size. Level of living and financial well-being in neighborhoods or communities have an impact on individual choices. Economic growth, population increase, and unemployment have ramifications on age of retirement, as illustrated by examples from China and Britain. Strategic planning can identify major trends and influences that affect providers, elders, and resource allocations to guide decisions related to external subsidy and such mutual aid arrangements as major reliance on volunteers and self-help.

Policy

Lifelong learning in an educative society is an attractive ideal, but in the United States there has been relatively little government legislation or policies by nongovernmental organizations in support of elder education. Even when such priorities are established, they are subject to retrenchment when poor economic conditions or competing priorities cause restrictions in educational services to older adults. The success of the political process on behalf of elder education depends on the strength of support for educational opportunities expressed by older adults and their allies. Strategic planning is an effective way to generate and coordinate such support.

Ideas from several of the other chapters are pertinent to education for elders. Content and methods, related to adult education for cultural affairs, health, and basic skills, are important to some elders. Methods analyzed in relation to part-time and distance education are also relevant to education for elders, especially those in rural areas and with limited geographic mobility. General program strategies described in chapters on cultural minorities and community problem solving are useful for elder education programs that deal with barriers to change.

11

Rural Development

Many U.S. adult education providers serve rural residents. The agricultural extension program through the Cooperative Extension Service (CES) of the land-grant universities provides a large and visible example. In addition to other CES program areas (such as home and family life, youth work, and community resource development), additional contributions to rural adult education are provided by schools, community colleges, other higher education institutions, government agencies, banks, social work agencies, religious institutions, library systems, and voluntary associations. Together, they address many aspects of rural life, especially when rural community development activities are included. This chapter explores strategic planning for rural adult education in the United States and in other countries, with special attention to societal influences that are distinctive in the rural context. Although the focus of this chapter is on adult education related to agricultural production, attention is given to other aspects of rural social systems that are mainly covered in other chapters, such as family life, social and educational services, youth employment, and general quality of life. Most of the rural adult education programs are nonformal and may not fit stereotypes based on formal education.

Features of Rural Adult Education

In spite of the large service areas of some rural adult education providers, sparse population allows field staff members to interact with people associated with various government and nongovernmental providers and other parts of the rural social systems in the service area. This personal contact encourages a systemic versus an individualistic perspective on rural development, and it helps staff members include key stakeholders in the planning process. Advisory groups encourage local input. In part because important resources (such as knowledge, equipment, supplies, and credits) may be located outside a rural service area, a crucial function of agricultural extension and many other types of rural adult education is linkage between client and resource systems. Other adult education providers may focus on serving individual participants with an established curriculum and faculty. For many rural adult education programs engaged in systemic linkage, however, a crucial aspect of planning is analysis of a dynamic social, political, and economic context, in addition to the widespread primary reliance on educational needs assessment for responsive programs. Clientele analysis and market segmentation (type of production, level of living, gender, educational level) remain important to identify and serve major subpopulations. This attention to segmentation is illustrated by the traditional CES emphasis on farmers who are early adopters, in contrast to the program reorientation required to serve the late adopters and laggards (Crouch and Chamala, 1981). However, providers and clients are influenced by local contingencies (such as economic conditions and political priorities) that the external aspects of strategic planning should consider (Axinn and Thorat, 1972, chaps. 8 and 14; Rivera and Gustafson, 1991; Sanders, 1966).

Relations between the provider agency and its parent organization can also be affected by the rural setting. After more than seventy-five years, a large provider such as the CES can develop standard procedures bordering on bureaucratic. Therefore, planning should encourage responsive, innovative, and transformative interactions among multiple stakeholders to achieve commitment to achievement of shared goals. Such flexible collaborative relationships can also strengthen decision making regarding staffing, resources, and accountability. In practice, of course, extension staffs located in a rural service area may be more integrated into local social systems than to the parent organization some distance away. In U.S. land grant universities, faculty specialists from various

fields associated with CES provide a major source of recommended
practices, research findings, and other knowledge that extension
staff members seek to share with rural families in their service area;
this situation differs from agricultural extension field staffs in many
developing countries that lack university affiliations but may be
associated with regional agricultural research centers. In some settings, it may be more crucial to strengthen the links of extension
staff with research than with rural families.

Most adult education programs related to rural development
aim to promote change, which typically entails issues related to
differing priorities and values. Again, there are both similarities and
differences regarding rural development in the United States and in
other countries. In the United States about 3 percent of the work
force produces food and fiber, and there are surpluses. An additional
25 percent works in agribusinesses. In some developing countries,
more that 80 percent of the population live in rural areas, largely
engaged in agriculture, and there are shortages. In both settings,
there is typically some tension between costs and benefits of rural
production and the costs and benefits of urban consumption. Sometimes rural poverty is the price of cheap food for city dwellers. Furthermore, production agriculture (for sale, in contrast with
subsistence agriculture for use by the farm family) has become international (regarding supply and price fluctuations and trade
policies).

Strategic planning can help leaders of adult education for
rural development articulate a compelling vision of their agency's
mission in light of conflicting values and priorities. Identification
of emerging trends allows leaders to use their vision of desirable
future directions to interpret trends regarding threats and opportunities that their provider agency should address. Government agricultural prices affect extension's role in such issues as inequality
and emphasis on rural development (Compton, 1989; Crouch and
Chamala, 1981; Rivera and Gustafson, 1991; Williams, 1968, chap.
3). Long-term planning is important because major improvements
take many years to accomplish.

Distinctive features of leadership for rural adult education
reflect conflicts between rural and urban values. The parent organization for rural extension is a major influence, and one function

of strategic planning is to strengthen relations with the parent organization, especially to achieve agreement of the scope and goals of extension education and desirable outcomes of rural development. However, issues such as cheap food for city dwellers due to efficient commercial agriculture versus rural values associated with small family farms reflect remote influences like government priorities and economic conditions. Effective extension leaders relate to both resource systems and client systems for which tradition, change, education, and risk taking are important factors.

The examples and rationale in this chapter help to illuminate six broad themes important for strategic planning. One theme focuses on the *goals* of rural development and leadership to define program scope, obtain resources for extension education, and maintain satisfactory relations with the parent organization. A second theme is an appreciation of major *trends*. A third pertains to local *contingencies,* including social change and cultural values that affect participation by rural adults in extension activities. A fourth entails collaboration with *stakeholders* in other organizations that can contribute to rural development. The fifth theme is *staff* recruitment, retention, and development—a long-standing concern in efforts to strengthen extension. The sixth theme is *policy* and agency directions. The chapter concludes with implications for strategic planning and implementation related to these themes.

Cooperative Extension Service

When President Woodrow Wilson signed the Smith Lever Act in 1914 to create CES, the legislation formalized evolving educational efforts to strengthen agriculture and rural life that had begun more than a century before and continue today. Many antecedents paved the way for passing the Smith Lever Act. Included were activities by Benjamin Franklin begun in the colonial period to systematize study of agriculture, which included his founding in 1785 of the Philadelphia Society for Promoting Agriculture. Other developments in individual states included establishment in the early 1880s of state boards of agriculture that conducted extension activities, the start of farmers' institutes in state agricultural colleges in the mid 1800s, the work of Seaman A. Knapp as a federally supported agricultural agent in several southern states in the early 1900s, and the Commission on Country Life appointed at that time by President Theodore Roosevelt; the commission recommended a nationwide system of extension. The crucial point for strategic planning was that the Smith Lever Act was the culmination of these grass roots efforts, not the source of them.

Throughout, the basic CES mission has remained much the same: to help rural people to help themselves by provision of research-based, practical education regarding agriculture, home economics, youth work, and community development through non-formal adult education that encourages people to apply what they learn. Over the years, legislative amendments, administrative guidelines, foundation interests, and agreements by the Extension Committee on Organization and Policy have highlighted priority areas within the basic mission—farm safety, pest control, nutrition, pollution, and youth development.

As its name suggests, CES is a cooperative effort, not a federal system. It is a decentralized nationwide educational partnership that includes three levels of government and collaboration among many local organizations. Memorandas of understanding regarding priorities, needs, objectives, program areas, and finances have been exchanged between the Federal Extension Service of the U.S. Department of Agriculture and CES in the land-grant universities, based on CES agreements with county governments in their state. Representatives of the learners, producers, groups, and organizations engaged in rural development participate in planning in many ways, including planning and advisory committees. A major function of local CES field staffs (such as county agents or advisers) has been linkage between the state and national policies and resources and local clients in their rural social systems (Havelock, 1969). Participant fees have been negligible in a government-subsidized effort with total annual budgets from all three levels about $1 billion; there is much variation from state to state, but more than one-third of this amount comes from state funds and less than one-third from the county level. For more than a decade, increasing competition for other uses of limited tax funds at all three levels has been an increasing challenge to CES.

Although the basic CES clientele related to rural development has been rural families, mainly those associated with agriculture, there have been shifts. Seventy-five years ago, about one-third of the U.S. population lived on farms and ranches, compared with about 3 percent today. CES has also served consumers and the 25 percent of people engaged in agribusiness. CES programs have been concerned with all aspects of rural life at individual, family, and community levels and (as noted earlier) have included home economics and youth programs, along with community resource development. Some CES programs have served urban clients, such as the expanded food and nutrition education program for low-income homemakers. Throughout, CES educational programs have been nonformal as legislation prohibited use of CES funds for credit and degree courses. Over the years, as the numbers of farm families and rural legislators declined and as food surpluses rather than shortages have been a policy concern, there have been gradual shifts of CES funds to urban programs.

CES programs depend on contributions by both paid staff and unpaid volunteers. The staffs include university faculty members who serve as local county agents; subject matter specialists from many departments who assist the county field staffs with program development, materials preparation, and local staff and volunteer development; county, district, and state level administrative personnel; and support staff at all levels. In the late 1980s nationwide, there were about sixteen thousand professional CES staff members and about four thousand paraprofessionals. By contrast, almost three million volunteers helped to plan and conduct CES programs. In many states, about six full-time equivalent volunteers were estimated for each staff member. Thus, learning is central not only for the tens of millions of participants in CES activities, but also for the staff and volunteer activities that have pervaded the organization. In addition to staff development activities by CES staff, university departments have taught courses related to extension education for county and state CES staffs. In the 1960s, the W. K. Kellogg Foundation supported a center at the University of Wisconsin for advanced study in extension administration; in the 1990s, the foundation and the university again cooperated in a National Extension Leadership Development program, this time more oriented toward emerging views of leadership, global issues, and organizational transformation.

At the county level, mission, finances, staffs, and participants interact. For example, in a midwestern county with 100,000 population (of whom about half lived on farms and in small rural towns), the county CES staff consisted of three full-time educators and a secretary. Although local offerings covered home economics, youth development, and community development, this part of the program focused on agricultural extension. Program objectives and content reflected the prominent types of agricultural production and agribusiness in the county (such as crops grown and animals raised), along with pertinent topics related to economics, sociology, and engineering. The county government board of supervisors influenced goals, provided financial support and office space, and helped select staff. County CES staff prepared and implemented plans collaboratively with many related people. Some staff members complained that planning and reporting took about one-quarter of their time and restricted their responsiveness. Recent budget reductions compounded the problem as they tried to do more with less staff time. The annual budget was about $130,000 from all sources, of which about 75 percent was for staff salaries. About 40 percent of the people engaged in agriculture or agribusiness in the county had some contact with CES activities each year. The most active participants averaged more than five hours a week; they tended to be more educated and successful than the rest, and many also helped with planning and conducting programs.

Many societal trends and issues have affected such county CES programs in recent years. The clientele has become increasingly educated, specialized, and productive. Rural values encourage these people to remain in agriculture and benefit from that decision. Higher rates of participation in CES activities by the more successful have been both a result of and influence on CES program priorities, and have widened the gap between "haves" and "have nots." This disparity has been addressed as a problem area. The amount of new knowledge and technology has continued to increase, which makes the linkage function of CES still very important. The economic aspects of agriculture have been highly influential (including fluctuating supply and fairly constant demand, general economic conditions, drops in land values, and indebtedness) and have created severe crises for some farmers. Over the years, large increases in productivity due in part to technology, larger farms, and concern about surpluses have contributed to declines in legislative representation, priority, and appropriations for CES. These declines have resulted in staff reductions, changing program priorities, and strained collaborative relations.

There was far more strategic planning for CES during the 1980s than for most any other type of U.S. adult education provider, and the planning reports took into account most of the foregoing issues and societal influences. The general conclusion was that CES has provided predominantly rural adults with responsive, research-based, practical, future-oriented education. Over the years, there has been a consistent mission and evidence of impact, but the mission has evolved in response to changing circumstances. Strategic planning has assisted in refocusing specific goals and program areas on desirable emerging future directions.

However, the societal environment in which CES has functioned in recent decades has been turbulent, and there are differing views of achievements and desirable directions. CES has been responsive to legislation and to urban residents familiar with extension who moved from rural areas in providing programs such as urban gardening, urban youth programs, and nutrition education for low-income urban families. Critics have complained that extending programs to urban areas has neglected traditional rural constituencies, that recommended farming practices contribute to environmental degradation, that sustainable agriculture has been being neglected, that an agribusiness emphasis has lowered the quality of some produce, and that increased credit farming has led some farmers to bankruptcy.

Yet other frequent reports have praised past accomplishments and urged new directions. Commendable features include strong ties to both knowledge and client systems and the multiplier effect of extensive use of volunteers. A general conclusion is that CES has had a targeted clientele, effective methods, dedicated staff, and satisfactory accountability, along with its clear mission. Impact evaluation studies have substantiated benefits. Planning reports and recommendations since 1979 have emphasized strengthening agriculture, individual and family-life skills, natural resources, small business development, cooperation between research and both public and private extension, public policy issues, and international development. The public image of CES is positive. Almost 90 percent of the public is aware of CES; more than one-quarter of households have used extension, two-thirds of whom live in metropolitan areas; more than 90 percent of users are well satisfied with CES services, and more than 80 percent of users want public support for CES maintained or increased. CES provides an unusual example of extensive and effective use of strategic planning in recent years to address a combination of changing external conditions and internal inertia (Charters and Hilton, 1989; Extension Committee on Organization and Policy, 1987; Forest, 1983; Knox, 1987a; Merriam and Cunningham, 1989, chap. 25; Rivera and Gustafson, 1991; Sanders, 1966; Williams, 1968, chap. 4).

Other U.S. Rural Development Programs

Rural development has been far broader than agricultural extension. Additional societal influences are pertinent to planning, and many other adult education activities within and beyond the CES has taken them into account. In addition to people engaged in production agriculture, nonfarm rural employment in schools and small businesses in rural towns and trade centers has been affected by extractive industries such as agriculture, forestry, fishing, and mining. Projections for such natural resource–related commodities are for continued surpluses and low prices. Related policy issues include deregulation, relaxation of antitrust, increased social security taxes and unemployment benefits, and tax laws favoring capital-intensive urban development. There is clearly much interdependence between rural and urban areas. The most prosperous rural areas have the strongest urban and international connections. Other influences include pricing and production controls, migration between rural and urban areas, and agribusiness.

Some rural development policies are obviously inadequate—from an insufficient rural service sector (such as education and health) to import substitution policies. On the average, U.S. farm families derive more than half of their income from off-farm employment. Rural occupational retraining programs are important for many members of farm families making the transition to urban employment. The aggregate result of many public policies has been to subsidize large farms over small ones and to favor urban development over rural. There has been broad support for a four-pronged approach to rural development, focused on farms, families, commitments, and farm labor (Summers and others, 1988). Environmental scanning for strategic planning related to rural development has identified ten broad societal influences. They are an aging society, information technology, environmental stewardship, social issues and values, economic restructuring, a multicultural society, changing families, health and wellness, individual and social roles, and globalization (Sadowske and Adrian, 1990).

Parts of CES beyond agricultural extension have addressed most of these societal influences with many educational programs to help rural residents and policy makers understand the issues, clarify and solve related problems, and attract and use needed resources. Included are home economics extension programs concerned with home and family life, nutrition and health, youth development, aging, conservation, changing roles, public issues, and leadership. Many rural women prominent in local and state leadership positions have benefited early in their careers from extension leadership training. Youth development includes training and assistance to adult leaders of 4-H clubs for rural youth (long part of CES) and other youth-serving agencies. A recent emphasis in some states has been issue-oriented programming, such as youth at risk. Community resource development programs have helped rural and some urban residents improve community problem solving in relation to many issues: economic restructuring, environmental issues, social services, education, and international relations.

In contrast with most developing countries where most people live in rural areas, in the United States and many technologically advanced countries rural residents are a small and shrinking minority subculture that should be better understood if strategic planning for rural development is to be successful. Contrary to widespread urban stereotypes, rural settings, life, and residents are varied, and strategic planning should help programs address this diversity. Although low population density is typical, many other differences exist. On the one hand, some rural areas have experienced declining population for decades; young people have left for lack of jobs, the population is aging, and the towns are dying. On the other hand, some rural areas near urban centers or that diversified their economic base have experienced great vitality and are attractive places to live. For many people, the attractiveness of rural life is bound up in values such as a slower pace, importance of family life, more emphasis on natural resources than cultural attractions and specialized health care, and personal outlooks such as independence and self-reliance. Rural education should consider such characteristics and values, as well as draw on rural communication networks and the advantages of distance education, in the provision of a broad range of programs that include general education, family life, community development, and occupational education (Merriam and Cunningham, 1989, pp. 537–549).

Many types of adult education providers in addition to CES have served adults in a typical rural county. Most public school systems have had adult education offerings, including general education and public issues, vocational agriculture (such as a short course for young farmers) home economics, and adult vocational education for nonfarm occupations. A community college and one or more other higher education institutions whose service area includes the rural county furnish a variety of courses and workshops within commuting distance. Distance education programs that use some combination of correspondence study, radio, television, and educational telephone networks consider rural adults an important part of their clientele. Some financial institutions sponsor educational activities and counseling to help people who take out loans to succeed so they are able to repay them. Larger rural enterprises such as school systems, agribusiness, and hospitals provide staff development and educational benefits. Hospitals and clinics also offer patient education to promote wellness as well as recovery. Religious institutions provide adult religious education, and some community agencies sponsor educational activities for adults associated with them. Residents of most rural counties are served by at least a half-dozen providers of adult education opportunities. Some rural library systems, CES county offices, or community colleges assemble information about local adult education activities to help interested adults become aware of the alternatives. In localities where such program information is compiled, the listing is also useful for strategic planning.

The adult education offerings of all providers serving a rural area can include almost any topic if there is sufficient local interest; for distance education, there may be only one participant in a county. About half of local programs are typically work related: agriculture, forestry, fishing, mining, and many other local non-farm occupations. Another common subject area deals with various aspects of family life, nutrition, housing, and youth development. Some programs pertain to improved quality of life such as health, religion, recreation, and access to community programs and services, especially for the elderly, disadvantaged, and minorities. Some community education programs have focused on leadership development and community problem solving on issues such as small business development and preservation of natural, energy, and environmental resources. Other topics include local history and international relations. Strategic planning by a provider can review the range of available program topics both to avoid needless duplication (given the sparse population) but more importantly to identify gaps in available offerings that in similar counties elsewhere had been filled by successful programs. Similar to the contrast between an urban shopping mall with many specialty shops and a rural general store, a small population does not allow as great a variety of specialized adult education offerings as in a large city with hundreds or thousands of providers. However, in rural areas, it is much easier for adult education leaders to know many of the other local providers and program offerings. This familiarity can create substantial collaboration, complementarity of offerings, and strategic planning both to make the most of a provider's market niche and to maximize responsive adult education opportunities.

Rural Development in St. Lucia and Cameroon

This section focuses on agricultural extension in two countries. It begins with an example from St. Lucia that reveals societal influences that on balance are favorable to improved agricultural production and rural development. The second example from Cameroon illustrates societal influences that have mainly hindered rural development. Influences from both examples recur in many developing countries and have implications for strategic planning in various countries.

St. Lucia

The second largest island in the Windward Group in the Caribbean and located close to the South American continent, St. Lucia is a volcanic country composed of peaks and valleys. Much of the land is dense with vegetation. The primary crops are bananas (the primary export crop), coconuts, and vegetables. In addition to a private specialized banana growers' association extension service, the Ministry of Agriculture Extension Division has served farm families growing various crops for decades and in recent years has begun coordinating the work of extension officers from other divisions of the Ministry of Agriculture.

During the 1980s, St. Lucia and seven other Caribbean countries worked to strengthen their agricultural extension programs, with assistance from eight mostly land-grant universities that constitute the Midwest Universities Consortium for International Activities (MUCIA) through the Caribbean Agricultural Education Project (CAEP). Early, CAEP assisted the extension division in each of the Caribbean nations to analyze their programs. Deficiencies identified included inadequate staff training in extension organizations, poorly defined goals, conflicting lines of authority, insufficient incentives, and unreliable program monitoring; another problem was regional support services that were poor in resources, loosely coordinated, and inadequately connected to national efforts. Among the strengths identified in each country were examples of successful farmers who reported benefiting from extension, a genuine desire by farmers and staff to improve extension's effectiveness, and approval by national government cabinets of the national extension improvement plan. Among the objectives of MUCIA assistance to the Caribbean Extension Services through CAEP were aiding improvements in extension management, staff development, and program planning; rewarding excellent extension work; and evaluating projects. As international assistance declined, informal cooperation with MUCIA continued, and the project was renamed the Agricultural Research and Extension Project.

The project helped extension staff members to analyze local contingencies to help make their extension activities responsive and beneficial. They emphasized systems-oriented analysis in each growing region and consideration of each farm as a business and household unit to help farmers identify problems and opportunities in their farming system. A method introduced in the Caribbean in 1986 was the Sondeo (a rapid survey of a farming system by a multidisciplinary team that gathered and analyzed information from many points of view). Its purpose was to help farmers and extension staff working with them quickly identify major constraints and opportunities to deal with them using available resources and technology. The CAEP assistance by MUCIA was only one of the international influences in agricultural extension in St. Lucia. The CAEP effort helped extension staff understand and deal with many of these and domestic influences on their planning and to identify some that deserved additional attention (which are noted at the end of this example). The construction of an international airport affected the St. Lucia economy generally, including demand for produce by tourists and U.S. and U.K. export markets, domestic preferences for foreign food, and resistance to paying more for local produce. Weather and terrain affects the local economy in general and agriculture in particular. For example, weather attracts tourists and creates the ability to grow some crops, but the alternation of heavy rains and dry weather on steep terrain creates problems of soil conservation and road maintenance. Other international influences are various organizations (other than MUCIA) in the Caribbean and hemisphere that provide technical assistance, external finances, supplementary equipment, and staff development assistance.

Extension functioning is also affected by the national government, especially the Ministry of Agriculture, regarding leadership policy support for extension; the recent consolidation of extension, which was formerly conducted independently by several divisions and bureaus, had an additional impact. The government (namely the Ministry of Agriculture) is the main source of funds for extension. Other local organizations, such as the St. Lucia Development Bank, helps by providing both credit to farmers and workshops on loan procedures. In addition to minimal government funds, extension receives various amounts of funding from external sources. Individual extension agents are restricted by limited resources, but these limitations are dealt with in part by collaboration with various organizations: private sector extension, local farm groups, and educational institutions that had previously educated agents but began providing direct assistance to farmers.

In addition to market forces and government practices, extension itself is a major influence on Ministry of Agriculture policy and planning regarding opportunities (new crops), constraints (roads), and increasing emphasis on specific crops. Extension staff development, a major way to increase effectiveness and extension impact, includes staff participation in a regional diploma program and contributions by various international organizations to technological and program development proficiency, which most extension staff members appreciate.

There are also multiple influences on farmer participation in extension activities, which in turn contribute to achievement of farmers' and extension's goals. Continued improvements in extension efforts improve its image and encourage involvement to the extent that it is congruent with farmer values. The participation of farmers in extension activities is for the purpose of improving practices, which often depends on availability of resources to make this change (such as ability to pay for the basic costs of inputs; availability of land, labor, and capital; and fit with farm and family expectations). Farmers anticipated benefits from improved farm practices would lead to increased income and higher quality of life. Extension goals for participation were both general (to help clients to help themselves by taking greater responsibility for their own lives) and more specific (increased citrus production; control of disease, weeds, and insects; and field harvesting and packing to reduce rejects). Evidence of beneficial results from extension inspired more farmers to participate and persist. The results have been increased production and income; better marketing procedures, management, and use of technology; and even improved roads as part of the infrastructure.

Some influences on participation were identified for future attention through strategic planning. Educational level of farmers affects involvement; half are illiterate. This consideration suggests emphasis on personal contact and oral communications. The average numbers of farm contacts by agents were low but increasing. Casual contacts by agents encouraged more formal participation, but only 40 percent of the agents live in their service area. The recommendation to use group meetings coincided with the willingness of local farm groups to cooperate. Nevertheless, it is contrary to the individualistic values of many farmers (especially nonparticipants) which include resisting organizational participation. Perhaps strategic planning could identify promising solutions from similar extension programs that extension staff members in St. Lucia could adapt to their situation (Resource A, Campbell and Sandmann).

In addition to agricultural extension, there are a range of adult education programs in St. Lucia that contribute to rural development. The Ministry of Education has offered an adult literacy program, religious institutions and labor unions provide educational activities for their members, enterprises supply vocational education, and the University of the West Indies gives extension courses in St. Lucia and other Caribbean locations. These educational opportunities are available to farm families in their various life roles: family, community, and nonfarm employment for men and for women (Bird, 1975; Gordon, 1979, 1985; Midwest Universities Consortium for International Activities, 1987).

Cameroon

Cameroon, in West Africa, is a strikingly different case. Agricultural extension has been one of the main forms of adult education in Cameroon, guided by the Division of Extension of the Ministry of Agriculture. However, the effort has been very fragmented. Other divisions of the ministry, such as Cooperatives and Community Development, have conducted separate extension activities. In addition, literacy programs are provided by the Ministry of Education and health education programs by the Ministry of Health. The Ministry of Planning and Economic Development coordinates the independent agricultural extension and rural development activities of commodity organizations, such as producers of cocoa, coffee, palm oil, and cotton. These organizations have concentrated on large commercial producers. By contrast, the programs of the Ministry of Agriculture Division of Extension are intended to assist small (low-resource) farmers mainly engaged in subsistence agriculture, who are reluctant to participate in extension programs because they believe that the balance of costs and benefits are not favorable to them. Disincentives include negligible cash crops, negative image of extension, little encouragement by their reference groups, inadequate resources to take advantage of government programs, and few anticipated benefits. People interested in strategic planning might wonder what accounts for this discouraging situation.

Unfortunately, most of the societal influences hinder extension. The Ministry of Agriculture has several goals and priorities that restrict extension education for small farmers. Ministry goals reflect broader government economic plans for modernization and diversification of the economic base. These focus on larger commercial farms that produce export commodities yielding domestic tax funds and foreign currency for national development. The independent international and commodity-oriented extension efforts also focus on larger, commercial farms. The result is that the Ministry of Agriculture has few expectations and provides modest financing for extension programs, especially for low-resource farmers.

The extension field staff typically grew up in an urban area, completed formal education, and then started to work for extension in a rural area where the local language of the low-resource farmers was unfamiliar and where inadequate extension funds restrict staff members from spending much time in contact with most of the farmers in their district. As a result, many of the farmers perceive extension field staff members as people who mainly appear around harvest time to assure that they sell cash crops at controlled prices through the government, not outside the system for higher prices. Although their efforts are supplemented by international volunteers, the social distance between farmers and staff members and the limited amount of in-service education provided for them severely restricts their effectiveness. They give little attention to other aspects of rural development, although adult education activities by other ministries do so (Resource A, Nyemba (b)). The extension service at one time functioned in similar ways in Uganda and other African countries.

Other Countries

Agricultural extension and rural development have been important aspects of adult education in most countries. Their successes and failures illuminate planning issues relevant to many national settings. The brief examples in this section are from Asia (India, Bangladesh, Thailand, China, and Australia), the Middle East (Jordan and Israel), Africa (Kenya and Tanzania), Latin America (Chile), and Europe (Sweden, Portugal, and the United Kingdom). Each example focuses on societal influences with implications for strategic planning.

India

India has used various extension systems to increase agricultural productivity. Early community development approaches were usually too diffuse, and there were limited improvements in productivity. India was an early country to try the controversial Training and Visit system (T & V), supported by the World Bank (Benor and Harrison, 1977; Bhatnagar, Desai, and Reddy, 1986; Crouch and Chamala, 1981). The T & V system mainly addresses inadequate extension personnel management, linkage between researchers and extension field staff, and ways to encourage extension agents to have sufficient regular contact with local farmers and avoid conflicting demands to perform noneducational services.

In response to critics of T & V, advocates later clarified that it was intended mainly to train and manage more extension personnel whose numbers and contact time with farmers would become sufficient to achieve extension objectives; it was assumed that other arrangements would be made to select clients able to achieve (or to increase other ingredients essential for) greater productivity due to policy changes, improved infrastructure (such as roads and markets), and provision of other services (such as input supply, credit, marketing, and literacy).

In practice, field staff members are oriented by experts (specialists) about recommended practices for their district and expected to explain the practices to contact farmers whom they visit every two weeks. The contact farmers tend to be prominent and successful, and they are expected to share information about the recommended practices with other local farmers and encourage them to adopt them, as well as use the practices themselves. Agents are also expected to obtain information about educational needs and conditions of local farmers for the experts as input to their research and planning of future recommended practices.

There are mixed findings from research and evaluation studies regarding the extent to which the T & V system helped rural development. More successful farmers who already possess most of the ingredients of increased productivity typically use information about recommended practices to great advantage. Irrigation is a frequent example. Small (low-resource) farmers who lack essential ingredients benefit little (Chouhan and Rai, 1984). Critics of T & V urge increased attention to relationships between agents and small farmers that would give more attention to holistic approaches to rural development (such as health, family, inputs, markets), use of indigenous knowledge, and direct farmer contact with experts without dependence on agents and contact farmers. These objectives might be accomplished by combining T & V with the extension activities of Farming Systems Research and Extension or with comprehensive rural development approaches that consist of more holistic analysis and recommendations for improvement (Feder and Slade, 1986; Feder, Lau, and Slade, 1987; Howell, 1982).

A contrasting approach was use of community development projects or local farm training centers (associated with universities, associations, or research centers) where small farmers discuss problems and solutions with peers, using both indigenous and expert knowledge (Nagel, 1980; Prasad, Choudhary, and Doval, 1985). In such integrated approaches, agriculture is discussed as one of the complex and interwoven problems to be resolved to produce balanced growth. Strategic planning can help identify the elements of T & V, farming systems, and farm training centers that most require attention in a specific area to allow a synergistic effort to produce balanced rural development.

Bangladesh

Local social systems can undermine as well as support rural development. During the 1970s in Bangladesh, the government, the International Development Association, and the World Bank funded three thousand mechanically drilled wells in the northwestern region intended to enable twenty-five to fifty small farmers around each well to use the water to irrigate a second crop of rice during the dry season and thus solve their families' problems of poverty and hunger. Local irrigation cooperatives were to be formed that were expected to pay less than $300 of the more than $12,000 it cost to drill each well. Initially, the project seemed a success. However, a few years later, poverty increased in the region, and it was discovered what caused the actual failure of the project. Rural villages in that district generally included a rich landlord who was the only one who could afford to pay the cooperative's financial contribution; this individual would obtain the names of area farmers to apply as a cooperative, which only existed on paper. The landlord paid the fee and located the well on his property, which was less than half the land the well was capable of irrigating. His water charges to small farmers on adjacent plots were so high that most could not afford the hourly rates. Some of those who did became so heavily indebted as a result that they had to surrender their land. The project thus compounded the poverty that it was intended to solve. This example illustrates the importance of strategic planning, including multiple sources of information for needs assessment and contextual analysis for early identification of major potential situational threats to program success.

Thailand

Efforts to reduce rural poverty in other countries also confront opposition from powerful local elites like landlords and middlemen who exercise great control of local resources and the flow of outside resources as well. In Thailand during the early 1980s, rural development trends were described by rural people as increasing inequality, relative poverty, depletion of natural resources and the environment, instability of production, and underemployment. Constraints to rural development included population growth, language barriers, lack of educational opportunities, cultural customs, and government practices that discriminated against the poor. However, there were also local assets that enhanced the potential for rural development: indigenous knowledge, a spirit of cooperation, local organizations (such as Buddhist temples), supportive cultural practices, availability of mass media, availability of time and labor, and marketing potential. Proposed development strategies included integrated rural development, action-based participatory research, policies that favored the poor, and use of local organizations (Sungsri and Mellor, 1984; Supote and Akin, 1984).

Urban-rural tensions were also evident in the effort begun in the mid 1980s to decentralize and "ruralize" the nonformal literacy education program of the Adult Education Division (AED) in Thailand with policy and financial support from the Thai central government and the World Bank. The AED initiated the decentralization process, which began with establishing lifelong education centers in twenty-four provinces. Nonformal education was mainly concerned with adult literacy in a country that was 80 percent rural. The AED was marginal to the Ministry of Education, whose urban-oriented preparatory education programs (elementary and secondary education for young people) were supervised regarding curricula and budgets by provincial education officers in each of Thailand's seventy-one provinces and their counterparts in the twelve education regions. The provincial education officers had little familiarity with or interest in the nonformal education programs but used their fiscal powers to resist decentralization. They were aided by ambiguity that resulted from the clash between the strong government tradition of centralization and support for the AED decentralization plan. As a result, many provincial centers were slow to shift their programs from urban to rural needs. A major inhibitor of decentralization and freedom of action by the new centers was long delays after budget approval in the actual disbursement of funds (Armstrong, 1984).

This example reveals the tension between an adult education provider agency and a preparatory education–oriented parent organization that has occurred in many countries at national, regional, and local levels. The usual result is that an adult education agency's efforts to be responsive to the needs and circumstances of adult learners are frustrated by policy and financial controls by parent organization officials who want greater conformity with the dominant preparatory education system. Resolution of this conflict and improvement of the adult education function pose a particularly difficult challenge to strategic planning; the adult education agency must try to maximize the advantages and minimize the disadvantages of a symbiotic relationship.

In 1979, the AED was upgraded to the Nonformal Education Department, with five regional centers and an office in each province. Beginning in the early 1970s, the department began to articulate a curriculum rationale based on a Buddhist worldview. The rationale, known as Khit-pen, emphasized individual harmony with the environment as the goal and critical thinking as a means. The rationale was consistent with the Thai cultural context but did challenge two cultural norms strong in rural areas: personal resignation to circumstances and the tradition of not overtly challenging the opinions of superiors. Although the approach was ambiguous, staff training was inadequate, and many local literacy education practitioners had difficulty applying it to practice, the rationale attempted to combine both conservative (emphasis on harmony rather than conflict) and progressive elements (empowerment through critical thinking and problem solving). The major parts of the critical-thinking process that was advocated were consideration of the problem, analysis, information collection, use of knowledge and experience to try to solve the problem, consideration of the results, and (if those were not satisfactory), revision of procedure until harmony was achieved. This problem-solving emphasis in the adult literacy program was somewhat controversial and produced mixed results, but it shows the challenge to planning when many societal influences (religious beliefs, cultural norms, and government policies favoring harmony, preferences of some rural adults, and education for increased critical thinking for personal and rural development) coalesce (Bernard and Armstrong, 1979; Hugkuntod and Tips, 1987).

Another example of rural development education in Thailand was a participatory research approach to adult education for members of local cooperatives for small farmers (Verhagen, 1984).

Many societal influences contributed to marginalization of small farmers in the village: population growth, smaller land holdings, declines in public lands and water sources, unstable yields and markets, modernization of local economies with loss of local control to international market forces and generally declining commodity prices, inadequate concern for the poor by wealthy village elites and by government, disappearance of traditional crafts, and nonfarm rural work that was too capital intensive for small farmers.

Formation of local cooperatives for small farmers was tried, as part of a broader rural development effort to support and defend them, promote self-reliance and member participation, and intervene at higher levels to create a climate conducive to progress. Functions of cooperation included collective planning and decision making, increased local monetary resources and income-generating activities, and enhanced bargaining power and local control related to agricultural production. Collaboration sought to combine advantages of both the government (continuity of responsibility, access to expertise, independence from foreign donors), and nongovernment organizations (staff members who were able and long-term advocates of rural poor; providers that were more flexible and less political). Education for cooperative members was village based, action oriented, and for entire families. Attention was also given to linkages with government and other development agencies to create a climate conducive to success of the local cooperatives (technical assistance and at least acceptance by powerful elites). The tradition of patron-client relations encouraged small farmers to look upwards rather than sidewards for cooperation. In some villages, local leaders felt that the burden of the rural poor was becoming too heavy and were willing to support the development of cooperatives for small farmers and provide some protection against other members of the elite.

Local field staff members engaged in education for cooperative members, lived in a village, assisted with planning and implementation of an initial successful project, and also worked with people in higher-level service centers. They focused on helping people to help themselves and advised active participation and self-sufficiency in running the cooperative organization as well as in achieving rural development and increased productivity. Compared to conventional approaches, a participatory approach to education of cooperative members emphasized adaptation of cooperative organizational structure and educational activities to local contingencies. However, distinctive features of the participatory approach were active participation by members in decision making and mobilization of local resources and local focus on strengthening economic conditions for the poor majority of small-farmer households. Initial development activities were followed by natural expansion of other small cooperatives nearby, facilitated by small-farmer leaders as multiplying agents; then larger regional arrangements were created by voluntary association. Field workers were assisted in drafting their own work plans, provided monitoring and self-evaluation, and conducted local educational activities for leadership and member development of small farmers to promote active and effective participation and self-sufficiency. This approach reflected the firm belief within the cooperative movement that adult education should respect the worth and ability of members to work with others in the community to improve their situation.

China

The potential for rural development can be enhanced during periods of political and economic modernization. This fact has been illustrated in China since the late 1970s following the chaos of the cultural revolution. Between 1949 and 1979, there was heavy emphasis on grain production and little diversification of the rural economy, which had a stable structure and a 3 percent annual growth rate for gross value of agricultural output. Since the late 1970s, when food shortages were severe, China has become one of the world's most efficient food producers in terms of output per acre. It feeds 22 percent of the population of the world on only 7 percent of its arable land. Since then, per capita food consumption has increased by almost one-half. In contrast to traditional practices on collective farms that required little education, the introduction of technology and modern practices has increased the centrality of education for farm families, for those engaged in rural nonfarm occupations (about 20 percent of the rural labor force), and for those who have moved to urban areas. Economic reforms to create a socialist market economy provide powerful incentives for farmers close to urban areas to become rich by selling their productive output, after they meet government quotas.

There are many providers of rural adult education—village technical schools for rural adults operated by townships, adult secondary vocational schools, county agricultural extension units, distance education (TV universities, Radio Broadcasting School of Agriculture), and spare-time middle schools. Topics are varied: selection of improved seeds, protection against pests and diseases, maintenance of farm machinery, animal husbandry, rural crafts, and financial management. But recommended practices have been ahead of actual farming practices. It has been estimated that inadequate education is the main reason why 70 percent of available technology and modern procedures are unused by most farmers. County extension centers have combined local experimentation with extension activities. Women have increasingly participated because of their major role in agricultural production as well as in family and community life generally. Part of the educational effort has been staff development for the more than a half-million experts who help plan and conduct rural adult education activities (Chu, 1985; Hunter and Keehn, 1985; Wang, Lin, Sun, and Fang, 1988; Wenqing, 1987). During the transition of the 1980s, societal influences helped rural adult education much more than they hindered. In similar transition periods in other countries, strategic planning should help adult education leaders recognize the implications of emerging trends.

Australia

Over the years, agricultural extension in Australia has been somewhat unusual and fragmented. The national commonwealth government's contribution has been unique, emphasizing agricultural research but providing limited financial or administrative support to state governments. The states have varied greatly in their extent and arrangements to conduct extension directly and to support some applied research. The University of New England at Armidale, New South Wales, has been unusual in directly assisting rural extension. In most states, local extension work has been done by district field officers prepared in various branches of farming, assisted by regional supervisors and specialists. Additional extension activities have been provided by voluntary associations, private consultants, commercial firms, and various government agencies (Axinn and Thorat, 1972; Williams, 1968).

Jordan

A contrasting case from the Middle East suggests ways in which government ministries and nongovernment organizations (NGOs) can each contribute to rural development. Jordan is a small country with less than 6 percent of the land area suitable for agricultural production. An annual population growth rate of more than 4 percent has made agricultural extension important for increased production. As in other countries, Jordanian farmers vary in their situations and educational need (to which extension should be responsive). The three main sources from which farmers have learned to improve their practices are other farmers; the relatively new formal extension activities (such as the Ministry of Agriculture, Department of Agricultural Research and Extension); and activities by NGOs (such as nonformal extension by more than sixty large or medium-sized private companies, many of which have offered international technical assistance). Other ministries have also had extension functions related to rural development. In response to criticisms of agricultural research and extension during the mid 1980s, the Ministry of Agriculture (MOA) has sought to strengthen them in collaborative ways.

MOA extension field agents typically have B.S. preparation but receive little in-service education. Various specialists assist them, but few do so full time. Recommendations to improve the relatively weak extension methods and impact mention the various mechanisms that could be used to enhance linkages between agricultural research and farmers. Included are a farming systems research project, greater involvement by research organizations, use of mass media, and sharing of research farms. The existing level of informal cooperation provides the basis for progression to greater collaboration and systemic linkage (Woods, 1987).

Israel

Israel is another Middle Eastern example, but one atypical of agricultural education in developing countries and industrialized countries alike. It is an approach influenced by arid land, high immigration, and rural settlements. In the early years, Israeli extension education helped people new to the country and to agriculture achieve the transition from shortages of fresh food to using irrigation and other methods to produce surpluses. In the following decade, the trends were from mixed farming to specialization and from only local production to greater exports. More recently, rural trends have included new techniques to save water and labor, new intensive crops especially for export, and industrialization of rural areas.

Extension field agents work closely with local communities in this small country in which they are also able to know many people associated with extension. Exclusive focus on extension activities and in-service education (including a diploma course and a master's degree in extension education) have helped agents deal with rapid changes in agriculture. Such in-service education has included topics related to the varied sociocultural backgrounds of farmers and responsive educational programs. This orientation is especially important for planning in settings characterized by diversity and change (Crouch and Chamala, 1981, vol. 1, chap. 14; Rivera and Schram, 1987, chap. 11).

Each of these Middle Eastern countries has similar characteristics: arid climate, immigrants, and regional political tensions. Israel's early use of extension and technology has contributed to its distinctive achievements in rural development. In recent decades, many African countries have experienced major problems related to rural development and imbalances between agricultural production and consumption. The following examples from African countries describe extension approaches that comparative perspectives might enhance.

Kenya

In Kenya, a former British colony in East Africa with a population of twenty million people, about 80 percent are engaged in agriculture or related occupations. Rural development is provided by the National Extension Program (NEP) of the Ministry of Agriculture and by NGOs. In the early 1980s, Kenya changed from a typical developing country system (characterized by Ministry of Agriculture control of highly centralized, preestablished programs, separated from teaching and research). Between 1981 and 1985, Kenya modified NEP activities in several ways so that it would contribute more to national development. One change was introduction of the T & V system, organized within districts, in which subject-matter specialists worked with extension agents to prepare training packages, which they used with local farmers on a fortnightly visit schedule.

In most districts, there are training centers for farmers, and there are other ways in which farmers are involved in NEP activities and in their own organizations, such as the Agricultural Society of Kenya. Incentives to encourage participation include commodity price reviews; loans for investment in the form of seeds, fertilizer, or water; and a guaranteed minimum return schedule on their investment in case of insufficient production. There are incentives for extension staff, such as salary levels comparable to other government employees, professional career ladders, and fringe benefits and allowances. Some of the achievements since the changes in the NEP are a motivated field staff, cooperation from farmers, improved practice adoption, interest from farmers in new technology, support from local leaders, participation by women's groups, a uniform management system, clarity of staff duties, improved linkage with research, and regular staff training sessions. Commodity organizations have been encouraged to assist, as have private NGOs—banks, businesses, industry, voluntary organizations, and cooperatives (Rivera and Schram, 1987, pp. 149–162).

An example of an NGO is Farming Systems Kenya, which provides two- to five-day training courses on farm management for small-scale farmers, along with in-kind credit to use for farm supplies to increase yields and move into a cash economy. The program is quite successful, especially with livestock, maize, and beans (Maina, 1988–1989). International assistance has benefited several of the NGO rural development programs in Kenya.

Tanzania

Tanzania's first president, Julius Nyerere, was a strong proponent of adult education, self-help, and rural development. Major national development programs related to literacy, health, and rural development included extensive and well-planned adult education components; these were assisted by the Institute of Adult Education, which pioneered development of concepts and procedures for participatory research (Hall, 1979; Kassam, 1982). Thus, by 1979, when an innovative training program was begun for government community development specialists, there were many reasons why rural development had long been a high priority for the national government and for local villagers. The project was initially under the office of prime minister; in 1985, it was transferred to a new ministry of community development. The initial regions selected had high potential for increased agricultural production. The broad program goals were to develop a rural development training system focused on increased production and income by strengthening management of decentralized rural development institutions, expanding rural services, and enhancing self-help activities by farmers and cooperatives. A national program coordinator worked with a committee representing all ministries responsible for aspects of rural development. Trainers came from all cooperative ministries in each region. This cooperative, decentralized, and multidisciplinary approach was used for all aspects of the program, including planning, finance, staffing, and participation.

This systemic approach to helping farmers farm better contrasted with earlier disjointed efforts that had stressed adoption of separate practices. Village attendance at program activities was about 80 percent, and attrition was negligible. Such enthusiastic local participation was created through encouragement of farmers' initial interests and anticipated benefits, by the multiplier effect of peer support, by the generally positive image of national modernization and social change efforts, and through inclusion of a broad range of participants to minimize the negative effects of social stratification. Traditional values were the main negative influence at the outset. They reflected inertia but also risk avoidance and skepticism about the appropriateness of recommended practices. The collaborative staffing approach was seen in the staff development emphasis and some cooperative use of educational technology. A 1984 impact evaluation study revealed that agricultural production increased threefold in most cooperating villages.

The financing came mainly from governmental appropriations, in-kind contributions by cooperating organizations, and an international assistance grant from the U.S. Agency for International Development (USAID), which was very helpful in initiating and conducting this demonstration program. However, political differences between the two countries in the mid 1980s led in 1985 to an early termination of USAID's assistance. This caused major reductions of the program, but it continued satisfactorily at a slower pace. The program demonstrates the potential problem of dependence on international assistance (in contrast with its evident benefits) that strategic planning should address (Resource A, Isinika).

In countries like Tanzania, community development and participatory research approaches that emphasize farmer initiatives and integrated rural development have focused on ties between extension field staff and local villages; however, inadequate incentives can limit increases in productivity. Use of farming systems research and extension in countries such as Liberia and Lesotho has helped inform researchers about the interdependent aspects of farming so that they could make pertinent recommendations but has tended to neglect other aspects of rural development (Shaner, Philipp, and Schmehl, 1982). This neglect has also occurred in T & V systems that emphasize management of extension and adoption of specific agricultural practices (as illustrated in Kenya). Agricultural extension has evolved in the various states of Nigeria in relation to national trends and other extension providers (Axinn and Thorat, 1972). Strategic planning should help extension leaders understand the main systemic features of rural development and identify points at which to strengthen the two-way linkage that extension can achieve with both client systems in the local rural areas and with external resource systems such as research centers, educational institutions, government ministries, and educational NGOs (Havelock, 1969; Swanson, Sands, and Peterson, 1990).

Chile

Sometimes an NGO approach to rural development seems necessary, when government opposition or neglect of a subpopulation has eliminated many extension alternatives. This situation occurred in a rural information program in Chile that took place between

1979 and 1982 but that ended for lack of resources and without evidence of increased agricultural production or standard of living. Perhaps its main accomplishment was to bring together scattered groups and demonstrate nationwide benefits of collaboration within the framework of an authoritarian society. The program was aimed at the 20 percent of the country's population who lived in very dispersed locations in a country a few hundred miles wide and thousands of miles long and where mountain ranges and some desolate areas provided geographical barriers to human contact.

A major influence was social stratification that has occurred in many Latin American countries with a tiny wealthy elite, a small middle class, and large numbers of poor people who inhabit rural areas and increasingly urban slums. For more than a century, Chile has had a larger and more stable middle class than in most Latin American countries; it lives mainly in Santiago (where one-third of the population resides) and in a few other major cities and owns the haciendas. The stratification reflects the social distance between European immigrants (who are generally middle or upper class) and the native Mapuche (who are typically rural poor). In recent decades, an unsatisfactory economy (especially during such peak crisis periods as the inflation in 1973 and the unemployment in 1982) has worsened already widespread rural poverty and adversely affected adult education providers, programs, and participants. Although basic literacy rates for Chile are higher than most Latin American countries and there have been efforts to achieve educational reform and combat adult illiteracy for more than sixty years, the educational level of peasants is low. The lure of upward mobility and the relative quality of life and available social services, have caused peasants to move to the city, and rural areas have been depleted and impoverished.

The long-standing hacienda patron system of rural society was altered in the land reform efforts of President Allende between 1970 and 1973, but Allende's reforms were somewhat reversed during 1973 to 1989 by the Pinochet government. The Pinochet government and the elite opposed unions and other such organizations. This authoritarian government has a powerful influence on many rural development efforts, related to both program objectives and constraints of program functioning (such as restrictions on formation of local organizations, freedom of assembly, and media content).

The purpose of the rural information program was to work around some of the restrictions on local adult education programs by use of mass media—one of the few sources of information helpful to poor peasants—as a backup to local educational programs and as a way to increase feelings of solidarity among a dispersed subpopulation. The information program was coordinated and conducted by an NGO, in collaboration with organizations committed to nationwide rural development. Given these goals, little impact was expected unless rural groups contributed. Although some peasants listened to the radio broadcasts and read the publications, the program was unable to involve them in the production of materials. Rural family and close friends constituted powerful reference groups for peasant communications and actions, which distance education methods were unable to penetrate. Other unsettling influences included the breakdown of the hacienda system, shifting policies on land redistribution, and the guild as a powerful elite group.

Cooperating national organizations contributed to program policy, plans, and staff development. The staff development that they provided to local field staff members who worked with peasants was crucial to increased peasant participation in educational activities and use of media produced by the program (Resource A, Gajardo). Since the change of government in 1989, the severe restrictions on local adult education programs have been reduced, a situation that has allowed conducting programs that combine media with popular participation in more integrated rural development programs.

Europe

Adult education for rural development has also occurred in Europe and in other technologically advanced countries around the world. Preparations for altered international relations related to the European Community (EC) reorganization in 1993 have been an influence on rural development that reflects both domestic and international influences. Sweden (not an EC member) and Portugal offer contrasting cases. Many adult education providers, including agricultural extension, serve rural Sweden. As in the United States, about 3 percent of the work force is engaged in farming, and 35 percent of the farms account for 70 percent of the total agricultural production. Most of the remaining farms are part-time enterprises in which an average of 70 percent of family income is from off-farm work. Thus, rural development is closely associated with urban development. The government's goal is for rural quality of life (employment, education, social services) to be comparable to urban living. Yet a priority has remained to make more effective use of rural resources to bolster local economies in order to reduce vulnerability due to overdependence on government assistance (such as policy support for part-time farming), to promote integrated rural development, and to coordinate urban and rural development (Summers and others, 1988). Sweden's extensive and diversified adult education opportunities constitute a major asset for assisting with many aspects of this multipronged approach to rural development.

As a country with 70 percent of the population living in rural areas, Portugal's decision to join the EC set in motion international forces likely to transform both rural and urban life. Rural extension programs have been a major part of adult education for rural development, which in recent years has included content on self-management (de Melo, 1983; Resource A, de Melo). Since 1989, EC funds and the Portuguese Ministry of Agriculture have encouraged local and regional cooperatives, associations, and local development agencies to work together and with national and European networks to provide educational activities for agricultural development. Initial extension activities focused on progressive farmers but have now begun to serve a broader range of people to promote rural development, sustainable agriculture, and balanced development of human and natural resources.

In Britain, agricultural extension has had a strong technical base but weak connections with universities, except in Scotland (Williams, 1968). During the multiyear preparation for 1993, rural extension has been exploring the implications of the EC for rural people and policy makers. A contribution of strategic planning would be to enlarge the range of stakeholders so that people beyond the agricultural sector might more readily recognize likely trends and use a broader range of adult education providers to help the population prepare for the coming transformation likely to entail massive population shifts from rural to urban ares.

Strategic Planning

This section suggests the implications of the foregoing programs for strategic planning. The planning issues that are explored are goals and scope, trends and directions, contingencies, stakeholders, staff, and policies.

Goals

The scope of rural development programs by a type of adult education provider varies greatly from location to location because of both the content of rural development needs and the program offerings of other adult education providers serving that district. In unusual situations in which the rural economy is basically healthy, many farming and related enterprises are productive, and a range of occupational and nonoccupational adult education programs are serving the rural population well, a new offering can be very focused in scope and responsive to an emerging trend. Examples of responsive programs include education for introduction of a new crop to respond to a shift in consumer demand or vocational education for nonagricultural occupations to help underemployed rural people prepare for urban occupations. These goals are illustrated in the examples from the United States, Israel, and Sweden. At the other extreme, in a district plagued by rural poverty, substandard production, inadequate inputs, undeveloped markets, unsatisfactory agricultural policies, and insufficient adult education offerings to provide assistance for comprehensive rural development, a major adult education provider should seek an effective strategy for unilaterally or collaboratively providing a multipronged educational effort. This must address various aspects of the rural economic and social systems and related urban and policy influences likely to produce constructive changes (Axinn and Thorat, 1972; Swanson, Sands, and Peterson, 1990). Most of the preceding examples shared many of these characteristics.

Between these two extremes, strategic planning for rural adult education should help providers make preliminary decisions about desirable and feasible program scope. Realistic expectations depend on clear understanding of desirable outcomes to be achieved, undesirable outcomes to be avoided, current resources and circumstances, and additional resources and assistance that are required for progress to occur. The examples from Cameroon, Bangladesh, and Chile reveal some deterrents to success. It is important to limit program size so that success is possible with available or obtainable resources. This type of diagnosis occurs especially at early stages but throughout effective community development projects. The examples from St. Lucia, Tanzania, and Portugal demonstrate more comprehensive approaches.

Trends

Strategic planning should also identify major incentives and disincentives for change by people in various roles whose assistance seems necessary if desirable rural development is to occur. Too often, these efforts fail because the focus is too narrowly on male farmers and too little attention is given to educational activities for other family members, suppliers of essential inputs (seed, equipment, fertilizers), wholesalers who link producers to consumers, and policy makers who should better serve the vital interest of the rural population (McGrath, 1969; Rice, 1974). As illustrated in the example from Tanzania, early in a rural development effort it is desirable to focus on objectives for which there is high potential of improvement for rural people and for cooperation among stakeholders from adult education providers and organizations connected with intended changes. An ongoing major planning outcome should be guidance to help stakeholders agree on program mission (scope and major intended outcomes). Thus, stage of development is an important consideration (Axinn and Thorat, 1972; Daines and others, 1986; Rivera and Schram, 1987). Attention should also be given to economic outcomes, conservation of natural resources, and enhancement of human resources.

Although a better understanding of societal influences can help decide on program scope and goals, a major use of conclusions is to select strategies for rural development that try to make use of desirable influences and reduce the effect of undesirable ones. Social change occurs over time, and recent trends can influence future directions. For example, understanding of the early roots of the U.S. Cooperative Extension Service (including NGOs and volunteerism) helps explain the ongoing adaptive process necessary to fit internal strengths and weaknesses to external demands and constraints.

Appreciation of this process of organizational change within a larger social system also has implications for extension leaders in other national contexts. These people may be prompted to discover whether in their provider agency and service area there are the required ingredients for achievement of rural development goals and whether emerging trends are likely to help or hinder. Illustrative societal conditions and trends include general economic conditions, proportion of the population engaged in agriculture, educational levels of the rural population, governmental modernization trends and policies related to rural development, resources allocated to extension, rate of change in agricultural technology, urban-rural relationships and opportunities for off-farm employment, migration trends, and the international environment (such as consequences of the formation of the European Community). Strategic planning should include environmental scanning to identify major societal trends and directions likely to affect rural development efforts (Botkin, Elmandjra, and Malitza 1979; Crouch and Chamala, 1981; Theobald, 1987).

Contingencies

The essence of strategic planning combines factual information and value judgments. Values are usually implicit when basic rural development planning decisions are made about goals, methods, and resource allocations. The process of strategic planning helps make such judgments explicit—for example, when values clarification is used to resolve conflicts and achieve consensus among stakeholders. Attention to values should be given in many aspects of planning. There should be respect for distinctive rural values and community benefits, understanding of diverse subcultures among the rural population, specification of the values implicit in planning assumptions, recognition of major values associated with alternative program goals, attention to values implicit in procedural decisions (such as extent of participant involvement in planning), appreciation of gender differences, and extent of rural-urban bias in rural development policies (Nesman, 1981). The examples from China and Tanzania indicate how traditional rural values can deter modernization.

The extent of the social systems that a rural adult education provider seeks to understand can be extensive. A two-way systemic linkage model helps identify related systems to consider for planning purposes (Havelock, 1969; Swanson, Sands, and Peterson, 1990). An early stage of strategic planning can ensure that those relationships are satisfactory and warrant little additional attention (in contrast to relationships that require more detailed attention as planning proceeds). This preliminary reconnaissance stage also helps identify potential stakeholders to participate in major strategic planning activities. Three types are included within the macrosystem of growing conditions (such as temperature, soil, and rainfall) and the societal context of the service area (such as a district) for which a local or regional adult education leader has responsibility. One is the organizational system of the linkage agency—for instance, an extension service or NGO that also promotes technology transfer. A second is the client systems that the agency seeks to serve. The third is the variety of resource systems that the agency seeks to connect with clients so that an ongoing mutually beneficial exchange occurs.

There are various systems to which an agency might relate that could be analyzed in strategic planning. In addition to some basic background information about each, the important information is the relationship between the agency and each system. The systems are interrelated, so they influence each other. The following are categories of systems that could be pertinent to rural development in a specific setting:

1. Local cultural systems that influence each subpopulation of clients, such as extended family, local associates, religious and ethnic communities, powerful local elites.
2. Political and administrative systems (including national pol-

icy makers), regarding community development and agricultural development priority and policy, regional and local government, and corresponding governance arrangements of NGOs like cooperatives.

3. Parent organization systems to which the agency is related— for example, the ministry of agriculture or land-grant university for extension services.

4. Other provider organizations in the service area to be considered regarding collaboration, complementarity, or competition.

5. Funding or in-kind resource systems that support rural development programs.

6. Educational institutions and research institutes that may provide staff development for agency personnel, as well as serve as a major source of organized knowledge from research and development activities to include in technology transfer and recommended practices. This relationship can also help strengthen the continuum of preparatory and continuing education, advance lifelong learning, and avoid imposition of inappropriate formal education procedures on nonformal popular education of adults.

7. Indigenous knowledge reflected in successful traditional practices, which tend to be adapted to local conditions and can be combined with formal knowledge.

8. Technical inputs (such as credit, equipment, seeds, fertilizers, and other tools and supplies required for improved agricultural production) related to desirable changes to be made in various aspects of rural development: agriculture, health, family life, social services, and off-farm employment.

9. Marketing systems, including fair prices for produce or other outputs of rural occupations.

10. Risk management or other benefits that reassure and help rural people to make changes that are in their best interests and to overcome risk avoidance, one of the major deterrents to adopting recommended practices.

People associated with each of these systems likely to be important for implementation of plans should be identified as stakeholders in the strategic planning process (Axinn and Thorat, 1972, chap. 15;

Chambers and Jiggins, 1987; Compton, 1984, 1989; Swanson, 1985; Swanson, Sands and Peterson, 1990; Rivera and Schram, 1987).

Stakeholders

Leadership for rural adult education entails more than identification of potential stakeholders. It also includes arranging for able people from important stakeholder categories to participate effectively in the strategic planning process and to help implement plans. One result of this cooperation is collaboration between the provider agency and some of the related organizations and systems. Because practices are adopted locally and effective adult education agencies are decentralized to the extent that they are able to work well with local client systems, some of the collaboration that strategic planning can strengthen should be with local social systems to which potential clients belong. Because there are often various adult education providers in a service area, strategic planning should alert agency leaders to major offerings of other providers and encourage cooperation where appropriate. Because ties between both client and resource systems are important, a combination of stakeholders and collaborative relationships related to both types of systems should be considered. Financial and policy support is seldom adequate, so strategic planning should encourage assistance from rural, urban, national, and international sources—both governmental and NGOs. Contributions by NGOs can be seen in the examples from Thailand cooperatives and from Kenya. International assistance was influential in examples from St. Lucia, India, Bangladesh, Kenya, and Portugal. Because potential collaborating organizations vary greatly, strategic planning should help agency leaders to be flexible in the forms of cooperation that take place (Haverkort, 1988; Merriam and Cunningham, 1989; Rivera and Schram, 1987).

Staff

Agency staff members and volunteers are crucial to planning and implementation. A systemic perspective can help those who work in the local service area to use their personal contact with many of the related systems and stakeholders to strengthen linkage and agency effectiveness. An important staff proficiency is interpersonal relations. The range of adult educators engaged in rural development is likely to include various disciplines and specialties to address the diversity of rural people and development goals. If the volunteers, field staff members, specialists, and administrators are able and well prepared, they constitute a major asset for planning and implementation. Positive instances occurred in the United States, India, Australia, Israel, Kenya, Tanzania, and Chile. If agency workers and volunteers lack these qualities—and in addition spend much of their time of noneducational tasks—it will be difficult for agency programs to succeed. Negative examples include Cameroon and Bangladesh. The strategic planning process can serve as a staff development activity, as well as help to identify whether staff members should be added, developed, or helped to find more suitable occupations. Planning results can also help match staff and volunteer abilities and work responsibilities. Sometimes the conclusion is that given current staffing, some program directions may not be currently feasible (Charters and Hilton, 1989; Merriam and Cunningham, 1989).

Policies

Policy makers at local, regional, national and international levels influence rural adult education in various ways, including legislation, administrative regulations, and resource allocation. Most countries have some type of agricultural extension, but the specific arrangements and goals differ greatly. Policies may be aimed explicitly at rural adult education and extension or more often at agricultural or other aspects of rural development, which in turn affect educational programs. In many countries, there is no coherent rural development policy, and decisions are perceived to reflect other goals: national development, industrialization, or international trade balances. Irrelevant goals can increase rural resistance to extension. In such instances, strategic planning can be used to build consensus about desirable rural development policies or at least counteract antirural policies that sometimes are by-products of broad political or economic forces. Recommendations that 1 to 2 percent of agricultural gross domestic product should be involved in agricultural extension, compared to the 0.5 percent that is typically allocated, can be used in strategic planning to seek increased government commitment. The planning process can also identify excellent examples of well-developed and effective rural adult education programs that can help policy makers appreciate their benefits (such as in the United States, St. Lucia, China, and Tanzania), as well as determine unproductive programs and provide a basis for suggesting new program directions. The examples from Cameroon and Chile illustrate the severe problems resulting from low priority. Policy makers tend to be the most difficult category of stakeholders to include in the strategic planning process, so special attention should be given to inducements, appropriate forms of participation, and outcomes that they value (Crouch and Chamala, 1981; Molnar and Clonts, 1983; Rivera and Schram, 1987, chap. 3; Swanson, Sands, and Peterson, 1990).

Most of the societal influences on rural adult education are generally also reflected in the specific local contingencies in the village or rural area in which a field staff member works. A potential benefit of strategic planning at the agency level is that it can alert the staff members to specific local contingencies likely to be very influential on that program. The resulting insights can be useful locally; when shared with agency staff in other locations, it can enrich the overall planning process. The many aspects of rural life are interrelated, a fact that can make analysis difficult. Some of these factors are terrain, weather, economic conditions, local resources, powerful elites, low-resource farms, health conditions, family relations, human resources, and local leadership. For example, great inequalities between rural men and women may require unusual program approaches, especially if women are gatekeepers for the practices to be changed but men insist on representing the family at educational activities (Axinn and Thorat, 1972; Kamfwa, 1982; Nxumalo, 1982; Rivera and Schram, 1987; Robertson, 1984; UNESCO, 1986). Strategic planning should help local staff members and volunteers recognize and deal with major local contingencies that can have an impact on programs, as well as provide responsive organizational arrangements.

One of the most important but arduous tasks of strategic

planning is to focus on future directions. The main reason for planning is to affect decisions and actions that should occur in the future. However, past traditions, assumptions, habits, and standard procedures make it difficult for many people to shake off their usual mind-sets and be open to the possibilities of an improved future. The idealism of some of the people who work in rural development programs is an asset in this regard both for their own efforts and encouragement of peers. Because constructive social, organizational, or personal change is usually dependent on elements of stability and continuity, effective strategic planning can help identify such elements of desirable stability that can be used to reassure people who are apprehensive about proposed changes. Global perspectives on personal and social aspects of change and new ways to view old problems can help leaders develop a compelling vision that can inspire others to join in concerted efforts on behalf of rural development (Crouch and Chamala, 1981, chap. 22; Botkin, Elmandjra, and Malitza, 1979; Harman, 1988). Some strategic planning activities should help stakeholders reflect on their current vision of goals and procedures, explore alternative perspectives, and agree upon desirable directions that they will help to achieve. Extension advisory groups have enabled rural citizens to contribute to responsive programs.

Rural development sometimes also involves program areas dealt with in greater detail in other chapters, such as basic education and literacy, community problem solving, health education, and distance education.

12

Health Education

In April 1991, several organizations (including the American Dietetic Association) reported both good news and bad news that reflects the essence of the challenge to leaders of health education for adults. One report was based on a recent U.S. survey related to the National Cholesterol Education Program (designed to lower the risk of heart disease and cardiovascular illness, cancer, and diabetes). The good news pertained to knowledge and attitudes related to diet, cholesterol level, and risk of illness. Increasing proportions of U.S. adults were aware of this relationship. About two-thirds of adults had recently had their cholesterol level checked (about twice the average proportion seven years earlier), and more than one-third knew their level (almost ten times the proportion seven years earlier). In one study, more than half the men aged twenty to seventy-four had cholesterol levels that were too high. The bad news was that most adults with high cholesterol levels were doing little to change their eating habits to reduce their risk. Only about 15 percent were eating less fat, and most people at risk were not changing their eating habits.

Especially with an aging population in which an increasing proportion of illness is chronic and a majority of health problems are related to life-style, the main challenge to health educators is to broaden their strategy beyond dissemination of information to individuals and instead to use more comprehensive collaborative strategies likely to affect performance. Such comprehensive efforts

378

require strong leadership, including strategic planning with multiple stakeholders.

Features of Health Education

Shifting awareness, knowledge, and attitudes about life-styles are the product of desirable social changes on which deliberate health education programs can build. For example, a Wisconsin medical report in April 1991 indicated that fewer than 14 percent of Wisconsin young college graduates between eighteen and thirty-four years of age in the late 1980s smoked, compared with more than half of the young adults who had not completed high school. This higher rate of smoking reflected both higher proportions of the less educated who started smoking and smaller proportions who quit. Almost three-quarters of the high school dropouts started smoking in contrast to half that proportion for young adults who attended college. Fewer than a quarter of the dropouts quit smoking, compared with twice that proportion by people who attended college. Leaders should plan comprehensive health education efforts that address influences related to lifestyle and values. In a democratic society, it is important to do so in ways that focus on individual responsibility and empowerment, as well as to include a multipronged effort aimed at other people in the interdependent social systems in which at-risk adults function. There are broad situational influences. Health education and environmental education are interconnected.

Such holistic approaches have reflected international influences such as the Health for All campaign of the World Health Organization (WHO). Preventive and community health objectives also depend on contributions of primary-care physicians (such as family practice and internal medicine), who in turn interact with various specialists in medicine and the health professions. Collaboration is also desirable from people from other fields influencing diet, exercise, and stress, which affect heart disease and related illnesses. These fields include mass media, government, enterprises, recreation, and educational institutions. In some countries, such as Japan and China, traditional Western medical practices with their curative emphasis have been combined with ancient health traditions with their preventive focus (such as meditation for stress reduction).

Especially for health promotion, a distinctive feature of leadership is vision to select an approach that gives attention to both individual responsibility and community support. Strategic planning can contribute to a comprehensive approach that includes cultural values, social change, related social services, collaboration, and public priorities.

The examples and rationale in this chapter relate mainly to four planning themes. One theme is the focus on outcomes related to improved health and the changes that various people can make to achieve such outcomes. A second theme concerns the influences on participation: social stratification, high-risk populations, cultural values, social change, government priorities, and the like. A third is the various approaches that can be taken to health education as they relate to agency mission and collaboration with other providers. The fourth theme is leadership to succeed in comprehensive approaches, due to a compelling vision and broad cooperation, sometimes enriched by international perspectives. The chapter concludes with implications for strategic planning.

Minnesota Heart Health Program

In 1980, the Minnesota Heart Health Program (MHHP) began as a decade-long, multiple-strategy, population-wide preventive approach to use of education to help three midwestern communities reduce risk of cardiovascular disease. This ambitious research and demonstration project, largely funded by the National Institutes of Health, recognized the probability of powerful and widespread societal influences on hypertension and cardiovascular diseases and explored the efficacy of group and community-level screening, education, communication, and skill training in health promotion (Blackburn, 1992; Blackburn and others, 1984; Mittelmark and others, 1986; Murray and others, 1986).

The comprehensive communitywide mobilization entailed collaboration by the University of Minnesota, mass media, adult education providers, professional education, medical education, and those involved in preparatory education of youth; cooperation was also obtained from workplaces, food stores, and restaurants. In addition to adults at risk, educational and communication activities were aimed at their family members, health professionals, work sites, and the general community. This project built on previous public health projects that explored the relationships between education, prevention, community cooperation, increased awareness, and improved performance. During the 1970s, the North Karelia project in eastern Finland (Puska and others, 1981) and the Stanford project in northern California (Farquhar and others, 1977; Farquhar, 1990) contributed to planning, testing of program components, and preliminary projects in preparation of the MHHP. During the 1980s (as we will see later), a similar Heartbeat Wales project was conducted in Britain with WHO encouragement (Resource A, Nutbeam).

The Minnesota communitywide educational campaigns had five related parts designed to increase public awareness of risk factors related to heart health and to encourage action to reduce those risks (Blackburn, 1992; Blackburn and others, 1984). This multipronged community development approach was based on a rationale that community dynamics are composed of interrelated social systems with norms and values that influence individual behavior and that contribute to social learning (which reflects people's awareness, incentives, and perceived ability to change). The approach also drew on ongoing action research as a valuable source of feedback to guide leadership (Bandura, 1977; Lewin, 1951). Project evaluation was designed to demonstrate relationships between parts of the campaign process, the extent to which campaign exposure saturated various subpopulations, and desirable changes in performance and reduction of risk (Bracht, 1990; Murray and others, 1986).

One part of the campaign was use of mass communication, such as broadcasting and mailings. Within two years, nearly complete saturation of the adult population in the selected communities was achieved in the forms of awareness of the program, encouragement of participation in direct education activities, and in some instances explanations that led to changed performance. Information campaigns, however, tended to widen the knowledge gap. The more informed adults gained much more from the campaign than the less informed adults. This problem was offset by recognizing that people used multiple channels for more complex topics, by tailoring messages for various subpopulations (especially understanding of the health topic, such as including positive and negative reasons in messages for more educated adults), and by integrating mass communications with other parts of the campaign.

A second part of the campaign was direct education—participation in risk-factor screenings, drop-in health education centers, self-help programs, and adult education classes. Those who participated made significant improvements in risk factors (such as lower blood cholesterol, lower blood pressure, and less fat and sodium in restaurant meals). There was no reduction in smoking. More than half of the adults contacted in the campaign attended health factor screening and education sessions that averaged seventy-five minutes and that included testing for risk factors and reporting results, provided videotapes and print materials that explained how to change one's behavior, and concluded with a twenty-minute segment during which a health educator discussed results and suggestions with the person and family members. Unfortunately, about 40 percent of the population declined to attend one of the free screening and education sessions. Adult education classes were effective for those who attended but attracted only 5 or 6 percent of the population.

The third part of the program was continuing professional education workshops for physicians, dentists, nurses, nutritionists and other health professionals. Such health professionals were an important influence and resource for diagnosis, patient education, and reinforcement of messages from other parts of the campaign. There was evidence of changes in medical practice toward greater attention to prevention. For example, there was general consensus regarding treatment of high cholesterol levels. Recently graduated physicians had greater interest in preventive cardiology than those who graduated some years earlier. Practices and priorities in health care constrained attention to prevention, a situation that again emphasizes systemic influences (Blackburn, 1992; Kofron and Associates, 1991).

The fourth part of the effort was an extensive youth education program that included revision of school health education curricula and attention to 4-H clubs, youth campaigns, and children's events. Inclusion of parents was effective for children up to the sixth grade. This school-based family approach promoted healthy practices for young people at a stage in life when habits were being formed, helped recruit parents to adult programs, and promoted familywide decisions regarding eating, exercise, and smoking.

The fifth part consisted of all other community-based activities conducted by campaign task forces on smoking, exercise, and diet, or centering on special work site and medical center projects. Because societal influences encourage excesses of consumption and unhealthy habits of eating, smoking, drinking, and physical activity, part of the campaign addressed enhancing an individual's capacity for change by seeking to modify societal norms, values, and policies. A collaborative effort with community leaders and organizations achieved involvement in the campaign, which combined attention to government regulations, economic incentives, and public information with special cooperation by restaurants and grocery stores to reach people at the times when food-related decisions were made (Blackburn, 1992; Bracht, 1990).

The broad involvement by people in the demonstration communities contributed to long-term adoption of desirable public health practices. Participation of more than half the adult community, including policy makers, gatekeepers, and organizational leaders, fostered a sense of ownership of personal and situational changes that interacted and reinforced each other to sustain progress. Including educational activities aimed at policy makers helped to produce such societal changes as the availability of low-fat menu options, smoke-free work environments, health and safety practices, and provision of physical fitness recreational activities. Public support for such policy interventions complemented the main emphasis in a democratic society on educational and motivational strategies for health promotion based on individual understanding, intention to change, and choice (Blackburn, 1992; Loken, Swim, and Mittelmark, 1990; Murray and others, 1986).

Other U.S. Programs

The MHHP campaign during the 1980s was one of the more comprehensive, impressive, and well-documented preventive health education programs. It combined the expertise of the university, government funds, and broad-based participation by community organizations. But, of course, there are many other kinds of health education programs for adults.

Alcoholics Anonymous

Another very successful example is Alcoholics Anonymous (AA), which contrasts with MHHP in many ways. Many of its early members and the professionals who work with alcoholics regard AA as the greatest single therapeutic tool in the treatment of alcoholism. AA began in 1935 when two alcoholics (a physician from Ohio and a stockbroker from New York) found hope in mutual support after years of despair because their efforts to stop drinking had failed. Within a decade or so, the main features and guidelines of AA developed, and it spread rapidly as many groups were formed. In the 1990s, AA continues to be a major method of combating the alcoholism that afflicts eighteen million U.S. adults and has been the exemplar for dozens of self-help groups that have formed to combat other health and social problems.

Typically, the part-time local AA coordinators and most everyone else associated with the AA groups in a local community were once active alcoholics who found AA a big help in achieving and maintaining sobriety. Throughout, the emphasis has been on these autonomous local self-help groups. Although AA is not a formal organization with dues and officers, there is a national General Service Board (composed of both alcoholic and nonalcoholic members) that provides publications and assistance. Over the years, AA has resisted use of government funds. With the exception of direct donations, which support modest part-time staff salaries and office expenses, local AA programs have few financial resources. The emphasis is on self-support as well as self-help. At each weekly meeting, voluntary contributions are used to pay for expenses like room rental. Members may divide contributions between the local office and the national General Service Board office (which also derives income from sales of books and pamphlets).

The main purpose of AA is to help chronic alcoholics recover and remain sober by not drinking alcoholic beverages. New members share at least two characteristics: an alcohol addiction and a desire to stop drinking. Many AA members believe that success is likely only after an alcoholic concludes that the problems associated with alcohol are so great that sobriety is desirable. Joining AA is easy. Anyone who says that he or she is a member is. In recent decades, people whose lives have become unmanageable because of alcohol addiction are likely to know about the organization. Many are referred to AA by members, clergy, family, or formal treatment. Community residents and social agencies are generally supportive. Persistence is encouraged by small-group support, an informal setting, use of first names only, discussion of problems with less guilt than is usual outside AA, and the AA guidelines that emphasize living one day at a time. Similar separate groups for family and friends of alcoholics recognize that they too are affected and can be assisted in helping instead of hindering recovery. Program success has been widely acknowledged, and programs have been started in other countries even though some members initially have substituted their dependency on alcohol with a dependency on AA. Moreover, some alcoholics seem to benefit more from individual counseling, perhaps due to AA's emphasis on group support and spiritual fellowship.

When there is demand for additional groups, the coordinator works with some experienced and successful members who serve as volunteer leaders. In the collaborative learning setting of a self-help group, the emphasis is on learning from peers instead of experts, on combining individual responsibility and group support. As new leaders gradually assume responsibility, it reinforces their values related to sobriety. Alcoholics who join AA tend to be middle-class adults who relate to its very social fellowship. The majority are men, mostly in their thirties and forties. Alcoholics with less status, with less experience in voluntary associations, and who have difficulty sharing feelings in groups often drop out. Old and new members are welcomed to each weekly session with much support and are encouraged to discuss their alcoholism frankly and to see it as a disorder creating dependency and obsession, not a sign of moral degeneracy. Members gain more objective knowledge about alcoholism from reading the many AA publications. In the past, participants would usually tell their stories, acknowledging that they were alcoholics but no longer active. However, over the years, less attention has been given to anecdotes and more to the benefits of sobriety and the contributions of AA. Understanding and commitment to twelve steps and twelve traditions are central to AA beliefs. Meetings typically conclude with the Serenity Prayer: "God grant me the serenity to accept the things I cannot change, the courage to change the things I can, and the wisdom to know the difference."

A major societal influence on AA has been the severity of problems associated with alcoholism. Another is the positive image of AA, based on the evident success in helping many alcoholics become and remain sober, on the growing amount of pertinent research findings, and increasing acceptance by people in the helping professions and by the general public that alcoholism is a complex health problem and not just the result of a character fault. A negative factor is the emphasis on alcohol consumption as reflected in advertising, availability, and portrayal in the mass media. Other negative influences are: the inclination of alcoholics to use places that serve spirits as places to go to deal with loneliness, discouragement, and stress and the tendency of people who want an alcoholic to become sober to use guilt, a tactic that usually becomes part of the problem instead of part of the solution (Resource A, Knox (b)).

Nutrition Education

A major implication of AA for strategic planning is the success of self-help groups for many health and social problems. Self-help groups were one part of MHHP. However, in distinct contrast to MHHP, AA focuses on individuals and primary groups, curative instead of preventive, and depends on informal groups and self-support. Although the Expanded Food and Nutrition Education Program (EFNEP) of the Cooperative Extension Service (CES) has used support groups, the emphasis has been on nutritional counseling by paraprofessional nutritional aides working under the supervision of professional home economists—an approach differing from both MHHP and AA.

The EFNEP clients have been rural and urban low-income homemakers who generally buy and prepare the food for their family. The main program goals have been to improve family nutrition and health, while reducing expenditures for food. Nutritional aides visit homemakers in their homes, discuss ways to improve nutrition and reduce costs, jointly make plans with homemakers, and periodically monitor and reinforce progress. This basic individual counseling approach in homemakers' homes is sometimes supplemented by informal meetings in the neighborhood to provide group support. Follow-up and other evaluation studies demonstrated that EFNEP has been very successful. It shares with MHHP a preventive approach, but one focused on individual homemakers as gatekeepers of family nutritional decisions.

Other Approaches

There have been many other types of health education programs for adults, in addition to a few communitywide campaigns (such as MHHP) and many self-help groups (such as AA). Local self-help groups have been developed for dozens of physical and mental health problem areas—weight loss, diabetes, drug abuse, widowhood, child abuse, and terminal illnesses. Some of them have ties to health-related associations with broader education and promotion goals such as the Heart Association or the Cancer Society. Patient education by health professionals and educators associated with private or group practice or through hospitals and clinics address various goals: prevention, recovery, and adjustment. Secondary and post-secondary institutions with health education programs sometimes include outreach activities for adults. The earlier EFNEP example by CES was based in the home economics (and especially food and nutrition) expertise of the land-grant universities.

Some health education for adults is short term and focuses on cure or adjustment by patients and on support and assistance that include their family and friends. Family members have been associated with cause and cure of various health problems. By contrast, long-term preventive approaches encourage environmental and life-style changes. Examples include exercise programs by community agencies (such as the YMCA-YWCA) and programs on weight loss or smoking cessation that stress health education to help break old habits and replace them with more desirable ones. The necessity of strategic planning is evident for comprehensive communitywide campaigns (such as MHHP) that entail extensive collaboration. However, the leadership and the inclusion of multiple stakeholders are also important for many targeted health education programs that benefit from leaders using situational analysis and familiarity with other providers and resources.

Heartbeat Wales

Five years after MHHP began, a similar health promotion and education project began in the United Kingdom. As with MHHP, the U.K. project chose a government-financed comprehensive and collaborative health promotion strategy that used multiple points of intervention to achieve cumulative results. Special attention was given to societal influences on healthy life-styles and to educational and health promotion activities to obtain cooperation from enterprises and government (Merriam and Cunningham, 1989, chap. 38).

The Welsh Heart Programme, or Heartbeat Wales as it was colloquially known, was launched in March 1985. Sponsored by the Health Education Council and the Welsh Office, Heartbeat Wales was established as a demonstration project to test the feasibility of reducing risk factors for cardiovascular and heart disease (CHD). Although Heartbeat Wales was also concerned with life-style and health in general, the nutrition and diet component of the program was emphasized.

In December 1981, the Welsh Medical Committee recommended that there should be mass prevention through education, geared to the promotion of healthy living habits in the population. Paralleling this professional concern, there was a growing awareness in government departments of the high incidence of life-style–related diseases in Wales. In addition to this awareness of the scale of the problem relative to other industrialized countries, a number of national and international committees highlighted the fact that the high incidence of cardiovascular disease could be reduced through the application of existing knowledge about preventive and health promotion measures.

For administrative purposes, the Heartbeat Wales project was established as a department of the University of Wales College of Medicine, and the director of the program was appointed to the first chair of health education and health promotion in the United Kingdom. The establishment of Heartbeat Wales within the framework of a highly regarded university medical school provided added credibility in the eyes of the public and a degree of academic respectability to the health sector.

From the public perspective, it would appear that there was a lack of understanding about the impact of the Welsh life-style overall upon the population's health. One in four Welsh men and one in eight Welsh women did not reach the age of seventy-five years because of heart disease or stroke. In stark contrast to most other Western industrialized countries, Britain had not seen a significant decline in CHD mortality, particularly in middle age, over the previous decade and a half. There was evidence from inter- and intranational comparisons that the major cardiovascular diseases were substantially preventable.

The strategy comprised four complementary approaches designed to embrace both the demand and supply aspects of food consumption—namely, public education, changes in food ingredients, improvements in consumer information and food labeling, and increased access to and availability of those foods that figure prominently in a healthy diet. The progress of Heartbeat Wales as a practical demonstration project coincided with a conceptual evolution of health promotion at the international level and in particular with the Regional Office for Europe WHO. The developments were mutually supportive, with Heartbeat Wales reinforcing and being reinforced by the statements outlined in the Ottawa Charter for Health Promotion.

There was increased concern about health, as opposed to illness, during the lifetime of the project. This fact was reflected in an increase in mass media coverage of prevention. Heartbeat Wales collaborated closely with the Open University in the development of a distance learning course on cardiovascular disease prevention for primary health care practitioners. Cooperation with television occurred during 1986 with a coproduced, ten-part series about healthy eating broadcast from October to December. Information packs and health kits supported the programs. By the midpoint of the series, 37 percent of Welsh people had watched at least one program. The success of the high media profile was illustrated by a survey conducted one year after the launch: 53 percent of the Welsh population were aware of Heartbeat Wales, and 97 percent of those considered it a worthwhile enterprise.

Organizations in both the commercial and public sectors (such as the health authority) changed their stance, and there was higher priority accorded to health than was previously the case. In a similar vein, government policy also gave health promotion a higher priority. In addition to providing Heartbeat Wales with a real increase in funding during the first two years, the secretary of state for Wales established an all-Wales health promotion agency, the Welsh Health Promotion Authority, in April 1987. (However, successive administrations of both parties when in power have yet to demonstrate a real concern for health as an essential element of agricultural policy.)

Heartbeat Wales addressed the feasibility of intervention on a major scale, and the conclusions of the WHO and other expert bodies were accepted as the basis for planning. The 1982 WHO Expert Committee described three policy options for cardiovascular heart disease prevention: a population approach, a high-risk strategy, and secondary prevention. In Heartbeat Wales, the most effort was directed at a population approach, although support was also provided for certain high-risk and secondary prevention programs.

One of the first tasks of the project team was to establish a climate of opinion conducive to policy development, professional support, and public involvement. The following decisions were therefore taken at the outset:

- Involve key political figures in a practical way.
- Generate a widespread mass media campaign.
- Formulate a consultation document.
- Open a dialogue with as many organizations and potential allies as possible.
- Disseminate information that would assist the advocacy process.

One of the lessons learned from the Heartbeat Wales's experience was that there had to be a policy with which politicians, professionals, and the public could identify. At the outset of the program, the Health Education Council and the Welsh Office had established a multidisciplinary steering group for the project, comprising eminent representatives from a number of key professional groups within Wales. Negotiations about policy development likely to contribute to an improvement in the Welsh diet were entered into with a number of organizations outside of the health sector. Not the least of these was the food industry. One of the more innovative aspects of the Welsh Heart Program's work was its association with commerce and industry, primarily with the food industry. Detailed nutritional analyses were included on the labels of products, together with a simple guide ("low fat" or "high fiber"). Healthy foods were included at a reduced price in promotional exercises by some food chains.

The dairy industry was not universally in favor of the nationally accepted dietary guidelines, but a major milk distributor and retailer in south Wales helped Heartbeat Wales promote semi-skimmed and skimmed milk by taking one penny off the cost of a pint and delivering a promotional leaflet to every household served by its delivery men. The food industry in Wales was prepared to cooperate if there was a commercial advantage in terms of market share, public relations, or added value and if the approach was based on collaboration rather than criticism.

Two important aims were thus achieved with the formal launch of the program: first, the program was given a more positive image than that of disease prevention; second, the necessity for multisectoral participation and action was placed firmly on the political and public agenda. The personal involvement of elected politicians at national and local levels in high-profile public events remained a continuing theme of the program.

Establishing support from the food industry was only one of a number of alliances formed in the early part of the program. There was also agreement among the project team members that support and involvement from the voluntary sector would be crucial. Support came not only from the health sector and government departments, but also from the education sector, commerce and industry, and nongovernmental organizations.

The experience of Heartbeat Wales led to a number of conclusions that may be of value to others involved in health promotion policy development (Resource A, Nutbeam).

- The process of policy formulation is organic in nature and can begin at any level within an organization or sector. Indeed, it frequently starts at several levels simultaneously.
- Health promotion must start at the point of existing policy. It must be seen to be relevant to the current agenda of those called upon to reorientate their activities.
- Health promotion is by definition a positive concept, and it is only rarely that there needs to be "winners" and "losers." Heartbeat Wales adopted the principle that everyone should win as a result of the health promotion process. Collaboration rather than confrontation should be the general rule.
- It is essential to have an entry point that is meaningful and credible from the political decision makers' point of view. Proposals must be specific and based upon a clearly defined need.
- Negotiating ability is essential for those charged with an advocacy role in health promotion, and a comprehensive information base is a prerequisite for effective negotiation. Equally, personal and organizational communication skills are of fundamental importance.
- Although it is important to establish a plan of action based upon consultation, it is also essential to remain flexible within the agreed aims of the program.
- It is imperative to generate a climate of public acceptability for health promotion prior to and throughout the policy development process. This can be achieved through genuine participation by community groups, through market research, and through mass media coverage.
- Persistence is a virtue. A negative response at one level does not necessarily mean that there will be a similar reaction at other levels of the same organization.
- Peer endorsement and the exchange of ideas are important when dealing with the issue of professional development.
- Policy proposals must be demonstrably feasible in practice. A program of education and training is essential where new

knowledge and skills are required to implement changes in working methods.

- The use of local demonstration projects can be a valuable precursor to more comprehensive policy agreements.
- Most importantly, simultaneous action in a number of sectors is preferable to a concentration of effort in one sector only. Multisector action can lead to mutual reinforcement in the policy development process, one sector agency spurring others to action.
- It is undesirable and logistically impossible for the central agency to undertake or endeavor to control all activities. The consequence would be a shift from a role of innovation and advocacy to that of program maintenance, which would stifle progress. Furthermore, it is essential to engrain health promotion policy into professional and organizational practice so that developments will be maintained once the project, such as Heartbeat Wales, is discontinued. This result will not occur without a devolution of responsibility to a local level.

Heartbeat Wales supported the proposals for the prevention of cardiovascular disease outlined in a report by the Welsh Council of the Royal College of General Practitioners. The council's report stressed the importance of appropriate education, including in-service training for all members of the primary health care team.

A follow-up survey in 1988 indicated that improvements had occurred during the first three years of the project. There were already improvements of several percentage points in risk indicators such as eating high-fiber and low-fat foods, engaging in regular active exercise, and not smoking.

In summary, Heartbeat Wales was a comprehensive community approach using information and education as ways to reduce health risks, especially regarding nutrition and circulatory disease. International ideas and public policy were taken into account. The government provided the main financial support. Project staff helped develop policy consensus and utilized collaborative planning with many diverse groups at Welsh and local levels. Commitment to shared values and goals helped reduce resistance from some organizations. The collaborative approach sought the cumulative effect of interventions at multiple points in the social system (Catford, 1990; Nutbeam and Catford, 1987; Parish, Catford, and Nutbeam, 1987; Resource A, Nutbeam).

Other Countries

As MHHP was one unique communitywide health project among a wide range of health education programs for adults in the United States, so Heartbeat Wales was an exceptional and comprehensive approach that was undertaken along with various other health education programs worldwide. This section provides diverse examples from countries around the world and with differing levels of technological development. A major theme illustrated by these examples is empowering underserved adults through strengthening decentralized primary health care. This priority on equity and self-reliance in decentralized health education strategies reflects international commitment since the 1978 conference at Alma Ata in the Soviet Union toward self-help health promotion integrated with related aspects of social and economic development. A related theme is the combination of traditional and Western health and medical practices (Merriam and Cunningham, 1989, chap. 38). Each example focuses on societal influences on health education approaches and implications for strategic planning.

Australia

Women's health for predominantly working-class women between the ages of forty and sixty living in the Sydney, Australia, metropolitan area is the focus of a program initiated in 1983 and based in a hospital. The content emphasizes self-help and self-referral related to topics such as menopause and breast self-examination and women's changing roles in relation to family, work, and community. The hospital provides women's health manual training workshops for people engaged in a wide variety of health and helping professions. Workshop participants attend a four-day workshop based on an extensive resource manual that covers health content, instructional methods, and information on resources for instructors and midlife women. Workshop participants then serve as instructors for a wide variety of educational activities for midlife women.

Commonwealth government funds helped initiate the program, and the New South Wales Department of Health then started providing financial subsidy to support the hospital that provided the training workshops and other cooperating hospitals. The program is cost effective because of the multiplier effect; workshop participants eventually serve as instructors for many and varied health education activities over the years. However, a major negative influence on this successful program is uncertainty about continued funding.

The workshops and related staff development activities for instructors are augmented by the fourteen modules of the resource manual, a thirteen-minute videotape, and a companion book especially published to provide information that is not readily available. During the year or so after the initial set of training workshops, the participants conducted health education activities for more than a thousand women, and follow-up evaluations reported many desirable changes that resulted. Among the societal influences on planning the project are trends toward health promotion, consumer movement, self-care, alternative health, and the women's movement. These—along with growing recognition of the relation between health condition and social class level—contribute to initiation, support, and cooperation; to mass media coverage; and to participation in subsequent health education activities by working-class women in the middle years. The project planners did little to affect societal influences but recognized and benefited from them (Resource A, Degeling, Bennett, and Everingham).

This was but one of many health education programs for Australian adults, which also address such topics as occupational health and safety, alcohol and drug dependency, AIDS, diabetes, and nutrition. These programs are provided by various organizations, including hospitals, which also offer healthy-living programs for the community (for example, stress management for middle-aged adults and exercise for elders [Tennant, 1991]).

Canada

Two Canadian health education programs show contrasting approaches to health promotion for working-class adults. In Ontario Province, HealthLine: Center for Corporate Health Promotion is a collaborative venture of Humber College and Etobicoke General

Hospital, in conjunction with an advisory board that includes members from Toronto-area enterprises. Their cooperation is important because HealthLine arranges with enterprise managers for provision of contract programs in enterprises on a cost-recovery basis. All instructors are certified following a training course to work with HealthLine. The self-supporting program provided for each enterprise is tailor-made but is for all levels of staff, from blue-collar workers through senior management. HealthLine services include needs assessment, specialized program design and implementation, and evaluation. Regardless of audience, content, and length of program in an enterprise, all HealthLine courses are medically based, personalized, and performance oriented and include resource manuals, follow-up, confidential referrals, and cost sharing. Content includes health-style assessments, weight loss, smoking cessation, stress management, physical fitness, life-style analysis, and cardiac crisis management. This approach serves more blue-collar adults, in part because of the work-site location (Resource A, Pratt).

Another health education program in Ontario was aimed at Canadian Indians throughout the province. The initiative was taken by the Union of Ontario Indians (UOI), formed to advocate the views of its forty-six-member bands to various levels of government. This initiative was encouraged by a 1979 policy of the Federal Department of Health and Welfare that emphasized Indian control over Indian health. Although Canada's standard of living was among the highest in the world, social and living conditions of Native Canadian Indians were far below national averages, as reflected in unemployment, poor housing and water supply, infant mortality, youth suicides, accident rates, and alcohol abuse. UOI constituted a Health Steering Committee (HSC) to prepare a health policy as a basis for negotiations with various government agencies. During two and a half years, HSC used a rotating planning subcommittee to conduct ten workshops of three to five days' duration. Each workshop was planned around a health topic in which participants learned from resource persons and each other to solve specific community problems. Consciousness raising was a priority, and the approach reflected the Alma Ata declaration on preventive health care, which viewed health as not the mere absence of disease but as a balance of physical, mental, spiritual, and social elements based on respect for whole people in their environments. Participants who had been suspicious of education as an alienating force from the majority culture responded positively to the HSC approach that reflected the native people's experience and traditional indigenous knowledge (Cervinskas, 1984).

Republic of Ireland

A certificate course of study for people who deal with drug and alcohol addiction problems, provided by Maynooth College, twenty miles west of Dublin, Ireland, demonstrates another approach to health education. Need for the course reflected reports and analysis of addiction in Ireland, advice of course instructors, and public debate about the importance of educating parents, helping professionals, and community leaders about alcohol and drug abuse as family and social problems. A full-time college extension administrator devoted part time to coordination of the course, which consisted of twenty weekly two-hour class sessions, plus readings and a course project. The instructors planned the course with potential participants, family members, and various interested people. The course included guest resource persons and audiovisual materials. The intent of the program was to help participants become more able and confident in coping positively with those experiencing drug and alcohol problems in work, family, and community settings, with special attention to earlier intervention and collective responses.

The government Department of Health provided a small initial grant for program development and publicity, but the college provided no financial subsidy. Thus, fee income covered all direct and indirect expenses. Instructors and guest lecturers had many contacts with course clientele, which contributed to attraction of participants and course relevance. Yet without a national policy on alcohol and drug problems, health responses were few and scattered. The general lack of qualified full-time specialists in alcohol and drug addiction reduced the multiplier effect that might have occurred if certificate course graduates had been available to teach other people. The course certificate had little status, so did little to attract participants, many of whom were interested in career advancement. Distance and limited public transportation between the college, where the course was held in the early years, and Dublin, where most potential participants were located, were also barriers to participation. Plans were made to offer the course in Dublin in the future (Resource A, McCann).

Kenya

In contrast to the foregoing examples from technologically advanced urban countries (with the exception of the program for Canadian Indians), many of the following ones from developing countries emphasize family and community development approaches to strengthen the technical and social infrastructure (such as diet and water supply) that influences causes of illness and scope of health education. Two examples from Kenya are illustrative of such approaches. A community-based primary health care project in western Kenya used adult and nonformal education for community involvement in collectively defining adults' concepts of health and identifying their health priorities. Project staff trained local "first-aider" health workers in a two-month program composed of one week in the community and one week in the health center. This was followed by six to eight weeks of gradual assumption of health education activities; under the guidance of project staff, these workers helped local people understand how to prevent disease and promote good health by changed practices related to diet, nutrition, sanitation, and water supply. Another project in Kenya conducted by the National Christian Council of Churches, with assistance from World Education, Inc., focused on adult education for collective problem solving related to social and economic conditions, including health. In this approach, the initial emphasis was on helping local groups to set priorities regarding social and economic improvements, to engage in critical analysis of connections between these priorities and healthful practices, and to pursue ongoing learning activities for using available resources, increasing confidence, and extending general community involvement.

Each of these Kenya projects reveals program impact on health practices of individuals and on community environmental conditions such as sanitation and water supply. Implications for strategic planning include health education goals that extend beyond treating the symptoms of illness to addressing situational causes. These improvements are not within the total control of individuals or governments, but entail cooperation, a commitment to equitable distribution of social services and benefits, and recognition of interrelations between health and community development (Clark, 1980).

Nigeria

In each country, people in some roles can help or impede health education efforts depending on whether or not they are effectively included in program planning and implementation. For example, some years ago in Nigeria, neglect of traditional midwives discouraged expectant mothers from using a modern new maternity center; but once midwives were given a role, they became supportive, and many women began to use the maternity center. For these and other health education activities, people in related roles (such as husbands and mothers-in-law) can become valuable allies if included (Osuhor and Osuhor, 1978).

Tanzania

Especially for communitywide mobilizations, it is helpful to focus on a specific health problem. This fact was illustrated in 1979 in Bunju, Tanzania, a village of fewer than two thousand people on the Indian Ocean about twenty miles from Dar es Salaam. There the village council working committee on health decided that the most serious health problem was a parasitic disease that affected two-thirds of the people. After a two-year adult education campaign to inform and mobilize people on treatment, control, and prevention of this parasitic disease, the incidence was reduced by about half.

Few villagers had previously understood the symptoms, causes, or means of prevention. The disease was so pervasive that many believed blood in the urine to be normal. Because such symptoms were not recognized, treatment was delayed. Educational activities taught local teachers and village leaders about the disease.

These individuals then helped to conduct educational meetings, used audiovisual aids, showed microscope slides to explain the problem, and convened study circles to discuss solutions.

At first, men and women attended separate sessions to become study circle leaders because women avoided discussion in mixed groups. As they gained proficiency and confidence, however, this separation became unnecessary. The ongoing functional literacy campaign included health content. Related projects focused on building latrines and on filling and spraying useless swamps and ponds to kill the snails that served as necessary hosts for the parasitic flatworms that caused the disease.

As the project progressed, outside adult educators turned over increasing amounts of the educational process to local people who then understood that they had both a right to health services and a responsibility to maintain them. Nearby villages learned of the project and began their own with support from the Ministry of Health (Cervinskas, 1984). Other community development and functional literacy programs during the previous decade helped pave the way for this focused health education project.

India

Sometimes oppressed subpopulations have been unaware of major causes of their health-related problems. In 1977, a Gram Vikas development team set out to help Khond tribal people in Orissa, one of the most economically backward states in India. Khonds in one area had a literacy rate of less than 5 percent and few educational, health, or social services. The Khonds lived in small, isolated forest villages, and depended on selling firewood and fruit; they were exploited by nontribals who employed them, sold them illegal alcohol, and loaned them money with the result that many mortgaged their land, trees, and livestock. The development team recognized the great influence of powerful elites and the fact that progress depended on local initiatives and awareness of causes of oppression, leading to collective solutions.

Development team members began work with eleven villages, where people had relied mainly on indigenous medicines. The team began by dispensing medicines that provided dramatic relief from malaria or tuberculosis. These efforts helped win people's confidence and give team members credibility to discuss larger issues. Village meetings began by discussing modest health programs: immunization, curative medicine, maternal and child health, and health insurance. Village meetings became monthly health education events that analyzed causes of ill health such as sanitation, poverty, alcoholism, and exploitation.

Within three years, the program had spread to ninety-one villages, and a multitiered health care system was established, with more serious cases referred to nearby dispensaries or to a regional hospital for very specialized services. Local people discovered that they could work with the government to achieve a healthy environment. They were able to redeem their mortgaged land and trees and set up credit unions to protect their improved economy. The educational process that began with adult health education helped tribal people to awaken and become more empowered (Cervinskas, 1984).

Another comprehensive community development approach to health education in India was taken by the Hayden Hall Center, a quasi-independent social service center affiliated with St. Joseph College, located in Darjeeling in the hill country in the northern corner of west Bengal. Started in 1969 as an emergency response to help rehabilitate urban landslide and fire victims in the region (which includes a large rural and urban disadvantaged population primarily of Nepali origin), Hayden Hall's social service mission included nonformal health education for the rural poor who lacked social services. At any one time, half the full-time staff of forty-five and hundreds of paraprofessionals and volunteers were working with people in rural villages. Center staff members set policy and made plans mainly with the clientele, and gave special attention to staff, volunteer, and local leadership development to enable villages to become more self-confident and self-reliant.

One part of this effort was a paramedic training program for village women, which included a three month nonformal training course at the Darjeeling Center to become village-level health workers. When a woman returned to her village, she was able to help in 80 percent of health problems and to see that those problems that she could not treat received proper referral and care. Special

attention was given to maternal and child health, tuberculosis eradication, and family nutrition education. Yearly refresher courses
were given to review and update training. Center policies were
somewhat influenced by the college, which provided funding along
with international religious sources (which the positive image of
the center helped attract). There was little formal collaboration.
Political unrest in support of greater autonomy for the Gurkas affected the program by preventing travel in the area, thus restricting
assistance (Resource A, Burns). This example shows how external
religious organizations can be very responsive to a minority clientele but encounter some resistance from the government and some
local elites that do not want the power structure disrupted.

Colombia

Sometimes indigenous health educators have experienced conflicting roles as members of a local community and as government
officials within that community. That situation happened among
local health promoters who worked with indigenous Sikuani peoples at the Orinoco River Basin of eastern Colombia, South America, along the border with Venezuela. The Sikuan numbered almost
twenty thousand people who lived in small, scattered villages along
the river.

　　Historically, the Sikuan had been a self-sufficient, nomadic
people who engaged in hunting and gathering, supplemented by
slash-and-burn agriculture to produce cassava and by trade with
other indigenous tribes along the Orinoco and Amazon river systems. As settlements in Colombia had moved eastward and in Venezuela had moved westward, the Sikuani territories had shrunk.
Their mobility reduced, these people had been forced to establish
villages. The Sikuani continued to speak their native language,
maintain their oral culture, practice traditional medicine and rites,
and use traditional healers. Changing food consumption, along
with accumulated waste from and proximity of domesticated animals, resulted in malnutrition, water pollution, and increased incidence of diseases such as infections, intestinal parasites, respiratory
illnesses, diarrhea, tuberculosis, and malaria.

　　In 1984, the Regional Health Service, with financial and in-kind support from several nongovernmental organizations (NGOs) and the regional trade center, began to modify the in-service education for local health promoters, which appeared to be ineffective and a source of frustration for promoters and village leaders. Previously, the three months of training that the health promoters received had been based on a manual oriented toward Western medicine and highland conditions around Bogota (regarding nursing techniques, recommended diets, urban phamaceuticals, and public sanitation and water systems). The inappropriateness of this information contributed to a widening gap between villagers and some of the health promoters. Some of the health promoters had abandoned health-related practices, values, and concepts learned in childhood and tried to promote recommended practices. Conflict and alienation also resulted because some health promoters stopped hunting and fishing to support themselves and instead waited for patients to request medications. As salaried Regional Health Service employees, some health promoters became indigenous elites separate from the local community that had selected them—to the point that in some villages, local leaders even confiscated promoters' salaries to finance community projects.

The modified training program reversed this alienation by a participatory approach in which health promoters became bridges between Western and traditional health concepts and practices. They worked with villagers to recover and analyze indigenous knowledge and to discuss health problems and possible solutions. Regional Health Service consultants who provided in-service training for several years helped the health promoters to evolve health practices that promoted health as well as to cure illness in ways that combined the best of Western and traditional practices, adapted to local circumstances. Potable water projects helped accommodate both tradition and progress and had the support of women whose walking time to fetch water and work in the fields had increased greatly with permanent settlements. These had also encouraged use of baby bottles and formula so relatives could take care of young children, but polluted stream water still caused illness. Health education began with breast feedings and sterilizing water and baby bottles; it then extended to nutrition, hygiene, family economy, and infant illness and mortality. Installing wells in villages became part of a broader strategy: clean well water was used for drinking and cooking; however women continued to go to streams for water for bathing and laundering (which allowed continuation of related social activities such as chatting and matchmaking), and men learned how to maintain and repair well and water system equipment.

Local health promoters became indispensible mediators between traditional and Western medicine. To help rural doctors understand the perspectives and practices of indigenous patients, health promoters accompanied referrals with bicultural case histories that included traditional diagnoses and treatments by shamen and grandmothers and suggestions by the health promoters about adaptation of health services to Sikuani conditions (Herrera and Lobo-Guerrero, 1988).

Chile

In the early 1980s, a similar participatory approach was used by a Family Health Group (FHG) in conjunction with a small primary health care clinic northwest of Santiago, Chile. They sought to serve seventy thousand poor people, many in shanty towns with high unemployment and unsanitary conditions. Despite the vertical health system and an adverse political climate of a military government, FHG staff trained local women to lead health education for small groups of young women. The training program covered both health content and educational procedures, with an emphasis on broad community participation for self-sufficiency through active learning based on personal experience and analysis of personal and collective realities. The women who participated that had ties to the community continued as health educators there, compared to women without such ties who discontinued when there was no room for them to work in the clinic (Cervinskas, 1984).

These examples regarding use of indigenous health leaders from rural Colombia and urban Chile illustrate the importance that strategic planning consider the indigenous culture of the community to be served and the roles of the local educators in relation to both the clientele and government health service and clinics with which the health educators are connected. In each instance, the people who conducted the in-service education programs helped the local health leaders understand this relationship, demonstrated the participatory approach to be used, and worked with them over time until they were functioning satisfactorily.

Strategic Planning

Leadership of health education activities for adults can gain special benefits from comprehensive planning because human health is interconnected with many other aspects of life and is affected by various societal influences. Comparative perspectives are valuable because understanding of health education in other national settings helps reveal powerful implicit cultural values that shape behavior of clients and staff; each group uses its ethnocentric lens to interpret health-related practices, influences, and results (Conner, 1988; Marsick, 1988b). The programs in different national settings reflect four broad themes important for strategic planning. These pertain to outcomes, participation, approaches, and leadership.

Outcomes

Because of the complex array of influences and results associated with health and illness, specification of intended outcomes and anticipated benefits can contribute greatly to planning and conducting health education programs that have desirable cumulative impacts on health promotion and illness reduction. Different goals make it difficult to select specific performance indicators to guide program development and evaluation and to focus resources and activities to achieve desirable ratios between costs and benefits. An increasing portion of health education for adults goes beyond patient education by health professionals to aid recovery from illness. It concentrates on primary health care and especially promotion of health and prevention of illness. The preventive emphasis was central in examples from Minnesota, Wales, Australia, Kenya, Tanzania, and Chile. This expansion of scope from curing illness to promoting health changes the influences and strategies of health education and makes specification of health education objectives and anticipated personal and societal benefits especially important.

Early efforts regarding preventive medicine and public

health in the United States concentrated on individual awareness in the community, whereas public health efforts in some developing countries placed more importance on community infrastructure (such as sanitation and water supply) with relatively less attention to individual choice. This community focus was prominent in the examples from Tanzania, India, and Colombia. It has become increasingly clear that attention to both personal and societal aspects of health promotion is important in all national settings, awareness may not result in improved performance, and improved facilities may not result in effective use. Achievement of some health education and promotion goals requires policy changes by government or enterprises. As shown by the example regarding alcohol and drug abuse in Ireland, lack of policy support can impede acquisition of support. Leaders of health education programs can use strategic planning to increase consensus among major stakeholders regarding intended outcomes at individual, group, community, and national levels. This consensus enables leaders to work with stakeholders to select specific performance indicators. Such an approach was emphasized in the Tanzania example. These indicators can be useful in various ways, including helping stakeholders understand program goals in concrete terms, selecting effective learning activities and materials, monitoring and addressing external influences on the program, and (especially) evaluating program impact (Abbott and Mejia, 1988).

Participation

The second theme regarding health education leadership involves use of strategic planning to identify, understand, and in some instances respond to pertinent societal trends by seizing opportunities, deflecting threats, and occasionally helping to achieve social change. Health education programs function within dynamic environments, including both abrupt change and gradually emerging trends that both help and hinder health conditions and educational programs to improve them. In the United States, an aging population, urban living, technology, and cultural values contribute to life-style–related illnesses caused by stress, lack of exercise, smoking, fat consumption, alcohol and drug abuse, automobile use, and poor health and safety practices. Comparative analysis of societal influences can assist strategic planning by helping to compensate for the culture-bound views, values, and practices of clients, health educators, and policy makers. International influences were apparent in the examples from Minnesota, Wales, Kenya, Darjeeling, and Colombia. As emphasized at the Alma Ata conference on health promotion and primary care, analysis of external influences is important to recognize causes of illness and to extend health education beyond curing the illness of individuals.

Strategic planning can help leaders focus on societal influences that are especially important in their situation. Comprehensive programs (such as the Minnesota Heart Health Program and Heartbeat Wales) have used strategic planning to address various societal influences and increase program impact. The other examples in this chapter each reflect some of the major external influences that seemed important in that setting. Review of the differing external influences and program approaches in various environments can help leaders recognize those that are particularly important to consider in their own situation. The following are a few of the many types of societal influences that leaders might assess.

- Level of health care capability, related to national economic and technological development and community infrastructure (partly reflected in examples from technologically advanced and from developing countries)
- Costs of health care in relation to people's ability to pay, including public concern about this issue (a background issue in MHHP)
- Distribution of health care between majority and disadvantaged subcultures (disparities that can occur within as well as between countries were seen in the examples from Canada, India, Colombia, and Chile)
- Understanding and responsiveness to indigenous and minority subcultures (as illustrated by the Sikuan in Colombia)
- Basic community infrastructure and resources related to health and illness in the urban or rural region, such as territorial restrictions, transportation, sanitation, and water quality (ex-

ample of Sikuan in Colombia, midwives in Nigeria; see also
Barrow, 1981)
- Political commitment to health promotion and access to health
  care (Allegrante, 1984)
- Opponents of improved health (as illustrated by the Khond in
  India)

Situational analysis (using some of the methods illustrated
by MHHP) can enable health education leaders to go beyond evident direct influences on clients and educational activities and take
into account more distant economic, political, and social influences
that may affect health education indirectly. For example, economic
conditions affect government support for health education, including seed money grants to initiate demonstration projects as well as
ongoing subsidy of programs that serve less-advantaged subcultures. Mass media attention to health education topics can increase
public awareness, including response by clients and support by policy makers. International initiatives, such as WHO's Health for All
campaign, can stimulate and reinforce national policy support for
local efforts. Increasingly, Western health care practices that emphasize high-technology cures for individuals are being combined
with traditional practices and beliefs, many of which emphasize a
holistic balance between body, mind, and spirit within the context
of group and environment. Strategic planning by a provider can
identify the societal influences that warrant attention in that setting
(Colle, 1977; Werner, 1988).

Approaches

The third theme regarding health education leadership relates to
program approaches that health educators can use. There are many
types of health education programs. Some are highly decentralized
and depend on volunteers and very little on government funding.
In an example such as Alcoholics Anonymous, the focus is on the
individual and a supportive self-help group. The EFNEP example
was counseling oriented. A second approach that was mentioned
only incidentally as part of comprehensive approaches in the United States and Britain is curative patient education by health professionals for middle-class participants. A third approach (seen in
many of the foregoing examples) entails selection and training of

local people to serve as paraprofessional health workers; these perform some combination of tasks—treating many illnesses, referring patients with more serious illnesses, organizing public health projects to prevent illness, and at the very least providing health education for primary care. A fourth approach is the comprehensive health promotion program (such as the examples from Minnesota and Wales) that include educational activities for multiple stakeholders. Additional approaches are demonstrated by other components of comprehensive approaches, such as use of mass media to increase awareness of risk factors for certain audiences or educational activities for policy makers in government or enterprises aimed at reducing health hazards related to alcohol abuse, smoking, air or water pollution, and fat consumption for which collective action is essential. Health education leaders can use strategic planning to help decide the one or combination of approaches to select and adapt to fit the purposes, societal influences, audience, staff, and resources that constitute the local contingencies within which planning occurs. The success of very selective approaches aimed at only one type of stakeholder usually depends on the contribution of other health promotion efforts for the remaining stakeholders (Feurerstein, 1982; Nichter and Nichter, 1986).

Especially when major health improvements are important and social change is involved, strategic planning requires working with multiple stakeholders: clients, staff members, policy makers, and sometimes other audiences, such as the general public and even detractors who oppose health promotion for indigenous people. As was noted especially in conjunction with Heartbeat Wales, it is difficult and probably undesirable to control a comprehensive health promotion centrally. Instead, participation by multiple stakeholders in strategic planning can help win and maintain voluntary cooperation, especially at the crucial stage of implementation of plans.

In democratic societies, a crucial aspect of cooperation depends on persuasion and education to achieve clients' voluntary participation, individual responsibility, and personal empowerment to achieve satisfactory health. Client understanding and commitment are especially important when many health problems are associated with individual life-styles and values. Personal perspectives on the costs and benefits of current health care are also major influences on collective public policy decisions about issues such as pollution, health, and safety rules.

Another stakeholder category consists of people associated with health care systems. Included are physicians, nurses, dentists, pharmacists, social workers, and people in many allied health occupations, most of whom contribute to patient education and other forms of health education in addition to provision of health care. The examples from developing countries in this chapter about paraprofessional health promoters reflect various combinations of health education, health care, and client advocacy. For primary health care for low-income populations, selection and training of local health education workers depend in part on accessibility of health care; this in turn is affected by location, patient fees, and client perspectives on health care workers. Strategic planning should contribute to health education activities that help both clients and staff members contribute to healthy living.

Of course, as seen in several programs (especially regarding alcoholism in Ireland), the causes, cures, and prevention of many forms of illness involve stakeholders beyond clients and health care workers. These include clients' families and friends, educational institutions, nongovernment organizations and voluntary associations, government agencies, enterprises in which clients work, retail outlets such as food stores and their suppliers, and the mass media. The examples from Ireland, Australia, Kenya, and Chile illustrate ways in which planning of workshops and manuals can be used to orient paraprofessionals and other local health educators to working with various stakeholders (Abbott and Mejia, 1988). The comprehensive programs from Minnesota and Wales indicate ways to encourage cooperation from more remote stakeholders, such as people associated with enterprises and government. Strategic planning can help health education leaders identify the desirable mix of local and remote stakeholders to include in planning and implementation.

Leadership

For some health education activities (such as patient education to promote compliance with medication or other activities to promote recovery), the focus can be on the individual patient, and the educational activity can be provided by a member of the health occupations. By contrast, for many primary-care health promotion activities, there is generally a more diverse set of local and remote stakeholders, a situation requiring more formal strategic planning to achieve significant personal and social change. The WHO-related examples (such as the comprehensive health promotion project in Minnesota and Wales) are cases of collaborative planning that includes multiple points of intervention to achieve cumulative results. Successful conduct of such comprehensive, multipronged health education approaches entails educational leadership characterized by effective communication and negotiations, a compelling vision of worthwhile goals, the ability to be an able champion, and persistence. To win and maintain cooperation, leaders can use the process and results of strategic planning to discover the combination of costs and benefits that each stakeholder considers a mutually beneficial exchange. For volunteers and members of NGOs, this exchange may focus on service to others and personal growth; for members of health occupations, the exchange may focus on a multiplier effect of collaboration and reduction of risk factors; and for representatives of government agencies or enterprises, it may concentrate on efficient service delivery and increased productivity. A typical feature of comprehensive health promotion for primary care is to integrate health with broader family and community concerns. As might be anticipated, women served as local health educators in many of the examples cited.

As reflected in many of the examples, successful local health educators work well with both indigenous clients and policy makers in the government agency or NGO with which they were connected. Selection for health education orientation of people already well connected with local community organizations and groups contributes to success, as does explicit analysis of relations between local and national social systems. Especially for health education aimed at change of habits (such as breaking addictions to alcohol, drugs, and nicotine), effective local health educators emphasize both individual responsibility and mutual support from reference and self-help groups. As we saw in the examples of Nigerian midwives and Colombian shamans, local opinion leaders can enhance health efforts if they are supportive and can nullify these efforts if they are opposed. When social changes to promote health necessitate policy alteration and political decision making, attempts to obtain support by powerful allies and to build consensus may include parallel activities to increase support and to reduce opposition. Religious beliefs may assist or impede. The Heartbeat Wales program illustrates a positive, win-win approach. Strategic planning provides a vehicle for broad involvement to identify crucial local and remote influences in the specific instance; these can strengthen the plan and increase commitment by key stakeholders to its implementation (Adelson, Watkins, and Caplan, 1985; Allegrante, 1984; Conner, 1988; Marsick, 1988b).

Themes relevant to health education occur in other chapters—for example, in those on rural development, in-service education and continuing professional education (regarding workplace learning for all enterprise members as well as for members of health occupations who conduct health education activities), and cultural programs (regarding family life education programs that include health topics). In all instances, strategic planning is especially valuable when collaborative, comprehensive programs are planned to increase impact on performance. Comparative perspectives can also help identify societal influences.

13

Community
Problem Solving

A small but important portion of educational programs for adults in the United States aim at community and organizational development and social change, in contrast to most adult education aimed at development and change at individual and primary-group levels. Though limited in extent, adult education for community problem solving and social change has a long history. From Thomas Jefferson through John Dewey and Eduard Lindeman to William Biddle and Myles Horton, adult education has been seen as an essential ingredient in community functioning and social progress in a democratic society. Many people have assumed that U.S. society is relatively free of political tyranny and economic oppression, and thus adult *education* for community and organizational problem solving could be successful in bringing about desirable changes. It has also been assumed that adult educators in other times and places who faced more totalitarian regimes had to give higher priority to social *action* to deal with conflict and resistance to change.

Education for Community Development

The social and organizational change targeted by specific U.S. adult education programs for community problem solving have varied greatly, but some procedures and rationales have dominated. Social change focus encompasses urban, industrial, rural, agricultural, economic, and social development. Educational activities designed to accomplish such changes have used somewhat different terminology and procedures. Examples include community development, popular education, action research, volunteer development, participatory research, and organizational development. In each instance, educational activities have been the process and result of an effort to include a broad cross section of people in educational activities to enable them to work together to solve organizational or community problems that have usually entailed consciousness raising, empowerment, and structural transformation.

Adult education for community or organizational development has often aimed at learning how to bring about structural transformations that alter the balance of power between the hegemony of a powerful elite and the larger numbers of organization or community members who wanted more active roles in working toward solutions or goals they valued. Educational activities have included attention to substantive issues and improvement, but also the process of leadership development, dealing with conflict, communication, teamwork, and human relations. Because the usual goal for the participants has been action and change, there has typically been resistance (and even conflict) especially from people who believe that their practices and advantages would be diminished. As a result, issues regarding values, power, and performance are more central in education for community problem solving than in many other types of educational programs for adults.

Community and organizational development programs have varied worldwide in their relationship between education and change. In countries and subcultures that are democratic and egalitarian and that have a relatively equitable balance of power, societal equilibrium has been assumed, and organizational and community development activities have been focused on individual change to achieve agreed-upon goals of modernization and improvement of human capital with a minimum of structural change in the political and economic system. By contrast, in totalitarian and oppressive countries and subcultures in which people feel exploited, revolutionary structural change sometimes seems to be the only solution to organizational and community problems. Under such circumstances, adult education is often employed to empower people with unredressed grievances through emphasis on ideolog-

ical solidarity and training for guerrilla war. To promote such revolutionary change, conflict resolution is seen as less important than
helping subjugated people understand societal causes of their personal problems and use conflict to consolidate support for desirable
changes.

A third approach has provided an alternative to either personal development (to enable individual adults to solve problems
within a largely satisfactory system) or leadership development (to
assist exploited adults in joining forces to overthrow an oppressive
regime). This alternative and popular educational approach focuses
on democratic reform to help broad coalitions of people to engage
in praxis, which entails attention to both enhanced proficiency and
desirable action to achieve gradual improvements.

Because action and change are central to adult education for
organizational and community development, there has been much
attention to ethical issues regarding relationships between education
and change. Most adult educators believe that desirable goals do not
justify use of procedures characterized by indoctrination, coercion,
and flagrant manipulation of participants. Such misuse of ostensibly
educational activities violates values that educators prize—freedom
of inquiry, critical thinking, volunteerism, and respectful treatment
of people—as ends in themselves and not just as means to achieve
someone else's purposes. However, it is also evident that organizational and community problem solving typically addresses issues
that affect various subgroups with differing viewpoints and that
education creates influence. As a result, value judgments are fundamental to both goals and procedures of organizational and community change. Organizational development includes people from
multiple groups in the solution of organizational problems that
require their participation. Similarly, community development
means including people from multiple organizations and segments
of the community. This diversity of viewpoints contributes to conflicts of values and aspirations that are part of the challenge to educators who provide leadership for community problem solving.
Such programs are comprehensive because they address multiple
stakeholders whose understanding and support are essential for constructive social change.

A distinctive feature of transformative leadership for community problem solving is an inspiring vision of community improvement shared by supporters as they deal with some opposing values by powerful elites that resist such changes. Community problem solving programs confront various influences, such as deterrents to participation, political priorities, economic conditions, and social change. Strategic planning and implementation help leaders address such influences.

Consensus building occurs at some stages in the process as people from multiple subpopulations explore the symptoms and causes of problems or opportunities that confront them, seek to clarify desirable goals or solutions, master procedures to achieve shared goals, inventory available resources, acquire additional resources, and encourage people to contribute to goal achievement. The following examples illustrate some contrasting ways in which adult education for community problem solving occurs in various national settings, with special attention to societal influences and implications for strategic planning by local adult education providers.

The examples and rationale regarding community problem solving pertain to five themes. One is the participation of adults, which depends on intended outcomes, cultural values, and social trends. The second is contextual influences, including both local contingencies and more remote political and economic forces. A third theme is resource acquisition, which sometimes requires collaboration. A fourth is compelling leadership, which helps define a distinctive niche for the provider agency and provide staff and volunteer development opportunities. The fifth theme is specification of program goals and mission from among the alternative approaches that have been taken to community problem solving (continuity, reform, radical). The chapter concludes with implications for strategic planning.

Highlander Research and Education Center

For six decades, Highlander Research and Education has functioned as an unique provider of adult education aimed at community problem solving and social change. Because most adult education providers have been somewhat marginal to bureaucratic organizations, the vitality of the provider agency has frequently reflected inspirational leadership by founders or subsequent directors whose vision and energy attracted people and resources to the cause. Highlander was such an example. Myles Horton, founder and director of Highlander, was similar to other persuasive advocates of using adult education to achieve greater equality (such as Saul Alinsky in Chicago and Paulo Freire in Brazil). His beliefs greatly shaped the functioning of Highlander, and he confronted great resistance to his efforts from the power structure. Program successes and setbacks have been affected by powerful contemporary societal trends and influences. A few examples from Highlander's long and colorful history have rich implications for strategic planning by providers engaged in educational programs for community problem solving in other times and places.

Horton established Highlander Folk School in Monteagle, Tennessee, which the state chartered as a school in 1930. As a result of local opposition in 1961, its charter was revoked and property confiscated, mainly on the grounds of violation of the state segregation statute. However, a new charter was granted under the name of Highlander Research and Education Center, which continues to operate in New Market, near Knoxville, Tennessee. Horton continued to be active in Highlander through the 1980s, and his programs and beliefs are reflected in the following examples of adult education for community problem solving (especially from the 1950s and 1960s). These were associated with education for citizenship and were related to the civil rights movement for black Americans in the southern states.

Throughout its history, Highlander's adult education programs were tied to social movements on behalf of increased equity and community change. During the 1930s and 1940s, the focus was on residential workshops for labor union staff and members. This partnership ended in the late 1940s when Highlander's emphasis on democratic values and individual responsibility for self-development in a community context ran counter to the interest of union officials who wanted to strengthen their roles and unions as pressure groups. The founding and early decades of Highlander showed the impact of societal dislocations from the Great Depression and

World War II and a resulting radical ferment that resulted in creation of other experimental colleges during that period.

From the outset, some basic guiding principles became evident as Horton made decisions about goals and procedures. One basic belief was the importance of staff members' immersing themselves in the community setting in which they sought to help people help themselves; close ties were considered vital to the staff's understanding and responsiveness. Another was that education was value laden and that espoused neutrality was implicit support for the status quo. Whole-community approaches that included social change were important because some problems such as discrimination did not have individual solutions. Promoting reform from outside the system was important because efforts to do so within it were usually coopted and thus reinforced the system. Highlander's purpose was not to accomplish social change by direct social action but to educate people to enable them to solve their own problems in their own ways. This open-ended educational approach was guided by convictions regarding democracy, freedom, and brotherhood and helped participants think for themselves about symptoms and causes regarding their current situation and desirable changes—goals, ways to achieve progress, and self-confidence. However, individual action remained the learner's responsibility.

Such beliefs and values guided Highlander's educational programs for people seeking to end segregation. The postwar climate for change was more positive than earlier decades, when Highlander had tried to initiate educational programs for southern farmers and labor groups that did not materialize because the initiative came from Highlander and not from the people themselves. Yet during the 1950s, there was a revolution of rising civic expectations by hundreds of thousands of black people who during the war gained new experiences in the military services and in factories and cities. Highlander responded, and with modest foundation support expanded its community leadership residential workshops lasting from less than a week to more than three months on topics like citizen participation, voter registration, health, housing, and school desegregation. Whites and blacks participated together in educational programs on concepts and procedures for community leadership for nonviolent action for social change. Many of the emerging black leaders of such civil rights groups as the Southern Christian Leadership Conference took part, and the Student Non-Violent Coordinating Committee was formed following student participation in a 1960 Highlander workshop. A hymn popular at Highlander activities and arranged by Horton's wife, Zilphia—"We Shall Overcome"—became a rallying cry for the civil rights movement.

An early demonstration of residential citizenship schools for development of local leaders for community problem solving focused on Johns Island, the largest (about thirty miles across) and most populous (about six thousand predominantly black residents) of the Sea Islands close to the South Carolina and Georgia coasts. In 1954, a female Charleston school teacher and a Johns Island black male leader who operated a few buses to transport residents to work in Charleston, South Carolina, attended a Highlander workshop. The black leader described his extensive local efforts for community betterment and his assistance to his bus passengers in helping them to read so that they could pass the literacy test and become registered voters. Horton later spent time with him on Johns Island getting to know him, the people, and their situation and concluded that the conditions were favorable for a demonstration project. Horton helped him involve others in the leadership process, and foundation support assisted local people to help with the teaching about literacy and citizenship. This indigenous self-help approach spread to other Sea Islands and eventually to the southern states generally.

Several features of Highlander's educational programs on Johns Island contributed to their success there and elsewhere in the South. Director Horton believed that community leadership programs should be responsive to the requests and circumstances of local people, that organizational structure should be minimal to serve program and participant needs, that Highlander's limited energy and resources should not be spent for coordination of large-scale programs better handled by indigenous organizations, and that the focus should be on intensive residential education programs for adults held mainly at Highlander, not direct political action. The essential characteristics of the citizenship programs on Johns Island (such as indigenous leadership, responsiveness and adaptation to local expectations and circumstances, and education for empowerment of minorities to enable them to provide effective, local nonviolent leadership for constructive social change in the interests of equity and democracy) were readily adaptable to the entire South.

The parallel emergence of the civil rights and desegregation movement resulted in Highlander's working with various regional and local civil rights, welfare leagues, voter crusades, and similar organizations. The hundreds of citizenship education programs and teacher training workshops held at Highlander and throughout the South helped educate and inspire thousands of black people, many of whom subsequently took action as citizens to help bring about social change. Many of the black leaders of that era and subsequent decades were participants and teachers in Highlander programs. A quiet woman from Alabama (Rosa Parks) felt liberated and free of discrimination for the first time in her life at an integrated 1955 Highlander workshop; a year later, she risked arrest by refusing to sit in the back of the bus reserved for blacks, an act that precipitated the Montgomery bus boycott and the eventual breakdown in the segregation of business establishments there.

Martin Luther King, Jr., and the Southern Christian Leadership Conference (SCLC) focused on demonstrations against unjust segregation laws but in 1960 encouraged participation in Highlander leadership and citizenship training programs that had enabled tens of thousands of black people to register to vote. Soon thereafter, SCLC set up its own educational program with the help of Highlander (which was also working with other organizations). Workers in local citizenship education programs were beaten and jailed for helping blacks register, especially in areas where blacks greatly outnumbered whites and increased black voters would change the political balance. During the 1960s and early 1970s, these educational programs, associated with Highlander, dramatically increased the number of black registered voters, local leaders, and elected officials and in general brought about a major shift in political power, legislation, and practices related to racial segregation and civic empowerment in many southern states.

As the geographical scope of programs and cooperating organizations broadened, planning guidelines emerged. The focus remained on responsiveness to local needs and circumstances and on educational programs to enable local leaders to act effectively on behalf of social change in the spirit of democracy, equity, dignity, and brotherhood. Educational workshops emphasized development of local leadership to address emerging local circumstances. The group experience reinforced solidarity and commitment to progress along with down-to-earth discussion of practical politics, such as a 1966 workshop Highlander held in Atlanta for all fifty black candidates for public offices in Alabama. However, Highlander stressed that the learning process began before a workshop and should continue long afterwards in dealing with local contingencies and in broadening the indigenous leadership base (as learners in workshops became teachers in subsequent peer teaching activities in their own communities). Highlander educational activities had a symbiotic relationship with the community action activities of the cooperating organizations. Both were influenced by and contributed to the regional civil rights movement and the process of desegregation. There were several influences on Highlander's success. Paid and volunteer program leaders, who were purposeful, well organized, courageous, and determined, focused on helping people learn how to solve their own problems and then follow through. Highlander workshop participants stated in the group their intention to make a difference back home. Participants were attracted who had great potential and commitment to address a compatible cluster of related issues in their community, and they participated in educational activities that explored these within the context of action. This approach helped them apply what they learned (Adams, 1975; Bell, Gaventa, and Peters, 1990; Tjerandsen, 1980, 1983).

One Highlander program during the later 1970s illustrates a participatory research variation on the community problem-solving theme, which emerged in recent decades. Major floods in Appalachia during 1977 encouraged regional efforts to analyze land ownership patterns as an influence on solution of local community problems in this poor, mountainous (relatively densely populated) rural area rich in resources. The Appalachian mountains in the eastern United States stretch from Maine at the north to Alabama at the south. Along with agricultural and recreational land use, for almost a century coal mining has been a major industry in central Appalachia and adjacent areas. Most of the local lands were owned by large corporations from outside the region, and practices such as strip mining by absentee corporations were associated with local community problems: flooding related to strip mining, low tax base, and poor services.

The Appalachian Regional Commission (ARC), the government agency concerned with regional development, focused on urban centers and maintained that rural land-related problems were neither extensive nor severe. An ARC study dealt with settlement patterns, not ownership patterns. A coalition of citizen groups from the region interested in rural development, the Appalachian Alliance, formed the Land Ownership Task Force, which with assistance from Highlander attempted to demonstrate how citizens can study their own problems. They sought to train local citizens to engage in participatory research, to promote collaboration among interested organizations for constructive action, and to use findings to mobilize support for land-related social change.

Highlander and the task force provided regional coordination of county- and state-level citizens' groups interested in participation in the study and collective action based on the findings. A 1979 Highlander workshop for potential participants from eighty counties in the region interested in land reform helped decide on specifics of the study plan and procedures. Later, state and regional workshops decided on study procedures—reporting content, format, dissemination, and follow-up activities. Study staff members and a hundred volunteers went to county courthouses to collect information about land ownership and taxation. It took almost two years to collect the information, analyze it, and prepare the report. The benefit of the report for task force members was that it documented their beliefs that much of the land and mineral rights were owned by a few people and enterprises outside the area and that mineral rights were assessed low for property tax purposes. This situation depressed the tax base and services for the residents of the region.

The combination of citizens' groups and educational institutions in the planning, conducting, and reporting of the study had several benefits. The ARC government agency resisted dissemination of the task force report, so the citizens' groups that had approved the study plan and that were crucial to the collection of ownership and tax information from county courthouses also helped with reporting, including arranging for community meetings and other activities to increase public understanding of the problem along with causes and solutions. A history of popular participation and organizational activity increased involvement in the participatory research process and in related training activities. Training for citizen participation in collection of information from courthouse records was more successful than training for interviewing and preparing in-depth case studies. Especially in counties where people had been concerned about land use issues, there was strong response to activities by Highlander and the task force to educate and mobilize on behalf of social change and community problem solving. Many educational activities were provided, such as workshops and meetings at Highlander and other locations, television and radio broadcasts, films, and pamphlets.

The goal of the participatory research approach for some leaders was radical social transformation, in the belief that solution of many community problems depended on redistribution of land and wealth. They were frustrated that this larger quest was not embraced by most participants, who focused on specific local issues related to absentee corporate and government ownership of the land. The leaders' use of participatory research was a reflection of their belief that such study could not be neutral; such assumed neutrality served to reinforce the current situation instead of revealing the sources of oppression, which would empower people to resist that domination. Although some of the radical leaders found it difficult to combine such theory with practice in their own careers, they were gratified that after the study was completed some participants reflected on a larger vision of social transformation and became more open to alternatives (Gaventa and Horton, 1981).

Both the civil rights and the land-use examples from Highlander reveal some implications for strategic planning of adult education for community problem solving. There was strong ideological commitment by provider agency leaders to radical social change for greater equity and democracy that helped them in acquiring resources to support a small staff to work with many energetic volunteers. Volunteer commitment depended on a clear focus and compelling vision of related problems and timely issues sufficient to sustain participation (in contrast with a broad purpose such as community improvement). The central staff and volunteer leader role was to help concerned citizens help themselves by assuming responsibility to make decisions to solve their own problems. Thus, education was for empowerment of people to take informed action in their community roles beyond the educational program. An understanding by program leaders and participants of community power structure, dynamics, and planned change helped them all contribute to successful programs that led to open-ended efforts by those engaged in community problem solving. Workshop participants made public commitments to each other to work toward constructive local change, which increased program impact.

Other U.S. Programs

Highlander's distinctive approach has been but one of many ways in which adult education was used on behalf of community problem solving in the United States.

County Boards

A sharp contrast is provided by a Community Information and Education Service (CIES) project. This was sponsored by the University of Illinois and five community college districts in central Illinois to serve elected volunteers who were members of forty-five county governing boards in that area (Resource A, Schweitzer, Lauts, and Kozoll). Local citizens elected to county boards acted as members of the main policy-making group that dealt with public issues and community problem solving in predominantly rural counties. Newly elected members were expected to learn much about the issues and problems they were expected to solve.

As recipients of CIES assistance, county board members were part of local government, unlike Highlander participants, many of whom were combating the local power structure. Also, in contrast with Highlander's antiestablishment ideological position, the University of Illinois (as a land-grant and state institution) supports the educational, political, and economic structure of the state. In the

CIES project, the university took the initiative to assemble considerable resources to assist county board members to improve their policy making and problem solving. It had a long-standing, statewide outreach mission, which included subsidized rural development programs through the Cooperative Extension Service (CES). The university was aware of potential foundation interest and prepared a grant proposal to the W. K. Kellogg Foundation, in collaboration with state government and five regional community college districts. Other cooperating organizations included higher education institutions and professional associations.

Among the public issues that confronted county boards were economic development, health care delivery, hazardous waste disposal in local landfills, inadequate jail facilities, and maintenance of roads and bridges. Because elected board members had other occupations, there was a limited amount of time that they could spend on their part-time county board responsibilities, including in-service education. Between 1981 and 1986, about eight thousand board members and other local officials and community leaders participated in about two hundred CIES-related educational activities, including more than fifteen hundred county board members who took part in seventeen teleconference programs through the CES TeleNet educational telephone system. (This system provided microphones and speakers in a meeting room in each county, which allowed participation with a minimum of travel time.)

Anticipated benefits and evidence of desirable outcomes in the early years of the project helped convince the Kellogg Foundation to approve major grant support at the outset and to extend some support beyond four years. Attitudes toward benefits also encouraged county board members to participate and the cooperating organizations to collaborate. The foundation grant that covered most early direct costs and the use of the CES TeleNet system were major influences on the effort, which continued beyond the period of foundation assistance. The university's image, resources, and history of service encouraged cooperation, and the collaborative approach and commitment to project goals in the parent organizations of all providers (university, community colleges, state government) contributed to program functioning generally, including planning, participants, staff and finance and in-kind contributions.

A 1984 survey revealed substantial benefits from CIES participation, including both progress toward solution of community problems and broadening of local participation in additional educational activities and decision making. The project staff members also concluded that audio teleconferencing for limited time periods was an acceptable and efficient method in the context of a wider range of face-to-face educational activities, that this use of university-based educational technology tended to diminish contributions by local community colleges, and that some counties were not supportive of the project due to competition from other local activities for time, money, and attention. The CIES approach lacked participant fervor to correct structural inequities, entailed more collaboration among resource systems, and received less resistance from the power structure than was the case for Highlander programs. Strategic planning for both approaches depended on a multiplier effect as participants used what they learned to broaden the base and strengthen local leadership for community problem solving. CIES continues to provide about nine educational programs annually and publishes various booklets, audiotapes, and videotapes for county government officials.

Participatory Literacy

Some participatory approaches to local community problem solving have focused on a narrow segment of the population with little power, such as functionally illiterate adults. Most adult basic education programs (developed within the white, middle-class norms used to judge the cultural patterns and needs of nonreading adults), have sought to socialize nonreaders into mainstream society. By contrast, participatory literacy programs have attempted to be responsive to the backgrounds, oral cultures, aspirations, and educational needs of low-literate adults. These adults have sometimes resisted the imposition of majority culture and values, and staff members and learners have planned and conducted programs collaboratively to address social change as well as individual progress (Fingeret and Jurmo, 1989). Within the large and diverse population of functionally illiterate adults in the United States, oral subcultures exist in tension with the literate majority culture. This situation can occur in part because some members of the oral sub-culture serve as scribes for nonreading friends and acquaintances.

Advocates of a participatory literacy approach have urged practitioners and learners to work together on behalf of collective action to change societal conditions that shape learners' lives. Humanistic education methods of group learning have been recommended to enhance social skills, problem solving, and self-confidence. Advocates give special attention to understanding distribution of power in society and learning how and why people participate in community decision making and problem solving. Learners and practitioners tend to be inexperienced and reluctant to address political and economic constraints, so advocates have urged them to include both collaborative strategies that promote solidarity among participatory literacy activists and approaches that emphasize potential benefits for learners, community, and democracy. Commitment to a participatory approach is deemed essential because practitioners and learners lack experience addressing social change. Regional educational activities by associations and educational institutions for practitioners and learners have been considered by activists as valuable sources of training, networking, and encouragement. Throughout, the focus has been on empowerment of members of oral subcultures to use basic skills to serve their own purposes.

Workplace Programs

Learner-centered literacy programs that stress collaborative learning also take place in the workplace, reflecting the increasing importance for most U.S. workers of problem solving, reading, writing, math, and use of computers. Enterprises, labor unions, and educational institutions have collaborated on such participatory literacy programs to enhance work-related problem solving in ways similar to community-based programs. Basic skills include learning to learn and use of computers and other forms of technology as part of explicit strengthening of learning strategies. Authentic materials such as newspaper articles, application forms, and visuals stimulate a high degree of interest in discussion and writing about social issues. These create real-life language learning situations to enable participants to improve their problem solving.

Collaborative teaching and learning (built on learners' strengths) help participants rethink their self-concepts. Learning activities are both supportive and challenging to stimulate group interaction to discuss, read, and write about provocative issues related to work, health, family, and community. Instructors and participants learn from each other through open-ended questioning and analysis of issues from personal and collective perspectives central to problem solving. Strategic planning shows a multidisciplinary rationale for active participation by functionally illiterate adults in their own empowerment.

Liberatory Education

Educational technology has sometimes been used as a vehicle for adult education for community problem solving. In the late 1970s, the Interactive Media Project took place for residents from a poor neighborhood of Rockford, Illinois, to help them overcome patterns of noncommunication and noncooperation that fragmented neighborhood groups and separated them from city government. The project was cooperatively planned with local residents and entailed training them to use video cameras to record scenes and interviews related to neighborhood problems as a vehicle for increasing public understanding and mobilizing to achieve solutions. Creation and showing of videotapes to neighborhood groups and government officials increased interest, understanding, and action. As residents used the media, they discovered that though the technology was not a substitute for their political literacy, the process of preparing the videotapes developed solidarity and collective leadership and it was their voices, not the technology, that influenced public policy. Neighborhood people may have been more inclined to express opinions and attend meetings because of the videotaping, and policy makers may have been more impressed with the dramatic portrayals of neighborhood problems that the videotapes allowed; however, the ongoing benefit was not dependence on technology but liberation from apathy as a result of success in their social change efforts (Wilson, 1983, pp. 40-44). Local progress reflected the leadership of community education staff who used video equipment to promote critical reflection by neighborhood residents on the relationship between public issues and personal problems, which led to constructive action. As state funding ended and with it the loan of the video equipment, the Rockford residents arranged to retain it.

During the same time period, a Hispanic neighborhood of Chicago experienced another kind of liberatory education. During the 1970s, neighborhood residents referred to their very successful adult education center of the Chicago community college system as Universidad Popular. Serving a neighborhood with widespread poverty and unemployment, the center had a governing board comprised of students, staff, and local residents who set policy, approved curriculum, and hired and evaluated staff. They resisted efforts of the college system to increase administrative control of the center and as a result lost more than $200,000 of college subsidy. Part of the dispute pertained to center emphasis on empowerment and structural change, in addition to center autonomy. Liberatory education addressed more than personal advancement; it also advocated collective action to correct social and economic conditions that local residents found oppressive.

Similar community-based and controlled adult education programs for Hispanics also occurred during the 1970s in other parts of the United States. One example was Liberacion Learning Center for rural south Florida farm workers and migrants. The center's largely volunteer staff used Freire-inspired culture circles to discuss educational topics in relation to daily problems and societal influences. Another example was Project Literacy initiated by educators and community activists in the Mission district of San Francisco; these individuals based literacy education in biweekly discussion and critique of housing, jobs, and human rights to achieve goals regarding self-identity, collective consciousness, and struggle to reduce marginalization and oppression. A third example was Instituto del Progreso Latino, an adult alternative high school on the near West Side of Chicago where the student council made decisions on policy, priorities, and hiring and deliberately kept funding diversified to maintain community control.

Among the many influences that made it difficult to start and continue such community-based adult education providers were widespread hierarchical organizations in U.S. society and extreme emphasis on individualism that fragmented neighborhoods and undermined solidarity on behalf of social change (Kasworm, 1983).

Community-Based Programs

During the same period, community-based programs were serving people in rural areas and small towns, where sparse population and distances to educational resources constituted distinctive impediments to rural adult education generally. Programs such as the University for Man in Manhattan, Kansas; the Southern Appalachian Labor School in Montgomery, West Virginia; and the Southeast Community College in Cumberland, Kentucky, were examples of small programs of this type, which collaborated with other organizations and emphasized capacity-building in service to rural adults to help them recognize and solve local community problems. Project ENLIST in western Minnesota used available technology to improve rural adult education by strengthening collaboration among many providers in the region, including community colleges, universities, technical institutes, public school–based community education programs, libraries, and telecommunications providers. This cooperation enriched the community development assistance available from the University of Minnesota Cooperative Extension Service by greatly increasing access for rural residents. A federal grant helped initiate this collaborative effort, which resulted from collaborative leadership and strategic planning (Kasworm, 1983).

Tuskegee

Another example of rural community development is provided by the Human Resources Development Center at Tuskegee Institute. For more than a century since its founding by Booker T. Washington, Tuskegee has focused on helping rural poor black people, and the center concentrates on fifteen counties in central and southwest Alabama. These were some of the poorest counties in the United States, and in spite of much outward migration in recent decades, in most of the counties blacks are more than half the population.

In this agricultural region, few blacks own their own farms but work as tenant farmers or hired hands until unemployment, poverty, and health problems cause many to move away. As a predominantly black institution with four thousand students, Tuskegee has worked with the people who remain in those counties. In 1968, the W. K. Kellogg Foundation provided an initial grant to launch the center, and over the years additional financial support was provided by other private philanthropic foundations and by federal and some international agencies. The state of Alabama was supportive of the idea, but little state or local financial assistance is furnished. There is a national advisory council.

A distinctive feature of the center's educational approach to serve the rural poor is heavy reliance on indigenous local people as effective center staff and rural change agents. They plan with local people, rather than for them, in various program areas—community education, agriculture and resource development, occupational retraining, food and nutrition, and business development. For example, the Mott Foundation supported a project to increase community participation in rural schools in three counties by bringing together parents, teachers, and local citizens to enable parents to become more active in program planning and implementation (Stubblefield, 1981, chap. 9).

Michigan State

A contrasting example of land-grant university outreach for local community problem solving was offered by the Institute for Community Development at Michigan State University during the same time period. This multidisciplinary institute used consultation, workshops, and publications to serve Michigan groups and organizations engaged in community problem solving: human relations commissions, government offices, religious institutions, voluntary associations, chambers of commerce, and neighborhood ethnic groups. Publications included a guide for affirmative action, a career opportunity directory, and a community planning and zoning handbook.

Institute planning reflected some basic beliefs about community problem solving. One was that various organizations would welcome planned change if perceived benefits exceeded costs. Moreover, organizations and institutions would have to devote their time and resources if change was to occur; their willingness to help would demonstrate their conviction that the change was desirable. The distinctive contribution of the institute was to clarify alternatives and to help related community groups agree on a recommended course of action that solved the problem. Value-laden issues related to community problems and various solutions tended to be controversial, which affected the community development process and the image of the institute (Stubblefield, 1981, chap. 4).

Ongoing social change creates dilemmas and conflicts, to which community development activities by the Institute and other providers respond in an effort to use democratic decision making based on reasoned choice between alternatives. As such, community development is an educational process for participatory democracy that tries to avoid the extremes of either social planning by experts or social action such as political confrontation. The community development educator seeks to increase consensus regarding desired improvements and reduce resistance to change. Educator roles include consultant, process expert, facilitator, and sometimes temporary resident of the local community. It is recommended that the community development educator understand social systems and change, possess consulting capability, and be flexible in using expertise in specific situations. Staffing is crucial to the success of community problem solving, which depends on the ability of staff members and leaders to appreciate human behavior in individual, group, organizational settings to help local people deal with conflict and change in ways that promote progress (Stubblefield, 1981, chap. 2).

Study Circles

A specific method to help grass roots groups to work together to discuss and solve local problems and public policy issues is the study circle. As previously noted, this has been used for this and other purposes for more than a century in Sweden and other Scandinavian countries. As an instrument for social change by working-class adults, study circles enable members to identify community problems of importance to them and to work together on solutions. There have been various ways in which assistance has been provided to local study circles. One is orientation sessions for study circle organizers and discussion leaders. Another is a community problem-solving study guide that describes procedures to help community residents identify community problems, influences, and strengths and develop and implement a plan of action to correct the deficiencies and improve the strengths.

In one example, local residents in an upstate New York mill town who wanted to preserve a historic local church met for six weekly meetings to conduct surveys and interviews regarding the church's social history and architecture and to use the new and existing information to apply for government designation as a historic site. The success of this study circle encouraged the formation of study circles to study other historic sites in the community. Swedish study circles also inspired U.S. labor unions to explore societal trends and their implications for future directions (Oliver, 1987; Stubblefield, 1981, chap. 8).

Study circles and community development activities in adult education for community problem solving were established by the 1930s in various states, including Virginia, Washington, Michigan, and California. By the 1950s, innovative use had been made of radio and television in California and Missouri, where study circles discussed ideas from broadcasts. Resulting insights regarding community problem-solving methods contributed to subsequent Peace Corps and VISTA approaches.

Associations

Although most adult education participants have been volunteers for learning, the connection between adult education and volunteerism is especially crucial when the objective is community problem solving. One reason is that adult education participants seldom achieve social change by themselves but typically do so through participation in voluntary associations related to the intended change. Another reason is that the experience of participating in an association helps volunteers learn in many ways that serve as prerequisites for adult education activities and as adjuncts as an adult applies the benefits of education to a specific community problem-solving activity. Furthermore, opportunities for educational participation and personal growth are a major benefit to many volunteers and help to compensate them for the time and effort they contribute. Thus, planners of adult education for community problem solving should provide both individual and organizational benefits for volunteers to encourage their continued participation and results. Although volunteers and organization paid staff members share many characteristics, the volunteer's motivation is especially dependent on the nature of the volunteer role and the satisfactions associated with it. Furthermore, it appears that volunteer goals and preferred types of learning activities in organizations that emphasize social change (where the commitment was to social ideals and a vision of a better future) differ somewhat from those in other types of organizations that stress the organizational mission, or the volunteer group, or maintenance of the organization. Strategic planning for social or organizational changes should be responsive to such differences (Merriam and Cunningham, 1989, chap. 8).

Organizational Change

When the goal of an adult education activity is social change, the target of the effort is seldom the broad social problem or source of oppression but instead more concrete aspects of organizational functioning—desegregation of educational institutions, equal opportunity employment, equitable taxation, or enterprise productivity. Thus, community and organization change may be closely connected. Planned organizational change has been the objective of many organizational development and quality management efforts. The most promising approaches to organizational change are characterized by effective two-way linkages between client and resource systems that include combinations of rational planning, group interaction, problem solving, and attention to power differentials. Organizational change can be greatly influenced by support or opposition by opinion leaders and cosmopolitans who are influential inside and out of the organization. The ease with which change agents can encourage members to try an innovation has been associated with the extent to which it is easy to understand, has clear advantages, is compatible with the organization, is divisible so can be implemented in parts, is low risk, and allows members to try it out on a trial basis. Proposed organizational changes that lack these features may take much more planning and resources.

Five interrelated components of planned organizational change deserve attention in strategic planning. They are (1) linkage between knowledge resources and organization members, (2) sources of knowledge and innovative ideas, (3) needs assessment to understand local circumstances, (4) open development and decision, and (5) support for implementation in the forms of release time, advocacy, assistance, and recognition for progress. Planning can strengthen these components, as well as attend to external influences that especially affect organizational change and assure that change agents have requisite expertise to guide strategic planning (Lindquist, 1978).

Another rationale for planned change that has been mainly used for organizational development but that is also applicable to community problem solving is action science (Argyris, Putnam, and Smith, 1985). Action science approaches have been used to solve human relations problems where solutions entail improved communication, conflict resolution, and teamwork. By diagnosing the sources of organizational problems (by making explicit the relationship between performance and both espoused theory and theory in practice), action science procedures help organizational members learn about the desirability of goals as well as effective methods of working together to achieve them. Learning about interpersonal relations serves as a way to improve organizational performance. Recent quality improvement procedures share an emphasis on broad participation by organization members in learning and decision making. Action science and quality improvement concepts and procedures can be used to enhance proficiencies of educational leaders engaged in organizational and community development.

Comprehensive Programs

Another aspect that is important for the success of community problem solving and for the proficiencies of those who plan such programs is conducting multipronged comprehensive programs that serve many stakeholders. Exclusive reliance on bottom-up educational programs for less-advantaged and power-poor segments of the population is unlikely to have much impact on social change, especially if the sole focus is on individual advancement. Other prongs of an all-encompassing approach can serve close associates in family, primary-group, and organizational settings, as well as policy makers whose legislation and guidelines can either advance or retard progress. Such equity issues are becoming increasingly important as cultural minorities are becoming a collective majority in the United States (they have already been so for years in some other countries). Use of adult education as an instrument of social policy to achieve greater equity, productivity, and democracy has increased in recent decades, but enabling legislation, appropriations, and administrative guidelines reflect external support on behalf of adult education to achieve valued goals, more than concerted effort by adult educators. Practitioners have avoided political activity and have seldom addressed broad policy issues. A benefit of concerted efforts by leaders from various segments of the adult education field is that such collaboration strengthens comprehensive programs for multiple stakeholders; the complementarity of various providers allows each to reach categories of learners that they serve best. Almost by definition, adult education for organizational and community problem solving involves working with a range of stakeholders to increase attention to consensus, conflict, cooperation, and constructive change. In such complex and interdependent social systems, progress typically depends on movement within various subsystems. Community development planners should judge when the likely aggregate benefits of comprehensive programs warrant the considerable investment required (Quigley, 1989, chaps. 5, 10, and 11).

Participatory Research

Recent attention to participatory research for community problem solving in the United States reflects efforts throughout this century to increase adults' involvement in the process and to use the conclusions of inquiry from both here and abroad (Hall, forthcoming). Examples include rural extension to help people help themselves and action research to improve school practices. In action learning projects in organizations and in analysis by citizens' groups of land ownership and taxation, a central concept has been the praxis between education and action. As people concerned about an organizational or community problem participate in an inquiry process to analyze symptoms, causes, solutions, and implications, they generally develop greater understanding and commitment to act individually and collectively on that understanding. This action component has been especially important in organizational and community development where inertia and resistance are so powerful. Participatory research approaches have been especially attractive in other countries in which political and economic resistance to change appears to be even more strong (Anyanwu, 1988; Brown, 1985; Corey, 1953; International Council on Adult Education, 1981; 1982; Merriam and Cunningham, 1989, pp. 153-154).

Adult Education in Latin America

Participatory research and other forms of popular education for adults aimed at empowerment and liberation constitute only part of the variety of educational programs for adults in Latin America and the Caribbean. Central and South American countries vary greatly in size, population density, urban-rural relations, political and economic conditions, ethnic tradition, and even languages. These national differences influence innovative approaches to nonformal education that have evolved there. This section provides a brief overview of various types of adult education generally in the region before presenting some examples aimed at community development and problem solving. Because in most of the region Spanish (and Portuguese in Brazil) is the national language, it will be referred to as Latin America, even though in Central America and the Caribbean, English, French, and other languages predominate in a few countries; indigenous languages are also widely used in rural areas throughout the continent. This section can contribute to a comparative perspective in interpreting the subsequent examples from Latin American countries in relation to societal influences on adult education in other parts of the world.

Before detailing differences between varied adult education

programs and their major societal influences, it is important to note that there have been some widespread common features. Some of the most creative programs have been intended to increase the democratic participation of large numbers of economically and politically oppressed adults in some countries, most of them economically impoverished indigenous peoples who had lived there for thousands of years before Western colonization. Other general social and economic problems in Latin America include the outward flow of agricultural produce, natural resources, educated people, and foreign debt payments to the United States and other industrialized countries. One result of turbulent political and economic conditions over the years has been alternating growth and retrenchment of many adult education programs, some of which have faced government opposition. Independent provision of adult education by separate government ministries, nongovernment organization (NGOs), and other providers has contributed to great fragmentation among adult education programs.

In many Latin American countries, extreme social stratification and concentration of power in a small wealthy elite—in contrast to a large majority of poor, largely illiterate people, have reduced the positive relationship between educational level and economic advancement that is assumed in the United States and other technologically developed countries and that has been a strong incentive for adult education participation. Also, technological conditions and changes have sometimes been accompanied by undesirable cultural changes. Such paradoxes have helped focus adult education efforts on desirability of directions, outcomes, and impact. The resulting emphasis of some popular education programs has been on consciousness raising about societal and structural influences on personal problems; this is viewed as a first step toward liberation from economic and political oppression that would enable participants to take action to participate in the solution of community problems closely associated with their quality of life. The educational process for popular education sometimes entails active learner involvement in program decision making, including helping participants compare a vision of a just and equalitarian society with their real and perceived political, social, and economic conditions (Capanema, 1985; Freire, 1970; Furter, 1983; LaBelle, 1986, 1987; Pyne, 1984; Torres, 1990; Villarroel, 1983).

However, popular education for individual liberation and social reform by nonviolent means is only one form of adult education in Latin America. Two other broad approaches have been (1) adult education to enhance human capital and maintain equilibrium and continuity without structural change and (2) adult education for radical structural change, including training for guerrilla warfare and revolutionary conflict. The following discussion begins with a short summary of adult education to enhance human capital and maintain equilibrium, followed by brief mention of adult education for radical change; however, it mainly provides a review of popular education programs for reform and concludes with comments on major societal influences.

Most of adult education to enhance human capital in Latin America is provided by educational institutions or is the product of a preparatory education orientation in which experts disseminate information to dependent learners. The educational institutions, broadcasting stations, military service, or other providers tend to be extensions of the government and to emphasize achievement of national goals related to continuity, stability, unity, planning, productivity, and citizenship. Even distance education and external degree programs for adults are targeted at socialization with a preparatory education rationale. Economic goals are central, including technical specialization in work or education related to literacy, health, or family planning; these are intended to contribute to increased productivity, flexibility to adapt to economic fluctuations, and economic development. Although the result might be individual mobility, most such programs are aimed at preserving the existing economic and political power structure by teaching adults how to fit in. Not surprisingly, such human capital–oriented adult education has not produced much structural change. The following brief examples illustrate these programs.

Brazil

The consciousness-raising approach to literacy education of Paulo Freire, to be described later in this section as an example of popular education for reform, has become well-known worldwide as a Brazilian contribution to adult education for community development. However, much of Brazilian adult education over the years has taken a human capital approach. The government's adult literacy efforts, occurring in 1915, 1949, 1952, 1958, 1961, 1965, and 1969, were mostly ineffective; they had inadequate national resources and little local leadership. In the 1950s and 1960s, NGOs such as the Catholic Church also provided adult literacy programs, including some using television and Freire's approach in the northeast.

From the late 1960s until the early 1980s, the Brazilian Literacy Movement (MOBRAL) was the most widely heralded literacy campaign in Latin America. Impetus for this government initiative included a populist president between 1961 and 1964 for whom increased adult literacy strengthened political support. Until 1983, only literate adults could vote, and large proportions of poor people were illiterate. However, high inflation rates and ideological differences with the power structure contributed to a military takeover in 1964. During the next few years, economic conditions improved somewhat, but when civilian government was resumed in 1985 and some economic expansion occurred following the generally recessionary conditions of the previous decade, the traditional power structure was little changed. There existed a small urban elite and large rural estates on the one hand and pervasive poverty, illiteracy, and ill health on the other. This situation was compounded by one of the world's largest foreign debts.

MOBRAL was established to coordinate various literacy and related programs. The first classes began in 1971; by 1975, $130 million, largely raised from a sports lottery, donations by enterprises that received tax credits, and local contributions, had been spent. Indications of program impact were mixed. Area program supervisors worked with municipal commissions that provided some subsidy, and literacy teachers were semivolunteers who received small payments. In the planning, MOBRAL goals were humanistic, and ideas were obtained from many ministries to strengthen nonformal adult education beyond the school system. Early programs were varied and included literacy, cultural, health, and vocational education. As MOBRAL began functioning, its goals became more pragmatic and were aimed at increased economic production. Unfortunately, the Brazilian economy did not expand enough to absorb new literates, a fact discouraging participation and support. This was in spite of efforts such as the technology of scarcity that used various methods including radio and television to suggest supplementary ways in which people might improve their living standards without outside resources. Additional problems included shortages of funds and staff. Most program participants were adolescents and young adults. By the early 1980s, MOBRAL programs were decentralized, and functional literacy education for adults was no longer a priority as the focus shifted to education for the young (Dave, Ouane, and Ranaweera, 1986, chap. 1; LaBelle, 1986; Hunter, 1985; Torres, 1990; Verhine and Lehmann, 1982).

Mexico

In the early 1980s, the Mexican government created the National Institute of Adult Education (INEA), patterned on the Brazilian MOBRAL model, to coordinate all adult education policies and programs related to the Secretariat of Education. The creation of INEA reflected the conclusion that the series of national arrangements for adult education—beginning with the National System of Education (SNEA) in 1976—were not fulfilling their mission, as reflected in declining enrollments and increasing attrition; the main clientele was middle-class youngsters who were completing their secondary education through an open system. The creation of INEA also reflected abundant resources from the oil boom. INEA used decentralized coordination at the provincial level for public libraries in various rural areas and for bypass of adult education: elementary and secondary education, job training, and community education. Participation, especially for men, was discouraged by increased employment rates, reduced leisure time, occupational devaluation of primary school certificates, and the long duration of studies. Instructors were young and inexperienced, and in-service education was inadequate. Contradictory visions of adult education in relation to economic and political institutions was evidenced in planners who wanted closer connections between education and labor, compared with critics who complained that education reinforced the hegemony of the dominant majority culture. Until 1987, INEA enjoyed strong financial support despite a serious financial crisis and claimed substantial progress in adult literacy, vocational education, and educational modernization. After the change of national government in 1988, increasingly severe economic problems contributed to shifting from basic literacy education to postliteracy and bilingual programs and dropping job training programs with the hope that they would be continued by the private sector, a hope that was rarely realized (Torres, 1990, chap. 4).

Colombia

In the early 1980s, Colombia also increased coordination of adult education through the National Education Campaign (CAMINA). The purpose of CAMINA was to increase equality of educational opportunity by improving access, cultural and recreational activities, technology transfer, unified cultural identity, and the quality of teacher training. Adult education programs coordinated by CAMINA began as early as 1903, including night school centers for adults, community action programs, literacy campaigns, and distance education. In a country of twenty-eight million in 1983, about 18 percent were illiterate. About 40 percent lived in mountainous and rural areas, so mass media helped increase access to educational opportunities. About half of the population was mestizo, about 20 percent white, and the remainder mixed.

The National Ministry of Education provided about 80 percent of adult education through CAMINA, such as basic primary and secondary education, distance higher education, and technology transfer. Other ministries also contributed to the CAMINA effort. The Communications Ministry has furnished radio and television since 1967 for distance education, with out-of-school youth comprising 60 percent of the learners. The Work Ministry offered rural and urban vocational education for the unemployed and for occupational advancement, and the Health Ministry supplied health education and assistance to elders. Agriculture supplied integrated rural development, nutrition education, and agricultural education for commercial farmers and campesinos who farmed small plots; Home Affairs supplied community development; and the Defense Ministry supplied military training. Difficulties included insufficient incentives for adult learners, inadequate financial support, and incomplete consolidation by public and private providers of adult education (Dave, Ouane, and Ranaweera, 1986, chap. 2).

Venezuela

The example of adult education in Venezuela shows the influence of oil wealth on the economy. Before the 1960s, Venezuela mainly exported agricultural products. A sharp economic depression during 1960–1963 set back several modernization programs of the period, including literacy education. In the mid 1960s, the oil industry boomed again, and a new petrochemical industry was launched. As a founding member of OPEC, Venezuela more than quadrupled the price of its oil in 1973 and in 1976 nationalized the petroleum industry, actions that enriched the elite but did little to alleviate the poverty of the masses. The oil glut and international recession of the late 1970s created economic stagnation in Venezuela that continued through the 1980s and was accompanied by inflation, unemployment, investment in foreign markets, and inability to repay foreign debt. These problems prompted diversification to reduce heavy reliance on oil. As a result, only 20 percent of the population remained in rural areas because of the heavy migration to the cities, including the marginal areas around them.

From the late 1950s until the early 1970s, illiteracy declined from almost 60 percent to less than 25 percent. Illiteracy rates were higher in rural areas. In the mid 1980s, unemployment exceeded 40 percent. The Adult Education Division of the Ministry of Education addressed adult basic education directly through literacy campaigns and school-based programs and indirectly through mass media. In spite of the cooperation of other ministries in the National Adult Education Commission begun in 1977, the results were disappointing because of underfunding due to the economic crisis, lack of coordination, unsatisfactory teaching, irrelevant content, and lack of postliteracy opportunities. Many new literates had little opportunity or reason to read and write so lapsed into illiteracy. Courses and other educational activities were offered by the division through local Popular Culture Centers and Cultural Extension Centers. Almost two-thirds of participants were under age twenty.

Adult secondary education was conducted by the Ministry of Education, which set graduation standards and awarded certificates of completion. Although it had the potential for postliteracy activities, the teaching tended to be instructor centered and to lack relevance, so attrition was high and use in daily life was low. Higher education institutions also provided continuing education courses, but their noncompletion rates were also high. Other programs included teacher training centers, environmental education, arts and crafts training, and rural training programs for workers in agricultural and rural enterprises. These human capital programs reflected both economic goals and economic conditions (Dave, Ouane, and Ranaweera, 1986, chap. 4).

Nongovernmental Organizations

Throughout Latin America, nonformal education for adults has been offered by various organizations other than government and educational institutions which are referred to as nongovernmental organizations (NGOs). In the following examples, providers cooperated with government and educational institutions. (By contrast, other NGO programs were characterized as popular education for reform.) NGO providers included churches and nongovernmental organizations. In recent years, in some countries, the Roman Catholic Church has been one of the few institutions sufficiently powerful to provide alternative adult education programs. Cooperatives provide a second educational chance for some members. In Colombia since 1957, the continuing education program of the Family Benefit Fund (CAFAM), created by more than four thousand affiliated enterprises, has furnished various educational opportunities for low-wage employees. In cooperation with Nova University in the United States, CAFAM provided postgraduate education for adult education instructors between 1976 and 1978. In Venezuela since 1958, the National Institute of Educational Cooperation has worked with enterprises, and voluntary associations have supplied similar support to adult education for upgraded human resources, including adult education instructors. Also in Venezuela during the 1970s and early 1980s, a private institution, Simon Rodriguez Experimental University, provided in-service education for adult education staff in cooperation with Florida State University. In various countries, large enterprises typically offer occupational education for staff members. Technology transfer is sometimes accomplished through nonformal arrangements such as health education by pharmacies or agricultural extension by farm supply stores or informal groups of local farmers. As noted, mass media such as radio and television have supported distance education programs. The collective result of the adult education from such a variety of providers is fragmented, but it has increased educational opportunities for adults to advance and become more productive within the existing social order. Although such programs have done little to accomplish structural change or reduce social stratification, there is evidence that workers who receive in-service education are more productive than those who do not.

Radical Endeavors

In contrast with the foregoing overview and examples of adult education for enhancement of human resources, in some countries adult education has been associated with conflict, revolution, and radical structural change. In such programs, content has included military training for guerrilla warfare and ideological education regarding class consciousness and broadened participation in the political process. The overthrow of an oppressive totalitarian regime creates an opening of the social system and an increased optimism by people that further education can lead to an improved quality of life. In the attempt to topple an oppressive regime, the poor risk being used as a battering ram against the elite. Adult education contributes to solidarity by providing a rationale for the cause as well as preparation to succeed. Most of the successful literacy campaigns occur in revolutionary euphoria when educated volunteers are willing to teach a combination of literacy skills and political ideology and when illiterate adults believe that their chances for a better life are greatly improved and that further education will help them. Prime examples are Cuba (with the emphasis on primary education for adults) and Nicaragua (with the emphasis on secondary and postsecondary education for adults). In other countries, such as Argentina, Brazil, and Chile, the opening of the social system has been accompanied by increased adult education (Carnoy, 1974; LaBelle, 1986, 1987; Martin, 1983; Torres, 1990; Youngman, 1986).

Nicaragua

The Nicaraguan literacy crusade, as analyzed by Miller (1985) is an insightful example of a political transformation and empowerment approach that made use of a literacy campaign. The government-sponsored national crusade was a first step after the fall of the oppressive Somoza dictatorship to create a new democratic society. The primary crusade mission was political action to transform social power relations and help citizens become owners of the revolution. The educational aspects were secondary. They were to liberate and empower learners as fully participating members of the new society by helping them to acquire literacy as a means to help them build the country as active citizens. Political support for education and health was in part an affirmation of people's dignity and self-worth. The effort was aided by the revolutionary zeal of the new generation of leaders.

The young government planned a short intense national campaign soon after taking power, as a way of demonstrating commitment to the poor. The chaos of reconstruction and intense time pressure affected the development of materials, but they were revised as the campaign progressed. People from various countries composed the national training team, which used a training pyramid to prepare eighty volunteers in a two-week workshop, followed by a one-month field practicum. These volunteers then trained 600 people in two weeks, who prepared 12,000 in one week (phase three), who then trained 100,000 (phase four). From design to implementation, the elapsed time for the training program was less than six months.

Ten days before the phase three workshop, the earlier decision to use mainly young and liberal university students in phase three was reversed, and a political determination was made to utilize more conservative elementary and secondary school teachers instead. At the last minute, another political decision was made to use massive numbers of secondary school students in the final instructional phases in rural areas; the result was a logistical nightmare.

It was concluded that even though many illiterate adults learned to read and write, the chief beneficiaries of the campaign were the staff and volunteers. In general, the crusade was managed as the insurrection had been, without long-term planning and a vision of the future but by a quick response to the moment and the immediate situation. Yet the crusade was successful in many ways, and more than one-fifth of the population participated, 460,000 as students of literacy and 95,000 as students of actual conditions in the nation (students and teachers). At the outset, the recent revolution contributed to political will and national unity. There was resistance from vested interests, and the continuing conflict between Sandinistas and U.S.-backed Contras contributed to economic problems that affected the ongoing literacy education effort, which had equivocal political priority. The child-centered and bureaucratic ministry of education restricted the adult education approach. The participatory research approach used in the first phase of training was one of the distinctive contributions, but it was damaged by time pressure and limited resources. The revolution contributed to the literacy crusade, but it raised expectations regarding educational and occupational opportunities that could not be fully met, a failure that created frustration. There were many unique features of this generally successful experiment in personal empowerment and national transformation, which illustrates how literacy education is closely connected to politics, ideology, and organizational behavior (Miller, 1985).

Reform

Popular education constitutes a third approach between the extremes of equilibrium and conflict, based on a rationale of nonviolent reform. Community and organizational development procedures are used in adult education activities that combine basic education for masses of illiterate oppressed people with consciousness raising regarding political and economic causes of their personal problems. Such popular education empowers learners for involvement in political action for popular liberation.

A wellspring of rationale and methods for popular education has been Paulo Freire, whose *Pedagogy of the Oppressed* (1970) rejects a banking concept of traditional education. Instead, the emphasis is on social rather than individual empowerment to raise the consciousness of oppressed people through cultural circles that engage them in dialogues regarding their problems and the underlying causes. Illiterate and disenfranchised people endure a culture of silence; they lose hope and internalize society's low regard for them. Through praxis, in which they engage in critical reflection within the context of action, they better understand the political and economic forces on their lives. This understanding enables learners to gain a vision of a utopian future, to take informed political action to improve conditions, and to gain confidence in their ability.

During the 1950s and 1960s, Freire evolved his rationale and methods working with poor people in rural northeast Brazil. The improvements that learners sought included democratic government, responsive services, land reform, and economic development. Such changes were understandably unpopular with the elite of the Brazilian power structure, so such adult education programs were suppressed and Freire worked for some years in Chile and other countries. With a change of government and international fame for his writings and ideas, Freire returned to Brazil in a major leadership position in adult education.

Argentina

Not all popular education programs concern rural literacy education. An urban example that used television for health education occurred during 1973–1974 in Santa Fe, Argentina, as part of a health campaign in poorer neighborhoods (barrios) to reduce disease-carrying insects produced by unsanitary conditions. The slogan was "we are all responsible." The Ministry of Health and local authorities worked with local barrio committees to organize teleclubs that met in people's homes to view and then discuss a series of eight programs, which included local residents as actors. The program objectives were popular participation, solidarity, and orientation of residents to active participation. Teleclub coordinators received a discussion guide to help the eight to fifteen participants engage in lively discussion and explore practical applications. Benefits included improved sanitation and health, along with the ongoing tele-clubs that enabled interested residents to discuss other community problems to be solved (O'Sullivan-Ryan and Kaplun, n.d.).

Popular Education

In general, popular education programs have tried to avoid heavy involvement by government and educational institutions in the belief that they would impede structural changes and reforms. Instead, popular education programs usually seek mobilization of social action for structural change. The popular education rationale is that collective action is required by participants and their associates if progress is to occur for large numbers of poor, disenfranchised, and powerless adults who are dependent on the dominant elites in their country. Popular education programs do not generally advocate violent overthrow of the regime but provide nonformal education as a means to alter the balance of power in society by gradual transformations toward greater democracy and equity. A limitation of popular education has been that though consciousness raising has prepared participants to take advantage of opportunities that occur, the programs lack linkage to social action. Once awakened, some participants became frustrated over structural influences rather than liberated from them. Popular education, community development, and participatory research share goals and procedures but differ in rationale.

The participatory research rationale in Latin America emphasizes learner involvement in planning the educational activity, especially analysis of change related to the conditions that engender poverty, dependence, and exploitation. Because such changes inevitably result in resistance from the power structure, some participatory research rationales involve a preliminary phase that precedes typical steps for organizational or community problem solving. The preliminary phase includes definition of a provisional strategic goal, analysis of local and external obstacles, and specification of major societal influences, including sources of resistance. This preliminary phase enables participants to select and understand their actual strategic goal, assess feasibility, and then choose objectives, activities, and proficiencies to be mastered (Dubell, Erasmie, and de Vries, 1981; Enyia, 1983; LaBelle, 1986; Luft, 1984).

Economic Forces

All types of educational programs for adults in Latin America reveal broad economic, political, and social influences that affect agency planning. As shown in several examples in this section, economic conditions and shifts are a powerful influence, especially during modernization to market economies. Economic dependency includes personal dependence of many poor people on resources controlled by a small elite and national dependence on agricultural products and raw materials exported to industrialized countries.

As with many countries in recent decades, economic woes have been compounded by high foreign debt payments. In the mid 1980s, three Latin American countries owned one-third of the total international debt in the world, and Chile had the world's highest per capita international debt. However, there have been some promising trends. In late 1991, compared with 1989, inflation rates decreased and economic growth rates increased, after a decade of no growth, crippling inflation, rising foreign debt, deficits, and protectionism. Improvements reflected public acceptance of unpopular economic policies—reduced buying power, government layoffs, privatization, and reduced government spending on social programs. Economic trends of the past decade did not help the poor, with 44 percent of the Latin American population considered living in poverty in 1990 compared with 40 percent in 1980. The political trend was toward democracy; there were democratically elected governments in all Latin American countries except Cuba and Haiti in late 1991. (In early 1979, there were military dictatorships in Argentina, Bolivia, Brazil, Chile, Ecuador, Paraguay, Peru, and Uruguay.) Paradoxically, international aid related to adult education expanded educational opportunities for individuals but achieved little structural change and tended to widen the gap between the haves and have nots.

Political Forces

Political power has been a major influence on Latin American adult education in recent decades. Popular education especially is understandably perceived as a threat to repressive regimes, some of which ban all group meetings. Government support and cooperation are often frustrated by bureaucratic struggles among various ministries, with some exceptions as noted in this section. Adult educators who seek to empower the poor and reduce dependency confront power relations in which the large numbers of poor insiders contend with the hegemony of elite outsiders who control resources. As a result, widespread pessimism makes it difficult to attract and retain participants in educational programs. This situation contributes to the separate types of programs (human capital, conflict, and reform), each serving different purposes and learner expectations.

Social Forces

The contrasts between Latin American countries are striking. Adult illiteracy rates in 1980 vary from less than 10 percent in Argentina and Uruguay to more than half in Guatemala and three-quarters in Haiti. However, some of the greatest contrasts occur *within* countries, and these population characteristics are especially influential on adult education. Population growth, combined with widespread poverty and migration from rural areas, has created huge urban slums. The existence of small, powerful elites based in cities and on large rural estates, large numbers of powerless indigenous and other poor people, and a relatively small middle class has produced distinctive kinds of adult education purposes and clienteles. Values such as democracy and equity are interpreted quite differently by people in various parts of the power structure. Even participation in adult education to enhance human capital seems unattractive when unemployment rates are high during extended depressionary periods.

Adult education has been buffeted by economic, political, and social conditions and has had little impact on achieving desirable structural change. Funding and staffing fluctuate greatly, generally much below levels of expectations. Fragmentation in types of providers and government ministries confound collaboration. In spite of all of these problems, some comprehensive programs have been planned and partially implemented, but even they typically have had little direct influence on policy making. It is within this context that adult education for community problem solving has occurred (Brock and Lawlor, 1985; Dave, Ouane, and Ranaweera, 1986; Dubell, Erasmie, and de Vries, 1981; Jeria, 1989; LaBelle, 1986, 1987; Torres, 1990).

Chile

This section concludes with two examples of popular education for reform by NGOs for rural community development in Chile during the 1970s. These illustrate deterrents to program planning and implementation arising from an oppressive military regime. Started in the early 1970s under a socialist government, an educational program set out to teach basic skills to poor rural people in impoverished provinces to promote socioeconomic development and reduce poverty. Although the general effort continued in Chile and several other Latin American countries during the 1970s, the 1973 military coup and junta in Chile resulted in an authoritarian regime, which banned organizations and collective action and restricted social participation, especially in rural areas. Under these extreme circumstances, the related local educational providers declined because there was a lack of support from the community, loss of its ability to participate, and shrinking resources to address the related problems of poor people. At the national level, this situation resulted in an understandable goal displacement and shift from education for empowerment (to be achieved through literacy for rural men) to vocational education for urban women. This emphasis contributed to traditional curriculum and teaching, instead of the planned popular education approach of nontraditional facilitation of learning and an integrated curriculum built around adult life concerns. The types of local cosponsors very much shaped the clientele that was attracted. Although the original benefits were to reduce poverty, the actual program that resulted had little impact on it (Duke, 1985, chap. 6).

In the late 1970s, under the same authoritarian regime, another popular education attempt was made to help poor rural adults solve community problems related to poverty. Because of continuing restrictions on rural organizational and group activities, the national Rural Information Program used radio broadcasts and publications (newspapers and magazine supplements) to stimulate, assist, and strengthen local cooperative organizations. Use of mass media seemed viable because peasants were isolated and their cooperative organizations did not meet regularly. In a political and economic context that paralyzed trade union activity nationwide and caused peasants to struggle with many economic, social, and political problems related to their survival, the program made some modest gains. The few local cooperative leaders and instructors who received training helped prepare contributions for communication media, which increased public understanding of rural problems and possible solutions, strengthened solidarity among cooperative members, and enriched materials that local cooperatives could use in their educational activities. The program was one of the very few means available for the voice of the rural population to be heard, a fact that enhanced local optimism and cooperation. However, a government agrarian policy that drastically reduced technical assistance, loans, and incentives for cooperatives and other peasant organizations hastened their deterioration (especially of the least advantaged), and many organizations disappeared. There was little indication that the communication program improved rural living and working conditions. By the early 1980s, the program ended for lack of resources. Perhaps the main contribution was to maintain hope and contact in rural areas until a return of a democratic regime at the end of the 1980s, when political conditions allowed resumption of popular education for community problem solving (Gajardo, 1983; Resource A, Gajardo).

These and other examples of popular education in Latin America demonstrate the extreme resistance that can confront adult education for community problem solving and the importance of strategic planning to maximize program impact and continuance under difficult circumstances.

Other Countries

Adult education for community problem solving has occurred in all types of countries in all parts of the world. The following brief examples from Tanzania, Thailand, Australia, Japan, Italy, and

Canada illustrate some additional societal influences that have implications for strategic planning.

Tanzania

Tanzania has provided a distinctive example of adult education for community development. Located in East Africa and including the Great Rift Valley and Mt. Kilimanjaro, Tanzania gained independence in 1961, and a few years later joined with another former British colony, Zanzibar. Ninety-eight African (composed of 127 ethnic groups) and 2 percent European and Asian, Tanzania and its unity and community development efforts were affected by Swahili as the official and national language, an overwhelmingly rural and economically impoverished agricultural countryside, a one-party (TANU) socialist political system, and Julius Nyerere, the founding president and enduring leader who was a strong champion of adult education and community development. The sequence of government ministries for community, rural development, and adult education had somewhat fragmented policies and programs related to community problem solving. However, adult education was prominent in the Arusha Declaration of 1967, the sequence of five-year development plans, and numerous presidential statements, which reflected its part and government priority. Included were education for socialist self-reliance, rejection of individualistic material wealth as a major criterion of social merit, and government commitment to eliminate poverty, ignorance, and disease. In general, the educational and social goals were more fully achieved than the economic goals.

Government-supported adult education addressed various aspects of community development, with modest contributions by nongovernmental organizations, religious institutions, and private enterprises. Functional literacy campaigns and ongoing efforts reduced an illiteracy rate from more than 80 percent to less than 20 percent. Local community development workers organized both literacy courses and self-help projects related to health, sanitation, transportation, and housing. Moreover, literacy and postliteracy educational activities were connected to various other adult education program areas that together contributed to problem solving. Radio broadcasts and local discussion groups were used for political education tied to early elections. Traditional African practices of shared labor and wealth were revived to offset colonial dependency; cooperative villages were created to increase population density and social services, and the cooperative movement was encouraged.

In 1969–1971, district adult education officers and local adult education instructors worked with organizers from the University of Dar es Salaam Institute of Adult Education in combined radio broadcasts and local discussion groups to help celebrate Tanzania's tenth anniversary and adult education year. This cost-effective effort paved the way for a well-planned and much more extensive preventive health education campaign a few years later. The Man Is Health campaign also drew on radio broadcasts and oral communication to mobilize and inform people; along with positive use of social pressure and participatory group discussion, this effort achieved increased understanding, improvements in health and sanitation, and grass roots political organization and solidarity. The success of this program was due to an able adult education field staff, strong national political support, integrated rural development, interministerial cooperation, limited scope of campaign content, relevance to all intended audiences, and use of various forms of communication. In 1973, nearly two million Tanzanians participated through seventy-five thousand radio study groups that included nearly 40 percent of all adults between fifteen and sixty years of age.

In 1971, a delegation went to Sweden to study its folk schools. By 1976, Tanzania had established a network of one Folk Development College for every two districts in the country. Each college could accommodate from fewer than fifty to more than two hundred community leaders for residential educational activities to support comprehensive community development. Short courses ranged from a few weeks to six months, and long courses lasted up to two years. Shared financing with villages and colleges did not materialize, so the national government paid most of the costs. Limited finances restricted follow-up. The Kibana College provided inservice education for the staff members of other colleges.

Various adult education activities related to community development were interconnected at some points. Rural newspapers (developed with Norwegian support) provided postliteracy opportunities and content for community development projects. The newspapers were also used in Folk Development Colleges. Almost three thousand rural libraries also furnished postliteracy resources for community problem solving, as did the correspondence courses developed with Swedish support. Workers' education served urban adults with vocational education, partly by correspondence courses. Adult education publications assisted various programs, and a coordination section of the directorate of adult education helped with planning, budgeting, personnel, equipment, materials, and evaluation. Agricultural extension was related to the Ministry of Agriculture. As noted earlier, instructional radio was one form of educational technology related to local discussion groups. This linkage and collaboration were possible because of advanced planning and strong policy support.

In spite of ideological commitment to community development and self-help, lack of economic progress, inequality for women, and inadequate local initiative contributed to fragmentation of adult education activities. Annual government expenditures for adult education were more than 10 percent of the total education budget. Adult education was a major beneficiary of an estimated $10 billion in aid from Sweden and many other Western donors over a period of twenty years. International trade, including rising oil prices and falling payments for exports such as coffee and sisal, damaged economic development, which began to improve in recent years following economic reforms (Dave, Perera, and Ouane, 1985b; Hall, 1974, 1977, 1985; Hall and Dodds, 1974; Kassam, 1974, 1982; Nyerere, 1976; Oomen-Myin, 1983).

The pioneering contributions by Hall and his associates in Tanzania and subsequently in the International Council on Adult Education have contributed much to the theory and practice of participatory research (Hall, forthcoming). The focus is on empowering oppressed people by helping them learn about the sources as well as the symptoms of their oppression and about the procedures that they can use to create and use knowledge for their advancement. Participatory research (sometimes referred to as action research-evaluation) entails creating knowledge, raising consciousness and understanding, and mobilizing for action for social change. The emphasis has been on production and use of socially constructed knowledge to counteract dependence on the hegemony of the majority culture by oppressed people who seek social change and increased power. The concentration on local initiative, process assistance, experiential learning, and empowerment has contributed to use of participatory research in many different settings outside Tanzania, including in the Highlander Land Ownership Task Force and in various programs in Latin America.

Thailand

For two decades, adult education for empowerment and community problem solving in Thailand has reflected a Buddhist tradition. Government-supported adult education was evident following the 1932 revolution and change from absolute monarchy to democracy. One of the six guidelines for national development was that education shall be provided fully for the people. The first literacy campaign during the early 1940s reflected the war environment and governmental commitment and support. Postwar expansion of adult education went beyond illiteracy and citizenship to include vocational education, life improvement, and leisure activities. The UNESCO Fundamental Education Center established in Thailand in 1954 to prepare people for rural adult education emphasized functional literacy, rural development, health, agriculture, and social welfare. In subsequent decades, the scope of adult education continued to broaden to include also industrial, political, moral, and cultural development. In the late 1960s, the Thai Division of Adult Education departed from the UNESCO approach to work-oriented functional literacy. In 1969, the division and especially its director advanced a humanistic philosophy for adult education, based on Buddhist beliefs regarding harmony and happiness combined with critical thinking and problem solving.

This evolving approach to adult education for self-help was known as Khit-pen (also discussed in Chapter Eleven). It stressed enabling people to learn, think, do, and solve problems. The underlying belief was that active participation and self-reliance should guide people's striving for complete development in which they were subjects and not objects of development activities. The 1977

National Scheme of Education recognized rural-urban disparities related to political, social, and economic conditions, and the Fifth National Economic and Social Development Plan reflected broadened acceptance of Khit-pen beliefs. However, adult education for reflective thinking conflicted with deep-rooted Thai traditions of learning by memorization and not challenging the authority of learned teachers and other authorities. Such resignation and apprehension about the consequence of challenging the power structure moderated the empowerment that resulted, a result that was exacerbated by the ambiguity of the Khit-pen philosophy.

In recent years, multipronged local adult education activities have focused on self-reliance in community problem solving. Guidelines have included integrated development, decentralized local participation in community-based education, and assistance from distance education and volunteers. Priority for rural social and economic development has been shown in development of a coordinated educational system for improving self-reliance (Armstrong, 1984, Bernard and Armstrong, 1979; Hinzen, 1989). This Thai example shows how traditional values can both help and hinder adult education for community development.

Australia

Some community development efforts focus on local government— for example, a local government education program during the 1980s in the state of Tasmania, Australia. The program purpose was to use media and workshops to encourage citizen participation in local government to counteract low voter registration and participation (only 20 percent of those registered voted). The program was conducted collaboratively by the recently formed Local Government Education Association and the Adult Education Section of the local College of Technical and Further Education. Financial and in-kind support for the program came from several sources. For example, the section and the association conducted workshops led by experienced city council members entitled "Win an Election" and "Dealing with Your Council" and charged fees to participants, which were used to pay workshop leaders at the regular college pay scale. Association members helped plan and conduct activities, and their association dues helped pay for media campaigns to publicize the public issues and educational activities about them. The mass media (such as television stations and newspapers) were very cooperative. However, the association's proposal for financial support was rejected, as was its application for nonprofit status. Although participants reported that the educational activities were beneficial, few of them became registered voters or ran for public offices as a result. The impact was personal rather than community development (Resource A, Holderness-Roddam). Low public interest, government retrenchment, and low college priority ended this program; however, in the early 1990s, the coordinator's interest was sufficient for him to volunteer to initiate a similar program entitled Community Action Skills, which distributed leaflets to interested citizens.

Japan

Since 1945, adult education for local empowerment and problem solving in Japan has emphasized social and political transformation to democracy despite a strong nationalist tradition, family solidarity, and reverence for authority. One contributor to the transformation has been social education for adults through Kominkan (citizens' public halls), which changed historic village centers into nonformal education agencies. These learner-centered educational programs, strengthened by the social education law of 1949, have become the prominent providers of adult education and have served various purposes, including democracy, community cooperation, and local leadership. Cooperating universities and the National Training Institute for Adult Education have furnished research and in-service education for social education staff members. The high rate of economic growth following 1955 has accelerated urbanization, which has disrupted traditional family solidarity and its insulation from national intrusion.

Social education has helped to build communities (Thomas, 1985; Yamaguchi, 1986). For example, during the 1970s, in the hot-spring resort town of Yufuin with a population of twelve thousand, some young adults formed the Society to Think about the Future of Yufuin. The initiative came from some young managers who had left Yufuin to work in Tokyo or Fukuoka but had returned to succeed their fathers. These people were concerned about the effects on their community of creeping urbanization from nearby cities. This spontaneous mutual-help group and its growing number of supporters benefited from social education activities. The society addressed three problem areas. One was enterprises, including tourism and preservation of old thatched houses and replacement of declining rice production with increased agricultural production (such as shiitake mushrooms and cottage-industry production of bean paste and miso pickles). A second problem area was the environment, including renewal of a depopulated area in the center of town and zoning for orderly growth at the fringes. A third problem area was human resources, including problems of juvenile delinquency and the assistance needed for older adults. The social education program helped local citizens solve their problems by promoting communication and solidarity and by encouraging cooperation between citizens' groups, such as between the society and local government (Resource A, Moro'oka).

Italy

Another approach to community development was taken during the 1980s by a professor of adult education and some of his colleagues and students at the University of Florence in Italy, who took the initiative to collaborate with friends who worked in city government in the nearby industrial city of Prato. A varied set of educational programs became the joint effort of the city government and the university. The city was a source of funds and encouragement. The university was a source of ideas, students, and contacts with local adult education programs. The adult learners benefited from enriched educational opportunities and awareness of options. Staff members in adult education programs in the city of Prato received assistance from university students from the department, who in turn gained practical experience. The department sought to create and disseminate new knowledge about community-based adult education. The professor was concerned that local economic values might become the main influence on community priorities and policies. The educational focus was on social rather than individual change, and the main intended outcome was to broaden citizen participation in the educational, social, cultural, and economic life of the community and to strengthen collaboration between educational providers, enterprises, and city government (Resource A, DeSanctis).

Canada

Sometimes dramatic events have prompted adult education for community problem solving. This situation occurred in 1985 in Buchans, a one-industry mining town of about 1,600 people in the center of Newfoundland, Canada. The previous year, the mining company had closed the mine, no other industrial alternative existed, and unemployment soared to 90 percent. The university adult education division had already pioneered use of educational technology for community development. After intensive planning, it conducted an intensive three-day program (using a mobile, low-powered transmitter) viewed on the television sets in each of the 350 households in the community. This allowed narrowcast interactive television with phone-in capacity that was set up in less than a day. (After that, a smaller, more mobile transmitter was used that required even less staffing).

During the three days, the program issues focused on the town's future, with live, interactive television that used local people in key roles. Phone call-ins included local residents and outside resources from enterprises, the government, and the mayor of a former mining town that had made a successful transition. Because of the urgency, only two months were required for preparation instead of the usual six. More than 95 percent of the households participated, and the direct costs were paid by a $10,000 government youth activity grant. The main benefit was that all community members could interact (in the nonthreatening setting of their own homes) in a discussion of the problem and their options. This approach helped transform residents from passive dependence to greater commitment in seeking solutions to their own employment problems and to the future of their community. The community development worker helped with the planning, the three-day event, and the follow-up. Outside assistance included early retirement of workers, help with relocation to other communities, and assistance in locating replacement enterprises to provide employment opportunities (Resource A, Curran).

Strategic Planning

The following summary of implications for strategic planning is based on the examples just given and on pertinent writings on community development (Araiyo, 1978; Bunch, 1982; Hollnsteiner, 1979; Merriam and Cunningham, 1989, chaps. 7, 8, and 33; Nesman, 1981; Stromquist, 1986). The specifics of adult education for organizational and community development vary greatly from situation to situation and within and among countries, and some of these local contingencies are noted in the following implications for strategic planning. However, there are also some general implications at the level of the local provider agency, which include suggestions of the ways that agency leaders can analyze their societal context as a basis for decision making. This concluding section covers mobilization of participants, contextual influences, linkage with resources, transformative leadership, and alternative approaches.

Participation

The mobilization of participants for community problem solving has usually focused on the adults who were adversely affected by current conditions—those who suffered most from the problems to be solved. In developing countries, the announced intended beneficiaries of community problem solving have been the have nots (largely the rural poor and increasingly in many countries the urban slum dwellers). Typically, cultural minority subcultures and especially indigenous peoples are heavily represented in economically less-advantaged categories. They confront many deterrents to educational participation: poverty, illiteracy, poor health, and location. Nevertheless, a major deterrent has been their attitudes, which have created invisible barriers to progress. Such attitudes include fatalism (external locus of control, low sense of efficacy), low self-esteem and self-confidence (internalization of cultural stereotypes and beliefs about social stratification), lack of a sense of solidarity with others who share their plight (sometimes even conflict with other minority subcultures), and in general a lack of optimism and hope that they can do anything to improve their life (based in part on unfamiliarity with how social, economic, and political arrangements affect them and in part on feelings of powerlessness to improve their situation). Another deterrent has been resistance from powerful elites, as illustrated by examples of Highlander and Universidad Popular in Chicago and from Brazil and Chile (Barrow, 1981, 1983; Torres, 1983, 1990; Zabala, 1982).

These factors suggest why community development leaders have emphasized consciousness raising and solidarity. Most writers on community development and the designers of some projects discussed here (especially Universidad Popular, Tuskegee Institute, and participatory literacy and popular education in Latin America generally—examples from Nicaragua, Brazil, and Chile) have concentrated on mobilization of the poor as an essential early planning stage in a process that includes their active participation in decision making to help them to help themselves and become active members of society. As in voluntary action generally, much depends on responsiveness to basic needs and current stage of progression so learners can express and explore their concerns and recognize likely benefits of their efforts. In some instances, the intended participants in adult education for community problem solving have been local officials. As the examples from Illinois and Tasmania indicate, they may be in a position to affect decisions, but inertia may be a problem. A two-pronged effort (perhaps by separate adult education providers) aimed at both the disenfranchised and local officials might be an effective strategy in some situations.

Context

Adult education for problem solving in organizational and community settings usually confronts major societal influences to be understood and reflected in strategic planning. Most examples and guidelines demonstrate that it is crucial to understand the community and organizational context from tacit knowledge born of long immersion in the societal context and from deliberate analysis and consensual validation of perceptions regarding conditions, threats, and opportunities. Understanding the local context was stressed in examples such as Highlander, Rockford, Tuskegee, Tanzania, and Italy. Explicit analysis is important because contrasts between the interpersonal networks that characterize minority subcultures on the one hand and the hierarchical organization of many economic and political organizations on the other make understanding and cooperation difficult from either position. Such contextual analysis, when combined with typical adult education needs assessment, allows planning that takes major influences from a dynamic external environment into account as well as learner preferences. Contextual influences include international and domestic economic, political, ideological, and organizational dynamics.

Social change both contributes to many of the community problems to be solved and creates conditions that help mobilize efforts to solve some of them. At the early stage of social movements, adult education can help people understand influences and options. Highlander was responsive to the beginnings of the civil rights movement in the southern United States, the Nicaragua literacy crusade occurred right after the revolution, and a social education program contributed to efforts to protect a Japanese resort town from urbanization. Popular education in various Latin American countries was especially effective around the time of the opening up of political systems. The Canadian one-industry town where the mine closed experienced a crisis that fostered unusual solidarity and participation in exploration of future directions. Such social upheaval can create a focus on issues and rising expectations that stimulate enthusiasm and initiatives for change by people who had earlier endured oppression or accepted unsatisfactory conditions. Established institutions such as universities and government can also serve as providers, as illustrated by examples from Illinois, Minnesota, Tuskegee, Michigan State, Brazil, Mexico, Colombia, Argentina, Tanzania, Thailand, Australia, Japan, Italy, and Canada. Urban and rural settings each have distinctive problems and influences, many associated with population density. Solutions also depend on degree of urbanization, such as lack of resources in rural areas and coordination of resources in urban areas. In developing countries, the urban bias of the powerful elite is a severe impediment to the solution of rural problems. Strategic planning can help both urban and rural citizens understand actual interdependence and discover solutions that have advantages for both groups.

Resources

Although only one of many societal influences, economic conditions have a powerful effect on adult education programs because financial resources affect all of their aspects (subsidy of providers, participant affluence and ability to pay, occupational opportunities that influence learner motivation, enterprise support for education, and policy support for nonoccupational adult education). Adult education for community problem solving usually requires government or NGO subsidy, both of which are tied to national economic conditions. National support for adult education reflects both priority and economic conditions, which in developing countries especially may be affected by outflow of resources. National economies (such as the examples from Mexico and Venezuela) with heavy dependence on a few commodities, such as oil or coffee can be more vulnerable to price fluctuations than more diversified economies (a situation that can create great discontinuity in support for adult education over the years). This is particularly the case for programs on community problem solving; enterprise support provides a buffer for occupational education. Extreme social stratification influences the types of community problems to be solved and allocation of resources for adult education for community development. In most instances, analysis of economic conditions as they relate to a specific provider agency, clientele, country, time period, and economic system is a crucial part of strategic planning for community development, even more so than for other types of adult education (Swett Morales, 1983).

When planning community development programs to assist the poor or minority subpopulations, the economic and political power structure is a major factor to consider because it tends to be a major source of resistance to change. Community problem solving is more likely to occur when there is national support, which usually reflects the values of the majority culture and the elite power structure. Their support or resistance is quite different according to whether the political system is democratic and egalitarian or totalitarian and oppressive. Where possible, strategic planning should give special attention to solutions to community problems for which there is broad support from people who want relief from the problem and who can contribute to the solution. When consensus is impossible, separate educational activities for people in the client system and for policy makers may be effective. Strategic planning can include a sufficiently broad range of stakeholders and information to identify the main societal influences likely to help or undermine the specific program.

Leadership

Transformational leadership requires working with stakeholders to agree upon a compelling vision of desirable goals that warrant cooperation. As illustrated by Highlander's work with civil rights workers and by the pedagogy of the oppressed in Brazil, inspirational leadership can build local support and solidarity within the client system that can be especially important at early stages of community problem solving when internal confidence may be low and external resistance great. The values and beliefs that undergird transformative leadership include both goal desirability and commitment to process guidelines such as democracy, communication, and equity. For community problem solving, empowerment to help people to help themselves is such a basic value. Consciousness raising reflects that value, whereas indoctrination does not. Community development usually involves conflicts of values, which place a premium on able leaders who can deal well with values clarification, conflict resolution, planning, communication, and other process aspects of leadership.

Leadership contributions from various stakeholders often change during a community development project (as seen in the Highlander example). Early stages of community development may be especially open ended as staff members or volunteer leaders work with various stakeholders to analyze the symptoms, causes, available resources, and strategies to obtain needed resources, deal with resistance, and implement solutions. Outside change agents can help obtain valuable ideas and resources, but local leaders must be developed who are well selected, trained, placed, paid, and inspired.

Staff and leadership development is crucial as both a process and outcome of community development. Sometimes goals are displaced, such as the program in Chile that aimed to serve rural men but actually reached urban women. As powerful forces shape community and organization development efforts, it takes strong leadership to persist in pursuit of desirable and feasible goals, but also to adapt strategies to local contingencies as necessary.

Strategic planning can help community development leaders focus on feasible as well as desirable objectives and to identify indicators of progress toward goal achievement. The participation of citizens in most adult education for community problem solving depends on their enthusiasm and commitment, which in turn depend on early, recognizable success. Even more than for most adult education programs, it is difficult to specify performance indicators and evidence of progress in community development activities. Personal gain and progress are insufficient outcomes when evaluating community problem solving activities in which intended outcomes entail social change. Evaluation of impact includes the multiplier effect as learners use what they learn in taking local action with their associates. It is difficult to assess such changes and to attribute them to educational activities. Strategic planning can alert leaders to the importance and difficulty of such impact evaluation, as well as to suggest feasible performance indicators likely to encourage continued participation by learners and other major stakeholders. Such specification can also help clarify and build commitment for the often vague mission of community development programs (Humphrey and Meyer, 1985).

The contextual analysis and environmental scanning emphasis of strategic planning makes it especially valuable for strengthening linkage with resources important to the success of the community development effort. The specific resources to be acquired depend on the type of problem to be solved and on local contingencies. Usually, the most important ones to be mobilized are human resources within the community. Local people's indigenous knowledge, time, and cooperation are crucial for planning and implementation of the community development activity, as well as utilization of the solutions that result. (This fact was illustrated by the Rockford example.) External resources include ideas, money, and educational technology, which may come from NGOs, government, or philanthropic foundations. (These sources were illustrated by the Michigan State and Minnesota examples. Foundations also provided support in Highlander and the Illinois and Tuskegee programs.) As necessary as such external resources generally are to assist early stages of community development activities, it is also important not to flaunt them but to phase them in and out with care to prevent dependency and the stifling of enthusiasm and mobilization upon which long-term success depends (Avalos, 1985; Darkenwald and Merriam, 1982; Grossi, 1984). Whether the government or an NGO is a stakeholder and supporter, linkage is important, and strategic planning can strengthen both local initiative and external support.

Approaches

As indicated in the section on adult education in Latin America, there have been some quite different approaches to adult education for community problem solving: human resources, reform, and conflict. The approach to be selected depends on local contingencies, usually the severity of the problem and the resistance from the power structure. However, there are some guidelines for success in most community development activities. One is openness of communication, planning, and decision making so that participants contribute to planning and also learn cooperative action. A second is to start small and begin slowly so that early successes and failures can be used to modify the effort before expanding. A third is to provide sufficient preparation before, support during, and follow-up for implementation (Bown, 1977; Compton, 1982; Curtin and Varley, 1986; Erasmie, Lima, and Pereira, 1984; Hamilton, 1984; Hollnsteiner, 1979; Northmore, 1986).

As indicated in most of the projects discussed and the related rationale, fragmentation constitutes one of the main barriers to successful adult education for community problem solving. Strategic planning provides a way to involve stakeholders from local client systems and from various resource systems, such as NGOs and related government ministries. (Collaboration among providers was illustrated by examples such as Illinois, workplace literacy, Minnesota, Colombia, Venezuela, Japan, and Italy.) Such a comprehensive approach to planning can be combined with multipronged educational activities for categories of adults related to the problem to be solved. These coordinated educational activities can complement each other by addressing various parts of the larger social system in which the problem occurs and can increase the momentum for change. Inertia and resistance will occur in most settings, but a concerted effort is more likely to succeed than one that addresses only one part of the problem. Thus, collaboration is an important ingredient in adult education for community problem solving.

The central themes in this chapter on community development are pertinent to those in other program areas—rural development, nonoccupational programs related to citizen role, and health education. In such adult education programs, strategic planning helps leaders strengthen support from major stakeholders related to the problem and its solution.

14

Strengthening
Strategic Leadership:
Guidelines from
Worldwide Practice

This concluding chapter draws on the examples and planning implications in the preceding twelve chapters to provide a rationale and guidelines for strategic planning and leadership in this emerging era when adult education agency *leadership* is becoming a societal imperative. The rationale is informed by comparative perspectives that are essential for *comprehensive* programs that have a major impact on performance. Too many programs begin with high hopes but conclude with the disappointing result that they did not make much of a difference.

Rationale for Strategic Leadership

In the various program areas and national settings in which societal influences on adult education agency functioning have been studied, examples of comprehensive programs have been located and analyzed. Such comprehensive programs are typically distinguished by synergistic efforts by one or more agencies to provide coordinated educational activities for various categories of adults related to an important social issue that merits such collaboration.

Synergy refers to enhanced energy and impact because a problem area is addressed by multiple programs and by cooperation among providers. In contrast to adult education programs aimed at individual advancement (which are also important), synergistic leadership of comprehensive adult education programs depends on a comparative perspective on societal influences and external stakeholders. The following rationale for agency leadership focuses on strategic planning and implementation as a process that enables leaders to gain stakeholder commitment to shared goals and encourage contributions to goal achievement.

The underlying concern addressed by this book is that it is increasingly important to strengthen the impact of adult education, and traditional reliance on delivering educational programs to individual adults is inadequate to the new realities of the twenty-first century. The rationale and guidelines that follow reflect some fundamental questions that tie comparative perspectives to strategic leadership. Why is leadership important to strengthen adult education agencies and their provision of comprehensive programs? Why are so few adult education practitioners now providing such synergistic leadership? How can more adult educators be helped to do so? The rationale is responsive to the first and second of these questions. In answer to the third question, the chapter furnishes ten guidelines for strategic leadership.

Why is leadership important? In any organization, the essence of leadership is working with other members for planning and implementation. One or many people associated with an organization can contribute, and in best practice the leadership function is broadly shared. Leadership for planning entails gaining member commitment to shared vision, mission, and goals. Leadership for implementation of plans requires guiding member contributions so that goals and objectives are achieved. *Strategic* leaders are future oriented as they use some form of strategic planning to seek agreement on desirable agency goals and to achieve cooperation for implementation of the plans.

When an adult education practitioner plans and conducts a course or arranges for other instructors to do so, many planning and implementation decisions may be implicit. As illustrated in Chapter One, such individually oriented approaches may be inadequate when the goal is major program impact on performance in a problem area such as literacy, rural development, rehabilitation of inmates, or health promotion. Such progress calls for more comprehensive adult education programs, which typically involve concerted efforts by various adult education provider agencies. Serving one or several categories of learners, each agency is interested in some aspects of the total problem area. When a program coordinator arranges for an individual course, several categories of people have a stake in the success of the course, so they can contribute to planning and implementation. Included are the coordinator, instructor, learners who participate, and sometimes policy makers and supporters. Planning and implementation can be informal and implicit in the decisions that are made.

Comprehensive efforts in which multiple adult education programs are planned and conducted in concert to address an important problem area greatly broaden the range of stakeholders whose cooperation is necessary. The expanded range of stakeholders includes representatives of collaborating agencies and people associated with the problem area and major societal influences. This broadening of program scope increases the salience of societal influences and contextual analysis to understand them. Strategic leadership for adult education agencies that participate in comprehensive programs is synergistic because it affects decision making and releases energy by various stakeholders. It is thus especially important that strategic leadership formalize and make explicit the decision-making process to gain agreement on goals and encourage contributions toward their achievement. Such leadership entails effective communication among stakeholders and agreement on policy guidelines, along with supportive guidance, feedback, encouragement, and the recognition that is essential for cooperation.

The decision by an adult education agency to engage in a comprehensive program reflects commitment to a problem area and necessitates increased attention to contextual analysis. Compared with arranging for individual courses and workshops, collaboration with a broader range of stakeholders to conduct a comprehensive program (or at least to be aware of and build on their contributions) requires a strong commitment to the problem area to be addressed and confidence in its relevance to the agency mission. (Examples of problem areas include multicultural opportunities for minorities, health care, improvement for staff members, and comprehensive rural development.) To conduct a successful comprehensive program involves more than a long-range plan. Success depends on contextual analysis to parallel needs assessment in individually oriented programs. Contextual analysis can clarify provider agency mission and resources, contributions of other pertinent providers, and major societal influences likely to help or hinder the proposed comprehensive program and progress regarding the problem area. Most of all, successful comprehensive programs require cooperation by multiple stakeholders to implement the plans. Synergistic leadership promotes such cooperation.

A *comparative* perspective can enable adult education leaders to conduct comprehensive programs that have an impact. One benefit of strategic planning is specification of situational opportunities and threats. Examples of such societal influences include legislation, economic conditions, immigration, aging trends, and new knowledge. Comparative analysis across program areas and even national settings can help adult education leaders recognize both similarities and differences between providers as a basis for effective cooperation, harness societal influences that help, and deflect societal influences that impede the impact. Synergistic leadership is characterized by comparative perspectives that undergrid successful comprehensive and collaborative educational programs. Future-oriented strategic leadership for adult education is emerging in many program areas and parts of the world.

But why are so few adult education practitioners providing such strategic leadership? Several trends help explain this failure. Volunteerism may be both the greatest strength and the greatest weakness of adult education. The phrase "volunteers for learning" has been used to describe the adults who participate in a wide variety of part-time and short-term educational activities. The phrase also describes most of the people who help adults learn. Paid or volunteer, they typically do so part time without long-term arrangements; they have great commitment and enthusiasm for their special field but little familiarity with the broader field of adult education. As a result, part-time and short-term adult education instructors tend not to function like a faculty in a preparatory education institution in relation to general program directions and planning.

This part-time and volunteer feature of adult education instructors affects program coordination. The agency administrative function is also influenced by a lack of attention to the adult education function by the governing board of the parent organization with which most adult education agencies are associated. (The use of advisory committees often compensates for this.) With little leadership over program directions from instructional staff and governing board, the extent of strategic planning and leadership depends greatly on agency directors and administrators, who could include various stakeholders in strategic planning and implementation. In fact, this practice is infrequent for several reasons.

Most adult education agency directors and program coordinators have gradually advanced from instructional roles or transferred from administrative roles outside of adult education. Only a small proportion have obtained education or special preparation for adult education work, which would have provided them with an overview of the professional field and important proficiency areas. Many adult education administrators join an association of practitioners working in the same program area, attend meetings, and read publications but learn little about the broad field of adult education in other program areas and national settings (Knox, 1979; Votruba, 1981, chap. 1).

As a result, agency leaders tend to be fairly familiar with *internal* features of agency functioning, strengths, and weaknesses because information about participants, staff, enrollment trends, and agency finances is used in routine decision making. Planning time is likely to be devoted to activities like a management audit, budget request, or internal review. Fluctuations in enrollment and resources contribute to crisis management rather than planning. The general goals and specific problems seem so evident that it may not occur to agency administrators that taking time for planning is feasible, let alone desirable. (It is like the manager who was too overworked to take a course on time management.) High ideals and low resources are so characteristic of many adult education agencies that strategic planning is either unfamiliar or considered a luxury they can not afford. This is especially the case for future-oriented collaborative plans for comprehensive programs.

How can strategic leadership be improved? There are ten basic guidelines that are suggested for strategic planning and implementation. The guidelines reflect recent writings about leadership and strategic planning generally as they apply to adult and continuing education (Bennis and Nanus, 1985; Bown, 1985; Bryson, 1988; Fiedler and Chemers, 1984; Hall and Stock, 1985; Jarvis, 1987; Simerly and Associates, 1987, 1989). Each guideline emphasizes contextual analysis and comparative perspectives from various program areas and national settings. Examples are drawn from all of the preceding chapters to illustrate societal influences and implications for leadership to strengthen adult education agencies.

Guidelines for Planning and Implementation

Effective leaders for adult education use two fundamental procedures that are essential when they apply each of the following ten guidelines. One is planning to obtain stakeholder commitment to a shared vision of desirable future directions. The second is implementation to obtain contributions by stakeholder to the achievement of agency goals. The interpersonal relationships upon which such goal achievement depend are fragile and require ongoing attention. Adult education leadership has been likened to building sand castles on an ocean beach, where initial placement and frequent rebuilding are necessary to prevent the fragile structures from becoming victims to wind and wave. Established stable organizations (such as private enterprises, government departments, and preparatory education schools and colleges) generally have their own facilities, full-time staff, and other resources. By contrast, most adult education agencies lack full-time staff, a reliable pool of participants, and policy and financial support. As a result, many adult education leaders hold their agencies together by repeated temporary agreements that they negotiate for staff, facilities, financial support, volunteers, and collaboration. This situation makes the following guidelines essential for agency survival, let alone innovation. However, they should be adapted to the specific situation in which each agency functions. Although some guidelines necessarily precede others, they are not discrete steps, but interrelated components. Thus, the planning and implementation process is a spiral of successive approximations, with preliminary and parallel decisions about various guidelines followed by further refinements and adjustments as planning and implementation proceeds.

1. *Form a strategic planning committee that reflects major*

agency stakeholders. The effectiveness of this planning committee depends greatly on the members who are selected and the administrative support that is provided. The range of committee members should include people familiar with the strengths and weaknesses of internal agency functioning. These internal members usually predominate, especially those from such stakeholder categories as administrators, instructors, participants, and policy board members. Committee membership should also include people familiar with external opportunities and threats related to desirable future directions. These external categories may include parent organization leaders, funders, public policy makers, and cosponsors. The scope of membership should be wide enough to engender sufficient support but not so broad that the committee becomes unwieldy or diffuse. The individual members should have sufficient stature to have the confidence of their constituency and the flexibility to make plans; they should not just serve as messengers for the real decision makers in their constituencies (a situation that can create inertia and frustration). For example, a public health promotion coordinating committee might include adult educators from health associations and educational institutions, along with members from health professions, government, the media, and retailers. Winning and maintaining the support of stakeholders depend on mutually beneficial exchanges in which their contributions to agency planning and implementation are balanced by benefits that they value (Beder, 1986; HR&H Marketing Research, 1987; Kotler and Fox, 1985). Desirable results of such mutually beneficial exchanges can be seen when tutors, participants, board members, and other people related to a local adult literacy agency involve themselves in strategic planning and then take action to implement the plans by strengthening agency programs and external cooperation.

Assembling and working with a strategic planning committee can be greatly facilitated by a person, acting in the role of a process champion, who coordinates selection of committee members and works with them to arrange staff support and encourage consensus building and implementation. The example of the midwestern community college initiative to establish an educational maintenance organization based on sharing of educational technology, as well as the more successful similar effort in the Southeast, reflects the crucial contribution of an enthusiastic process champion who generates support and persistence.

It tends to be relatively easy to obtain internal cooperation and to assess local influences. People associated with an agency usually have commitment to and familiarity with agency functioning. Of course, their cooperation depends in part on the specific goals toward which strategic planning is aimed. In the CIES project for county board members in Illinois, there was great agreement among those involved. But there can also be resistance by some stakeholders (such as the retailers in the Heartbeat Wales health education project) and even conflict (as with some landowners and government officials related to the Highlander Land Ownership Task Force project). Stakeholders from other parts of the parent organization can be specially influential and important to include on a strategic planning committee so as to increase internal support for the adult education agency. Their influence can be positive (as with central administration support for a continuing higher education program) or negative (as with resistance from prison security for a correctional education program). The support of stakeholders depends in part on how much they value the benefits of the adult education function.

It is usually more difficult to obtain support from external stakeholders and to assess distant influences such as economic conditions, public policies, and population shifts. The example of statewide strategic planning for public adult education in California illustrates its usefulness for strengthening local programs. Examples from India and Saudi Arabia demonstrate the difficulty of harnessing positive societal influences and overcoming negative ones—in comparison with greater external support in the examples from Ireland, Australia, China, and Canada.

Adult education leaders can use broad representation on a strategic planning committee to strengthen agency linkage with both resource and client systems (Havelock, 1969; Liveris and Horvath, 1984). For example, this occurs when the plans are designed to involve medical school faculty members in conducting continuing education programs in community hospitals for physicians likely to refer patients to teaching hospitals (referrals are important for professors' teaching and research). In distance education, collaboration with other adult education providers depends on familiarity with their programs, as illustrated by Edison College's use in New Jersey of materials developed by a similar agency in New York State and by a Netherlands open university's utilization of procedures developed by the U.K. Open University. Among the many other examples of collaborative planning and implementation are cooperation among prisons, associations, and educational institutions in correctional education and extensive interorganizational collaboration that has characterized the Cooperative Extension Service over the years.

Representation of adult learners on a strategic planning committee is important for several reasons. The main reason is that they are the primary program beneficiaries, and program success requires their participation; their representation on the committee can thus serve as part of the needs assessment and can increase program relevance. Direct investment in strategic planning can help clarify pertinent client characteristics, such as enabling younger planners to understand the actual diversity of older adults that elder education programs can address. In general, client involvement in strategic planning of programs for less-advantaged adults can enable more well-educated planners to understand their differing cultural values. For example, both poor and rich farmers should participate in the planning of rural adult education, and minority group members should take part in planning basic education programs for such groups as Hmong refugees. Deliberate inclusion of less-advantaged adults in strategic planning was seen in examples from Sweden, Czechoslovakia, Australia, and Canada. Making members of participants' reference groups part of planning and implementation is especially important where solidarity is a cultural value or a program outcome. Their contribution is illustrated in staff development activities aimed at organizational development in examples from Japan, Sweden, and the United States.

This rationale for representation on a strategic planning committee of all those concerned indicates why it is important to include external stakeholders and suggests the contributions that they can make (Mitroff, 1983). In practice, committee membership should reflect emerging issues and circumstances. Especially for planning comprehensive programs that need synergistic leadership, communication and cooperation among external stakeholders are essential.

2. *Clarify the agency mission so as to inspire stakeholder cooperation and guide planning priorities.* Leaders should provide the planning committee with existing materials regarding the agency mission and guidance for an early review of those materials (Keller, 1983). These can orient the committee members to the focus for planning and help them decide how much creation or revision of a statement is necessary. As previously stated, a major purpose of planning is to achieve a shared vision of desirable future directions for the agency. The planning process should help committee members agree on intended outcomes that they value. This consensus should be congruent with a brief mission statement. Such an agency mission statement has many valuable uses for leadership: identifying major stakeholders, emphasizing benefits they value, attracting staff and participants, distinguishing agency niche, setting specific agency goals and priorities, and encouraging contributions to goal achievement.

For a mission statement to be useful, it should reflect actual agency values and external mandates, not just serve superficial public relations purposes. For example, in an enterprise training and education department, a fundamental policy decision that greatly affects the staff development function is how much staff mobility is desirable. A policy in support of mobility would lead to a training department mission that would include cross training for jobs in other departments and supervisory training in support of staff development, lateral transfers, and promotion from within. The breadth of mission of adult basic education agencies ranges from a narrow focus on teaching reading and numeracy to a broad commitment to functional participatory, family, or workplace basic skills that enable undereducated adults to progress occupationally and in further education. For example, the *Jump Start* literacy report emphasized economic benefits, in contrast to the adult literacy effort in India, where the mandate was so broad that various people assumed that there were quite different missions. Examples of cultural education programs from Sweden, Italy, Ireland, and the United States show a focus on critical reflection, which can be controversial in some settings. The study of undergraduate programs for adults by the University of Maryland illustrates the use of findings to refine provider mission and to broaden the base of support. The strategic planning process should include a review of both explicit mandates and implicit values. This review can reaffirm a satisfactory mission statement or perhaps lead to revision or creation of one.

In fact, few adult education agencies have satisfactory mission statements and performance indicators to use in making planning and evaluation judgments about agency directions and program quality. Most agencies serve various categories of participants with a variety of educational programs. Separate adult education courses and workshops typically have objectives that respond to the educational needs and expectations of adult learners. Market-driven programs take this approach to attract participants, and subsidized programs do this to attract external support. Given such varied program goals and the absence of strategic planning, attention to agencywide mission is unlikely unless leaders appreciate the importance of a shared agency mission.

Provider agencies with focused missions tend to serve a specific clientele. For example, in Britain, education for elders is for older members who serve as learners, instructors, planners, coordinators, and policy makers; the mission is therefore to be responsive to the membership. In the United States, the mission of enterprise staff development is mainly to improve organizational functioning and productivity, and it is evaluated in terms of production, quality, sales, customer satisfaction, numbers of accidents, absenteeism, turnover, and grievances. The main criteria for judging mission accomplishment may vary among countries, such as the passing of an exam in China, career advancement in Germany, enterprise productivity in Japan, and in Sweden stimulation of innovation and creation of a learning enterprise. In continuing higher education divisions that only provide credit and degree courses in the evenings and at remote locations for the convenience of part-time students, the mission may be clearly to extend standard course offerings to additional learners; agency performance indicators may be enrollments, income, achievement, and alumni support.

Of course, many adult education agencies serve a wide range

of learners with many educational programs. This situation leads to a diffuse agency mission and lack of specific agency performance indicators, factors that make strategic planning more difficult. However, under these circumstances, it is even more important to generate energy and cooperation among major stakeholders—especially for comprehensive programs such as the Council of Europe projects to promote European solidarity and the Heartbeat Wales example of community-based health promotion.

Strategic planning should involve major stakeholders in an organized sequence of ongoing decisions to strengthen future agency functioning and service. A strategic planning committee can help establish a mission, which can then be implemented and further refined as agency staff members define specific policies with the help of major stakeholders. For example, the British Columbia correctional education effort included an alternative educational community approach negotiated between the educational institution that conducted the program and the provincial department of corrections that approved a mission statement (which the security staff of a local prison accepted). This process might entail accommodation of some conflicting values.

Another benefit of a clear mission statement is to help agency leaders address external influences. For example, if the mission of rural adult education is to contribute to integrated rural development, not just to transmit technical information to farmers, extension leaders must also include educational activities for people in other organizations. These offerings might be related to credit from financial institutions, availability of transportation facilities at harvest time, provision of inputs such as equipment and fertilizers, health conditions, opportunities for nonfarm employment, assistance from local cooperatives, and price-level policies for agricultural products. Representatives from each of these areas might engage in educational activities concerned with an aspect of comprehensive rural development.

A mission statement can also provide a rationale for subsequent action decisions to encourage innovation and agency survival. For example, distance education planning often makes use of new developments in educational technology (such as educational telephone, instructional television, and computer systems) that have great potential for reaching adult learners. However, most of the attention and resources are devoted to the technology, with inadequate attention to learner responsiveness and development of educational materials to use with the technology. A mission statement should enable stakeholders to recognize past mistakes and contribute to more balanced planning and development.

While enthusiastically promoting solidarity and cooperation among stakeholders, it is important for planning to avoid overcontrol, which discourages creativity and initiative. Such overemphasis on planning can be minimized in several ways. One is to restrict time devoted to it, usually to less than 10 percent. Another is to emphasize planning related to organizational values, culture, and policies, within which there is decentralization and delegation that give staff members and volunteer leaders latitude to use their creativity to develop programs and explore consistency with agency mission and policies. A third way is to encourage and reward entrepreneurial efforts that improve the quality and impact of current programs as well as pioneer new agency directions. Synergistic leaders can guide the planning process, including attention to mission, so that it contributes to agency vitality and broad involvement in successful comprehensive programs.

3. *Use contextual analysis to scan opportunities and threats in the external environment of the agency.* A major purpose of strategic planning is to enable an agency to be future oriented and to recognize emerging trends likely to affect its responsiveness, impact, and survival (Ascher, 1978; Brockett, 1988; Theobald, 1987). Contextual analysis includes environmental scanning, futures forecasting, and other procedures to understand current and emerging societal influences, many of which are implicit and require some analysis to identify and specify their implications for agency planning. Most adult education agencies are service oriented and responsive to adult learners in their particular area. For separate courses and workshops, needs assessment procedures specify learner characteristics and gaps between current and desired proficiencies that educational activities should address. For agency-level planning, especially for comprehensive and collaborative programs, contextual analysis is a parallel planning activity that helps specify societal influences along with resources and expectations of major

stakeholders. Needs assessment can identify what potential participants would like to learn and their request for financial assistance. Contextual analysis can reveal educational opportunities available from other providers and sources of diversified financial support for the agency. Strategic planning should use findings from past contextual analysis and improve the analysis process if it is inadequate.

Part of contextual analysis is the assessment of circumstances and emerging trends related to local contingencies, including characteristics of the provider agency, other providers, and the service area. Strategic planning should review findings from analysis of these local contingencies and make arrangements to supplement programs as required. Information about the provider agency and its parent organization should detail organizational purposes and resources and especially priorities related to agency mission. Information about other providers should include their current purposes and programs, as well as likely trends that can be used to project competition, collaboration, and complementarity. Information about the service area should evaluate the potential participants (market segments), availability of potential staff members and volunteers, access to educational resources, and policy support (such as legislation, tuition reimbursement by enterprises, and other forms of traditional assistance).

Strategic planning can provide perspective on these facts. For example, leaders of a continuing higher education agency can obtain information from their counterparts in similar institutions regarding such contingencies as the extent to which their parent organization requires full-cost recovery from participant fees or the degree to which participant fees are reimbursed by their enterprises. The conclusions can be used to recommend policy changes. Similarly, generalizations about the extent to which the vitality of university continuing professional education depends on strong linkage with both faculty members and members of the profession can be used to strengthen agency functioning.

Some findings from contextual analysis are related to both local contingencies and more remote societal influences. For instance, educational activities directed at quality improvement, such as quality circles, are greatly affected by such enterprise characteristics as financial condition, occupational profile, management style, type of product or service, and top-management support. In addition, studies of quality circles in Japan, Sweden, and the United States show that national characteristics are also influential. Rural adult education is affected by local contingencies that affect production (such as growing conditions, health problems, and social services), along with more remote influences, such as national policies, economic conditions, and markets for agricultural products. Because agency leaders are typically aware of indicators of local contingencies, contextual analysis usually refines and provides perspective on knowledge of the service area that had already been acquired informally.

Agencies are actually affected by more remote political, social, and economic influences than leaders tend to assume. Comparative perspectives can help agency leaders focus contextual analysis on understanding societal influences that are least well understood but most important for strategic planning (Botkin, Elmandjra, and Malitza, 1979; Crouch and Chamala, 1981; Hoghielm and Rubenson, 1980; Janne, Dominice, and James, 1980; Titmus, 1981; Vio Grossi, Hall, Stromquist, and Duke, 1986). For example, planners of elder education recognize demographic trends that result in larger numbers of older adults with satisfactory levels of income, health, and formal education. However, the success of educational programs for older adults also reflects life-cycle interests in cultural programs combined with technological contributions such as transportation and media. Planning of adult basic education programs in various countries reflects various societal influences that might be addressed in strategic planning. National steel industry trends had an impact on the plant in Wierton, West Virginia. Employee ownership heightened interest in learning, and government funding for literacy, together with volunteer activity, contributed to the ability of the library to provide literacy tutoring. In countries with many immigrants, government immigration policies affect educational programs for them. Strategic planning can use a comparative perspective based on familiarity with agencies in other areas of practice and national settings to identify relevant but remote influences.

Contextual analysis provides an early warning of emerging trends and issues. The societal context of many agencies is changing, turbulent, politicized, pluralistic, and ambiguous. Powerful economic conditions such as poverty, recession, inflation, agricultural markets, and trade balances affect agencies several ways. Some economic influences are direct (such as financial support for the agency), and some are indirect (such as the family budgets of potential participants and organizational budgets of enterprises and foundations). Strategic planning can identify other remote influences and implications for agency decisions (Ascher, 1978; Brockett, 1988; Coombs, 1985). For example, new knowledge and emerging trends in practice influence the offerings of continuing professional education providers. Distance education is affected by sparse population and expensive technology. Effective contextual analysis procedures can shorten the response time to allow agencies to offer timely and important programs.

Given these many influences, contextual analysis helps leaders identify the most salient ones. In India, a shifting government subsidy and ambiguous national program goals that made progress difficult illustrates the importance of agreement on at least a few indicators of agency performance to use for planning and accountability. In many educational programs for community problem solving, contextual analysis is so central that it tends to be implicit. In the Rockford example (which used videotape for communication about neighborhood problems), in the Highlander example on land ownership, and in many of the popular education examples from Latin America, one educational function was to mobilize exploited subcultures through increased awareness of structural influences on their condition. In these cases, participants were part of contextual analysis. It is less clear if and how adult education is used to help bring about change in other segments of society that are related to the community problem.

There are many specific contextual analysis procedures that agency leaders can employ to assess environmental opportunities and threats, many of which are not obvious and require some analysis to identify. Environmental scanning as used for continuing education at the University of Georgia provides a widely applicable example. Environmental scanning can be conducted by a policy board with subcommittee, staff, or consultant assistance. As described in Chapter Two, the following are elements of effective environmental scanning (Simerly and Associates, 1989, chap. 31): (1)

Encourage participation in occasional scanning activity by staff and volunteers throughout the agency; (2) arrange for competent coordination and staff understanding of scanning procedures; (3) select a practical taxonomy to collect and classify information about trends (social, technological, economic, and political); (4) have scanners agree to scan designated materials periodically for information about trends; (5) train scanners to prepare summaries; (6) have procedures to process, retrieve, and use summary information; (7) periodically review and evaluate the summaries to identify emerging trends, themes, and implications; (8) document actions taken as result of the total scanning process; (9) provide prompt and systematic feedback to the agency; and (10) evaluate and modify the process.

The extent of environmental scanning and other aspects of contextual analysis that an agency uses is tied to its size and resources, as well as the availability of such information from other sources. One advantage of collaborative activities (including comprehensive programs) is that they can enrich the contextual information available to agency leaders. Participation in associations with adult education practitioners from other areas of practice can also broaden comparative perspectives.

4. *Review internal agency culture and functioning as a basis for planning and change.* Strategic planning emphasizes external influences and future directions, but use of the conclusions largely depends on decisions and actions by people associated with the adult education agency and their working relationships. Therefore, agency leaders should review the way in which the agency functions. The understanding that results from this review has several uses. One is to assess the resources and commitment available for planning. A second is to identify likely resistance and openness to change. A third is to prepare for implementation of strategic planning conclusions that require modification of agency functioning. This internal review can be straightforward when leaders are familiar with the agency, it is small, and there has been recent experience with planned change. An internal review may be more complicated and difficult (and even more important) when leaders are new to an agency, when it is large and complex, and when lack of recent

organizational change makes it difficult to predict how members will react to the strategic planning process.

A holistic view of the agency as a social system aids both understanding of agency functioning and preparation for strategic planning and implementation. Such a systemic approach includes analysis of subsystems within the agency. Larger agencies are organized into parts or departments that fit its functions, tradition, and parent organization. For example, a community college continuing education division may be organized by general and vocational education areas of instruction. An enterprise training department may be structured according to roles performed by categories of staff members, such as sales, supervision, and data processing. A state university continuing education division may be organized in several ways—off-campus credit courses, noncredit workshops in a large conference center, and distance education based on correspondence study, broadcast television, and an educational telephone network.

Each subsystem, as well as the total agency, has a distinctive organizational culture that reflects shared values and typical ways of interacting. This organizational culture affects and is affected by participation in strategic planning. As open systems, agencies and their subsystems differ in their relations with their external environment of the service area (Katz and Kahn, 1978). Leaders of correctional education deal with such systemic relations as they work with inmates in relation to the prison culture, to the society to which the inmates expect to return after release, and to an alternative democratic culture that some correctional educators seek to create as a vehicle for rehabilitation.

Part of strategic planning is assessment of agency strengths and weaknesses. The process and conclusions of such assessment assist both planning and internal improvement, somewhat independent of societal influences and future directions. Self-study and staff development are some of the procedures for internal assessment. Sometimes analysis of agency culture and functioning is implicit—for instance, in the staff development department of an enterprise in which organizational development activities are emphasized or in a small elder education program in which members serve as learners, instructors, and coordinators (a situation that may reduce the distinction between internal and external relations).

As an open system functioning in its context, an adult education agency is influenced by relations with its parent organization, other providers in the service area, and more remote societal influences. Strategic planning can help leaders and other agency stakeholders understand agency strengths and weaknesses as they are affected by contextual influences, an appreciation that has implications for strengthening agency functioning. Sometimes close relations between external influences and internal functioning reflect agency mission. An example is an enterprise staff development department that emphasizes total quality improvement; all enterprise members are encouraged to improve relations with their "suppliers" and "customers" so that quality is improved. Another example is a distance education agency in which assessment and planning are ongoing activities related to proposals for new educational technology.

Agency leaders can include some external stakeholders in self-study teams or staff development activities as they review agency culture and functioning. Guidelines for such a review can give attention to external influences and implications for change. Broad agency participation in an internal review can also increase understanding and commitment related to the total process of strategic planning.

5. *Frame high-priority strategic agency goals.* Stakeholder agreement on goals is one of the two major purposes of leadership and strategic planning. (The other major purpose is commitment to implementation of goals to achieve progress, which is discussed in guideline six.) Stakeholders can help agency leaders identify strategic issues that are important to the agency's future. Attention to such issues can confirm agency goals that will continue to be important, as well as suggest objectives to be added or modified. An essential function of strategic planning is to use conclusions about internal agency strengths and weaknesses along with external opportunities and threats to some agency goals to which stakeholders are committed. These goals should reflect the values of the agency and the stakeholders.

To be useful for planning and implementation, the goals

should also be made operational to serve as criteria for decision making and evaluation. Such criteria take the form of performance standards, quality indicators, policies, and decision rules. The appropriate criteria vary with agency goals. For example, in enterprises where organizational policies and supervisory support influence staff development, criteria for individually oriented training might emphasize increased proficiency and improved performance. In a staff development agency focused on organizational development, criteria might stress improved communication, teamwork, conflict resolution, and enterprise productivity. In general, agency goal-setting procedures include values clarification and consensus building. Group members can list goals, discuss them for clarification, and then select those that have the most support. Formalizing the goal-setting process is especially helpful when expectations are ambiguous or conflicting.

As issues are analyzed and objectives are framed, it is important to consider both internal and external aspects. Internal aspects include agency resources and capability. External aspects include situational opportunities and threats. The process of goal setting should connect external opportunities with internal capabilities. Within the United States, few adult basic education agencies aimed at emancipation of undereducated adults and reform of the system contrast with the great majority of agencies that attempt to help participants progress within the existing system. Programs for minorities need goals that attract both participants and subsidy funds. Health education for individual patients entails more limited goals and stakeholders than a community-based preventive health campaign. Strategic planning should involve a range of stakeholders in framing high-priority goals that relate to both agency capability and major societal influences. For comprehensive programs with multiple providers, this can be one of the crucial aspects of planning and tests of synergistic leadership.

The objectives should be large enough to be inspiring but small enough to be feasible. The national adult basic education program in the Indian state of Tamil Nadu illustrates an instance where the ambiguity of goals allowed various stakeholders to interpret them quite differently. The general or specific nature of agency goals should depend on the program area and local contingencies.

They should also allow sufficient latitude for stakeholder initiative and creativity (Dave, Perera, and Ouane, 1985a; Faure and Associates, 1972). For example, collaborators in a distance education consortium that uses expensive educational technology may welcome detailed goals, policies, and performance criteria as a basis for cooperation and planning. By contrast, adult education for community problem solving in the United States and in other countries is often flawed by basic conflicts between poor participants and the elite policy makers who create general educational goals. Strategic planning should contribute to stakeholder agreement on high-priority goals; this is crucial for the other major aspect of leadership: selection of an action plan that stakeholders will help implement.

      6. *Select and implement an action plan to address the main issues and to encourage progress toward goal achievement.* The first four planning guidelines contribute to this and the preceding guidelines, whereas the final four cover ways to facilitate the planning process as it occurs. Agency leaders should help members of a strategic planning committee and other key stakeholders develop an action plan to move toward achievement of high-priority goals.

      As early as possible in the planning process, a strategic planning committee should make a broad policy decision about the general approach to implementation that is most likely to succeed under the circumstances. A comparative perspective can enable leaders to recognize alternative approaches from which to select. Effective leaders also understand local contingencies that favor one approach over another, the importance of coordination and communication for cooperative implementation, and development of an action plan that fits the major objectives. Attention to the details of an action plan is especially important for comprehensive programs that entail multiple providers and stakeholders who are learning to work together as well as implement planning goals. Health education provides an illustration of alternative approaches from which a planning committee might select. When combining use of mass media and human interaction, a health promotion campaign might select from many possibilities: orientation materials for leaders of decentralized self-help groups; patient education self-study materials and counseling by health professionals; orientation and support materials for local paraprofessional health aides; and a comprehensive program aimed at the creation of general awareness through the mass media, at patient education and counseling by health professionals, and at coordinated adult education activities for policy makers and business leaders. Another example of contrasting general approaches is adult education for community problem solving: one approach emphasizes development of human resources with little direct attention to structural change, one concentrates on gradual structural reform as a goal of educational activities, and one stresses education for conflict and radical structural change.

Within a chosen general approach, a strategic planning committee can use many procedures to gain commitment, delegate, and coordinate specific contributions to implementation of the action plan. Especially in comprehensive programs with multiple stakeholders who may have limited experience working together, leaders may give special attention to their commitment, development, and recognition. Leader coordination of the action plan includes making sure that together the cooperating stakeholders make all of the contributions necessary for implementation of the action plan. Stakeholders should also be committed to assist as required and encouraged to follow through until their part is completed. Staff development activities can enhance the ability of those involved to contribute, and recognition (from a thank-you and newsletter mention to a banquet and a job promotion) can encourage stakeholders to persist in the strategic planning process. Sometimes encouragement of these contributions is straightforward. In best practice, when there is broad agreement on goals and standards of achievement, the planning and implementation process can be very open and the benefits self-evident. The examples from the Netherlands of technology transfer and continuing education of engineers illustrate how progress can provide sufficient reward for major stakeholders.

This combination of stakeholder commitment, development, and recognition can be seen in staff development for total quality improvement in an enterprise. The essence of most quality improvement efforts is that all members of an enterprise take part in a prescribed process to make improvements in all aspects of the workplace. All members are expected to both perform their jobs and learn how to do them better. Work teams engage in projects to improve quality, and in the process team members require proficiencies, resources, and support. One contribution of an enterprise staff development agency is to provide workshops for staff members who serve as coaches for improvement of project team members. After an initial overview for all staff members about the quality improvement process, these workshops combine ideas from theory and practice to help coaches understand quality improvement goals and procedures along with practice, joining such ideas with insights they already have. The workshops offer simulated activities similar to ones coaches will use with team members. The workshops occur just after teams are formed (to benefit from members' heightened readiness to learn), give attention to motivation, are part of an action learning process, and focus on essential proficiencies of coaches—team building, conducting meetings, and using data for decision making related to quality. In this example, the improvement effort combines staff development with enhancement of quality. Thus, implementation of the strategic planning action plan for the staff development aspects should stress team member commitment to learning and change, workshop and coaching assistance to help team members learn and change, and recognition closely connected with the satisfaction and rewards of their work.

The implementation of an action plan can be very difficult, especially if the strategic planning goals are ambitious, the number of stakeholders is large, and the history of working together is limited. Under such circumstances, strategic planning leaders can use procedures such as pilot testing to adapt the implementation process as it proceeds. For example, in a distance education program with an initial overemphasis on technology, the implementation of the action plan might be adjusted to give more attention than anticipated to additional aspects of a successful program. Such aspects might be use of findings from evaluative feedback from learners to increase program responsiveness and learner appreciation of benefits. Another aspect might be increased attention to development of materials to use with the technology. Additional factors to emphasize might include improved interpersonal relations, increased staff expertise, broader program development procedures, and addition of local study groups. Trying such modifications on a limited scale as the action plan is implemented can contribute greatly to the success of the implementation of strategic planning. The following four guidelines amplify these ideas for the entire strategic planning process.

7. *Guide staff and volunteer development for people engaged in the total strategic planning process.* Effective agency leaders of strategic planning and implementation improve the expertise and promote the teamwork of people associated with the process. Especially for new, comprehensive programs, this focus on staff and volunteer development is important at all stages of strategic planning. Most of this assistance is nonformal and is part of discussing, orienting, planning, explaining, doing, and evaluating. The content covered by staff and volunteer development should be selected to increase the proficiencies and commitment of planning team members to explore policy directions and to prepare and implement plans. An additional purpose of this staff development is to promote contributions to planned organizational change to achieve planning goals by overcoming inertia. An example of individual and team growth in adult education for cultural minorities is program improvement and projects that include both paid staff and volunteers in activities that enhance their personal careers; this advancement comes as a benefit of working together to strengthen educational methods and materials.

Specific staff and volunteer development activities can be used to improve specific aspects of strategic planning and implementation. The following list contains some examples.

- Increased stakeholder agreement on a new mission for an adult basic education agency can be achieved by using the nominal group technique with representative stakeholders to identify high-priority goals.
- Greater understanding of the organizational culture of the Cooperative Extension Service can be obtained by new staff and volunteers who participate in a self-study of county office policies and procedures.
- Increased expertise in proposal preparation can be gained by distance education staff members as they study guidelines and

readings on increasing external support in preparing a grant application for better facilities and staff activities related to educational technology.

- Broader understanding of resource acquisition by an elder education agency policy committee can be created by a joint meeting with policy board members from successful agencies regarding ways to acquire money, facilities, and volunteer time.
- Effective action on behalf of continuing professional education can be better understood by a subcommittee related to strategic planning that explores working relationships between staff and volunteers.

Conducting nonformal staff and volunteer development activities relating to strategic planning can be improved if leaders understand and use pertinent concepts and procedures from the professional literature on helping adults learn (Brookfield, 1988; Cervero, 1988; Daloz, 1986; Knox, 1986, 1987c). Deliberate attention to this guideline is especially important for new and large-scale adult education programs with multiple stakeholders who have not all worked together before. For this scope of effort, handbooks are especially valuable (Bown and Okedara, 1981; Bown and Tomori, 1979; Houle, 1992; Merriam and Cunningham, 1989; Peters and Jarvis, 1991; Titmus, 1989).

8. *Evaluate strategic planning activities and use the conclusions to strengthen the process.* Strategic planning promotes change, and that usually generates unanticipated resistance. Various evaluation activities can monitor the planning and implementation process, test the feasibility of untried aspects, and reinforce progress. Formalizing the evaluation process so that judgments are made explicit and available for decisions about strategic planning is especially important when comprehensive programs are new and large.

One use of evaluation is to test parts of the strategic planning process with which members of the planning committee have little experience. Pilot testing helps leaders to identify benefits to be emphasized, as well as costs to be minimized and activities to modify. The example of the women's museum in Germany illustrates use of pilot testing of educational materials in cultural education programs.

Another use of evaluation is to monitor the planning and implementation process. Examples of such ongoing evaluation in adult basic education occurred in an Australian workplace literacy program and in an Irish community literacy program in which government support included ongoing assessment. Each example shows planning and implementation of educational materials to decide on the desirability of specific versus general content coverage. Tracking results can help planners analyze mistakes, identify shortfalls, resolve conflicts, and spot potential modifications to increase cooperation and progress. For example, monitoring adult education programs for immigrants might provide early warning of a major change in the backgrounds of participants (such as a drop in English language facility and familiarity with U.S. culture) or in opportunities for job placement for people who complete the program (such as a decrease in some types of job openings).

Constant evaluation of planning and implementation can have additional benefits. Because record keeping is standard for much of distance education, evaluation findings can be added to the data base for decision making, especially for future planning activities. Evaluative feedback can also be used to recognize progress and provide positive reinforcement for people engaged in strategic planning and implementation. Use of such feedback can be especially valuable in staff development activities in which distinctions between work activities, educational plans, educational activities, and organizational change can become indistinct.

Evaluation of the impact on performance of program implementation provides information to plan future programs that make a difference. For example, a recent review of the effectiveness of continuing medical education (CME) programs concluded that comprehensive approaches were far more effective in improving physician performance and health status of patients than those that only increased knowledge, only provided practice with new procedures, or only reinforced recommended procedures. The intensity and impact of comprehensive approaches resulted from varied CME methods combined with related educational activities for other health professionals and for patients (Davis, Thomson, Oxman, and Haynes, 1992).

Some of the data for judgments about strategic planning may be available from program evaluation, so these two activities should be coordinated to avoid needless duplication. Especially for comprehensive programs in which multiple providers collaborate, evaluation activities should be selective to minimize the burden on the program and to assess those aspects of planning and implementation that most warrant evaluation.

9. *Recognize the contributions of the people engaged in strategic planning.* The success of strategic planning depends on stakeholder commitment to the process. Without such commitment, plans are neither made nor implemented. Fortunately, most adult education stakeholders are service oriented and committed to the educational goals, qualities that provide a starting point for their assistance in implementation. However, these same people juggle competing time demands, and their continued contributions to strategic planning may depend on additional incentives and recognition.

Sometimes people whose cooperation is important to program success resist helping with strategic planning and implementation. For example, rural adult education may call for assistance from people who are initially reluctant to become involved in those projects. An early stage of strategic planning might call for the release of human interest stories of people who had discovered that it was in their best interest to start cooperatives for low-resource farmers, begin nonfarm rural enterprises, or expand rural social services. Recognition of contributions by and focus on benefits to stakeholders can both encourage their continued assistance and help broaden the base of those engaged in future planning. Another example from correctional education would be inviting security staff to participate in educational activities that they value as a personal benefit and as a way of winning their support for an innovative educational program for inmates.

Especially for comprehensive programs that bring together stakeholders from different program areas, the image of the program may be a crucial influence on cooperation. Recognition of contributions by people engaged in strategic planning can both reward them for their contributions and add to the program image that encourages assistance by others. Sincere recognition for important contributions can also enhance morale. This recognition can take many forms. For example, distance education planners might receive special assistance, free materials, and public recognition. Members of a staff development strategic planning committee might participate in an attractive retreat to review progress and next steps. The cultural education example of the National Issues Forum conference at the presidential library illustrates how inspiring that occasion was for the retired executive who became the volunteer coordinator in Grand Rapids. Sometimes appreciation by valued peers and the opportunity to meet interesting new colleagues in a comprehensive program can be a powerful form of recognition. The time and effort required to recognize valuable contributions by people engaged in strategic planning are surely less than that to recruit and orient their replacements if they feel unappreciated and withdraw.

10. *Provide transformative leadership for the entire future-oriented strategic planning and implementation process.* The foregoing guidelines suggest ways in which leaders can bring a future-oriented and comparative perspective to an adult education agency. Strategic planning and implementation elaborate two essential aspects of leadership: gaining the commitment of stakeholders to shared goals and their contributions to goal achievement. This tenth guideline is the most comprehensive. It entails obtaining and maintaining firm agreement on a shared vision of the provider's future at each stage of the process of strategic planning and implementation. Such leadership is transformative because all stakeholders are encouraged to contribute, and it is synergistic because this interaction can redouble the energy generated (Bogard, 1992; Boshier, 1985; Buttedahl, 1985; Fox and Mutangira, 1985; Knox, 1982a; Shorey, 1983; Simerly and Associates, 1987).

Transformative leadership is illustrated by a multicultural approach to adult education for minorities that emphasizes members of both dominant and subcultures learning from each other. Transformative leadership is also seen in community preventive health campaigns that include various stakeholders in parts of a comprehensive approach designed to have a major and cumulative impact on practice. Leaders of such programs recognize the freedom and latitude that are necessary to encourage local commitment and creativity.

Future-oriented strategic planning broadens the leadership focus beyond the usual preoccupation with internal agency strengths and weaknesses. Transformative leadership also includes attention to major societal influences that assist or impede agency functioning. Helping key people understand past assumptions and address emerging issues also characterizes transformative leadership (Harman, 1988; Jarvis, 1991; Senge, 1990; Stubblefield, 1988). In adult education for rural development and community problem solving, issues-oriented programming (such as youth at risk by the Cooperative Extension Service) shows such attention to emerging issues. In distance education, combining the potential of new educational technology with familiarity with related educational programs and a commitment to the human touch reflects several major contemporary trends.

The foregoing guidelines constitute components for strategic planning and implementation. The tenth one on transformative leadership should permeate the entire process. Transformative leadership is synergistic and allows multiple stakeholders to cooperate in comprehensive programs that make a difference. As educational programs for adults emerge from the margin and become part of a societal imperative in an era characterized by transformation, it is essential that agency leadership be strengthened. Creative instructors who are responsive to individual learners are necessary but not sufficient. Creative *leaders,* whose comparative perspective enables them to understand and harness major societal influences to strengthen comprehensive programs, are also necessary.

Resources

A. World Perspective Case Descriptions

B. List of Case Coordinators

C. Major Societal Influences on Educational Programs and Providers

A

World Perspective
Case Descriptions

This resource contains a listing of all 175 case descriptions from thirty-two countries prepared or assembled for the collaborative project World Perspective on Adult Education between 1986 and 1989. All case descriptions have been analyzed in the preparation of this book. Many have served as the basis for brief summary examples (and these are cited by author's last name). When they were published by the ERIC system, all of the case descriptions from each country were assigned an ED number and may be ordered on microfiche or paper copy. Each set of cases for a country contains a common overview section for the entire project. Thus, libraries with copies of the ERIC microfiche collection have available the packets of microfiche for all of the countries included in the World Perspective Project. For information about cost and arrangements to purchase case descriptions for any or all of the countries, contact the ERIC Clearinghouse on Adult, Career, and Vocational Education, 1960 Kenny Road, Columbus, Ohio 43210-1090, USA. Attention: World Perspective Case Descriptions of Educational Programs for Adults. In response, a listing and order form will be sent. Sets of cases have been published for Australia (Clark and Rooth, 1988), Finland (Tuomisto, 1987), and Germany (Reischmann, 1988). Carey has circulated the set of cases from Ireland.

Abel, W. *Residential Adult Education in Canada*, Canada. (ED 311 162)

Abrahamsson, K. *Corporate Classrooms,* Sweden. (ED 311 184)

Aksjoberg, T. *NKS School of Management (Correspondence School),* Norway. (ED 311 180)

Al Rasheed, M. A., and Al Sunbul, A. *Illiteracy Eradication and Adult Education,* Saudi Arabia. (ED 311 183)

Ansere, J. K. *Training Teachers by Distance Education Methods,* Ghana. (ED 311 168)

Anyanwu, C. N. *Guinea Worm Eradication Program: Community Education in Nigeria,* Nigeria. (ED 311 179)

Arvidsson, L. *Popular Education in Sweden,* Sweden. (ED 311 184)

Balde, M. (a). *Occupational Retraining in Office Skills,* Netherlands. (ED 311 178)

Balde, M. (b). *Open School,* Netherlands. (ED 311 178)

Benham, O., and Vickers, S. *School for Seniors,* Australia. (ED 311 160)

Berg-Ran, A.V.D. (a). *In-Service Training—Basic General Nursing,* Netherlands. (ED 311 178)

Berg-Ran, A.V.D. (b). *Part-time Course for Teachers of Nursing,* Netherlands. (ED 311 178)

Bleechmore, K. *Community Living Project,* Australia. (ED 311 160)

Bluff, E. *Trade Union Postal Courses Scheme,* Australia. (ED 311 160)

Brady, J. *Refresher Education for Company Directors,* Australia. (ED 311 160)

Bryden, D. *CPE for Veterinarians,* Australia. (ED 311 160)

Bugl, H., and Fehrenbach-Neuman, F. *Counseling Courses in Agriculture,* Federal Republic of Germany. (ED 311 167)

Burns, E. P. *Hayden Hall: A Community Development Approach,* India. (ED 311 172)

Campbell, D., and Sandmann, L. *Caribbean Agricultural Extension Program,* St. Lucia. (ED 311 182)

Collins, T. *Training of Community Enterprise Animateurs,* Ireland. (ED 311 173)

Conaty, M. *Extra-Mural Studies in Basic Counseling,* Ireland. (ED 311 173)

Cristovao, A.F.A.C. *Rural Extension Program Evaluation,* Portugal. (ED 311 181)

Crock, M., and Cottman, C. *Preparatory Studies,* Australia. (ED 311 160)

Curran, D. *Buchans Community Transition Project,* Canada. (ED 311 162)

de Melo, A. S. *Management Groups as a Method of Rural Extension,* Portugal. (ED 311 181)

de Ruiter, R. *Re-Entry Course for Women in Construction Trades,* Netherlands. (ED 311 178)

Degeling, D., Bennett, D., and Everingham, F. *Women's Health—The Middle Years,* Australia. (ED 311 160)

del Corno, L. *University of the Third Age—Orvieto,* Italy. (ED 311 175)

DeSanctis, F. M. *Educational Aims for the Year 2000: Adult Education for the City of Prato,* Italy. (ED 311 175)

Diggins, P. B. *Introductory Course to Educational Administrators,* Ireland. (ED 311 173)

Dircken, A. *Television Academy,* Netherlands. (ED 311 178)

DiSilvestro, F. R. *Indiana University Independent Study by Correspondence,* United States. (ED 311 188)

Dominice, P., and Finger, M. *Formative Research in Swiss French Agricultural Schools,* Switzerland. (ED 311 185)

Dong, M. *Postsecondary Education in China,* People's Republic of China. (ED 311 164)

Dong, M., and Zhu, Z. (a). *Aging Issue and Education for the Aged,* People's Republic of China. (ED 311 164)

Dong, M., and Zhu, Z. (b). *Chinese Adult Education—At Present and in Prospect,* People's Republic of China. (ED 311 164)

Donoghue, E. *Teacher Training Program—Health Education,* Ireland. (ED 311 173)

Donoso, P. *Centro El Canelo De Nos,* Chile. (ED 311 163)

Dow, J. L. *Discussion Program—Council of Adult Education,* Australia. (ED 311 160)

Gaskin, C. A. *Canada Congress for Learning Opportunities for Women,* Canada. (ED 311 162)

Gurthrie, C. A. *Human Resource and Organization Development,* Federal Republic of Germany. (ED 311 167)

Hartl, P. *House of Culture and Its Function in Adult Education,* Czechoslovakia. (ED 311 165)

Hassett, M. *Certification in Farming,* Republic of Ireland. (ED 311 173)

Haughey, M. *Distance Education at University of Victoria,* Canada. (ED 311 162)

Hernandez, I. (a). *Adult Education in Latin America,* Argentina. (ED 311 159)

Hernandez, I. (b). *Education and Elders,* Argentina. (ED 311 159)

Hoghielm, R. *Perspective on Municipal Adult Education,* Sweden. (ED 311 184)

Holderness-Roddam, B. *Increasing Citizen Participation in Local Government,* Australia. (ED 311 160)

Iceton, N. (a). *Social Developer's Network,* Australia. (ED 311 160)

Iceton, N. (b). *UNElearn Group Discussion Correspondence Program,* Australia. (ED 311 160)

Isinika, A. *Training for Rural Development,* Tanzania. (ED 311 186)

Israeli, E. *School for Parents, Teachers, and Children in a Distressed Moshav,* Israel. (ED 311 174)

Jayagopal, R. (a). *Literacy Program,* India. (ED 311 172)

Jayagopal, R. (b). *National Council for Hotel Management and Catering Technology,* India. (ED 311 172)

Jayagopal, R. (c). *Punjab Association,* India. (ED 311 172)

Jennett, P. A. *CPE Program for Family Physicians,* Canada. (ED 311 162)

Johnson, D. W. (a). *Libraries and Literacy—Tulsa,* United States. (ED 311 188)

Johnson, D. W. (b). *Libraries and Literacy—Weirton,* United States. (ED 311 188)

Kalela, J. *Union History Project: Study Circles Doing Research,* Finland. (ED 311 166)

Kassotakis, M. *In-Service Teacher Training in Greece,* Greece. (ED 311 169)

Kauppinen, J. *Beginning of Adult Education Planning at the Municipal Level,* Finland. (ED 311 166)

Kerr, D. *Marriage Enhancement,* Australia. (ED 311 160)

Kett, M. *Extra-Mural Studies,* Republic of Ireland. (ED 311 173)

Kilgenstein, P. *In-Service Training at Busch,* Federal Republic of Germany. (ED 311 167)

Knox, A. B. (a). *Adult Basic Education,* United States. (ED 311 188)

Knox, A. B. (b). *Alcoholics Anonymous,* United States. (ED 311 188)

Knox, A. B. (c). *Cooperative Extension Service (Local),* United States. (ED 311 188)

Knox, A. B. (d). *Credit Union Staff Development,* United States. (ED 311 188)

Knox, A. B. (e). *Helping Stock Brokers Cope with Stress,* United States. (ED 311 188)

Knox, A. B. (f). *National Issues Forum,* United States. (ED 311 188)

Knox, L. B. *YWCA Refugee Program,* United States. (ED 311 188)

Koskela, I. *Developmental Work Research Project at Adult Education Center,* Finland. (ED 311 166)

Kulic, R. *Basic Adult Education,* Yugoslavia. (ED 311 190)

LaNauze, H. *Women's Access Program,* Australia. (ED 311 160)

Letcher, M. *Carringbush Library,* Australia. (ED 311 160)

Lin, J. *A University Without Campus,* People's Republic of China. (ED 311 164)

Liu, Y. *A Survey of Beijing's Workers University Graduates,* People's Republic of China. (ED 311 164)

McCann, M. E. *Extra-Mural Studies in Drug and Alcohol Addiction,* Republic of Ireland. (ED 311 173)

McCarthy, L. *Family Life Education Premarriage,* Republic of Ireland. (ED 311 173)

McDonnell, J. A. *Welcare Program,* Australia. (ED 311 160)

Nyemba, J. A. (a). *AE Programs in Cameroon,* Cameroon. (ED 311 161)

Nyemba, J. A. (b). *Agriculture University Center in Extension Program Implementation,* Cameroon. (ED 311 161)

Okedara, C. (a). *Professional Continuing Education for Grade Two Teachers in Nigeria,* Nigeria. (ED 311 179)

Okedara, C. (b). *Women Education in Oyo State, Nigeria,* Nigeria. (ED 311 179)

Okedara, J. (a). *Correspondence Education,* Nigeria. (ED 311 179)

Okedara, J. (b). *Model Adult Literacy Classes,* Nigeria. (ED 311 179)

Okedara, J. (c). *Remedial Education,* Nigeria. (ED 311 179)

Oljaca, M. *Self Management at Worker's Universities,* Yugoslavia. (ED 311 190)

O'Neill, B. *Farm Management Home Study Program,* Australia. (ED 311 160)

Oosting, B. (a). *Medical Specialists,* Netherlands. (ED 311 178)

Oosting, B. (b). *Psycho-Geriatrics for Home Helps,* Netherlands. (ED 311 178)

Osolnik, M. R. *Nutrition Education,* Yugoslavia. (ED 311 190)

Pearson, T. G., and Cervero, R. M. *Continuing Medical Education,* United States. (ED 311 188)

Pevc, E. *Development of Training in Sava, Kranj,* Yugoslavia. (ED 311 190)

Pratt, D. I. *Health Line: Centre for Corporate Health Promotion,* Canada. (ED 311 162)

Pulkkis, A., Teikari, V., and Vartiainen, M. *Role of Training in Changing a Work Organization,* Finland. (ED 311 166)

Rebesko, B. *Veterinary Education in the Farming Population,* Yugoslavia. (ED 311 190)

Renschler, H. E. *Professional Training for Medical Specialists,* Federal Republic of Germany. (ED 311 167)

Ricci, M. *Adult Education in Bologna,* Italy. (ED 311 175)

Rivera, W. M. *Cooperative Extension Service (National),* United States. (ED 311 188)

Rouine, B. *Extra-Mural Diploma Course in Religious Studies,* Republic of Ireland. (ED 311 173)

Rundle, P. A. *Learning-Centered Social Services Model of ABE,* Canada. (ED 311 162)

Ryan, J. *Diploma in Management and Industrial Relations,* Republic of Ireland. (ED 311 173)

Salminen, L. *Experiments in Vocational Adult Education,* Finland. (ED 311 166)

Sari, M. *Protecting Our Environment,* Hungary. (ED 311 171)

Savićević, D. M. (a). *Correlation of Primary and Work Oriented Professional Education of Young People,* Yugoslavia. (ED 311 190)

Savićević, D. M. (b). *Research into and Training in Literacy,* Yugoslavia. (ED 311 190)

Schiele, S. *State Center for Political Education,* Federal Republic of Germany. (ED 311 167)

Schmoock, P. *Courses by Radio,* Federal Republic of Germany. (ED 311 167)

Schweitzer, H., Lauts, N., and Kozoll, C. *Educational Programs for Government Officials,* United States. (ED 311 188)

Skoda, K. *Czechoslovakian Adult Education,* Czechoslovakia. (ED 311 165)

Stark, E. (a). *Language School for Refugees,* Netherlands. (ED 311 178)

Stark, E. (b). *Management and Computer Education for Re-Entry Women,* Netherlands. (ED 311 178)

Stel-Overdulve, H.V.D. (a). *Advanced Nursing Course,* Netherlands. (ED 311 178)

Stel-Overdulve, H.V.D. (b). *Part-Time Training—Sick Care,* Netherlands. (ED 311 178)

Suortamo, M. *School for Teaching Automated Data Processing,* Finland. (ED 311 166)

Susi, F. (a). *Education for Adults in the Earthquake Region of Basilicata,* Italy. (ED 311 175)

Susi, F. (b). *Education Project of Molise: Creation of an Adult Education System,* Italy. (ED 311 175)

Swindell, R. *Self-Help Adult Education: University of the Third Age,* Australia. (ED 311 160)

Taigel, H. *Evening High School,* Federal Republic of Germany. (ED 311 167)

Takashi, F. *The Founding of a University for Senior Citizens,* Japan. (ED 311 176)

Thang, P. O. (a). *Basic Education for Adults in Sweden,* Sweden. (ED 311 184)

Thang, P. O. (b). *Labor Market Training in Sweden,* Sweden. (ED 311 184)

Tokatli, R. *Comparative Analysis of Literacy Education,* Israel. (ED 311 174)

Tone, R. *Extension Service and Its Role in Training Farmers—Slovenia,* Yugoslavia. (ED 311 190)

Tori, V. *Provincial Administration of Moderna,* Italy. (ED 311 175)

van Straalen-van Waard, B. *Pre-Retirement Education,* Netherlands. (ED 311 178)

Vartanian, F., Orlov, D., and Nazarova, E. *Continuing Medical Education,* Union of Soviet Socialist Republics. (ED 311 189)

Vepsalainen, K. *Instruction in Information Technology,* Finland. (ED 311 166)

Virtala, M. *Experimentation in Adult Education Centers,* Finland. (ED 311 166)

Werner, G. *Adult Education Center,* Federal Republic of Germany. (ED 311 167)

Wickert, R. *NSW Board of Adult Education—Literacy,* Australia. (ED 311 160)

Willen, B. *Distance Education at the University Level,* Sweden. (ED 311 184)

Wilson, E. (a). *Dutch as a Foreign Language,* Netherlands. (ED 311 178)

Wilson, E. (b). *Study House for Adults,* Netherlands. (ED 311 178)

Zuidhoff, E.R.T. *Dutch as a Foreign Language,* Netherlands. (ED 311 178)

Zuidhoff, R. *In-Service Occupational Training,* Netherlands. (ED 311 178)

B

List of
Case Coordinators

This resource lists the thirty-two countries from which case descriptions were obtained and the names of the World Perspective project case coordinators in each country who arranged for their preparation.

Country	Coordinator
Argentina	Isabel Hernandez
Australia	S. J. Rooth
Cameroon	Jean Nyemba
Canada	James A. Draper
Chile	Marcela Gajardo
China, People's Republic of	Dong Mingchuan and Zhu Zhongdan
Czechoslovakia	Kamil Skoda and Pavel Hartl
Finland	Jukka Tuomisto
Germany, Federal Republic of	Jost Reischmann and G. Dohmen
Ghana	Joe K. Ansere
Greece	Michael Kassotakis
Hong Kong	Charles Wong
Hungary	B. Laszlo Harangi
India	R. Jayagopal
Ireland, Republic of	Liam Carey
Israel	Eitan Israeli

Italy	Filippo M. DeSanctis
Japan	Kazufusa Moro'oka
Korea, Democratic People's Republic of	Nam Jin U
Netherlands	Barry J. Hake
Nigeria	Joseph Okedara
Norway	Odd Nordhaug
Portugal	Eduardo Figueira and Artur Cristavao
St. Lucia	Dunstan Campbell
Saudi Arabia	Mohammad Al-Rasheed
Sweden	Robert Hoghielm
Switzerland	Hans Amberg
Tanzania	Aida Isinika
Union of Soviet Socialist Republics	Michail N. Kulis
United Kingdom	Paul Fordham
United States	Alan B. Knox
Yugoslavia	Dušan Savićević

C

Major Societal Influences on Educational Programs and Providers

The main societal influences that emerged from the World Perspective project are listed here. Following each term are some phrases that help define it. These external influences affect various aspects of internal agency functioning, including anticipated benefits, agency planning, learner participation, staff members, financial resources, collaboration with other providers, staff development, educational technology, and actual outcomes. The chapters in which that type of influence is especially prominent are noted at the end of each description in parentheses.

1. *External policies:* Policies, plans, and guidelines of parent organization, local government, and other organizations that apply specifically to this program and agency (does not include national legislation, priorities, and appropriations). (Chapters Two through Seven, and Twelve)
2. *Parent organization:* All types of relations between a provider unit and its parent organization, if it has one. (Chapters Two, Five, Six, Seven, and Eleven)
3. *Enterprises and employers:* Relationship between places where adults work and their adult education participation, including commitment to human resource development, labor-management relations, and extent of enterprise training and development effort. (Chapters Five, Six, and Nine)

4. *Formal educational institutions:* Relations with formal educational institutions of all types and levels, as related to staff, participants, and other matters (does not include relations with parent organizations or collaboration with other adult education providers). (Chapters Two, Six, Seven, Nine, and Eleven)

5. *Other organizations:* Any other organizations (besides educational institutions, enterprises, and religious institutions) as they relate to adult education, including cultural organizations and community agencies (does not include voluntary associations, professional societies, and labor unions, which are classified as associations). (Chapters Three, Four, Eight, and Thirteen)

6. *Volunteers:* All sources and categories of volunteers who contribute to a program without pay. (Chapters Eight and Ten)

7. *Relative priority for adult education:* Societal priority for adult education as reflected in legislation, public policy, association resolutions. (Chapters Two and Seven)

8. *External financing:* All forms of program financial support, including multiple sources, ongoing government appropriations, temporary grant support, participant fees, reimbursement by enterprises, and influences of subsidy levels on program. (Chapters Five and Eight)

9. *Government:* National and state ministries, programs, and guidelines for local adult education. (Chapters Three, Four, and Eleven)

10. *National economy:* Satisfactoriness of the economy as reflected in Gross National Product growth, inflation, unemployment, and productivity. (Chapters Three, Five, and Six specifically, but all chapters to some extent)

11. *Image of adult education:* Media and other influences on image of specific program or general adult educational activities, which may be reflected in policy makers' perception of public support for adult education. (Chapters Six and Seven)

12. *Media use:* Extent of use of print and electronic media by adult population. (Chapter Five)

13. *Urban-rural relationship:* Relations between rural and urban

areas, including relative emphasis and population shifts. (Chapter Five and Eleven)

14. *Geographic characteristics:* Climate, terrain, density and distribution of population, total area, adjacent countries, and natural barriers. (Chapters Five and Eleven)

15. *International influences:* Economic, political, and national development influences by individual countries and international agencies. (Chapters Four, Nine, Eleven, and Thirteen)

16. *Cultural values:* Widespread values, beliefs, assumptions, and ideology, such as individualism, solidarity, spirituality, equity, productivity, and sense of national identity. (Chapters Seven, Eight, Ten, and Thirteen)

17. *Pluralism:* Extent of national pluralism versus centralization, which may be related to diversity of individual benefits (non-occupational) and flexibility of guidelines. (Chapters Four and Ten)

18. *Organized religion:* Both provision of adult religious education and relations between religious institutions and adult education generally. (Chapter Eight)

19. *Minorities:* Extent of minorities and immigrants. (Chapters Four and Seven)

20. *Social stratification:* General social class and stratification characteristics and influences on standard of living, life-style, poverty level, and ability to pay for educative activity (does not include level of formal education; includes social mobility). (Chapters Three, Four, Seven, and Nine)

21. *Educational level:* National and regional average level of formal education. (Chapters Three, Seven, Nine, and Eleven)

22. *Social services:* Extent of public social services available to adults, including those related to health, welfare, occupation, family, and educational counseling. (Chapters Eleven and Twelve)

23. *Powerful elites:* Extent of political, economic, religious, and social elites (including patron-client) that affect adult education programs, participants, and efforts to apply new learning. (Chapters Four and Thirteen)

24. *New knowledge:* New ideas, knowledge, and content from re-

search from home country, other countries, or other sources. (Chapters Six and Ten)

25. *Modernization:* Extent of deliberate modernization and technology transfer, including national trends regarding use. (Chapters Five, Six, and Nine)

26. *Health condition:* Indicators of health problems in adult population. (Chapters Ten and Twelve)

27. *Age distribution:* Proportions of population at various age levels. (Chapter Ten)

28. *Population change:* Extent of population increase or decrease. (Chapters Four, Ten, and Twelve)

29. *Social change:* Fundamental shifts, societal changes, gradual trends, and abrupt changes in any aspect of society (does not include deliberate modernization and technology transfer). (Chapters Four and Thirteen)

30. *Role performance:* Any aspects of role expectations, performance, and change that relate to participation in educative activity (does not include general family relations). (Chapters Six and Nine)

31. *Family:* Family size and relations; gender relations. (Chapters Four, Ten, and Eleven)

32. *Associates:* Outlook and interests of friends, associates, reference groups, voluntary association members, labor union members, and primary groups that serve as facilitators or barriers to participation in educative activity (does not include family role). (Chapters Four, Six, and Eleven)

33. *Expectations:* Indicators of changes in level of expectations for the future. (Chapters Three, Seven, and Thirteen)

References

Abbott, F. R., and Mejia, A. *Continuing Education of Health Workers: A Workshop Manual.* Geneva, Switzerland: World Health Organization, 1988.

Abrahamsson, K. *Adult Participation in Swedish Higher Education.* Studies in Higher Education in Sweden, no. 7. Stockholm: Almqvist & Wiksell, 1986.

Abrahamsson, K. *Adult Literacy and Basic Skills in Sweden: An Overview of Policy Issues and Research Needs.* Stockholm: Swedish National Board of Education and Swedish National Committee for the International Literacy Year, 1990a.

Abrahamsson, K. *The International Literacy Year in Sweden: A Journey Through a Changing Landscape.* Stockholm: Swedish National Board of Education, 1990b.

Abrahamsson, K. *Learning Rights for the Next Century: Improving Learning Options by a New Deal Between the Public and Private Interests in Adult Learning.* Division of Adult Education, Swedish National Board of Education, 1990c.

Abrahamsson, K., Hultinger, E., and Svenningsson, L. *Expanding Learning Enterprise in Sweden.* Stockholm: Swedish National Board of Education, 1990.

Adams, F. *Unearthing Seeds of Fire: The Idea of Highlander.* Winston-Salem, N.C.: Blair, 1975.

Adelson, R., Watkins, F. S., and Caplan, R. M. *Continuing Education for the Health Professions.* Rockville, Md.: Aspen Systems, 1985.

Adiseshiah, M. S. "Community Leadership Role Central to Education of the Elderly in India." *Convergence,* 1985, *18* (1–2), 82–87.

Adler, N. J. *International Dimensions of Organizational Behavior.* Boston: Kent, 1986.

"Adult Education for Social Change: All India Declaration on Priorities and Action." *Convergence,* 1982, *15* (4), 38–43.

Adult Literacy and Basic Skills Unit [England]. *Resourcing Adult Literacy and Basic Skills.* London: Adult Literacy and Basic Skills Unit, 1987. (ED 284 074)

Allegrante, J. P. "Potential Uses and Misuses of Education in Health Promotion and Disease Prevention." *Teachers College Record,* 1984, *86* (2), 359–373.

Allison, R. "The Soviet Military—Political-Education, Training and Morale." *Soviet Studies,* 1987, *39* (4), 674–675.

Al Sunbul, A. "ABE in Saudi Arabia." *Adult Literacy and Basic Education,* 1985, *9* (3), 144–153.

Anyanwu, C. N. "The Technique of Participatory Research in Community Development." *Community Development Journal,* 1988, *23* (1), 11–15.

Apps, J. W. *Higher Education in a Learning Society: Meeting New Demands for Education and Training.* San Francisco: Jossey-Bass, 1988.

Araiyo, J.E.G. "Adult Education, Community Enterprises, and Rural Development in Latin America." *Convergence,* 1978, *11* (2), 15–22.

Arger, G. *Promise and Reality: A Critical Analysis of the Literature Available in Australia on Distance Education in the Third World.* Armidale, Australia: University of New England, 1985. (ED 284 022)

Argyris, C., Putnam, R., and Smith, D. M. *Action Science: Concepts, Methods, and Skills for Research and Intervention.* San Francisco: Jossey-Bass, 1985.

Armstrong, G. "Implementing Educational Policy: Decentralization of Nonformal Education in Thailand." *Comparative Education Review,* 1984, *28* (3), 454–466. (ED 314 333)

Armstrong, P. F. "Towards an Analysis of the Curriculum of University Extramural Departments in Great Britain." In G. J. Conti and R. Fellenz (eds.), *Dialogue on Issues of Lifelong Learning in a Democratic Society: Working Papers from a British and North American Faculty Exchange.* Washington, D.C.: Commission of Professors of Adult Education, American Association for Adult and Continuing Education, 1985. (ED 260 212)

Arnove, R. F., and Graff, H. J. *National Literacy Campaigns: Historical and Comparative Aspects.* New York: Plenum Press, 1987.

Ascher, W. *Forecasting: An Appraisal for Policy Makers and Planners.* Baltimore, Md.: Johns Hopkins University Press, 1978.

Aslanian, C. B., and Brickell, H. N. *Americans in Transition: Life Changes as Reasons for Learning.* New York: College Entrance Examination Board, 1980.

Auganes, H. G. "Continuing Engineering Education in Norway: The Role of the Norwegian Institute of Technology." *European Journal of Engineering Education,* 1985, *10* (3-4), 235-237.

Avalos, B. "The Evaluation of Cultural Action." *International Journal of Educational Development,* 1985, *5* (3), 235-240.

Axinn, G. H., and Thorat, S. *Modernizing World Agriculture: A Comparative Study of Agricultural Extension Systems.* New York: Praeger, 1972.

Baden, C. (ed.). *Competitive Strategies for Continuing Education.* New Directions for Continuing Education, no. 35. San Francisco: Jossey-Bass, 1987.

Bandura, A. *Social Learning Theory.* Englewood Cliffs, N.J.: Prentice-Hall, 1977.

Bannerji, S. "Adult Education in India: A Village-Level Experience." *Prospects: Quarterly Review of Education,* 1981, *11* (3), 381-386.

Bard, R., Bell, C. R., Stephen, L., and Webster, L. *The Trainer's Professional Development Handbook.* San Francisco: Jossey-Bass, 1987.

Barron, B., and Mohan, R. P. "Recent Trends in Adult Education in Eastern Europe." *Adult Literacy and Basic Education,* Spring 1979, *3* (1), 48-57. (EJ 220 623)

Barrow, N. "Knowledge Belongs to Everyone." *Convergence,* 1981, *14* (2), 45-52.

Barrow, N. "Social Action and Development: A Liberating Power." *Convergence,* 1983, *16* (1), 46-51.

Baskett, H. K., Hamilton, A. B., and Bruce, A. *University Contin-*

uing Education: Strategies for an Uncertain Future. Paper presented to the Canadian Association of University Continuing Education, Winnipeg, Manitoba, 1985. (ED 262 241)

Bates, T., and Robinson, J. (eds.). *Evaluating Educational Television and Radio.* Milton Keynes, England: Open University Press, 1977.

Beaudin, B. P. *Facilitating Transfer of Learning to the Workplace.* Paper presented at the annual conference of the American Association for Adult and Continuing Education, Hollywood, Fla., Oct. 23, 1986. (ED 274 791)

Beckhard, R., and Pritchard, W. *Changing the Essence: The Art of Creating and Leading Fundamental Change in Organizations.* San Francisco: Jossey-Bass, 1992.

Beder, H. (ed.). *Marketing Continuing Education.* New Directions for Continuing Education, no. 31. San Francisco: Jossey-Bass, 1986.

Beder, H. *Adult Literacy: Issues for Policy and Planning.* Malabar, Fla.: Krieger, 1991.

Belenky, M. F., Clinchy, B. M., Goldberger, N. R., and Tarule, J. M. *Women's Ways of Knowing: The Development of Self, Voice, and Mind.* New York: Basic Books, 1986.

Bell, B., Gaventa, J., and Peters, J. *We Make the Road by Walking: Conversations on Education for Social Change.* Philadelphia: Temple University Press, 1990.

Bell, R., and others. *Correctional Education Programs for Inmates.* Washington, D.C.: National Institute of Law Enforcement and Criminal Justice, 1979.

Bellah, R. H., and others. *Habits of the Heart.* New York: Harper-Collins, 1985.

Benne, K. D., and others (eds.). *The Laboratory Method of Changing and Learning: Theory and Application.* Palo Alto, Calif.: Science and Behavior Books, 1975.

Bennett, C., Kidd, J. R., and Kulich, J. *Comparative Studies in Adult Education: An Anthology.* Syracuse, N.Y.: Syracuse University Publications in Continuing Education, 1975.

Bennis, W., and Nanus, B. *Leaders: The Strategies for Taking Charge.* New York: HarperCollins, 1985.

Benor, D., and Harrison, J. Q. *Agricultural Extension: The Training and Visit System.* Washington, D.C.: World Bank, 1977.

Bernard, A., and Armstrong, G. "Implementing an Educational Philosophy: 'Khit-pen' in Thailand." *Convergence,* 1979, *12* (4), 17–28.

Bertsch, G. K., and Persons, K. L. "Workers' Education in Socialist Yugoslavia." *Comparative Education Review,* 1980, *24* (1), 87–97.

Berwick, D. M., Godfrey, A. B., and Roessner, J. *Curing Health Care: New Strategies for Quality Improvement.* San Francisco: Jossey-Bass, 1990.

Best, F. *Adult Education for the Twenty-First Century: Strategic Plan to Meet California's Long Term Adult Education Needs.* Summary Report. Sacramento: Adult Education Unit, Division of Youth and Alternative Educational Services, California State Department of Education, 1989.

Bhasin, K. "The Why and How of Literacy for Women: Some Thoughts in Indian Context." *Convergence,* 1984, *17* (4), 37–43.

Bhatnagar, O. P., Desai, G. R., and Reddy, M. R. "Management of Agricultural Extension Under T & V System in India: An Overview." *Journal of Rural Development,* 1986, *5* (5), 561–571.

Bhola, H. S. "Why Literacy Can't Wait: Issues for the 1980's." *Convergence,* 1981, *16* (1), 6–23.

Bhola, H. S. "Non-Formal Education in Perspective." *Prospects: Quarterly Review of Education,* 1983, *13* (1), 45–54.

Bhola, H. S. *Literacy for Development: An African Perspective.* Paper presented to the African Studies Association, Madison, Wis., 1986. (ED 273 782)

Bhola, H. S. *Adult Literacy for Development in Zimbabwe: The Third Phase of the Revolution Examined.* Paper presented to the Canadian Association of African Studies, Edmonton, Alberta, 1987. (ED 279 898)

Bhola, H. S. *World Trends and Issues in Adult Education.* Kingsley and UNESCO, 1988.

Bird, E. "Adult Education and the Advancement of Women in the West Indies." *Convergence,* 1975, *8* (1), 57–67.

Blackburn, H. "Community Programs in CHD Prevention and Health Promotion: Changing Community Behavior." In M.

Marmot and P. Elliott (eds.), *Coronary Heart Disease Epidemi-
ology: From Aetiology to Public Health*. New York: Oxford
University Press, 1992.

Blackburn, H., and others. "The Minnesota Heart Health Program:
A Research and Demonstration Project in Cardiovascular Disease
Prevention." In J. D. Matarazzo and Associates (eds.), *Behavioral
Health: A Handbook of Health Enhancement and Disease Pre-
vention*. New York: Wiley, 1984.

Blair, L. H. *Technological Change and Employment in Western
Europe*. Research Report Series. Washington, D.C.: U.S. Department of Labor, National Commission for Employment Policy,
1985. (ED 263 404)

Blid, H. *Education by the People—Study Circles*. Stockholm: Swedish Workers' Educational Association, 1989.

Bock, J. C., and Papagiannis, G. J. (eds.). *Nonformal Education
and National Development: A Critical Assessment of Policy, Research, and Practice*. New York: Praeger, 1983.

Bogard, G. *Adult Education and Social Change*. Strasbourg,
France: Council of Europe, 1989.

Bogard, G. *Adult Education and Social Change*. Interim Report,
1989–1990. Strasbourg, France: Council of Europe, Council for
Cultural Cooperation, 1991.

Bogard, G. *For a Socializing Type of Adult Education*. Project Report, Adult Education and Social Change. Strasbourg, France:
Council of Europe, Council for Cultural Cooperation, 1992.

Boshier, R. (ed.). "Training of Trainers and Adult Educators."
Convergence, 1985, *18* (entire issues 3–4).

Botkin, J. W., Elmandjra, M., and Malitza, M. *No Limits to Learning: Bridging the Human Gap*. Elmsford, N.Y.: Pergamon Press,
1979.

Boucouvalas, M. *Adult Education in Greece*. Vancouver, Canada:
Centre for Continuing Education, 1988.

Bown, L. "Adult Education and Community Development: The
Nigerian Traditional Setting." *Convergence*, 1977, *10* (4), 53–62.

Bown, L. *Current World Trends in Adult Education*. Paper presented at the International Symposium on Adult Education,
Haifa, Israel, 1985. (ED 271 585)

Bown, L., and Okedara, J. R. (eds.). *An Introduction to the Study of Adult Education: A Multi-Disciplinary and Cross-Cultural Approach for Developing Countries.* Ibadan, Nigeria: University Press, 1981.

Bown, L., and Tomori, S. H. (eds.). *A Handbook of Adult Education for West Africa.* London: Hutchinson University Library for Africa, 1979.

Bracht, N. (ed.). *Health Promotion at the Community Level.* Sourcebooks for the Human Services, series 15. Newbury Park, Calif.: Sage, 1990.

Bradford, L. P. *National Training Laboratories: Its History, 1947–1970.* Bethel, Maine: Bradford, 1974.

Brasseul, P. "Senior Citizens Challenge Traditional Education: The French Experience." *Educational Gerontology,* 1984, *10,* 185–196.

Brett, K. "The Organization of Adult and Continuing Education in the British Higher Education Sector." *Journal of Tertiary Educational Administration,* May 1987, *9* (1), 65–75.

Brock, C., and Lawlor, H. (eds.). *Education in Latin America,* London: Croom Helm, 1985.

Brockett, R. G. (ed.). *Continuing Education in the Year 2000.* New Directions for Continuing Education, no. 36. San Francisco: Jossey-Bass, 1988.

Bron, M. *Adult Education and Disintegration Processes in Yugoslavia.* Reports on Education, no. 22. Uppsala, Sweden: Department of Education, Uppsala University, 1985. (ED 278 802)

Brookfield, S. (ed.). *Training Educators of Adults.* London: Routledge, 1988.

Brown, L. A. *Innovation Diffusion: A New Perspective.* New York: Methuen, 1981.

Brown, L. D. "People-Centered Development and Participatory Research." *Harvard Educational Review,* 1985, *55* (1), 69–75.

Bryant, I. *Radicals and Respectables—The Adult Education Experience in Scotland.* Edinburgh: Scottish Institute of Adult Education, 1984. (ED 278 835)

Bryson, J. M. *Strategic Planning for Public and Nonprofit Organizations: A Guide to Strengthening and Sustaining Organizational Achievement.* San Francisco: Jossey-Bass, 1988.

Bunch, R. *Two Ears of Corn: A Guide to People-Centered Agricul-*

tural Improvement. Oklahoma City, Okla.: World Neighbors, 1982.

Burge, E. "Beyond Andragogy." *Journal of Distance Education,* Spring 1988, *3* (1), 5–23.

Burge, E. J., Snow, J. E., and Howard, J. L. "Distance Education: Concept and Practice." *Canadian Library Journal,* 1989, *46* (5), 329–335.

Buschmeyer, H. *Aging and Adult Education in North Rhine–Westphalia.* Workshop Report from CDCC Project on Adult Education and Social Change. Strasbourg, France: Council of Europe, Council for Cultural Cooperation, 1991.

Buskey, J. (ed.) *Attracting External Funds for Continuing Education.* New Directions for Continuing Education, no. 12. San Francisco: Jossey-Bass, 1981.

Buttedahl, P. "The Training of Adult and Popular Educators." *Convergence,* 1985, *18* (3–4), 94–101.

Byrne, A. *Adult Education in the Gaeltacht.* Dublin, Ireland: National Association of Adult Education, 1987.

Callan, P. M. (ed.). *Environmental Scanning for Strategic Leadership.* New Directions for Institutional Research, no. 52. San Francisco: Jossey-Bass, 1986.

Campbell, C. P. "Human Resource Development in Saudi Arabia with an Emphasis on Skilled Manpower." *Canadian and International Education,* 1982, *11* (2), 87–102.

Capanema, C. F. *Continuing Education Needs in Latin America: A Report.* Unpublished report, 1985. (ED 272 672)

Carnevale, A. P., Gainer, L. J., and Meltzer, A. S. *Workplace Basics: The Essential Skills Employers Want.* San Francisco: Jossey-Bass, 1990.

Carnevale, A. P., and Johnston, J. W. *Training America: Strategies for the Nation.* Alexandria, Va.: American Society for Training and Development, 1989.

Carnoy, M. *Education as Cultural Imperialism.* New York: McKay, 1974.

Cassara, B. B. (ed.). *Adult Education in a Multicultural Society.* London: Routledge, 1990.

Castro, A., Stirzaker, L., Northcott, P., and Basch, P. "Applications of Computer Communications Technology to Distance Education." *Media in Education and Development* [England], June 1986, *19*, 92–96.

Catford, J. *Health in Wales, 1990.* Cardiff: Health Promotion Authority for Wales, 1990.

Cerna, M. "Lifelong Teacher-Education in the Czechoslovakian-Socialist Republic with Especial Reference to the Training of Teachers in Special Education." *Journal of Education for Teaching,* 1987, *13* (3), 285–288.

Cervero, R. M. *Effective Continuing Education for Professionals.* San Francisco: Jossey-Bass, 1988.

Cervero, R. M., Azzaretto, J. F., and Associates. *Visions for the Future of Continuing Professional Education.* Athens: Department of Adult Education, University of Georgia, and Georgia Center for Continuing Education, 1990.

Cervero, R. M., and Scanlan, C. L. (eds.). *Problems and Prospects in Continuing Professional Education,* New Directions for Continuing Education, no. 27. San Francisco: Jossey-Bass, 1985.

Cervinskas, J. *Organizing for Health.* Toronto, Canada: International Council for Adult Education, 1984.

Chamberlain, M. N. (ed.). *Providing Continuing Education by Media and Technology.* New Directions for Continuing Education, no. 5. San Francisco: Jossey-Bass, 1980.

Chambers, R., and Jiggins, J. "Agricultural Research for Resource-Poor Farmers. Part 1: Transfer-of-Technology and Farming Systems Research." *Agricultural Administration and Extension,* 1987, *27*, 35–45.

Charnley, A. H. *Paid Educational Leave in France, Sweden, and West Germany.* London: Hart Davis Educational, 1975.

Charnley, A. H., and Jones, H. A. *The Concept of Success in Adult Literacy.* Cambridge, England: Huntington, 1979.

Charters, A. N., and Hilton, R. J. (eds.). *Landmarks in International Adult Education: A Comparative Analysis.* London: Routledge, 1989.

Charters, A. N., and Associates. *Comparing Adult Education Worldwide.* San Francisco: Jossey-Bass, 1981.

Chi, M.T.H., Glaser, R., and Farr, M. J. *The Nature of Expertise.* Hillsdale, N.J.: Erlbaum, 1989.

Chickering, A. W., and Associates. *The Modern American College:*

Responding to the New Realities of Diverse Students and a Changing Society. San Francisco: Jossey-Bass, 1981.

Chisman, F. P. *Jump Start—The Federal Role in Adult Literacy: Final Report of The Project on Adult Literacy.* Southport, Conn.: Southport Institute for Policy Analysis, 1989.

Chisman, F. P., and Associates. *Leadership for Literacy: The Agenda for the 1990s.* San Francisco: Jossey-Bass, 1990.

Chouhan, V. L., and Rai, G. C. "Attitude of Tribal and Non-Tribal Farmers Towards Adult Literacy and Improved Agricultural Practices: A Study." *Indian Journal of Adult Education,* 1984, *45* (3), 26–31.

Chu, L. *Rural Women's Vocational Training for National Development.* Paper prepared for Rocky Mountain Educational Research Association, 1985. (ED 261 844)

Clark, N. M. "Adult Education and Primary Health Care." *Convergence,* 1980, *13* (4), 62–70.

Clark, R. J., and Rooth, S. J. *Case Studies in Australian Adult Education.* Armidale, Australia: Department of Continuing Education, University of New England, and New South Wales Board of Adult Education, 1988.

Clemson, D. W. "Supporting Evaluation in Kenya: Reflections on Experiences with the Kenyan Adult Literacy Programme." *International Journal of Educational Development,* 1985, *5* (3), 245–248.

Coleman, A. *Preparation for Retirement in England and Wales.* London: National Institute of Adult Education, 1983.

Colle, R. D. "The Traditional Laundering Place as a Non-Formal Health Education Setting." *Convergence,* 1977, *10* (2), 32–39.

Collins, Z. W. (ed.) *Museums, Adults, and the Humanities.* Washington, D.C.: American Association of Museums, 1981.

Commission on Museums for a New Century. *Museums for a New Century.* Washington, D.C.: Commission on Museums for a New Century, American Association of Museums, 1984.

Compton, J. L. "Sri Lanka's Sarvodaya Shramadana Movement: Promoting People's Participation in Rural Community Development." *Journal of the Community Development Society,* 1982, *13* (1), 83–104.

Compton, J. L. "Linking Scientist and Farmer: Re-Thinking Extension's Role." In *World Food Issues.* (2nd ed.) Ithaca, N.Y.: Cornell University Program in International Agriculture, 1984.

Compton, J. L. (ed.). *The Transformation of International Agricultural Research and Development.* Boulder, Colo.: Reinner, 1989.

Conner, R. F. "A Cross-Cultural Assessment of Health Promotion/ Disease Prevention Programs." *Evaluation and Program Planning,* 1988, *11,* 179–187.

Cooley, V. E., and Thompson, J. C. *Staff Development in Varied U.S. Geographical Regions: A Study of Attitudes and Practices.* Paper presented at annual conference of the National Council of States on Inservice Education, November 21–25, 1986. (ED 275 653)

Coombs, P. H. *The World Crisis in Education: The View from the Eighties.* New York: Oxford University Press, 1985.

Corey, S. M. *Action Research to Improve School Practices.* New York: Teachers College Press, 1953.

Corner, T. (ed.). *Learning Opportunities for Adults.* London: Routledge, 1990.

Corvalen, O. *Vocational Training in Latin America: A Comparative Perspective.* Vancouver, Canada: Centre for Continuing Education, University of British Columbia, 1977.

Cory, G. H. "Television Experiences in Other Nations." In M. Chamberlain (ed.), *Providing Continuing Education by Media and Technology.* New Directions for Continuing Education, no. 5. San Francisco: Jossey-Bass, 1980.

Council of Europe. *Final Activity Report on Education in Prison.* Strasbourg, France: Council of Europe, Committee of Ministers, 1989.

Craig, R. L. (ed.). *Training and Development Handbook: A Guide to Human Resource Development.* (3rd ed.) New York: McGraw-Hill, 1987.

Crookes, F., and Associates. *The Battle Creek Plan.* Battle Creek, Mich.: Kellogg Community College and Battle Creek Public Schools, 1988.

Crouch, B. R., and Chamala, S. *Extension Education and Rural Development.* (2 vols.) New York: Wiley, 1981.

Curtin, C., and Varley, A. "Adult Education and Community Development in the West of Ireland." *Community Development Journal*, 1986, *21* (3), 186–194.

Curzon, A. J. "Correspondence Education in England and the Netherlands." *Comparative Education*, 1977, *13* (3), 249–261.

Dahrendorf, R. *Life Chances*. Chicago: University of Chicago Press, 1979.

Daines, J., and others. *Just Listen Awhile: Voices from a Developing Country*. St. Paul: Office of International Agricultural Programs, University of Minnesota, 1986.

Daloz, L. A. *Effective Teaching and Mentoring: Realizing the Transformational Power of Adult Learning Experiences*. San Francisco: Jossey-Bass, 1986.

Daresh, J. C. "Research Trends in Staff Development and Inservice Education." *Journal of Education for Teaching*, 1987, *13* (1), 3–11.

Darkenwald, G. G., and Merriam, S. *Adult Education: Foundations of Practice*. New York: HarperCollins, 1982.

Dave, R. H., Ouane, A., and Perera, D. A. (eds.). *Learning Strategies for Post-Literacy and Continuing Education in China, India, Indonesia, Nepal, Thailand, and Vietnam*. Report no. 4. Hamburg, Germany: UNESCO Institute for Education, 1986.

Dave, R. H., Ouane, A., and Ranaweera, A. M. (eds.). *Learning Strategies for Post-Literacy and Continuing Education in Brazil, Colombia, Jamaica, and Venezuela*. Report no. 5. Hamburg, Germany: UNESCO Institute for Education, 1986.

Dave, R. H., Perera, D. A., and Ouane, A. (eds.). *Learning Strategies for Post-Literacy and Continuing Education: A Cross National Perspective*. Report no. 1. Hamburg, Germany: UNESCO Institute for Education, 1985a.

Dave, R. H., Perera, D. A., and Ouane, A. (eds.). *Learning Strategies for Post-Literacy and Continuing Education in Kenya, Nigeria, Tanzania, and United Kingdom*. Report no. 3. Hamburg, Germany: UNESCO Institute for Education, 1985b.

Davis, D. "Australian Women in a Changing Society: Perspective Through Continuing Education." *Convergence*, 1980, *13* (1-2), 99–109.

Davis, D. A., Thomson, M. A., Oxman, A. D., and Haynes, R. B.

"Evidence for the Effectiveness of CME." Journal of the American Medical Association, September 1992, *268* (9), 1111–1117.

De Brito, A. H. "Basic Problems of Continuing Engineering Education in Developing Countries: Transfer of Technology from Developed to Developing Countries by CEE." *European Journal of Engineering Education,* 1985, *10* (3–4), 247–250.

de Melo, A. *Adult Education in Portugal.* Studies and Documents, no. 16. Prague: European Centre for Leisure and Education, 1983.

Department of Adult Education, State Education Commission [China]. *Eradication of Illiteracy in China.* Beijing: National Commission for Adult Education, Department of Adult Education, State Education Commission, China, 1990.

Drews, W. "Education for Retirement in the UK and Northern Europe." *Adult Education* [England], 1981, *54* (3), 222–229.

Dubell, F., Erasmie, T., and de Vries, J. (eds.). *Research for the People—Research by the People.* Selected papers from the International Forum on Participatory Research in Ljubljana, Yugoslavia. Amersfoort: Netherlands Study and Development Centre for Adult Education, 1981.

Duguid, S. "Post Secondary Education in a Prison: Theory and Praxis." *Canadian Journal of Higher Education,* 1980, *10* (1), 29–35.

Duguid, S. "Democratic Praxis and Prison Education." *Harvard Journal of Criminal Justice,* February 1987, *26* (1), 57–65.

Duguid, S. (ed.). *Yearbook of Correctional Education, 1989.* Burnaby, Canada: Institute for the Humanities, Simon Fraser University, 1989.

Duguid, S. (ed.). *Yearbook of Correctional Education, 1990.* Burnaby, Canada: Institute for the Humanities, Simon Fraser University, 1990.

Duke, C. "Issues of Organizing Adult Continuing Education: The Context of Australian Trends and Examples." *Convergence,* 1984a, 17 (2), 3–14.

Duke, C. "Learning from and with Liberation: Report from ICAE China Symposium in Shanghai, May 1984." *Convergence,* 1984b, 12 (3), 4–11.

Duke, C. (ed.). *Combating Poverty Through Adult Education: National Development Strategies.* London: Croom Helm, 1985.

Duke, C. (ed.). *Adult Education: International Perspectives from China.* London: Croom Helm, 1987.

Duke, C., Rudnik, H., and Davis, D. *Immigration, Adult Education and Multiculturalism in Australia.* Canberra: Centre for Continuing Education, Australian National University, 1986. (ED 282 051)

Duke, C., and others. *Grassroots Approaches to Combating Poverty Through Adult Education.* Supplement to Adult Education and Development, no. 34. Bonn: German Adult Education Association, 1990.

Duning, B. S., Van Kekerix, M. J., and Zaborowski, L. M. *Reaching Learners Through Telecommunications: Management and Leadership Strategies for Higher Education.* San Francisco: Jossey-Bass, 1992.

Eastman, J. A. "The Different Organizational Requirements of Scholarship and Service." *Review of Higher Education,* Spring 1989, *12* (3), 279–292.

Edstrom, L. O., and others (eds.). *Mass Education: Studies in Adult Education and Teaching by Correspondence in Some Developing Countries.* Stockholm: Almqvist & Wiksell, 1970.

Elias, J. L. *The Foundations and Practice of Adult Religious Education.* (2nd ed.) Malabar, Fla.: Krieger, 1986.

Ellis, P. "Women, Adult Education, and Literacy: A Caribbean Perspective." *Convergence,* 1984, *17* (4), 44–53.

Enyia, S. O. *An Investigation of the Development and Application of Participatory Research Methods in Nonformal Education of Rural Adults in Developing Countries.* De Kalb: Leadership and Educational Policy Studies, Northern Illinois University, 1983.

Erasmie, T., Lima, L., and Pereira, L. C. "Adult Education and Community Development: Experiences from Programs in Northern Portugal." *Convergence,* 1984, *17* (4), 17–26.

Eurich, N. *Corporate Classrooms: The Learning Business.* Princeton, N.J.: Carnegie Foundation for the Advancement of Teaching, 1985.

Extension Committee on Organization and Policy. Futures Task Force. *Extension in Transition: Bridging the Gap Between Vi-*

sion and Reality. Virginia Cooperative Extension Service, November 1987.

Farmer, J. A., Jr., Knox, A. B., and Farmer, H. S. (eds.). *International Review of Education*, special issue on counseling and information services for adult learners, 1977, *23* (entire issue 4).

Farnham, D. "Training Trade Unionists in Britain." *Journal of European Industrial Training*, 1987, *11* (3), 5–12.

Farquhar, J. W. "Effects of Community-Wide Education on Cardiovascular Disease Risk Factors: The Stanford Five-City Project." *Journal of the American Medical Association*, 1990, *264* (3), 359–365.

Farquhar, J. W., and others. "Community Education for Cardiovascular Health." *Lancet*, 1977, *1*, 1192–1195.

Faure, E., and Associates. *Learning to Be: The World of Education Today and Tomorrow*. Paris: UNESCO Press, 1972.

Feder, G., Lau, L. J., and Slade, R. "Does Agricultural Extension Pay? The Training and Visit System in Northwest India." *American Journal of Agricultural Economics*, 1987, *69* (3), 677–686.

Feder, G., and Slade, R. "A Comparative Analysis of Some Aspects of the Training and Visit System of Agricultural Extension in India." *Journal of Development Studies*, 1986, *22* (2), 407–428.

Feurerstein, M. T. "Mobilization for Primary Health Care: Role of Adult Education." *Convergence*, 1982, *15* (2), 23–34.

Fiedler, F. E., and Chemers, M. M. *Improving Leadership Effectiveness*. New York: Wiley, 1984.

Fingeret, A., and Jurmo, P. (eds.). *Participatory Literacy Education*. New Directions for Continuing Education, no. 42. San Francisco: Jossey-Bass, 1989.

Flude, R., and Parrott, A. *Education and the Challenge of Change: A Recurrent Education Strategy for Britain*. Milton Keynes, England: Open University Press, 1979.

Fordham, P. "West and South: The Adult Education Dialogue." *Adult Education* [England], June 1986a, *59* (1), 6–13.

Fordham, P. "West and South: The Adult Education Dialogue." *Adult Education* [England], September 1986b, *59* (2), 98–105.

Forest, L. *Extension in the '80s*. Madison: Cooperative Extension Service, University of Wisconsin–Extension, 1983.

Fox, J., and Mutangira, J. "The Overseas Training of Adult Educators: An Evaluation of Programmes in Africa and the U.K.— Some Emerging Themes." *International Journal of Educational Development,* 1985, *5* (3), 241–244.

Fox, R. D., Mazmanian, P. E., and Putnam, R. W. *Changing and Learning in the Lives of Physicians.* New York: Praeger, 1989.

Freire, P. *Pedagogy of the Oppressed.* New York: Seabury Press, 1970.

Friedson, E. *Professional Powers.* Chicago: University of Chicago Press, 1986.

Frischkopf, A., and Braun, J. *Report of the Visit to Information, Guidance, and Counselling Centres in the United Kingdom.* Strasbourg, France: Council for Cultural Cooperation, 1981. (ED 245 111)

Fullan, M. G. "Staff Development, Innovation, and Institutional Development." *Changing School Culture Through Staff Development: The 1990 ASCD Yearbook.* Alexandria, Va.: Association for Supervision and Curriculum Development, 1990.

Furter, P. "Dependency and the Pedagogical Debate: Permanent Education in Latin America." *Compare,* 1983, *13* (2), 99–111.

Further Education Unit [England]. *Retraining Adults. Responding to the Educational/Training Needs of Unemployed Adults in Coventry.* FEU-REPLAN Project Report. London: Further Education Unit, 1986. (ED 275 817)

Gaber-Katz, E., and Watson, G. M. *The Land That We Dream of. A Participatory Study of Community-Based Literacy.* Toronto, Canada: OISE Press, 1991.

Gajardo, M. "Chile: An Experiment in Non-Formal Education in Rural Areas." *Prospects,* 1983, *13* (1), 83–94.

Garrison, D. R. *Understanding Distance Education: A Framework for the Future.* London: Routledge, 1989.

Gaventa, J., and Horton, B. D. "A Citizen's Research Project in Appalachia, U.S.A." *Convergence,* special issue on participatory research, 1981, *14* (3), 30–42.

Gayfer, M. (ed.). "Education and Older Adults." *Convergence,* 1985, *18* (entire issues 1–2).

Gelpi, E. *A Future for Lifelong Education.* Vol. 1: *Lifelong Education: Principles, Policies, and Practices.* Dorset, England: Direct Design, 1979a.

Gelpi, E. "Lifelong Education Policies in Western and Eastern Europe." In T. Schuller and J. Megarry (eds.), *World Yearbook of Education, 1979: Recurrent Education and Lifelong Learning.* London: Kogan Page, 1979b.

Gelpi, E. *Lifelong Education and International Relations.* New York: Croom Helm, 1985.

Giladi, M., and Reed, H. "Nonformal Education Unifies Life-Functions in the Kibbutz." *Community Development Journal,* 1985, *20* (1), 10–16.

Glanz, D. "Aging and Education in Israel." *Educational Gerontology,* 1984, *10,* 245–267.

Glanz, D. "Higher Education and Retirement: The Israeli Experience." *Higher Education in Europe,* 1985, *10* (1), 85–93.

Glanz, D., and Tabory, E. "Higher Education and Retirement: The Israeli Experience." *Educational Gerontology,* 1985, *11,* 101–111.

Glendenning, F. *Education and the Over-60s.* Keele, England: Beth Johnson Foundation, 1976.

Goldman, I. M. *Lifelong Learning Among Jews: Adult Education in Judaism from Biblical Times to the Twentieth Century.* New York: KTAV Publishing House, 1975.

Goldstein, I. L., and Associates. *Training and Development in Organizations.* San Francisco: Jossey-Bass, 1989.

Gooderham, P. N. *Adult Education Outcomes: A Status Attainment Approach.* Trondheim: Norwegian Institute of Adult Education, 1988.

Gordon, H.L.A. "University Adult Education in Jamaica: Origins and Characteristics." *Caribbean Education Bulletin,* May 1979, *6* (2), 15–49.

Gordon, H.L.A. "Adult and Non-Formal Education in the Third World: A Jamaican Perspective." In Kulich, J. (ed.), *Monographs on Comparative and Area Studies in Adult Education.* Vancouver, Canada: Centre for Continuing Education, University of British Columbia, 1985.

Gough, J. E., and Coltman, B. "Counselling the Distance Student: Fact or Fiction." Geelong, Australia: Centre for Educational Services, Deakin University, 1979.

Grebelsky, O., and Tokatli, R. *Literacy in Israel: Widening Horizons.* Jerusalem: Ministry of Education and Culture, 1983.

Green, J. S., Grosswald, S. J., Suter, E., and Walthall, D. B. (eds.). *Continuing Education for the Health Professions: Developing, Managing, and Evaluating Programs for Maximum Impact on Patient Care.* San Francisco: Jossey-Bass, 1984.

Gross, R. "Everyman's University: Open Learning in Israel." *Change,* 1978, *10* (11), 19–21. (EJ 192 718)

Grossi, F. V. "Research in Adult Education in Latin America." *Convergence,* 1984, *17* (2), 15–23.

Gueulette, D. (ed.) *Microcomputers for Adult Learning: Potentials and Perils.* Chicago: Follett, 1982.

Gugnami, H. R. "Adult Literacy by 1990." *Adult Education and Development,* 1985, (24), 106–113.

Gunther, J., and Theroux, J. "Developing Mass Audiences for Educational Broadcasting: Two Approaches." *Prospects: Quarterly Review of Education,* 1977, 7 (2), 288–298. (EJ 64 987)

Hall, B. L. "Mtu ni afya! Tanzania's Mass Health Education Campaign." *Convergence,* 1974, 7 (1), 71–78.

Hall, B. L. "Non-Formal Education: Redistribution of Wealth and Production." *Education in East Africa,* 1977, 7 (1), 1–9.

Hall, B. L. "Knowledge as a Commodity and Participatory Research." *Prospects: Quarterly Review of Education,* 1979, *9* (4), 393–407.

Hall, B. L. *Man Is Health: Tanzania's Health Campaign.* (2nd ed.) Toronto, Canada: International Council for Adult Education, 1985.

Hall, B. L. "Participatory Research." In *International Encyclopedia of Education.* Elmsford, N.Y.: Pergamon Press, forthcoming.

Hall, B. L., and Dodds, T. *Voices for Development: The Tanzanian National Radio Study Campaigns.* IEC Broadsheets on Distance Learning, no. 6. Cambridge, England: International Extension College, 1974.

Hall, B. L., and Stock, A. "Trends in Adult Education Since 1972." *Prospects: Quarterly Journal of Education,* 1985, *15* (1), 13–26.

Hamilton, E. "Adult Education and Community Development in Nigeria." *Graduate Studies Journal,* 1984, *2,* 63–75.

Hanaoka, S. "Training Courses by Japanese Computer Manufacturers." *Education and Computing,* 1986, *1* (4), 235–241.

Harman, D. *Illiteracy: A National Dilemma.* New York: Cambridge University Press, 1987.

Harman, D., and Brim, O. G. *Learning to Be Parents: Principles, Programs, and Methods.* Newbury Park, Calif.: Sage, 1980.

Harman, W. *Global Mind Change.* Indianapolis, Ind.: Knowledge Systems, 1988.

Harris, W.J.A. *Comparative Adult Education: Practice, Purpose, and Theory.* London: Longmann, 1980.

Hautecoeur, J. P. (ed.). *Alpha 90: Current Research in Literacy.* Hamburg, Germany: UNESCO Institute for Education, 1990.

Havelock, R. G. *Planning for Innovation.* Ann Arbor: Center for Research on the Utilization of Scientific Knowledge, University of Michigan, 1969.

Haverkort, B. "Agricultural Production Potentials. Part 1: Inherent, or the Result of Investments in Technology Development? The Influence of Technology Gaps on the Assessment of Production Potentials in Developing Countries." *Agricultural Administration and Extension* [England], 1988, *30*, 127–141.

Heffernan, J. M. *Educational and Career Services for Adults.* Lexington, Mass.: Lexington Books, 1981.

Heim, K. M., and Wallace, D. (eds.). *Adult Services: An Enduring Focus for Public Libraries.* Chicago: American Library Association, 1990.

Henriksson, K. (ed.). *Adult Education in the 1990s: Considerations and Proposals.* Stockholm: Swedish National Board of Education, 1991.

Hernandez, I. "Education and the Elderly Population in Argentina." *Educational Gerontology,* 1984, *10*, 219–231.

Herrera, X., and Lobo-Guerrero, M. "From Failure to Success: Tapping the Creative Energy of Sikuani Culture in Colombia." *Grassroots Development,* 1988, *12* (3), 28–37.

Hinzen, H. (ed.). "Adult Education in Thailand." *Adult Education and Development,* German Adult Education Association, September 1989, (entire issue 33).

Hirsch, H. "Higher Education in Retirement: The Institute for Retired Professionals." *International Journal of Aging and Human Development,* 1978, *8*, 367–374.

Hofstede, G. *Culture's Consequences: International Differences in Work-Related Values.* Newbury Park, Calif.: Sage, 1980.

Hoggart, R. *Continuing Education: From Policies to Practice.* Leicester, England: Advisory Council for Adult and Continuing Education, 1982.

Hoghielm, R. "Ideals and Realities in Competence-Giving Adult Education: An Examination of Swedish Municipal Adult Education." *Adult Education Quarterly,* 1986, *36* (4), 187–201.

Hoghielm, R., and Rubenson, K. (eds.). *Adult Education for Social Change: Research on the Swedish Allocation Policy.* Stockholm: Stockholm Institute of Education, 1980.

Hollnsteiner, M. R. "Mobilizing the Rural Poor Through Community Organization." *Philippine Studies,* 1979, *27,* 387–416.

Holmberg, B. *Theory and Practice of Distance Education.* London: Routledge, 1989.

Hopkins, D. "China's Successful Adult Literacy Campaign." *Adult Literacy and Basic Education,* 1986, *10* (2), 101–116.

Hopkins, P.G.H. *Worker's Education: An International Perspective.* Milton Keynes, England: Open University Press, 1985.

Horne, E. E. (ed.). *Continuing Education: Issues and Challenges.* New York: Saur Verlag, 1985.

Houle, C. O. *The External Degree.* San Francisco: Jossey-Bass, 1973.

Houle, C. O. *Continuing Learning in the Professions.* San Francisco: Jossey-Bass, 1980.

Houle, C. O. *The Literature of Adult Education: A Bibliographic Essay.* San Francisco: Jossey-Bass, 1992.

Howell, J. *Managing Agricultural Extension: The T and V System in Practice.* Agricultural Administration Unit Discussion Paper, no. 8. London: Agricultural Administration Network, 1982.

HR&H Marketing Research [England]. *Marketing Adult/Continuing Education—A Feasibility Study.* Project Report. London: Further Education Unit, 1987. (ED 287 067)

Huang, Y. K. "International Adult Basic Education." *Adult Literacy and Basic Education,* 1985, *9* (1), 49–56.

Hugkuntod, U., and Tips, W. "Planning and Implementation of Nonformal Education Projects in Rural Thailand." *International Review of Education,* 1987, *33,* 51–73.

Humphrey, C., and Meyer, C. *Peace Corps Programming in Small Enterprise Development: Three Case Studies and Analysis.* Washington, D.C.: Peace Corps, 1985.

Hunger Project. *Ending Hunger: An Idea Whose Time Has Come.* New York: Praeger, 1985.

Hunter, C. St. J. "Training Women Workers in Brazilian Favelas." *Convergence,* 1985, *18* (3-4), 129-132.

Hunter, C. St. J., and Keehn, M. M. *Adult Education in China.* London: Croom Helm, 1985.

Husen, T., and Postlethwaite, T. N. (eds.). *The International Encyclopedia of Education.* Elmsford, N.Y.: Pergamon Press, 1985.

Hutchinson, E., and Hutchinson, E. *Women Returning to Learning.* Cambridge, England: National Extension College, 1986. (ED 281 982)

Inglis, T., and Bassett, M. *Live and Learn: An Evaluation Study of Day-Time Adult Education in Coolock, Dublin.* Report Series. Dublin, Ireland: National Association for Adult Education, 1988.

International Council on Adult Education. "Participatory Research: Developments and Issues." *Convergence,* 1981, *14* (entire issue 3).

International Council on Adult Education. "Adult Education for Social Change: All-India Declaration on Priorities and Action." *Convergence,* 1982, *15* (4), 38-43.

International Council on Adult Education. "Education and Older Adults." *Convergence,* 1985, *18* (1-2).

Israeli, E. "The Israeli Experience in Adult Education." *Convergence,* 1978, *11* (3-4), 54-63.

Israeli, E. "Arabic Adult Education in Israel: The Present and the Challenge." *Compare,* 1980, *10* (1), 47-54.

Janne, H., Dominice, P., and James, W. *Development of Adult Education.* Final Report of the CDCC Project, no. 3. Strasbourg, France: Council for Cultural Cooperation, 1980.

Jarvis, P. *Adult Learning in the Social Context.* London: Croom-Helm, 1987.

Jarvis, P. (ed.). *Twentieth Century Thinkers in Adult Education.* London: Routledge, 1991.

Jeria, J. "Literacy in Latin America: The Development of Popular

Education." *Thresholds in Education,* November 1989, pp. 39–42.

Johnson, H. W. *Current Status and Trends of Adult Education in the Netherlands.* Unpublished Master's thesis, University of Minnesota, 1984. (ED 250 532)

Johnson, R. "Developments in Distance Education in Australia." *International Council on Distance Education Bulletin,* May 1991, *26,* 11–22.

Johnston, R. "Outreach Work with Unemployed and Unwaged Adults." *Adult Education,* 1987, *60* (1), 58–65.

Johnstone, J.W.C., and Rivera, R. J. *Volunteers for Learning: A Study of the Educational Pursuits of American Adults.* Hawthorne, N.Y.: Aldine, 1965.

Jones, D. J. *Adult Education and Cultural Development.* New York: Routledge, 1988.

Jones, D. J., and Chadwick, A. F. (eds.). *Adult Education and the Arts.* Nottingham, England: Department of Adult Education, University of Nottingham, 1981.

Jourdan, M. *Recurrent Education in Western Europe.* Windsor, England: NFER-Nelson, 1981.

Joyce, B., Bennett, B., and Rolhelser-Bennett, C. "The Self Educating Teacher." *The 1990 ASCD Yearbook: Changing School Culture Through Staff Development.* Alexandria, Va.: Association for Supervision and Curriculum Development, 1990.

Joyce, B., and Showers, B. *Student Achivement Through Staff Development.* White Plains, N.Y.: Longman, 1988.

Kahler, D. (ed.). International Seminar on Curriculum Development for Basic Education Programmers. Bonn: German Foundation for International Development, 1978. (ED 163 294)

Kairamo, K. (ed.). *Education for Life: A European Strategy.* London: Butterworth, 1989.

Kamfwa, F. D. "Contribution of Women's Clubs to Rural Development in Ndola Rural Development in Ndola Rural East." *Journal of Adult Education* [Lambia], September 1982, *1* (1), 42–55.

Kassam, Y. O. "Political Education vis-á-vis Adult Education in Tanzania: The Dynamics of Their Interaction." *Convergence,* 1974, *7* (4), 40–49.

Kassam, Y. O. "Formal, Nonformal, and Informal Modes of Learning: A Glimpse of the Tanzanian Experience." *International Review of Education*, 1982, *28* (2), 263–267.

Kasworm, C. E. (ed.). *Educational Outreach to Select Adult Populations*. New Directions for Continuing Education, no. 20. San Francisco: Jossey-Bass, 1983.

Katz, D., and Kahn, R. L. *The Social Psychology of Organizations*. (2nd ed.) New York: Wiley, 1978.

Keegan, D. *The Foundations of Distance Education*. London: Croom Helm, 1986.

Keeton, M. T. *A Study of Baccalaureate Curricula for Adults*. College Park: University College, University of Maryland, 1990.

Keller, G. *Academic Strategy, The Management Revolution in American Higher Education*. Baltimore, Md.: Johns Hopkins University Press, 1983.

Kelly, J. "European Cooperation in Continuing Engineering Education." *European Journal of Engineering Education*, 1985, *10* (3–4), 251–256.

Kenny, I. (ed.). *Lifelong Learning, Report of the Commission on Adult Education*. Dublin: Stationery Office, 1983.

Kidd, J. R. "Developing a Methodology for Comparative Studies in Adult Education." *Convergence*, 1970, *3* (3), 12–26.

Kimberly, J. R., Miles, R. H., and Associates. *The Organizational Life Cycle: Issues in the Creation, Transformation, and Decline of Organizations*. San Francisco: Jossey-Bass, 1980.

Kirsch, I. S., and Jungeblut, A. *Literacy: Profiles of America's Young Adults*. Report no. 16-PL-02. Princeton, N.J.: National Assessment of Educational Progress, 1986.

Knoll, J. H. *Adult Education in Federal Republic of Germany*. Vancouver, Canada: Centre for Continuing Education, University of British Columbia, 1981.

Knox, A. B.. "Life-Long Self-Directed Education." In R. J. Blakely (ed.), *Fostering the Growing Need to Learn*. Rockville, Md.: Division of Regional Medical Programs, Bureau of Health Resources Development, 1974.

Knox, A. B. *Enhancing Proficiencies of Continuing Educators*. New Directions for Continuing Education, no. 1. San Francisco: Jossey-Bass, 1979.

Knox, A. B. (ed.). *Leadership Strategies for Meeting New Chal-*

lenges. New Directions for Continuing Education, no. 13. San Francisco: Jossey-Bass, 1982a.

Knox, A. B. "Organizational Dynamics in University Continuing Professional Education." *Adult Education,* 1982b, *32* (3), 117–129.

Knox, A. B. *Helping Adults Learn: A Guide to Planning, Implementation, and Conducting Programs.* San Francisco: Jossey-Bass, 1986.

Knox, A. B. *International Perspectives on Adult Education.* Columbus, Ohio: ERIC Clearinghouse on Adult, Career, and Vocational Education, 1987a.

Knox, A. B. "Reducing Barriers to Participation in Continuing Education." *Lifelong Learning,* 1987b, *10* (5), 7–9.

Knox, A. B. "Strengthening Continuing Education Instruction." *Journal of Continuing Higher Education,* Summer 1987c, *35* (3), 18–20.

Knox, A. B. "Influences on Continuing Education Participation." *Journal of Continuing Education in the Health Professions,* 1990, *10* (3), 261–274.

Kofron, P. M., and Associates. "Physician Practice for Cardiovascular Disease Risk-Factor Reduction in Six Upper Midwest Communities." *Journal of Family Practice,* 1991, *32* (1), 49–55.

Komada, K. "Recent Trends in Adult Education in Japan." *Convergence,* 1977, *10* (4), 48–52.

Kotler, P., and Fox, K. *Strategic Marketing for Educational Institutions.* Englewood Cliffs, N.J.: Prentice-Hall, 1985.

Krajnc, A., and Mrmak, I. *Adult Education in Yugoslavia.* Studies and Documents, no. 4. Prague: European Centre for Leisure and Education, 1978.

Kulich, J., and Kruger, W. (eds.). *The Universities and Adult Education in Europe.* Vancouver, Canada: Centre for Continuing Education, University of British Columbia, 1980. (ED 194 769)

Kunzel, K. "Regional Development and Continuing Education: A Case for a Fresh Look at University Evolution in West Germany?" *Oxford Review of Education,* 1985, *11* (3), 305–316.

LaBelle, T. J. *Nonformal Education in Latin America and the Caribbean: Stability, Reform or Revolution?* New York: Praeger, 1986.

LaBelle, T. J. "From Consciousness Raising to Popular Education in Latin America and the Caribbean." *Comparative Education Review*, 1987, *31* (2), 201–217.

Landa, L. N. "The Algo-Heuristic Theory of Instruction." In C. M. Reigeluth (ed.), *Instructional Design Theories and Models*. Hillsdale, N.J.: Erlbaum, 1983.

Lappé, F. M., and Collins, J. *World Hunger: Twelve Myths*. New York: Grove Press, 1986.

Lee, C. "Basic Training in the Corporate Schoolhouse." *Training*, April 1988, pp. 27–36.

Lee, D. C. "Public Organizations in Adult Education in the Soviet Union." *Comparative Education Review*, 1986, *30* (3), 344–358.

Legge, D. *The Education of Adults in Britain*. Milton Keynes, England: Open University Press, 1982.

Lei, H. "Worker Education in China." *Prospects*, 1985, *15* (3), 389–397.

Levine, H. A. *Strategies for the Application of Foreign Legislation on Paid Educational Leave to the United States Scene*. New Brunswick, N.J.: Labor Education Center, Rutgers University, 1975.

Levine, R. A., and White, M. I. *Human Conditions: The Cultural Bases of Educational Development*. London: Routledge & Kegan Paul, 1986.

Lewin, K. *Field Theory in Social Science*. New York: HarperCollins, 1951.

Lewis, L. H. (ed.) *Addressing the Needs of Returning Women*. New Directions for Continuing Education, no. 39. San Francisco: Jossey-Bass, 1988.

Lichtner, M. *Comparative Research in Adult Education: Present Lines and Perspectives*. Rome, Italy: Centro Europeo dell'Educazione, 1988.

Lieberman, A., and Miller, L. *Staff Development: New Demands, New Realities, New Perspectives*. New York: Teachers College Press, 1979.

Limage, L. J. "Adult Literacy Policy in Industrialized Countries." *Comparative Education Review*, 1986, *30* (1), 50–72.

Lind, A., and Johnston, A. *Adult Literacy in the Third World: A Review of Objectives and Strategies*. Education Division of Documents, no. 32. Stockholm: Institute of International Education and Swedish International Development Authority, 1986.

Lindquist, J. *Strategies for Change.* Berkeley, Calif.: Pacific Soundings Press, 1978.

Lindsay, C. P., and Dempsey, B. L. "Experiences in Training Chinese Business People to Use U.S. Management Techniques." *Journal of Applied Behavioral Science,* 1985, *21* (1), 65–78.

Liveright, A. A., and Haygood, N. *The Exeter Papers: Report of the First International Conference on the Comparative Study of Adult Education.* Brookline, Mass.: Center for the Study of Liberal Education for Adults, 1968.

Liveris, M., and Horvath, N. "Continuing Education: A Cooperative Endeavor." *Journal of Tertiary Educational Administration,* 1984, *6* (1), 85–90.

Livingston, K. "Brokering in Distance Education, Australian Style." *Media in Education and Development,* March 1987, *20,* 10–13.

Loken, B., Swim, J., and Mittelmark, M. "Heart Health Program: Applying Social Influence Processes in a Large-Scale Community Health Promotion Program." In J. Edwards, R. S. Tindale, L. Heath, and E. Posavac (eds.), *Social Influence Processes and Prevention.* New York: Plenum Press, 1990.

Lowe, J. *The Education of Adults: A World Perspective.* Toronto, Canada: UNESCO Press and Ontario Institute for Studies in Education, 1975.

Luft, M. *Popular Adult Education: The Bolivian Experience.* Toronto, Canada: Luft, 1984.

Lumsden, D. B. (ed.) *The Older Adult as Learner: Aspects of Educational Gerontology.* Washington, D.C.: Hemisphere, 1985.

Lusterman, S. *Trends in Corporate Education and Training.* New York: Conference Board, 1985.

Lynton, E. A., and Elman, S. E. *New Priorities for the University: Meeting Society's Needs for Applied Knowledge and Competent Individuals.* San Francisco: Jossey-Bass, 1987.

McAllister, I. "Canadian Aid for the Training of Public Servants in Ghana and Zimbabwe." *Public Administration and Development,* 1987, *7* (3), 289–307.

McCormick, R. "Prospects and Problems for China's TVUs." *Me-*

dia in Education and Development, September 1984, *17* (3), 136–139.

McGrath, M. J. (ed.). *Guidelines for Cooperatives in Developing Countries.* Madison: International Coorperative Training Center, University Extension, University of Wisconsin–Madison, 1969.

McIlroy, J. "Continuing Education and the Universities in Britain: The Political Context." *International Journal of Lifelong Education,* January–March 1987, *6* (1), 27–59.

Mackenzie, K. D. *The Organizational Hologram: The Effective Management of Organizational Change.* Boston: Kluwer Academic, 1991.

McKenzie, L. *Adult Education and Worldview Construction.* Malabar, Fla.: Krieger, 1991.

MacKenzie, N., Postgate, R., and Scupham, J. *Open Learning: Systems and Problems in Post-Secondary Education.* Paris: UNESCO, 1975.

McLagen, P. A. *Models for HRD Practice: The Practitioner's Guide.* Alexandria, Va.: American Society for Training and Development, 1989.

McLean, M. "A World Educational Crisis?" *Compare,* 1986, *16* (2), 199–211.

Maina, P. M. "African Field Notes: Farming Systems, Kenya." *African Development Views as New Challenges Emerge,* 1988–1989, *2,* 44–45.

Manheimer, R. J. "Developing Arts and Humanities Programming with the Elderly." *Adult Services in Action.* No. 2. Chicago: Reference and Adult Services Division, American Library Association, 1984.

Marsick, V. J. (ed.). *Learning in the Workplace.* Beckenham, England: Croom Helm, 1987.

Marsick, V. J. (ed.). *Enhancing Staff Development in Diverse Settings.* New Directions for Continuing Education, no. 38. San Francisco: Jossey-Bass, 1988a.

Marsick, V. J. "Proactive Learning in Primary Health Care: An Adult Education Model." *International Journal of Adult Education,* April–June 1988b, *7* (2), 101–114.

Marsick, V. J., and Cederholm, L. "Developing Leadership in International Managers—An Urgent Challenge!" *Columbia Journal of World Business,* 1988, *23* (4), 3–11.

Marsick, V. J., and Watkins, K. *Informal and Incidental Learning in the Workplace.* London: Routledge, 1990.

Martin, D. "Pedagogy and Politics: Adult Education in Latin America." *Convergence,* 1983, *16* (4), 17–23.

Mathews, A. *Library Programs: Library Literacy Program, Abstracts of Funded Projects, 1986.* Washington, D.C.: U.S. Department of Education, 1987.

Maydl, P., and Savicky, I. "Comparative Research Project on Organization and Structure of Adult Education in Europe." *Convergence,* 1986, *19* (3), 61–69.

Maydl, P., and Associates. *Adult Education in Europe: Methodological Framework for Comparative Studies.* Prague: European Center for Leisure and Education, 1983.

Menges, R. J., and Mathis, B. C. *Key Resources on Teaching, Learning, Curriculum, and Faculty Development: A Guide to the Higher Education Literature.* San Francisco: Jossey-Bass, 1988.

Merriam, S. B., and Cunningham, P. M. (eds.). *Handbook of Adult and Continuing Education.* San Francisco: Jossey-Bass, 1989.

Mescon, T. S. "The Entrepreneurial Institute: Education and Training for Minority Business Owners." *Journal of Small Business Management,* Jan. 1987, pp. 61–66.

Mezirow, J. *Transformative Dimensions of Adult Learning.* San Francisco: Jossey-Bass, 1991.

Midwest Universities Consortium for International Activities. *The Caribbean Agricultural Extension Project: More Productive Agriculture Through Extension.* Columbus, Ohio: Midwest Universities Consortium for International Activities, 1987.

Midwinter, E. "The University of the Third Age in Britain." *Universities Quarterly,* Winter 1983–1984, *38* (1), 9–15.

Midwinter, E. (ed.). *Mutual Aid Universities.* London: Croom Helm, 1984a.

Midwinter, E. "The Social Determinants of Educational Policy in the United Kingdom and Their Effects on the Provision of Educational Opportunities for the Elderly." *Educational Gerontology,* 1984b, *10,* 197–206.

Millard, R. M. *Today's Myths and Tomorrow's Realities: Overcoming Obstacles to Academic Leadership in the Twenty-First Century.* San Francisco: Jossey-Bass, 1991.

Miller, V. *Between Struggle and Hope: The Nicaraguan Literacy Crusade.* Boulder, Colo.: Westview Press, 1985.

Mire, J. *Labor Education: A Study Report on Needs, Programs, and Approaches.* Madison, Wis.: Inter-University Labor Education Committee, 1956.

Mitroff, I. I. *Stakeholders of the Organizational Mind: Toward a New View of Organizational Policy Making.* San Francisco: Jossey-Bass, 1983.

Mittelmark, M. B., and others. "Community-Wide Prevention of Cardiovascular Disease: Education Strategies of the Minnesota Heart Health Program." *Preventive Medicine,* 1986, *15,* 1-17.

Miura, S. *A Methodological Study of the Citizens' Learning Network in a Small-Size City in Japan.* Paper presented to the national AAACE Conference, Louisville, Ky., 1984. (ED 251 604)

Molnar, J. J., and Clonts, H. A. (eds.). *Transferring Food Production Technology to Developing Nations.* Boulder, Colo.: Westview Press, 1983.

Moon, J., Webber, D., and Richardson, J. J. "Linking Policy Areas—IT Education, Training and Youth Unemployment in the UK and West Germany." *Policy and Politics,* 1986, *14* (2), 161-188.

Moore, M. (ed.). *Contemporary Issues in American Distance Education.* Elmsford, N.Y.: Pergamon Press, 1990.

Morin, L. (ed.). *On Prison Education.* Ottawa: Canadian Government Publishing Centre, 1981.

Moro'oka, K. "Continuing Education: The Japanese Approach." *Bulletin of the UNESCO Regional Office for Asia and the Pacific,* Sept. 1987, *28,* 47-64.

Morris, C. "Universities and the Third Age." *Adult Education* [England], September 1984, 57 (2), 135-139.

Morrison, J. L. "Establishing an Environmental Scanning System to Augment College and University Planning." *Planning for Higher Education,* 1987, *15* (1), 7-22.

Morrison, J. L., Renfro, W. L., and Boucher, W. I. *Futures Research and the Strategic Planning Process: Implications for Higher Ed-*

ucation. ASHE-ERIC Higher Education Report, no. 9. Washington, D.C.: Association for the Study of Higher Education, 1984.

Mouton, J. S., and Blake, R. R. *Synergogy: A New Strategy for Education, Training, and Development.* San Francisco: Jossey-Bass, 1984.

Mpogolo, Z. J. "Post-Literacy and Continuing Education in Tanzania." *International Review of Education,* 1984, *30* (3), 351–358.

Mugridge, I., and Kaufman, D. (eds.). *Distance Education in Canada.* London: Croom Helm, 1986.

Murchu, M. W. *Adult Education in Ireland.* Studies and Documents, no. 21–22. Prague: European Centre for Leisure and Education, 1984.

Murgatroyd, S. "Business, Education, and Distance Education." *American Journal of Distance Education,* 1990, *4* (1), 39–52.

Murray, D. M., and others. "Systematic Risk Factor Screening and Education: A Community-Wide Approach to Prevention of Coronary Heart Disease." *Preventive Medicine,* 1986, *15,* 661–672.

Mutahaba, G. "The Training and Development of Top Executives in Developing Countries—A Tanzanian Approach." *Public Administration and Development,* 1986, *6* (1), 49–59.

Nadler, L. (ed.). *The Handbook of Human Resource Development.* New York: Wiley, 1984.

Nadler, L., and Wiggs, G. D. *Managing Human Resource Development: A Practical Guide.* San Francisco: Jossey-Bass, 1986.

Nagel, U. J. *Institutionalization of Knowledge Flows: An Analysis of the Extension Role of Two Agricultural Universities in India.* Frankfurt, Germany: DLG-Verlag, 1980.

National Association for Adult Education [Ireland]. *Priority Areas in Adult Education.* Report Series. Dublin, Ireland: National Association for Adult Education, 1986.

National Institute for Educational Research [Japan]. *Non-Formal Education in Asia and the Pacific.* Report of a workshop in Tokyo, Japan, Nov. 1986. (ED 283 966)

Nesman, E. G. *Peasant Mobilization and Rural Development.* Rochester, Vt.: Schenkman, 1981.

Neumann, R., and Lindsay, A. "The Johnson-Hinton Report on Continuing Education: Some Implications for Higher Education." *Australian Universities' Review,* 1986, *29* (2), 45–47.

Neves, H. "Role of the Women's Movement in Literacy Campaigns: The Portuguese Experience." *Convergence,* 1982, *15* (3), 73–76.

Newman, M. *The Poor Cousin: A Study of Adult Education,* London: Allen & Unwin, 1979.

Nichter, M., and Nichter, M. "Health Education by Appropriate Analogy: Using the Familiar to Explain the New." *Convergence,* 1986, *14* (1), 63–72.

Niebuhr, H. *Revitalizing American Learning, A New Approach That Just Might Work.* Belmont, Calif.: Wadsworth, 1984.

Niemi, J., and Gooler, D. D. (eds.). *Technologies for Learning Outside the Classroom.* New Directions for Continuing Education, no. 34. San Francisco: Jossey-Bass, 1987.

Nji, A., and Nji, K. L. "Why My Mother Died Illiterate: For an Appropriate Technology in Adult Literacy Programs in Cameroon." *International Foundation for Development Alternatives,* 1985, *46,* 3–14.

Nordhaug, O. "Distribution of Adult Education: The Norwegian Case." *Adult Education Quarterly,* 1983, *34* (1), 29–37.

Nordhaug, O. *The Shadow Educational System: Adult Resource Development.* Oslo: Norwegian University Press and Oxford University Press, 1991.

Northmore, S. "A Community Development Model of Adult Education." *Community Development Journal,* 1986, *21* (3), 181–185.

Nowlen, P. M. *A New Approach to Continuing Education for Business and the Professions.* New York: Macmillan, 1988.

Nusberg, C., Gibson, M. J., and Peace, S. *Innovative Aging Programs Abroad: Implications for the United States.* Westport, Conn.: Greenwood Press, 1984.

Nutbeam, D., and Catford, J. "The Welsh Heart Programme Evaluation Strategy: Progress, Plans, and Possibilities." *Health Promotion,* 1987, *2* (1), 5–18.

Nwaerondu, N. G., and Thompson, G. "The Use of Educational Radio in Developing Countries: Lessons from the Past." *Journal of Distance Education,* Fall 1987, *2* (2), 43–54.

Nxumalo, S. "Income-Generating Project Develops Skills of Swazi Women." *Convergence,* 1982, *15* (3), 48–55.

Nyerere, J. K. "Declaration of Dar es Salaam: 'Liberated Man—the Purpose of Development'." *Convergence,* 1976, *9* (4), 9–17.

Nyirenda, J. E. "Radio Broadcasting for Rural Development in Zambia." *Journal of Adult Education* [Zambia], September 1982, *1* (1), 1–8.

O'Connor, A. *Nursing Staff Development and Continuing Education.* Boston: Little, Brown, 1986.

Odunuga, S. "Literacy Campaigns in Developing Countries." *System,* 1984, *12* (3), 235–242.

Okeem, E. O. *Adult Education in Ghana and Tanzania, 1945–1975: Socio-Cultural Determinants of Literacy Education and Extra-Mural Studies.* Nsukka: University of Nigeria Press, 1982.

Okun, M. A. (ed.). *Programs for Older Adults.* New Directions for Continuing Education, no. 14. San Francisco: Jossey-Bass, 1982.

Oliver, L. *Study Circles: Coming Together for Personal Growth and Social Action.* Cabin John, Md.: Seven Locks Press, 1987.

Omolewa, M. "The First Year of Nigeria's Mass Literacy Campaign and New Prospects for the Future." *Convergence,* 1984, *17* (1), 55–62.

Onushkin, V. G., and Tonkonogaya, E. P. *Adult Education in the USSR.* Studies and Documents, no. 20. Prague: European Centre for Leisure and Education, 1984.

Oomen-Myin, M. A. "The Involvement of Rural Women in Village Development in Tanzania." *Convergence,* 1983, *16* (2), 59–69.

Organization for Economic Cooperation and Development. *Yugoslavia.* Reviews of National Policies for Education. Paris: Organization for Economic Cooperation and Development, 1981.

Organization for Economic Cooperation and Development. *Education and Training after Basic Schooling.* Paris: Organization for Economic Cooperation and Development, 1985.

Oshima, K., and Yamada, K. "Continuing Engineering Education in Japan." *European Journal of Engineering Education,* 1985, *10* (3–4), 217–220.

Osuhor, P. C., and Osuhor, A. "Factors of Culture and Change in Health Education for Adults in Nigeria." *Convergence,* 1978, *11* (2), 63–68.

O'Sullivan-Ryan, J., and Kaplun, M. "Communication Methods to Promote Grassroots Participation: A Summary of Research Findings from Latin America." Report to UNESCO. Paris: UNESCO, n.d.

O'Toole, L. J. "Interorganizational Cooperation and the Implementation of Labor-Market Training Policies: Sweden and the Federal Republic of Germany." *Organizational Studies,* 1983, *4* (2), 129-150.

Parish, R., Catford, J., and Nutbeam, D. "Breathing Life into Wales: Progress in the Welsh Heart Programme." *Health Trends,* Cardiff, U.K.: May 1987, *19,* 23-27.

Payne, B. C., and others. "Method of Evaluating and Improving Ambulatory Medical Care." *Health Services Research,* June 1984, *19* (2), 219-245.

Payne, D. "Education for Adults in China." *Adult Education* [England], 1987, *59* (4), 356-360.

Pedler, M. (ed.). *Action Learning in Practice.* Aldershot, England: Gower, 1983.

Peters, J. M., Jarvis, P., and Associates (eds.). *Adult Education: Evolution and Achievements in a Developing Field of Study.* San Francisco: Jossey-Bass, 1991.

Peterson, D. A. *Facilitating Education for Older Learners.* San Francisco: Jossey-Bass, 1983.

Peterson, R. E., and Associates. *Lifelong Learning in America: An Overview of Current Practices, Available Resources, and Future Prospects.* San Francisco: Jossey-Bass, 1979.

Peterson, R. E., and Associates. *Adult Education and Training in Industrialized Countries.* New York: Praeger, 1982.

Pitman, W. "Education for a Maturing Generation in Canada." *Educational Gerontology,* 1984, *10,* 207-217.

Prasad, C., Choudhary, B. N., and Doval, A. M. *Krishi Vigyan Kendra Farm Science Center: Management and Operational Guidelines.* New Delhi: Publications and Information Division, Indian Council of Agricultural Research, 1985.

Puska, P., and others. *Community Control of Cardiovascular Diseases: The North Karelia Project.* Copenhagen: World Health Organization, 1981.

Pyne, P. "The USIDEC Clearing House Project: Adult Education and the Latin American Co-Operative Movement." *International Journal of Lifelong Education,* 1984, *3* (4), 305-316.

Queeney, D. S. (ed.). *An Agenda for Action: Continuing Professional Education Focus Group Reports.* University Park, Pa.: Office of Continuing Professional Education, Division of Planning Studies, Pennsylvania State University, 1990.

Quigley, A. (ed.). *Fulfilling the Promise of Adult and Continuing Education.* New Directions for Continuing Education, no. 44. San Francisco: Jossey-Bass, 1989.

Radcliffe, D. "U3A: A French Model for the Later Years." Paper presented at the annual conference of the Comparative and International Education Society, New York City, March 18–21, 1982. (ED 228 134)

Ramsden, K. W. "Continuing Engineering Education: The UK Scene and the Contribution of Cranfield Institute of Technology." *European Journal of Engineering Education,* 1985, *10* (3–4), 229–234.

Rangaswami, G. "Adult Education: A Viewpoint." *Indian Journal of Adult Education,* 1984, *45* (5), 13–16.

Reason, P., and Rowan, J. (eds.). *Human Inquiry: A Sourcebook of New Paradigm Research.* New York: Wiley, 1981.

Reed, H. B. "Conflicting Images of Nonformal Education." *Lifelong Learning,* 1987, *10* (6), 23–25.

Reischmann, J. (ed.). *Adult Education in West Germany in Case Studies.* New York: Verlag Peter Lang, 1988.

Reischmann, J. "Facilitating Adults' Learning by Coaching: Development and Evaluation of an Andragogical Model of Continuing Vocational Education Within Industrial Companies." *Learning Environments: Contributions from Dutch and German Research.* Berlin: Springer-Verlag, 1990.

Revans, R. W. *Developing Effective Managers: A New Approach to Business Education.* New York: Praeger, 1971.

Revans, R. W. *The Origin and Growth of Action Learning.* Lund, Sweden: Studenlihterafur, 1982.

Rice, E. B. *Extension in the Andes: An Evaluation of Official U.S. Assistance to Agricultural Extension Services in Central and South America.* Cambridge, Mass.: MIT Press, 1974.

Riche, M. F. "America's New Workers." *American Demographics,* February 1988, pp. 34–41.

Risler, M. "Adult Vocational Education in the People's Republic of China." *Adult Education and Development*, 1987, *28*, 175–190.

Rivera, W. M., and Dohmen, G. "Political System, Educational Policy, and Lifelong Learning—The Experience of Two Federally Constituted Nations: The United States and the Federal Republic of Germany." *International Journal of Lifelong Education*, 1985, *4* (2), 135–148. (EJ 317 906)

Rivera, W. M., and Gustafson, D. J. (eds.) *Agricultural Extension: Worldwide Institutional Evolution and Forces for Change.* Amsterdam: Elsevier Science, 1991.

Rivera, W. M., and Schram, S. G. *Agricultural Extension Worldwide: Issues, Practices, and Emerging Priorities.* London: Croom Helm, 1987.

Roberts, H. *Culture and Adult Education: A Study of Alberta and Quebec.* Edmonton, Canada: University of Alberta Press, 1982.

Robertson, C. C. "Formal or Nonformal Education? Entrepreneurial Women in Ghana." *Comparative Education Review*, 1984, *28* (4), 639–658.

Rogers, E. M., and Shoemaker, F. F. *Communication of Innovations: A Cross-Cultural Approach.* (2nd ed.) New York: Free Press, 1971.

Rojo, E. "Literacy and Politics in Latin America: The Case of Brazil, Peru, and Nicaragua." *Convergence*, 1984, *17* (2), 24–33.

Rongshu, C. "The Chinese Way." *Labour Education*, 1987, *67* (2), 30–32.

Rubenson, K. *Participation in Recurrent Education.* Paris: Organization for Economic Cooperation and Development, 1977.

Rumble, G. "Distance Education in Latin America: Models for the '80s." *Distance Education*, 1985, *6* (2), 248–255.

Rumble, G., and Harry, K. (eds.). *The Distance Teaching Universities.* London: Croom Helm, 1982.

Russell, R. *Further Education and Industrial Training in England and Wales.* Comparative Papers in Further Education, no. 12. Blagdon, England: Further Education Staff College, 1984. (ED 241 710)

Ryan, J. "Some Key Problems in Adult Literacy." *Prospects: Quarterly Review of Education*, 1985, *15* (3), 375–381. (EJ 332 206)

Sadowske, P. S., and Adrian, J. G. (eds.). *Outlook Report: Perspec-*

tives on the '90s. Madison: Cooperative Extension Service, University of Wisconsin–Extension, 1990.

Saha, A. "Training as a Major Factor in Japanese Economic Success." *Journal of European Industrial Training,* 1987, *11* (7), 13–16.

Sanders, H. D. (ed.). *The Cooperative Extension Service.* Englewood Cliffs, N.J.: Prentice-Hall, 1966.

Savićević, D. M. "Comparative Theory of Adult Education in Yugoslavia." *Convergence,* 1970, *3* (3), 43–47.

Savićević, D. M. "Adult Education Systems in European Socialist Countries." In A. N. Charters and Associates, *Comparing Adult Education Worldwide.* San Francisco: Jossey-Bass, 1981.

Saxena, J. C., and Sachdeva, J. L. (eds.). *Role of Adult Education and Mass Media for Civic Education.* Report of the Asian Pacific Seminar, New Delhi, India. New Delhi: Indian Adult Education Association, 1985. (ED 282 032)

Scheibl, H. J., and Bartz, W. J. "Continuing Education in the Federal Republic of Germany." *European Journal of Engineering Education,* 1986, *11* (1), 75–81.

Schlossberg, N. K., Lynch, A. Q., and Chickering, A. W. *Improving Higher Education Environments for Adults: Responsive Programs and Services from Entry to Departure.* San Francisco: Jossey-Bass, 1989.

Schmidt, H. G., Norman, G. R., and Boshuizen, H.P.A. "A Cognitive Perspective on Medical Expertise: Theory and Implications." *Academic Medicine,* October 1990, *65* (10), 611–621.

Schneider, G. "Adult Education in the German Democratic Republic." *Prospects: Quarterly Review of Education,* 1977, 7 (2), 263–271. (EJ 164 984)

Schön, D. A. *Educating the Reflective Practitioner: Toward a New Design for Teaching and Learning in the Professions.* San Francisco: Jossey-Bass, 1987.

Schuller, T., and Megarry, J. (eds.). *Recurrent Education and Lifelong Learning: World Yearbook of Education 1979.* New York: Nichols, 1979. (ED 182 432)

Schulz, J. H., and Davis-Friedman, N. O. *Aging China: Family, Economics, and Government Policies in Transition.* Washington, D.C.: Gerontological Society of America, 1987.

Schwier, H., and Piazolo, P. H. *Adult Education in the Federal Republic of Germany*. Contribution of the Federal Republic of Germany to the 4th International Conference of UNESCO on Adult Education. Paris: UNESCO, 1985.

Segal, D. R. "The Soviet Military—Political-Education, Training and Morale." *Contemporary Sociology: A Journal of Reviews,* 1988, *17* (2), 184–186.

Selman, G., and Dampier, P. *The Foundations of Adult Education in Canada*. Toronto: Canada: Thompson Educational Publishing, 1991.

Senge, P. M. *The Fifth Discipline: The Art and Practice of the Learning Organization*. New York: Doubleday, 1990.

Shale, D. "Innovation in International Higher Education: The Open Universities." *Journal of Distance Education,* Spring 1987, *2* (1), 7–24.

Shaner, W. W., Philipp, P. F., and Schmehl, W. R. *Farming Systems Research and Development*. Boulder, Colo.: Westview Press, 1982.

Sher, A. E. *Aging in Post-Mao China*. Boulder, Colo.: Westview Press, 1984.

Shorey, L. L. "Training for Formal and Nonformal Education: A Caribbean Perspective." *Convergence,* 1983, *16* (4), 57–64.

Sidel, M. "Adult Education in the People's Republic of China." *Convergence,* 1982, *15* (3), 37–47.

Silberman, M. *Active Training*. Lexington, Mass.: Lexington Books, 1990.

Simerly, R. G., and Associates. *Strategic Planning and Leadership in Continuing Education: Enhancing Organizational Vitality, Responsiveness, and Identity*. San Francisco: Jossey-Bass, 1987.

Simerly, R. G., and Associates. *Handbook of Marketing for Continuing Education*. San Francisco: Jossey-Bass, 1989.

Simmons, H. C. "Religious Education of Older Adults: A Present and Future Perspective." *Educational Gerontology,* 1988, *14,* 279–289.

Simmons, J. *The Education Dilemma: Policy Issues for Developing Countries in the 1980s*. Elmsford, N.Y.: Pergamon Press, 1980.

Skalka, J., and Livecka, E. (eds.). *Adult Education in the Czecho-*

slovak Socialist Republic. Prague: European Center on Leisure and Education, 1977.

Slotnick, H. B., Pelton, M. H., Fuller, M. L., and Tabor, L. *Adult Learners on Campus.* New York: Falmer Press, 1992.

Smith, M. "Adult and Continuing Education at the University of Western Australia." *Media in Education and Development,* June 1986, pp. 66–70.

Smith, R. M., and Associates. *Learning to Learn Across the Life Span.* San Francisco: Jossey-Bass, 1990.

Sobeih, N.A.A. "Nonformal Education in the Arab States: A Comparative Analysis." Paper presented at the annual conference of the International Society, Houston, Texas, March 21–24, 1984. (ED 243 744)

Soljan, N. N. (ed.). *Adult Education in Yugoslav Society.* Zagreb, Yugoslavia: Androgogical Centre, 1985.

Solmon, L. C., and Gordon, J. J. *The Characteristics and Needs of Adults in Postsecondary Education.* Lexington, Mass.: Lexington Books, 1981.

Southam. *Literacy in Canada.* Ottawa: Creative Research Group, 1987.

Steedman, H., and others. *Trends in Innovation in Continuing Education and Training.* Berlin: European Centre for the Development of Vocational Training, 1984. (ED 270 614)

Sternberg, R. J. *The Triarchic Mind.* New York: Penguin Books, 1988.

Stokes, K. (ed.). *Faith Development in the Adult Life Cycle.* New York: Sadlier, 1983.

Strom, R. "Intergenerational Learning and Curriculum Development." *Educational Gerontology,* 1988, *14,* 165–181.

Stromquist, N. P. "Decentralizing Educational Decision-Making in Peru: Intentions and Realities." *International Journal of Educational Development,* 1986, *6* (11), 47–60.

Stroud, J. S., and others (eds.). *Learning at a Distance: A World Perspective.* Edmonton, Canada: Athabasca University, International Council for Correspondence Education, 1982.

Stubblefield, H. W. (ed.). *Continuing Education for Community Leadership.* New Directions for Continuing Education, no. 11. San Francisco: Jossey-Bass, 1981.

Stubblefield, H. W. *Towards a History of Adult Education in America: The Search for a Unifying Principle.* New York: Croom Helm, 1988.

Styler, W. E. *Adult Education and Political Systems.* Nottingham, England: Department of Adult Education, University of Nottingham, 1984.

Summers, G. F., and others (eds.). *Agriculture and Beyond: Rural Economic Development.* Madison: Department of Agricultural Journalism, University of Wisconsin–Madison, 1988.

Sundqvist, A. "New Rules for Swedish Study Circles." *Western European Education,* 1983–1984, *15* (4), 83–95.

Sungsri, S., and Mellor, W. L. "The Philosophy and Services of Non-Formal Education in Thailand." *International Review of Education,* 1984, *30* (4), 441–455.

Supote, P., and Akin, R. *Villagers' Views on Rural Development: Potentials, Constraints, and Strategies.* Unpublished position paper on rural development in Thailand, 1984.

Sutton, P. *Basic Education in Prisons: Interim Report.* Hamburg, Germany: UNESCO Institute for Education, 1992.

Swanson, B. E. *Analyzing Agricultural Technology Systems.* Urbana: International Program for Agricultural Knowledge Systems, Office of International Agriculture, University of Illinois, 1985.

Swanson, B. E., Sands, C. M., and Peterson, W. E. "Analyzing Agricultural Technology Systems: Some Methodological Tools." In R. G. Echeverria (ed.), *Methods for Diagnosing Research System Constraints and Assessing the Impact of Agricultural Research.* Vol. 1: *Diagnosing Agriculture Research System Constraints.* The Hague: ISNAR, 1990.

Swedish Educational Broadcasting Company. *Radio and TV Aided Distance Education in Sweden.* Stockholm: Swedish Educational Broadcasting Company, 1988.

Swedish National Board of Education. *Adult Education in the 1990's.* Stockholm: Swedish National Board of Education, 1990.

Swett Morales, F. X. "Aspects of Financing Non-Formal Education." *Prospects: Quarterly Review of Education,* 1983, *13* (1), 55–60.

Swindell, R. *General Background and Statistical Information on*

U3A and BCAE. A report to the 1st national U3A [University of the Third Age] Conference, Melbourne, Australia, August 1988.

Swindell, R. *Characteristics and Aspirations of Older Learners from Twelve U3A Campuses in New South Wales, Queensland, and South Australia.* Queensland, Australia: Griffith University, 1990a.

Swindell, R. "Characteristics and Aspirations of Older Learners in an Australian University of the Third Age Program: Part 1, Survey Results." *Educational Gerontology,* 1990b, *16,* 1-13.

Taylor, M. C., and Draper, J. A. (eds.). *Adult Literacy Perspectives.* Toronto, Canada: Culture Concepts, 1989.

Taylor, R., Rockhill, K., and Fieldhouse, R. *University Adult Education in England and the United States: A Reappraisal of the Liberal Tradition.* New York: Croom Helm, 1985.

Tennant, M. (ed.). *Adult and Continuing Education in Australia: Issues and Practices.* London: Routledge, 1991.

Theobald, R. *The Rapids of Change: Social Entrepreneurship in Turbulent Times.* Indianapolis: Knowledge Systems, 1987.

Thomas, A. M. *Adult Illiteracy in Canada—A Challenge.* Ottawa: Canadian Commission for UNESCO, 1983.

Thomas, J. E. *Learning Democracy in Japan: The Social Education of Japanese Adults.* London: Sage, 1985.

Thompson, J. "Adult Education and the Disadvantaged." *Convergence,* 1983, *16* (2), 42-47.

Thoursonjones, M. "Unemployment, Schooling, and Training in Developing Countries—Tanzania, Egypt, the Philippines, and Indonesia," *Comparative Education,* 1986, *22* (2), 171-173.

Titmus, C. "Proposed Theoretical Model for the Comparative Study of National Adult Education Systems in Europe." *Society and Leisure,* 1976, *8* (2), 39-54.

Titmus, C. *Strategies for Adult Education, Practices in Western Europe.* Chicago: Follett, 1981.

Titmus, C. (ed.). *Lifelong Education for Adults: An International Handbook.* Elmsford, N.Y.: Pergamon Press, 1989.

Tjerandsen, C. *Education for Citizenship.* Santa Cruz, Calif.: Schwarzhaupt Foundation, 1980.

Tjerandsen, C. "The Highlander Heritage: Education for Social Change." *Convergence,* 1983, *16* (2), 10-22.

Todd, F. "Learning and Work: Directions for Continuing Professional and Vocational Education." *International Journal of Lifelong Education,* 1984, *3* (2), 89–104.

Tonković, S. "Education for Self Management." In N. N. Soljan (ed.), *Adult Education in Yugoslav Society.* Zagreb, Yugoslavia: Andragogical Centre, 1985.

Torres, C. A. "Adult Education Policy, Capitalist Development, and Class Alliance: Latin America and Mexico." *International Journal of Political Education,* 1983, *6* (2), 157–173. (EJ 286 010)

Torres, C. A. *The Politics of Nonformal Education in Latin America.* New York: Praeger, 1990.

Tuomisto, J. (ed.). *Adult Education in Finland,* 1987, *24* (1-2), 1–56.

Ulich, M. E. *Patterns of Adult Education: A Comparative Study.* New York, Pageant Press, 1965.

UNESCO. *An Orientation Seminar for the Arab States on the Development of Learning Strategies for Post-Literacy and Continuing Education in the Perspective of Lifelong Education.* UNESCO, Hamburg: Institute for Education, Unesco Institute for Education Project on Post-Literacy and Continuing Education, 1986.

Valentine, J. "Adult Functional Literacy as a Goal of Instruction." *Adult Education Quarterly,* 1986, *36* (2), 108–113.

van Enckevort, G., and Leibrandt, G. J. *The Open University of the Netherlands: Serving the Adult Learner by Distance Education and Improving Higher Education.* Unpublished report, 1987. (285 050)

van Meygaard, H. V. "The Relationship Between Engineering Education and Industry in the Netherlands." *European Journal of Engineering Education,* 1985, *10* (2), 177–184.

Verduin, J. R., Jr., and Clark, T. A. *Distance Education: The Foundations of Effective Practice.* San Francisco: Jossey-Bass, 1991.

Verhagen, K. *Cooperation for Survival: An Analysis of an Experiment in Participatory Research and Planning with Small Farmers in Sri Lanka and Thailand.* Geneva, Switzerland: International Cooperative Alliance, 1984.

Verhine, R. E., and Lehmann, R. H. "Nonformal Education and Occupational Attainment: A Study of Job Seekers in Northeastern Brazil." *Comparative Education Review,* 1982, *26* (3), 374–390. (EJ 273 114)

Villarroel, A. "Changing the Role of Adult Education Programs in Latin America." Paper presented at the annual convention of the International Studies Association, Mexico City, Mexico, April 5–9, 1983. (ED 235 093).

Vio Grossi, F., Hall, B., Stromquist, N., and Duke, C. *International Aid in Adult Education: Working Papers from the Kungalv Seminar.* Toronto, Canada: International Council for Adult Education, 1986.

Vladislavlev, A. P. "Continuing Education in Developed Soviet Society." *Soviet Education,* April 1979, *21* (5), 6–25.

Vladislavlev, A. P. "Soviet Union Serves Wide Learning Needs." *Convergence,* 1980, *13* (4), 74–75.

Vogel, L. J. *Teaching and Learning in Communities of Faith: Empowering Adults Through Religious Education.* San Francisco: Jossey-Bass, 1991.

Votruba, J. C. (ed.). *Strengthening Internal Support for Continuing Education.* New Directions for Continuing Education, no. 9. San Francisco: Jossey-Bass, 1981.

Wagner, D. A., and Puchner, L. D. (eds.). *World Literacy in the Year 2000.* Annals of the American Academy of Political and Social Science, vol. 520. Newbury Park, Calif.: Sage, 1992.

Wagner, R.M.K. "University Accommodation of Distance Education in Canada." *Journal of Distance Education,* Spring 1988, *3* (1), 25–38.

Walker, S. "A Comparison of Personnel Training Needs and Program Priorities for the Disabled in Ghana and Nigeria." *Journal of Negro Education,* 1983, *52* (2), 162–169.

Wang, M., Lin, W., Sun, S., and Fang, J. (eds.). *China: Lessons from Practice.* New Directions for Continuing Education, no. 37. San Francisco: Jossey-Bass, 1988.

Ward, K. "What Response Can Adult Education Offer to the Unemployment Crisis?" *Convergence,* 1984, *17* (4), 27–36.

Warner, M. "Review of Competence and Competition—Training and Education in the Federal Republic of Germany, the United States, and Japan." *Journal of General Management,* 1985, *10* (4), 97–104.

Weisbord, M. R. *Productive Workplaces: Organizing and Managing for Dignity, Meaning, and Community.* San Francisco: Jossey-Bass, 1987.

Wells, A. "Adult Literacy and Basic Education: The British Experience." *Adult Literacy and Basic Education,* 1985, *9* (1), 1-10.

Wells, R. L., and Goetz, D. N. *Adult Education in the Union of Soviet Socialist Republics.* Unpublished report, 1987. (ED 289 047)

Wenqing, Z. "Report of a Symposium on Rural Education in China." *Rural Education in China,* 1987, *39,* 24-29.

Werner, D. "Empowerment and Health." *Contact,* April 1988, *102,* 1-9.

Werner, G. A. *Recent Developments of Vocational and Professional Continuing Education in West Germany: Trends and Prospects.* Paper presented to national American Association for Adult and Continuing Education Conference, Hollywood, Fla., 1986. (ED 275 895)

Williams, D. B. *Agricultural Extension: Farm Extension Services in Australia, Britain, and the United States of America.* Melbourne, Australia: Melbourne University Press, 1968.

Williams, G. *Toward Lifelong Education: A New Role for Higher Education Institutions.* Paris: UNESCO, 1977.

Willis, B. "The Flight of the Pelican: Training of Aboriginal Adult Educators in Australia." *Convergence,* 1986, *19* (1), 32-38.

Willis, S. L., Dubin, S. S., and Associates. *Maintaining Professional Competence: Approaches to Career Enhancement, Vitality, and Success Throughout a Worklife.* San Francisco: Jossey-Bass, 1990.

Wilson, J. P. (ed.). *Materials for Teaching Adults: Selection, Development, and Use.* New Directions for Continuing Education, no. 17. San Francisco: Jossey-Bass, 1983.

Wilson, R., and Hooper, P. *Computer Assisted Learning in Basic Adult Education.* Payneham, Australia: Technical and Further Education, National Centre for Research and Development, 1986. (ED 286 062)

Wolf, J., and Waldron, M. W. "Measuring and Managing Variables for Continuing Education Programs in a University Setting: An Econometric Model." Paper presented to Canadian Association for University Continuing Education, Ottawa, 1986. (ED 275 844)

Woods, J. L. *Jordan's Agricultural Technology System*. Urbana: International Program for Agricultural Knowledge Systems, College of Agriculture, University of Illinois, 1987.

Woudstra, A., and Powell, R. "Value Chain Analysis: A Framework for Management of Distance Education." *American Journal of Distance Education*, 1989, *3* (3), 7–21.

Wright, P. C. "Andragogy and Vocational Education in China." *C.V.A./A.C.F.P. Journal*, 1985, *21* (2), 7–9.

Yamaguchi, M. "Japan's Experiences in Adult Civic Education." *Convergence*, 1986, *19* (2), 49–55.

Yong-Fan, H. "Continuing Literacy Work in China." *Prospects: Quarterly Review of Education*, 1982, *12* (2), 185–191. (EJ 271 849)

Youngman, F. *Adult Education and Socialist Pedagogy*. London: Croom Helm, 1986.

Zabala, A. "A 'Back-to-Front' Project in Peru: Starting with the Local People." *Convergence*, 1982, *15* (4), 44–53.

Zeng, Y., Li, G., and Wu, T. "Workers Education." In Wang and Associates (eds.), *China: Lessons from Practice*. New Directions in Continuing Education, no. 37. San Francisco: Jossey-Bass, 1988.

Zhang, X., Ren, Z., and Ruan, L. (eds.). *Proceedings: The Fourth World Conference on Continuing Engineering Education*. Beijing: Science Press, 1989.

Zhu, L. "Current Conditions of China's Distance Education and Countermeasures for Its Development." International Council on Distance Education. *Bulletin*, May 1991, *26*, 26–29.

Zuboff, S. *In the Age of the Smart Machine*. New York: Basic Books, 1988.

Name Index

561

Subject Index

A

Access, to part-time study, 31–35
Accreditation: for continuing professional education, 282, 285–286; for distance education, 164; and staff development, 190
Accreditation Council for Continuing Medical Education, 282
Action learning: and community development, 435, 437; and staff development, 192–193, 201–202, 208, 212, 213, 214, 215
Action plan, in strategic leadership, 490–493
Adult basic education and literacy: aspects of, 4, 68–103; comparative views of, 82–102; and correctional education, 220, 225–226, 228, 229, 230, 234; and distance education, 146; and extent of illiteracy, 68–71; programs for, 71–82; in schools, 71–77; staffing for, 71–72, 85, 86–87, 90, 96, 105; stakeholders for, 105–107; strategic leadership for, 471, 479, 484, 489, 493, 495; strategic planning for, 73–74, 94, 102–107
Adult education: background on, 1–3; basic education and literacy in, 68–103; for community devel-

opment, 5, 413–469; comparative views of, 3–10; continuing professional, 275–311; in correctional settings, 4, 216–238; in cultural programs, 239–274; at a distance, 133–178; for elders, 5, 312–335; in health, 5, 378–412; and hunger, 12–25; for minorities, 4, 108–132; parent agencies for, 6–7; part time, 31–67; for rural development, 5, 336–377; and socialization, 2; for staff development, 179–215; strategic leadership for, 1–30, 470–498
Adult Education Center (AEC) (Germany): and continuing professional education, 291; and cultural education, 262–263, 265
Adult Education Division (Thailand), and rural development, 356, 357
Adult Education Program (India), 86
Adult Learning Service of Public Broadcasting, 139
Adult Literacy and Basic Skills Unit (U.K.), 94
Adult Migrant Education Program (Australia), 118, 119
Africa: emigrants from, 122; hunger in, 12, 13, 15, 19–20

571